The
Harvard Crimson
Anthology

The Harvard Crimson Anthology

100 Years at Harvard

Edited by Greg Lawless '75
With a Foreword by Anthony Lewis '48

Houghton Mifflin Company   Boston   1980

Library of Congress Cataloging in Publication Data

Main entry under title:

The Harvard crimson anthology.

  1. Harvard crimson. 2. Harvard University —
Addresses, essays, lectures. I. Lawless, Greg.
II. Harvard crimson.
LH1.H3C533   378.744'4   80-20386
ISBN 0-395-27607-1

Printed in the United States of America

V 10 9 8 7 6 5 4 3 2 1

Acknowledgments

I AM GRATEFUL to many people. Friends and family count for most. They are important to any endeavor. Thanks go also to the most recent groups of Crimson editors, who have borne with my presence and given needed assistance with essential details all along the way. The Crimson's Trustees and Graduate Board were extremely helpful, giving encouragement and support — Frank Gilbert '52 and Bo Jones '68 should be singled out. A special thanks to Osborne Ingram '35, who has shown integrity and patience throughout. Numerous members of past News, Business, Editorial, and Photograph Boards have sent comments and suggestions — all displayed care and thought in helping to understand The Crimson and the events it covered — and researchers Daniel Swanson and Judy Kogan gave able assistance in researching the paper's files.

The backbone of any newspaper is its working staff, who deserve credit for their daily efforts alone. The same diligence they have brought to The Crimson's pages was also extended to this anthology. A very special thanks, then, for his insights to Pat Sorrento, one of the ablest production foremen around and also the best of teachers and a sometimes sage counselor to generations of Crimson editors. Thanks are also due to printer Lewis Brooks, especially for his reliable aid with reproductions, and to bookkeeper Aglaia Senese, who has always been generous with her time and assistance.

A warm thank you to Anthony Lewis, who, under the constraints of short notice and his many other responsibilities, has been kind enough to introduce this book.

A note of acknowledgment is due to all former Crimson editors; in addition to the few whose bylines appear here, many, many more contributed their ideas and performed all the thankless, anonymous tasks associated with putting out a good, solid newspaper. I would also like to thank Elizabeth Fishel, author of *Sisters: Love and Rivalry Inside the Family and Beyond* (Morrow; Bantam) for allowing me to reprint her article.

Finally, many thanks to editor Daphne Abeel for showing such good judgment and encouragement during the course of manuscript preparation.

Naturally, while the editing and headnoting of this anthology is the result of the collective efforts of many people, any mistakes, omissions, or grievous errors of interpretation are strictly the responsibility of this editor.

Contents

Illustrations

Adlai Stevenson in Boston during the 1952 presidential campaign. [126]

The 1965 march on Montgomery, Alabama, as covered by The Crimson. A marcher is beaten and hauled off. [146–47]

Secretary of Defense Robert McNamara argues with SDS member Michael Ansara '68. [150]

McNamara climbs on car and takes the microphone. [150]

President Nathan Pusey listens to a student debate Harvard's investments in southern corporations with discriminatory hiring practices, 1968. [161]

David Royce '53, '55½, '56 nominates a new Radcliffe president. [167]

Crimson managing editor George S. Abrams '54 presents *The Lampoon*'s Sacred Ibis to chief deputy delegate of the USSR to the United Nations. [183]

Harvard deans beg for funds, 1955. [192]

Ball out of control at the Harvard–Navy game, 1952. [201]

Baseball at Soldiers Field. [204]

Harvard scores a comeback against Yale on the football field, 1954. [214–15]

The Latin diploma controversy, 1961. [226]

Charles Schulz picks Snoopy as Radcliffe's new president. [248]

A plea for typewriters during exam period. [284]

Foreword

AFFECTION AND RESPECT bind me to The Harvard Crimson. It was the center of my life for nearly four years: an embarrassing statement, but true. From time to time I say to someone that I wish I had spent more time studying as a Harvard undergraduate, and less writing, editing, proofreading, talking, and sitting around at 14 Plympton Street, Cambridge, the Crimson building. But if I were so unlucky as to revert to the age of 17 and start over, it would not be any different. I had too good a time at The Crimson, I formed attachments, and I did learn something. I started college thinking that I might be an engineer. I left knowing that I would be a newspaperman.

But why would a reader without those personal connections be interested in a Crimson anthology? The question was answered, for me, when I read Greg Lawless's manuscript. For this is not a parochial book, dwelling on the lore of college journalism or on the fancies of undergraduate life in one age or another. It is more than a book about The Crimson or about Harvard University over the last hundred years. It is, I think, a piece of social history. We often learn about the general by looking at the particular in history. Reading the Sears Roebuck catalogue of 1896 tells us a good deal about the nature of American society then, its economics, its class assumptions, its moral attitudes. That is what happens as one reads this book: The microscopic world of Harvard, as The Crimson described and criticized it over the years, gives insights into the society.

It is not a Sears catalogue, I hasten to add. Even more important, it is not sociology. Nearly everything here is written in plain English. There is some elegance, and a good deal of humor. The self-righteousness that creeps into college newspapers (and is not exactly unknown in grown-up journalism) has somehow been pruned away by Mr. Lawless. But there is meaning in the enjoyment.

Take, for example, what used to be called the Condition of Women. What The Crimson has said on the subject is a capsule of changing social attitudes. In 1873 it addressed in an editorial the idea of opening Harvard to women. President Eliot of Harvard, it noted, "says that both male and female physicians agree in declaring that women are physically unfit for study." The president of Vassar, however, said its 400 students were healthy. The editors then ventured their own uncertain opinion, which was that it would be easier to establish a separate college for women than to open Harvard to them — a radical step that would change the policy of the College from caring for the whole man to "teaching, pure and simple, without any laws to control the students outside the classroom."

Ninety years later Professor John Kenneth Galbraith wrote a letter to The Crimson urging what must still have seemed radical to many readers: elimination of the "parietal rules" that for ages had governed when females could be in the male undergraduate Houses. Harvard was no longer an academy, he said, with scoutmaster types to protect the young "from the natural penalties of indolence, alcohol or lust." When students are admitted, Galbraith wrote, the bargain with them and their parents should be that they look after themselves. Then everyone at Harvard could worry about teaching and scholarship instead of debating the rules year after year. And "those who (one hopes on the basis of some special competence) are fascinated by the question of whether undergraduates are improved or damaged by fornication can organize private discussion groups or, if married, talk about it with their wives."

Reading the many pieces that touch on the status of women at Harvard made me feel ancient, so dramatically have attitudes changed since my day, 1944–1948. In 1947 The Crimson quoted Dean Mildred Sherman of Radcliffe as saying that "the process of saying goodnight" had "degenerated." I remember myself Dean Sherman's concern when The Crimson elected its first female editor, Joan McPartlin, Class of 1949. At that time Radcliffe College was still a separate institution. It had been founded in 1879, with Harvard professors walking across the Cambridge Common to teach segregated classes of women — more or less in line with The Crimson's 1873 prescription. The repetition of lectures was deemed inefficient during World War II, so Radcliffe girls were admitted to most Harvard classes in what was called "Joint Instruction." But as late as 1948 exams were still separate, and a Crimson story quoted an unnamed Harvard student as saying: "Girls are all right in classes, but in exams you have to concentrate."

In 1957 a Crimson editor (male) wrote a piece about how to date and impress Radcliffe girls; the humor still comes through today, but it is a bit like reading something from a Dead Sea scroll. Another piece in this book — from 1963, the same year as Professor Galbraith's letter — is a female editor's division of all Radcliffe into three flavors: peach, chocolate, and lime; my guess is that anyone writing such a thing today, however firmly tongue was pressed into cheek, would risk stoning.

The first woman member of The Crimson's Executive Board was Judith H. Blitman '61, photographic chairman. When she went down to Hyannis Port during the 1960 election to cover the victory of candidate John F. Kennedy '40, she did not get back to her Radcliffe House until 6 a.m. Her Housemother, waiting at the door, confined her to quarters in the evening for two weeks. That was only twenty years ago: hard to believe. To students today such an episode must sound more like 1860 than 1960.

Well, the end came fast. Radcliffe decided in 1969 to merge with Harvard. In 1971 the Faculty approved co-educational housing. And that same year The Crimson published an extraordinary article entitled "Paranoia: Walking the Streets," reprinted here, which conveyed with sensitivity and candor the feelings of women under sexual threat and molestation — in New York City or Cambridge. It portrayed a new psychological world: the one in which all of us live now.

In politics as on the status of women The Crimson has been

something of a barometer, indicating change in a particular slice of intellectual opinion. Before World War II a majority of the paper's board opposed rearmament and resisted support of the European democracies against Hitler; a letter from John F. Kennedy savaged the editorial position. With Vietnam The Crimson wavered as much as the rest of us, or perhaps a little more. It went from a call for American withdrawal (1963) to renewed commitment (1965) to gradual deescalation (1966) to support for the National Liberation Front (1969).

This book includes documentary accounts of some significant moments in recent American political history: a moving report of the speech by General George C. Marshall that launched the Marshall Plan; a story of the mobbing of Robert McNamara, which in a way marked the beginning of the anti–Vietnam War movement; the occupation of University Hall and the Bust, as seen from the inside; and a self-intoxicated description of a violent foray with the Weathermen.

The Crimson has not been relentlessly serious, and this book fortunately shows its frivolous side. There are good examples of humor: a deliciously nasty 1970 piece on the greening of Yale, for one. But I still treasure something of our day, little noted nor long remembered though it be. That was a fake issue of *The Dartmouth*, published on Saturday, November 9, 1946, when the Harvard-Dartmouth football game was to be played in Hanover for the first time in years. The issue of "the oldest college newspaper in America," as it proclaimed, was printed in Cambridge in carefully mimicked typeface and editorial style, and taken up to Hanover for distribution the morning of the game. The banner headline read:

SEVEN INDIAN STARTERS OVERCOME
BY FOOD POISON ON EVE OF GAME

A subhead was even more wonderful, I think: "Candy Ration Proved Toxic." Under it a story described the efforts of the police to unravel the crime. The chief had traced the poison to a box of bonbons delivered to the training table with a note "in female calligraphy." There was a stern statement from Dartmouth President John Sloan Dickey. And there was a front-page editorial:

BLOODY, BUT UNBOWED

Last night, tragedy stalked the campus. On the very eve of what is in many ways the most important game of the year, a mysterious food poisoning has risen to strike down more than half of the starting eleven. Whether the outbreak of ptomaine is the result of an accident or of evil design on the part of corrupt, twisted minds who feared that Dartmouth could never be beaten by fair means cannot be determined at this time. If it has been a plot, strong arms and keen minds stand ready to seek out the culprits and punish them.

Justice, as our President has so eloquently said, is blind-folded but not bleary-eyed. Already stunned sons of the Green are readying themselves to seek out the dastardly perpetrators of the plot, vowing to mete out vengeance with a mailed fist. To these men we say be avenged, but first be sure. As we said in the first paragraph, strong arms and keen minds stand ready to seek out the culprits and punish them . . .

When I said at the beginning of this foreword that I respected The Crimson, I was not referring only to the personal tie to the institution. I am a daily reader again — a resident of Cambridge — and I am impressed. Of course it is an irritating newspaper, and the Harvard administrators who have to bear its contumely deserve our sympathy. But it is a real newspaper now, taking much less for granted than we did in our day. The editors challenge received opinion, at Harvard and elsewhere. And a lot of the time they are right to do so.

ANTHONY LEWIS '48
Cambridge, 1980

The peace and war, prosperity and depression, cynicism and faith, liberalism and conservatism are captured in its pages.

— the editors of The Crimson, January 25, 1943

The
Harvard Crimson
Anthology

Harvard's History During the Last 100 Years: A Guide Through This Book

BECAUSE THERE HAVE BEEN few historical accounts of Harvard since its tercentenary in 1936, and because The Crimson has served as a faithful record of Harvard's history, this book is performing double duty to fill that void. So for those who are interested in Harvard's past century, but who have no interest in the trials and tribulations of The Harvard Crimson or the contributions its graduating editors have made to the world, the following is a handy guide to negotiating your way through the forest without getting caught in the thicket of Crimsoniana.

You can safely begin at the beginning with Chapter 1, "The University." All the italicized commentaries focus on Harvard history and most of the articles present many of the largest and most controversial issues facing the University during the past 100 years.

Once you've begun at the beginning, you will want to continue at the end, with the very last article in the final chapter: "Tell Me, How Can I Get Tenure at Harvard?" Even if you're not a prospective bright star in Harvard's brilliant sky of academicians, you'll find out a lot about how all those prestigious Harvard professors got where they are today, the means by which Harvard maintains its strong academic standing among universities around the world, and why those means may not serve Harvard well in the future.

By that time, you may want to know what all of those ivory-tower types have had to do with the real world. The introduction to Chapter 3, "Editorial and Politics," may help you along in that direction — it explains Harvard's role in the nation and in the world. Also, an article in that chapter, "Harvard Hears of the Marshall Plan," explains how one of the nation's most important postwar foreign policies came to be announced at Harvard.

For those interested in the social history of the University, Chapter 2, "College Life," is certainly worth reading. And in Chapter 8, read "The Three Flavors of Radcliffe," "Sex and Society: Coming of Age at Harvard," and "The Quest at Princeton for the Cocktail Soul," which deals with many of the same problems Harvard's exclusive club system has encountered. If you believe that we live as we laugh, many of the articles in Chapter 4, "Wit and Wisdom," serve equally well to help you understand what student life has been like at Harvard since the late nineteenth century. Portions of the introductions to Chapter 5, "Sports," and Chapter 7, "Arts and Criticism," also shed light on changes in University social life over the years, as do some of the last, more commentary-like articles in the chapter on sports. Two letters in Chapter 6, "A Harvard Mixer" and "Galbraith on Parietals," round out the social history.

One article included here presents a very good description of Harvard's buildings, their special features, and their place in American history: "Architectural Harvard," in Chapter 7, "Arts and Criticism."

And finally, two more articles in Chapter 7 are noteworthy: "Alumni Authors Have Long Tradition of Writing Novels About Harvard Life" and "Harvard and the Novel." They will direct you to just about all the novels concerning Harvard written since the nineteenth century, with critical appraisals of each.

Those are all the major signposts pointing you along the path of the University's history. If you read even a few of the articles recommended here — those in Chapter 1 on the University during the McCarthy era, for instance — you'll find that the course of Harvard University's history has been, at times, closely linked to the course of the nation's history, and you'll learn how Harvard in its fourth century has continued to make significant contributions to American life and learning.

A History of The Crimson Over Its First Century at Harvard

By Michael Ryan '72

January 24, 1973

To begin at the beginning would be a disservice to the past and the present. The earliest days of The Crimson have been chronicled and catalogued and codified times over and nothing we could say would add to the knowledge of the period or the people. That which is most recent is usually of most pressing interest, and so we shall begin with the most recent past, the last quarter century.

By relying on record rather than on recollection, this history will try to paint an accurate picture of The Crimson, with villains as well as heroes, weaknesses as well as strengths. There have been times when the paper has fallen down badly, when it has been rash and irresponsible, when it has been contented and lazy. Not all of the criticisms leveled at it over the years have been unwarranted. But the record shows that honesty, competence, and courage have always been the dominant virtues of Cambridge's Breakfast Table Daily, that talent, even in the darkest days, was always in evidence, and that no Crimson editor need be ashamed of his connection with the paper.

Although this narrative will not proceed chronologically, but will go from the tree to the acorn and back to the oak, one thing should become evident from The Crimson's history: The

Crimson editors of a hundred, and fifty, and twenty-five years ago share with the editors of today a spirit of dedication, of daring, and of confidence. The founder of The Magenta, who defied the dean of Harvard College in setting up his newspaper, was a spiritual ancestor of those editors who shook their fists at McCarran and McCarthy. Although the tenor of the editorial pages was politically conservative for most of the first half of its existence, The Crimson was always a paper which took its editorial duty seriously, and expressed itself on issues great and small. The oldest living graduate editor of The Crimson, who took his degree more than sixty years before the centennial, might not recognize the contemporary, five column, cold-type paper; he might frown at the practice of giving bylines; but he would certainly recognize the spirit of the paper. That, at least, has not changed.

For Academic Freedom: 1948–1960

A weary, somewhat discouraged man cocked his feet up on his desk yesterday and poured out the long, virtually untold story of his years in the Communist party at Harvard.

Apparently relieved to be free at last from the confining gag of the Fifth Amendment, Wendell H. Furry, associate professor of Physics, talked volubly and openly about his reasons for joining the party in 1938 and the nature of the cell here up until he quit in 1947.

Anthony Lukas's chronicles of the McCarthy era have become Crimson legend over the past two decades. The associate managing editor, Class of '55, applied the talent and style which later won him the Pulitzer Prize in producing some of the best writing and reporting in the paper. Along with Malcolm Rivkin '53, David Halberstam '55, and dozens of other Crimson editors, Lukas covered McCarthy's persecution of Wendell Furry and Leon Kamin '48, the Velde and Jenner witch hunts, the actions of McCarthy henchman G. David Schine '49, and all the other sordid chapters of what one survivor called "the bad old days." The early fifties were among the most intriguing in The Crimson's history. Editors never had to scrounge for news; it came at them from every direc-

Detroit News cartoonist Poinier plays off of The Crimson's name and its national reputation for its Academic Freedom Reports in this 1953 cartoon depicting Harvard's recently resigned President Conant being grilled by Senator Joseph McCarthy. Conant was then being considered for the position of German high commissioner. The scenario is entirely fictitious, as Conant's approval by the Senate Foreign Relations Committee was essentially pro forma, although it was marked by "fantastic, often ridiculous testimony" from right-wing groups, according to stories filed by J. Anthony Lukas '55. February 11, 1953. (Cartoon courtesy of the *Detroit News*)

tion, and they were up to handling it. Harvard's reputation as "the Kremlin on the Charles" was firmly entrenched. As Lukas recalled in the early seventies in *The New York Times Magazine*:

> After all, my most vivid memories of Massachusetts politics stem from the early Fifties when Senator Joseph McCarthy was rooting out "Communists" at Harvard, and Massachusetts was a stronghold of pro-McCarthy sentiment. When I went into Boston to cover the Senator's hearings as a young reporter for The Harvard Crimson, I often felt as if I were entering enemy territory. The crowds in the murky hearing room booed Harvard witnesses and one day a pasty-faced woman behind a Scollay Square lunch counter told me to "go back to Pinko U."

McCarthy jumped on Harvard with all the malicious glee of a teen-age bully who has found a smaller child to torment. A shameless publicity hound, he picked victims whose prominence would assure him widespread coverage — and Harvard was a perfect target; unsubstantiated rumors and vague charges against a half dozen or more Faculty members were the basis for McCarthy's vendetta. For several years, he made Harvard and Harvard professors his whipping boys, and The Crimson provided comprehensive coverage of the senator's three-ring circus. The Crimson's role in seeing Harvard through the McCarthy era should not be underestimated. Although it began its opposition to the Wisconsin senator uncertainly, the paper soon picked up steam in its defense of academic freedom, and served as a forum for the statements of such McCarthy foes as Erwin Griswold, Harlow Shapley, Kirtley Mather, Paul Buck, and, of course, President Pusey, whose opposition to McCarthy went back to his own Wisconsin days. In bringing the truth to the Harvard community, and in showing that others were standing up to the threat, The Crimson saved the morale of a University under siege.

McCarthy and McCarran set the tone of the early fifties, but they were by no means the only subjects The Crimson concerned itself with. In 1946, the paper had converted itself back to a civilian institution after three years of military operation.

As the army and navy moved out of Harvard, The Crimson had tackled the problems of reorienting both itself and the rest of Harvard. The new Crimson was larger, more diversified, and more aware of the world beyond the College Gate than its prewar predecessor had been. Its building, its layout, and its style were aired out and renovated after the war, and it gradually regained the cohesiveness which the war had destroyed. Harvard College got a new dean, Harvard undergraduates got the right to apply for two tickets to football games, and Harry Truman got The Crimson's endorsement as "a mediocre Democrat." Liberalism was the tone of the editorial page, and a history of the paper, written for its seventy-fifth anniversary, ended with speculation that women might some day be admitted to membership in the rank of Crimson editors.

The happy days of the postwar period were dimmed by the Korean War, and Harvard entered a season in hell. McCarthy ranted, and students were arrested and beaten by the carload in the "Pogo riots," when cartoonist Walt Kelly arrived in Cambridge for a 1952 speech about his creation. A number of Crimson editors landed in jail, in what would be the first of several times in the next two decades when the Middlesex County Jail would serve as a motel for Harvard students. The fifties had their own special flavor which has never been repeated. Parietals occupied dozens of editorial columns, and hundreds of news inches. The Freshman Smoker, the Student Council, and the all-College weekend became major issues, and The Crimson carried Coop ads for white bucks — $10.98 a pair. Relations with Massachusetts Hall were strained by the 1958 controversy over Memorial Church, but President Pusey and The Crimson were back on speaking terms by 1959, when the president made his decision to suspend Harvard use of funds authorized by the National Defense Education Act. The government monies, which provided a large amount of loan funds and outright grants every year, came with long and binding strings attached. Every recipient was required not only to sign a loyalty oath but also to sign a document attesting that the beneficiary had not been a member of a number of "subversive" organizations. The Crimson commented:

> By its refusal to administer federal funds for educational assistance, until policy on the required "loyalty oath" is thoroughly reconsidered, the University has acted wisely and honorably.

Wilbur Bender had succeeded Chester Hanford as dean of Harvard College after the war, and moved again in 1952 to become dean of admissions. In 1959, he retired altogether, and The Crimson recorded his resignation and replacement. In later years, the coverage of the University's labyrinthine procedures for the selection of new top officials would become a Crimson art. As the fifties ended, Harvard was calm, as the nation was calm. With McCarthyism safely in the background, the University pursued cultural exchange — now encouraged, rather than suspected, by the government. President Pusey attempted to set up an exchange with the University of Leningrad. On the home front, the paper continued to devote itself to the innocent and carefree matters of College life — where "College" finally began to include Radcliffe. The women on The Crimson, forced since the postwar period into a second-class citizenship in the "Radcliffe Bureau," began being elected to the Executive Board. The paper stood on the brink of its most turbulent decade.

Recording the College's Dark Period: 1960–1973

The Crimson of the 1960–1963 period ran a love affair with the White House of John F. Kennedy '40, a former Crimson editor. KISSINGER CALLS CRISIS SOVIET MISCALCULATION, read a headline during the Cuban Missile Crisis. The Crimson backed the president in his execution of foreign policy, and so did the associate professor of Government, Dr. Kissinger. In the days when his name was not a household word, and his consulting with the government was on a far less grand scale than his subsequent employment, Henry A. Kissinger '50 was a frequent topic in The Crimson. "Our sincerity is not at issue, our competence might be," Kissinger told a reporter about the nuclear-test-ban treaty. And almost every week at one point, Kissinger bombarded the paper with notices that he was canceling his subscription because of The Crimson's inaccuracy. His letter-writing campaign seemed to be his favorite hobby in the days before he worked his way up the ladder to fame. The Kennedy administration deprived Harvard of its senior dean, McGeorge Bundy of the Faculty of Arts and Sciences. While Bundy was to go on to notoriety in his later career, his reputation as dean was high. The Faculty liked and admired him; in fact they favored him over the president.

Drugs began to assume a new importance in society in the early sixties, when they suddenly became the property of the respectable middle class. At Harvard, two denizens of William James Hall, Timothy Leary and Richard Alpert, were using the "mind-expanding" drug psilocybin in experiments on students. Andrew T. Weil '63, now Andrew T. Weil, M.D., was The Crimson's drug expert at the time — even though he was also a 'Poonie — and did the bright, relentless, comprehensible reporting which led to the eventual banning of the experiments and termination of Leary and Alpert. The controversy spilled over more than a year. The Faculty debated, and the administration issued ukases. Elliot Perkins '23, the redoubtable master of Lowell House, probably spoke for almost the entire Faculty when he said: "Undergraduates shouldn't be involved in this or any other damned experiments." The vote of the Faculty to ban drug experiments made Crimson headlines, and eventually led to the termination of Alpert's contract, when he illegally administered the drugs to students and left Cambridge during term time without permission — and without making arrangements for his classes. The Crimson had played a large role in exposing the goings on in William James.

The Kennedy assassination brought to an end a Crimson era, and spelled the same numb disbelief and uncomprehending shock at Harvard which it caused all over the country. Although the paper remained liberal and Democratic, the war policies of the Johnson administration caused increasing alienation among the editors. At Harvard, a small, left-wing group called Tocsin gave way to a newer group called SDS [Students for a Democratic Society], which became more militant as the war escalated and the executive branch increased

The Crimson ran a love affair with the White House during the Camelot years. John F. Kennedy '40 was a member of The Crimson's Business Board. Here he is shown speaking at a Boston banquet one month before his assassination. October 23, 1963. (Copyright © 1963 Albert B. Crenshaw '64)

the level of warfare without consent of Congress, or the people. In 1967 a recruiter for the Dow Chemical Company was held in a room in Pierce Hall against his will; punishments were assessed on the students involved, and also on a large group of students who had signed a petition asking to be given equal blame with the actual perpetrators. The College was entering a dark period.

As strange as it seems, Dean Monro and Dean Fred Glimp after him had encouraged competition between the administration and SDS on the softball field. The games went well for several seasons, but the political situation in the nation had deteriorated to such a point that it seemed unlikely that students and administrators could ever see eye to eye on the role of the University. By April 1969, the situation was unsalvageable. While SDS and others demanded an end to military and military-industrial recruiting, Harvard expansion into poor communities, the ROTC program, and other connections between the University and war-related activities, administrators walked a fine line of distinctions and differentiations in seeking to reach a satisfactory balance of demands. The wheels of bureaucracy moved with excruciating tardiness, and this bureaucracy could not move fast enough to satisfy one segment of SDS. Although the group as a whole had voted to take no such action, a fraction of those in attendance at an SDS meeting on April 8, 1969, decided to occupy a building the next day. Shortly before noon on April 9, they did so, ejecting the deans in University Hall, and renaming the building "Che Guevara Hall." The crowds of students who gathered outside overwhelmingly opposed the occupation; there was talk of football players and other able-bodied students coming to remove the occupiers. Then, at dawn the next day, with no advance warning to the Faculty or the students, President Pusey ordered in the police. By the hundreds came police arrayed in combat gear and ready for violent action. They marched in and cleared the building with nightsticks and battering rams. Quite a few students were injured, a few seriously; a significant number of reporters were arrested and tossed in jail. In seconds, the mood of the University changed from antioccupier to antiadministration.

The Crimson was out with an extra soon after the Bust, just as it had issued an extra the day before, following the take-over. Crimson editors were among the group of reporters from the most distinguished publications in the country who were arrested, and Crimson photographers were among the many whose cameras were smashed by police billy clubs.

The anger which many members of the University community, students and teachers alike, felt at Pusey's unilateral, unprecedented action, was reflected in the editorial columns of The Crimson that spring. The mass meetings held in Harvard Stadium occasioned some of the paper's most thorough reporting, and relations with the administration deteriorated even more. For a generation of Crimson editors, the act of summoning riot-equipped police to the Harvard Yard stood as tantamount to treason.

The aftermath of the spring of 1969 brought many baffling moments for the executives of The Crimson. The task of making sense out of the post-1969 period is not an easy one; suffice it to say that The Crimson has made its own peace with the events of that year, and remains steadfast in its obligation to serve Harvard as a source of independent comment.

The Nixon administration did nothing to alleviate the seriousness of the Indochina war in the first years. After the 1970 invasion of Cambodia, The Crimson covered the activities of the Harvard people who went to Washington to lobby for peace. Michael E. Kinsley '72 would win a Dana Reed Prize and national reprinting for his article on the Harvard Faculty who went to the capital to confront their old colleague, Henry Kissinger. The spring brought riots as well, spin-offs from large-scale antiwar demonstrations in Boston, which caused damage of varying degrees to Harvard Square.

The selection of a successor to President Pusey engaged the attention of the University in 1970 and 1971. Scott W. Jacobs '71, the paper's executive editor, covered the search for a year, securing inside information more than once and publishing lists of the candidates on the Corporation's docket at frequent intervals. When Derek C. Bok was selected as president, Jacobs was ready to tell Harvard — and the world, through his connection with *Newsweek* — everything there was to be

Crimson Centennial Issue

The Weather
Cloudy 40s

The Harvard Crimson

VOLUME CLVI, No. 88 — CAMBRIDGE, MASS., WEDNESDAY, JANUARY 24, 1973 — FIFTEEN CENTS

U.S. INITIALS PEACE PACT

Treaty to Go Into Effect on Saturday
Includes Withdrawal Within 60 Days

By MARK C. FRAZIER

The light finally appeared at the end of the tunnel yesterday, as President Nixon televised an announcement that a truce in Vietnam will begin this Saturday.

Nixon said that Henry Kissinger '50, his national security advisor, had initialled an agreement which brings "peace with honor" to Indochina. He said the treaty will go into effect on Saturday, hours after it is formally signed.

The agreement calls for a pullout of all U.S. forces from Vietnam within 60 days, a return of all prisoners of war and an accounting of men missing in action.

No mention of ceasefire for Laos, Cambodia, or Thailand was made in Nixon's ten-minute address.

"We will do everything required by us, and expect them to do the same," Nixon said. The President said the United States would support Vietnamese efforts "to settle a peace among themselves."

The agreement will be released in its entirety today. It was made with the "full approval" of the South Vietnamese government, Nixon said.

"Let us be proud we didn't settle for a peace that would have abandoned our allies," Nixon said. "Let us be proud of the million young Americans who served in Vietnam. Let us be proud of those who sacrificed, who gave their lives, so that the people of South Vietnam might live in freedom, so that the world might live in peace."

Addressing all of the parties to the conflict in turn, Nixon offered a series of short tributes and invitations.

The South Vietnamese, he said, had "by your sacrifices developed the right to determine your own future." They would find the United States "friends in peace as allies in war," he said.

To the North Vietnamese, Nixon extended a request for reciprocal cooperation to "build a peace of reconciliation." He stressed that the United States would expect "scrupulous" observance of the settlement by the North Vietnamese.

Nixon said that the American people's steadfastness in supporting our insistence on peace with honor made the agreement possible. He thanked them also for bearing with his silence over recent actions in Vietnam.

"If I had talked, it would certainly have harmed and possibly destroyed chances for peace," Nixon said. He thanked the wives and families of POWs for having had "the courage to stand for the right kind of peace."

Yesterday's agreement is expected to differ only slightly from the settlement aborted last October. Though no mention

(continued on page 3)

President Nixon last night announced that Henry Kissinger '50, had initialled a peace agreement which meets the "full approval" of the South Vietnamese government.

Johnson Dies; 36th President Lies in State

By The Associated Press

The body of former President Lyndon Baines Johnson lay in state yesterday in the library in Austin, Texas, which he created as his own memorial and as a school for better government.

The closed, flag-draped casket rested on a raised platform in the Great Hall of the eight-story Lyndon B. Johnson Library on the University of Texas campus.

Johnson, the nation's 36th president, died Monday of what doctors described as "severe coronary artery disease." He was 64 and had been wracked by heart problems since the fifties.

Lady Bird Johnson stood with daughters Lynda and Luci and their husbands as the casket was carried by eight servicemen to the bier in the hall.

Johnson's widow wiped a tear from her eye as she embraced a family friend who had joined the line of mourners.

The body will be flown to Washington today and will be carried by Army caisson to the Capitol Rotunda, where the former President will lie in state until tomorrow morning.

President Nixon and other dignitaries are expected to take part in the hour-long procession up Constitution Avenue to the Capitol.

Nixon has declared Thursday a national day of mourning and called on people to assemble on that day "in their respective [illegible] memory."

Funeral services will be held at the National City Christian Church in Washington before the body is flown to the family cemetery near the LBJ Ranch. Nixon has provided Air Force One for transporting the former President's body.

Evangelist Billy Graham will officiate at final rites before Johnson is buried alongside his parents and grandparents in the graveyard which is situated in the Texas hill country in an area dotted with handsome oak trees.

LYNDON BAINES JOHNSON

AIR RAIDS

North Vietnamese forces nearly doubled their attacks yesterday across South Vietnam in a high point of activity before a cease-fire, the Saigon command announced Wednesday.

Scholars Evaluate LBJ's Role In Foreign, Domestic Spheres

By DALE S. RUSSAKOFF

Several Harvard professors and local educators yesterday assessed Lyndon Baines Johnson's double image—the architect of constructive reform programs at home and the author of disastrous foreign policies.

Doris Kearns, associate professor of Government, who helped Johnson write his memoirs, said yesterday that Johnson should be remembered in both roles because his administration left a double legacy.

"The Great Society created expectations—through civil rights and poverty programs—that life could be better," Kearns said. "You can cut back on programs, but nobody can kill these expectations."

Kearns said that Johnson's Vietnam policies created a public distrust of presidential power "which is an equally important and healthy legacy." She predicted that this legacy will be translated into changing military and economic power structures.

Johnson was a victim of "the American tyranny of benevolence," Kearns said, "the belief that he could make the world better for other people and the failure to realize that this was at the price of Vietnam's autonomy and independence."

These beliefs were the basis of the Great Society as well as his decision to escalate the bombing in Vietnam, she said.

"To understand why he made certain decisions in Vietnam is not to accept it," Kearns added. "There still were human choices."

(continued on page 3)

University Delays Immediate Action

Officials Appraise New Abortion Ruling

By EMILY WHEELER

Members of the medical and legal communities, as well as a spokeswoman for the National Organization for Women, yesterday indicated that under Monday's Supreme Court ruling on state abortion laws, the Massachusetts legislature can legally restrict abortions only during the last three months of pregnancy.

However, they stressed that they had not yet seen the complete decision of the Supreme Court.

Sen. Jack. H. Backman (D.-Boston), a long-time advocate of repealing abortion laws, said yesterday that the ruling invalidates present Massachusetts laws which permit abortions only if a pregnancy threatens a woman's mental or physical health. That determination is usually made by a hospital review board.

Backman added that the initiative for new legislation may have to come from abortion opponents rather than abortion advocates.

"Unless there is new State legislation, abortions are permissible in Massachusetts during the first six months," Backman said.

"The ruling states that regulation during the second trimester must have the goal of protecting a mother's health, but not of preventing abortion," Backman explained. "The problem is more difficult during the third trimester and most doctors would agree that an abortion at that time is not in keeping with normal medical procedures."

Backman predicted that the legislature would pass strict regulations curtailing a woman's right to an abortion during the third trimester of pregnancy, but added that such legislation may be redundant.

"If a woman is in consultation with a licensed doctor, one assumes he will use

(continued on page 3)

B&G Workers Unanimously Reject Contract; Some to Stage Unrelated Job Action Today

By CHARLES E. SHEPARD

Craftsmen in Building and Grounds last night rejected unanimously a proposed two-year contract and asked their representatives to re-negotiate provisions on wages, sick leave and parking.

The meeting was the first since negotiations began in November and was intended only as an "information meeting," Paul E. McWade, president of the Craftsmen Maintenance Counsel, said yesterday.

The bargaining committee made no recommendation at the meeting. The vote was to determine only whether the union members were interested in the contract.

The union's contract expired on December 8, and the craftsmen, who make up half of B&G, have been receiving pay under the old contract.

Between 50 and 60 craftsmen in the union also decided at yesterday's meeting to refuse to use their cars at work, beginning this morning, until the University increases significantly the mileage allowance they receive. The allowance is not part of the contract negotiations.

The University now pays 13 cents per mile to these drivers and has offered to increase this to 20 cents. The drivers usually travel about five miles a day. At the meeting last night the drivers were asking for allowances as high as $5 a day, complaining that 50 to 60 cents does not cover insurance and other costs.

McWade said that the University might eventually raise the allowance to $2, but

(continued on page 3)

Kilson Denounces Plan for Exchange With Black Schools

By DOUGLAS E. SCHOEN

Martin L. Kilson, professor of Government, yesterday released a memorandum opposing a proposal by a member of the Admissions Committee that Harvard should initiate an exchange program with black colleges.

In his memorandum, Kilson questions all the premises on which David Evans, assistant director of Admissions, proposed the exchange last month.

Evans said that Harvard has failed "to develop a sense of immediacy among its black students" to solve the problems confronting the black community in coming decades. He also said that black students are out of touch with the black community "because of the unrealities of Harvard—or any affluent college for that matter."

Responding to Evans' assertions, Kilson said that Harvard's "academic structure and related attributes have one primary

(continued on page 11)

Cronin's Strikers Win Reinstatement

By SETH M. KUPFERBERG

The State Labor Relations Commission ruled last night that Cronin's Restaurant must negotiate with the Harvard Square Waitresses Union (HSWU), whose strike against the restaurant began last January when James D. Cronin, the restaurant's owner, broke off bargaining.

The Commission held that Cronin's firing of eight HSWU members three days after the strike began showed anti-union bias and was therefore illegal. It ordered the waitresses reinstated in order of seniority, but rejected HSWU's demand for back pay for the time of the strike.

(continued on page 3)

Crimson Alumni and Editors Enjoy Panels, Speeches, Food

Some 400 Crimson editors, past and present, trooped over the red carpets and into the tapestry-hung dining room of the Harvard Club of Boston last Saturday, to celebrate the newspaper's hundredth anniversary.

Few enterprises have been led by and still claim the affections of such diverse men as Paul M. Sweezy '31 and Casper W. Weinberger, '38 who were both Crimson presidents.

Weinberger, who is the newly designated Secretary of Health, Education and Welfare was in Washington for the inaugural bash and could not attend the Crimson festivities.

But Sweezy, co-founder of the Marxist journal, Monthly Review, and author of several books on radical economics, was on hand to call President Nixon "fish-blooded" and to add, in a somewhat un-Marxist turn of phrase, "God save us from four more years of this monster." The audience overlooked this lapse into bourgeois rhetoric and applauded loudly.

In fact, after Sweezy had warmed them up, the audience proved their left-wing credentials by approving a statement calling on Nixon to sign the October peace agreements and to renounce publicly any future military intervention in Southeast Asia.

Harvard luminaries attending the dinner included President Emeritus James Bryant Conant '14, a former Crimson editor, President Bok, Radcliffe President Matina S. Horner, Dean Dunlop, and F. Stanton Deland Jr. '36, President of the Board of Overseers.

The Crimson weekend began with a cocktail party Friday evening at the 14 Plympton Street offices. Proving once again the old maxim about journalists and booze, about 200 Crimson staff members

(continued on page 11)

Police Apprehend 2 Alleged Robbers Inside Eliot House

By STEVEN REED

University police arrested two men with a revolver Monday night after the men had allegedly robbed an Eliot House student at gunpoint and fired a pistol past his head. A third man escaped.

The police, summoned by another Eliot House student to investigate three persons who had attempted to enter his room, arrested the two teenagers as they were leaving the House. A third man ran off as the police approached.

The three men allegedly robbed Richard P. White '74 of $26 in cash and a face mask valued at $10. White was unavailable for comment yesterday.

The incident was the second armed robbery arrest in a Harvard House in nine days. University Police arrested two men at the door of a Dunster House room on January 13.

Still Investigating

University and Cambridge police are still investigating the January 16 armed robbery at Mather House, in which four men pistol-whipped and bound two residents of a Mather suite and escaped with $750 worth of typewriters, stereos and radios.

Randy Nixon '74, a resident of Eliot House, called the University Police at about 10:30 p.m. Monday after three strangers came to his door asking for a fictitious "John Simmons." One of the men drew a pistol on Nixon, but he refused to admit them.

White told police Monday night that the three came to his door about 11 p.m. and asked for "John Simmons." When he

(continued on page 3)

The Crimson's front page on its hundredth anniversary. January 24, 1973.

known about the Law School dean and the reasons for his selection.

As the first century ended, yet another generation of Crimson editors, along with Pat Sorrento, the shop foreman whose patience with dilatory copy has made Job seem a piker; Miss Eunice Ficket, the Business Board's conscience, soul and spirit, who kept the details running; and those whose names have been forgotten all continued the pattern of their work, maintaining the tradition into the next century.

This narrative has been, to now, a rough chronicle of what has gone on at The Crimson since the last time the record was brought up to date; it is hardly as complete a narrative as perusal of recent bound volumes of the paper would provide. Let me encourage those who have the slightest interest in the subject to pursue it further, and let me offer the following sections as a rough history of the first three-quarters of the paper.

Beginnings: 1873–1883

"I won't philosophize, I will be read." An unusual contention for a college newspaper of the period, but nonetheless, this was the motto of the earliest version of today's Crimson — The Magenta, first published on January 24, 1873. Five of the six undergraduate newspapers founded in the nineteenth century had already folded: the last, the *Advocate*, held a position of seemingly unchallengeable strength in the Harvard community. Nonetheless, a handful of undergraduates were willing to make the attempt, once more, to give the University a newspaper.

The Magenta set its sights high; it would attempt fairness, accuracy, and encyclopedic coverage; it would avoid gossip, falsehood, and error: in short, it would try to please all of the people all of the time.

These were hardly fighting journalists, but these were not the days of great journalism, either. The worst newspapers of the period were the great yellow rags, the best were so genteel as to be stultifying — *The New York Times*'s masthead boasted, "It Does Not Soil the Breakfast Cloth." The Faculty of the College had seen to it that several earlier newspapers went out of existence after they had dared to print critical articles, and even a paper cofounded by James Russell Lowell, Class of 1838, had died from lack of readers. The bravest of the College papers, *The Collegian*, had boasted on its masthead "Dulce est Periculum" — "Danger Is Sweet" — and had run the risk of offending faculty sentiment. It too was closed down. The prospects of success for a new paper seemed bleak.

But The Magenta came into being at the dawn of Harvard's Golden Age, in the early years of Charles William Eliot, and no climate could have been better for fostering such an undertaking. The Faculty which had discouraged and disbanded the earlier newspapers was losing control over Harvard, as the school changed from a parochial college to the first great American university. Only in the light of Eliot's innovations could a newspaper survive where once the forces of academic conservatism had ruled unchallenged.

Yet even Eliot's liberalism did not mean that The Magenta would have an easy go of it with the administration. As Henry A. Clark, Class of 1874, The Magenta's first president and guiding spirit, later narrated the story in an earlier history of The Crimson, Dean Burney called Clark to his office for an explanation of the new paper and then

> expressed strong disapproval. I asked him whether the carrying out of the plan was officially forbidden. He said no, but that he wished us to understand that he thought the project very ill-advised. I reported what had taken place to the promoters, who decided to go ahead notwithstanding the Dean's advice to the contrary.

The Faculty, which a decade before might have banned the new publication outright, now held itself to a mild expression of outrage. The Magenta, on its part, largely observed the proper amenities in editorials, although it stood firm to a policy of identifying every editorial as the opinion of *all* the editors, not just the author. This policy was particularly useful, The Crimson's fiftieth-anniversary history relates, when the Faculty came round looking for the man who had referred to one of their number as "a little tin god on wheels."

The Magenta (named after the College color, it underwent a change in nomenclature in 1875, when the College went crimson) at first could not be recognized as what we would call a newspaper today. It appeared biweekly, a thin layer of editorial content surrounded by an even thinner wrapper of advertising.

The period of testing which The Magenta went through in the 1870s did not go easily. Even though the editors of the *Advocate* extended their editorial goodwill to the new paper, the community at large seemed unenthusiastic. The first issue promised a home delivery system for subscribers; the second retracted the offer because of lack of interest. The wrapper of advertising stayed at four pages until the fall of 1875 — two years without an increase. Also in 1875, in concert with the *Advocate*, The Magenta canceled its policy of credit to subscribers. "We have been in existence now for three and a half years, and during that time we have lost something like two hundred dollars on subscribers' bills . . . ," the business manager announced.

The formal systems of election and job classification which now exist at The Crimson seem not to have come into being in the 1870s. One became an editor simply by writing for the paper, or, presumably, by trying to sell advertising. Two editors were put in charge of each issue, and given the responsibility for writing the editorials, soliciting copy from other sources, and seeing the paper through the press. (Printing was done alternately at the Riverside Press and John Wilson & Sons, in Cambridge.) Periodically, meetings of the staff were called by the president, who would hang the Crimson shingle from an iron bar on the side of University Hall to summon editors to his room that evening.

As The Crimson rounded the corner into the 1880s, it seemed fairly sure of its place at Harvard. Its place at Harvard, though, was to be sharply redefined as it entered the second decade. The editors of the paper, larger in number and more ambitious in outlook than their predecessors, were eager to do something which more resembled the kind of journalism that big city newspapers were engaging in during that heyday of the American paper. The first attempt at a revision

The Magenta.

Vol. I.　　　　CAMBRIDGE, JANUARY 24, 1873.　　　　No. 1.

Contents.

Editorial.

FROM the *Treasurer's Statement* we learn that the Kirkland Fellowship at present amounts to about $6,300. It will be remembered that this Fellowship is being established by George Bancroft, who will pay $2,000 a year till the sum of $10,000 is reached, when the income will be devoted to the higher education of some student taken at the discretion of the Corporation from any department of the University. The student thus selected will be allowed to pursue his studies either in this country or in Europe.

WE have recently heard many complaints from the members of '74, of the sudden disappearance from the College Library of the books which contained the subject-matter of their themes. It would be well for the *favored* few to remember, in future, that books of this character are reserved for all, and that their disappearance is attended with great inconvenience to many.

IT has been suggested that if the gas in some of the College buildings were confined to narrower limits, instead of being allowed to escape until the basements are filled, it would be more conducive to the purpose for which it is intended. And furthermore, if a greater quantity could be furnished in the Reading Room it would be very acceptable. The afflicted inhabitants of Holworthy affirm that changes in the "twinkling of an eye" from light to sudden darkness are no unfrequent things in that building. Cannot some improvement in this line be made by those having the matter in charge?

WE wish the College would lay plank walks in the yard. As we wade through our classic enclosure on the sloppy days of the January thaw, or, when the signal-man at Washington turns the water into ice, as we gracefully measure our length in front of University, we think of this. We do not find fault with the management of our beloved institution, but we mildly hint that plank walks, such as are each winter laid on Boston Common, would be a blessing to Faculty and students.

WE earnestly request contributions from all members of the University.

THE excellent manner in which the College Chapel has been repaired certainly reflects great credit upon those having it in charge. The commodious gallery, which extends along three sides and contains three rows of seats, has greatly increased the seating capacity of the Chapel, and we think has not marred the beauty of its proportions. The windows of stained glass, each of which bears upon it the University motto, " Christo et Ecclesiæ," admit a very soft and mellow light. The fresco work, though of a plain and unassuming style, greatly improves the general appearance.

The first issue of The Harvard Crimson, then called The Magenta. January 24, 1873.

The Crimson.

Published Fortnightly by the Students of Harvard University.

CAMBRIDGE, FRIDAY, MAY 21, 1875.

WHEN the College color was changed, the question at once arose as to whether this paper should shed the discarded Magenta, and don the more popular crimson. We announced in our last number that a decision would be speedily made, and the title at the head of the page indicates the nature of that decision.

The considerations that led us to this step are very patent. The magenta is not now, and, as was shown in the meeting, never has been, the right color of Harvard ; accordingly the name, as applied to the paper, would be a mere vagary, or, worse, a solecism, in case another college should adopt magenta as its color. The general diffusion of the fact that crimson is Harvard's color will be somewhat difficult, and the difficulty would probably be increased if a paper existed at Harvard called the Magenta. The reasons that led the founders of the paper to choose Magenta as its name now dictate a change of that name to the Crimson. It was not the intrinsic value of the name, but its suggestiveness that recommended the Magenta, and so the paper was named, after the analogy of the *Dark Blue*, and other University papers. We believe that a title which at once localizes the paper among our exchanges as being issued at Harvard, and which calls up in the minds of undergraduates the entire body of interests of the University is most in consonance with the tendency and policy of the paper. Such a title the Crimson has now become. We change our name, therefore, that there may be no real change in our relations to the College, and, with a hope that this color may become a rallying word of victory before the summer is over, we present to our readers the first number of the Crimson.

Now that magenta has given way to crimson, we desire to make a suggestion of a practical nature. All who were at Saratoga last year, or at Springfield in '73, must have been surprised at the various shades that passed for magenta ; in fact, it seemed true that *verium et mutabile semper* magenta. Of late the manufacturers have made less magenta than formerly, and only one American house, it is said, imported a regular line of magenta ribbons ; naturally the ingenuous mercer sold any approximate shade as " *Harvard's* magenta," and that misty notion of colors in general, and magenta in particular, caused startling variations in the colors worn by Harvard men at the races.

Crimson, while a more popular color, has this same disadvantage, and unless some precaution is taken various shades will be sold for crimson. If arrangements could be made with some one house to manufacture and import for Harvard a given line of crimson ribbons which should be dyed after a fixed standard, the difficulty would be obviated. In this case, Harvard men would know just where they could buy the exact shade, and the enterprising shop-men of Saratoga could stock their counters with what was really Harvard's color, and not, as last year, sell quite another shade from the true one. Moreover, ribbon can be manufactured much more reasonably abroad, and the club ribbons furnished at a very reasonable price, and of satisfactory quality. Any large house would contract to furnish Harvard with all the ribbon needed, and then we could be sure of having it all alike. The suits, too, could be made there for less than is charged here, and the whole probably would cost less and be more satisfactory than at present. It is to be hoped that Harvard's color may never again run short, and that the crimson may hold and maintain its old place.

IN the past two weeks the various crews have done much in the way of improvement. Every boat, as it leaves the float, is subjected to the closest scrutiny, and as the time of the race draws

---

The Magenta changed its name when Harvard College changed its official color to crimson in 1875. "Magenta is not now, and . . . never has been, the right color of Harvard," the editors wrote. May 21, 1875.

in format was made in 1882, when a proposal for merger with the *Advocate* was rejected by a close vote of *Advocate* editors and The Crimson decided to move from a fortnightly publication to a weekly.

The editors of The Crimson had stood by for three years while not one but two dailies had been founded. *The Harvard Echo* in December of 1879 and *The Harvard Daily Herald* in January of 1882. While the adventurous and talented *Herald* moved in for the kill on the more stolid and less interesting *Echo*, The Crimson's editors were consigned to a back seat, serving as observers to a battle they wanted to join. After competing one term, *The Echo* quietly folded its tent and sneaked away to the land where newspapers whose time is past all go. *The Herald* had covered the field better than *The Echo* ever could; it was reporting Harvard news thoroughly, and exchanging news with *The Yale News* to keep the Cambridge readership aware of New Haven events. In its first year, it issued three eight-page extras after athletic events, most of them out within minutes after game's end. *The Herald* served the College's need for news, and the College read *The Herald*.

Nonetheless, starting a newspaper was expensive, then as now, and *The Herald* found itself facing a mounting deficit. At the end of the first full year, in June of 1883, the paper was running a $700 deficit. In this situation, and aware that the editors of the more established Crimson were eager to get into daily journalism, *The Herald* began to think of merger. The Crimson was eager, incredibly so, to make a union. The constitution of The Herald-Crimson was adopted on October 5, 1883, only four days after *The Herald* had gone for merger, and the daily Herald-Crimson hit the stands on October 8. Under the terms of the merger, the president of The Crimson was named president of The Herald-Crimson; the managing editor of *The Herald* became managing editor of the new paper. It was also agreed that, after one year, the name of the paper would be changed to The Crimson.

So The Crimson finally took the form which it would continue to have for the next 90 years. The dedication to poetry and literature in the pages of the paper had gone by the boards, and The Crimson would soon lose all connection, except in name, to the biweekly magazine which was its ancestor. But the hopes and ambitions, the dedication to journalism and hard work, which had characterized the first ten editors in 1873 would survive in their successors even to the present.

The Breakfast Table Daily: 1884–1904

The Crimson of the 1880s and 1890s was located, according to a past history, "in a front room one flight up in an old brick building on Massachusetts Avenue between Holyoke and Linden Streets, reached by an open wooden staircase at the back of the building."

The Crimson did quite a bit of moving around before coming to rest at 14 Plympton Street in 1915. Its original home was Stoughton 22, a room which was convenient at least to Yard dwellers, well stocked with punch for the convivial Crimeds, and, if a surviving photograph is to be trusted, comfortable. In 1885 The Crimson vacated Stoughton for the "front room one flight up." In 1895, the paper moved once again, this time to 1304 Massachusetts Avenue, in a building known as Hilton's block. Here the paper knew luxury at last, for it rented three stories worth of space: an upper floor for the president, managing editor, and Sanctum, a ground floor for the Business Board, and a basement for the candidates and printing presses. This arrangement lasted six years, until a move to the basement of the Union, on Quincy Street.

As it wandered around Cambridge, evolving toward the day when it would find a permanent home on Plympton Street, The Crimson gradually grew into a recognizable facsimile of a modern newspaper. Those were the days of rugged individualism, and the particular rugged individuals who edited the paper concerned themselves with sports to a degree that would startle the modern reader.

The foremost worry of the postmerger paper was a simple one — survival. The balance sheet of November 1883 reported a deficit of $600. That winter, an editor recalled, "The advisability of stopping the paper was discussed." But, by June,

The Daily Crimson had a surplus of all of $15, and was on its way to financial stability. In September 1884, the price of a year's subscription was raised to $3.50, and advertising had gone up. The paper's financial position remained healthy into the new century, and, in 1904, a permanent sinking fund was established from the annual profits to be used against capital expenditures and financial setbacks.

The spirit of the paper in those decades around the turn of the century was heady. Editors were eager for bigger and more ambitious projects, and threw themselves whole-heartedly into their work; it is not an accident that one biographer has quoted FDR as saying that his best training for the presidency of the United States was the presidency of The Crimson, for he ran the paper in a time when it rode high in the College community, when it was respected, and listened to, and when the president had more power on the paper than he ever had, before or since. From 1887 on, The Crimson became almost the official bulletin board of the University, and the Faculty used it often for all manner of official notices. Henry James, Class of 1899, president of The Crimson, wrote this description of a typical day at the paper in the December 1899 *Harvard Graduates' Magazine:*

> Roughly speaking, the reporting and first-draft writing is done by the candidates, who number from about forty, when a batch begins to try, to seven or eight when the most successful are elected editors. But as the poorest of them drop out or are dropped, the better ones are given more and more suggestions and assignments. If a candidate shows interest and industry, if he is accurate and reliable in writing up his news, and if he has any interest, intellectual, social, or athletic, which brings him into contact with some of the sources of College activity, he is pretty sure to be successful.
>
> At an hour in the morning depending on the time at which he got to bed the previous evening, and also on his lectures, the managing editor comes to the office and begins his day's work. After a glance at his memorandum books, he is ready to make out the list of assignments.
>
> This is the foundation of the forthcoming issue, but

while laying it he is never free from interruptions. Editors come in to find out whether they are to have work given them or not, and they sit around talking and laughing and poking fun at the managing editor while he tries to write, and they wait. Often other officers of the board appear with something to discuss. More than one person calls with the various purposes of pointing out that an organization in which he is interested has not been given enough prominence of late . . . A freshman is easy to dispose of. But if the caller is an instructor or a graduate, the task of pacifying him, of explaining the situation or, occasionally, making him see that he is asking for the impossible, may be both hard and unavoidable. A familiar classmate who rides his hobbyhorse into the office is likely to be attacked bodily, and dumped into a huge waste-paper basket near the telephone box, provided enough editors are present. The most exciting of all the morning interruptions can be caused by an angry business manager, who comes waving a printer's bill for extra work.

Before lunch time the assignment list is made out and hung up, and the office can lapse into quiet until evening. Those who come to it in the afternoon come to write and to be left alone.

By half-past seven the lights are lit and the copy box begins its merciless accompaniment to the printer's sharp cry, "Carp-e-e." This box is primarily an invention for conveying manuscript from the desk to the printing room. From then on, the managing editor's business is to keep his head, and to see that order and reason prevails in all matters concerning the paper and himself. Candidates come in with botched "stories" and wonderful excuses. All have to be attended to and set on the straight path promptly. Editors must needs be coaxed into getting down to their work, and then persuaded to keep at it until they are finished. Newspaper correspondents arrive and put the unvarying question: "Is there anything tonight?" and then leave for the time being, or else go to their side room to work according to the answer given by the managing editor . . . More interesting but less common are interruptions caused by the president of the board when he has some editorial question which he cannot settle alone. Indeed, so many and so various are the things which occur on a busy evening that one might say that the time which the managing editor can rescue from interruptions is none too much for the work of editing copy for the printers.

Little by little, as the hours wear on, the hurry and worry lessen, and the office becomes quieter and emptier, until only the proofreader remains for company. Finally the managing editor has nothing to do but to sit back in his chair and keep awake until he has been called up by the Associated Press, and the printers have told him that the paper is full and all is well . . .

Small as it is in itself, and little as the field in which it works must be recognized to be, The Crimson can still boast of accomplishments beyond its printed page. Of its most noteworthy successes, one of the most important has been that of providing against the dangers of vicious or foolish reporting of Harvard news in the daily press. It has done this by furnishing, to any responsible newspaper correspondent who applies, working accommodations and telephone facilities in its office, and also almost unrestricted access to the Crimson reports and articles before they are published.

As the College has grown, and become a University in fact as well as in name, The Crimson has grown and become more important and more necessary to every student. Whatever may be its deficiencies, it is a thorough news-chronicler. On one hand, it contributes a great deal to the College life of its editors. On the other, it is a daily bulletin and record, which now that the University has outgrown all unity and coherence, can boast of being in more than one way valuable and useful to its public.

The managing editor of today no longer has the superhuman responsibilities of his predecessor, and the copy box in the Plympton Street building drops away to a new, offset press, replete with computerized copy printer. Nobody yells "Carp-e-e," although choicer epithets are often used for a dilatory night editor. The practice of releasing unpublished stories to the public press, which had already been suspended once when Henry James wrote his article, died a natural death from old age somewhere in the twenties or thirties, its grave unmarked. But candidates still botch stories and give "wonderful excuses," and the flavor of a real newspaper is still there.

The twentieth-century Crimson prospered and with success came imitation, but not quite the imitation that is the sincerest form of flattery. On May 30, 1901, subscribers were confronted with the first issue of a new literary genre: the *Lampoon* Crimson parody. Diphtheria, anthrax, and typhoid, they discovered, were rampant at the Scientific School; the Corporation had rescinded President McKinley's honorary degree; and the fifty strongest men at Harvard would be awarded a varsity H. Nowadays Daniel Moynihan and Henry Kissinger are the targets of the humor, but the idea has remained the same. The development of the modern Crimson parody has closely paralleled the growth of the modern Crimson.

"The Crimesown" as seen by *The Lampoon* in 1902.

Finding a Home, and Settling In: 1905–1929

The quarters in the basement of the Union were becoming un-suitable for an expanding daily paper, and the desire for a building owned exclusively by The Crimson had increased over the years since the turn of the century. So land on Plympton Street was acquired in two steps — the first parcel by a committee of graduates and undergraduates, with Crim-son money, the second through a $6000 gift from Thomas Cole, of Duluth, Minnesota, father of F. L. Cole '15, then presi-dent. Cole's gift, along with a matching sum collected from graduates, was enough to get the project under way. Ground-breaking took place in the spring of 1915; the building was ready for occupancy by November. The Crimson Printing Company, which had shared the offices in the Union, installed itself in the Plympton Street basement; the *Alumni Bulletin* moved in downstairs. In keeping with its long-standing love of football, The Crimson issued its first number from the new building on the day of the Yale Game, November 20. A news story in the next issue made the justifiable claim that: "The ownership of its own building by the University daily sets a precedent for all other colleges and universities throughout the country." Although the building itself remained to be paid for, the *Bulletin* and Crimson Printing rentals made enough to meet the payments and cover taxes as well.

The new Editorial Board, established in 1911, was the most exciting thing happening at The Crimson in the new building. For the first time, late-night reviews of Boston and Cambridge plays were written, and run the morning after opening night. With the president no longer doing editorials single-handedly, the paper took a sharper editorial stance. The dark days of the prewar period were lightened only by a College-wide con-troversy over the number of beer ads which ran in The Crim-son. The editors were naturally reluctant to give up the adver-tisements — they were paid in kind.

The War to End All Wars depleted The Crimson as well as the College. Training camps sprung up to process men into soldiers, and Crimson editors volunteered in droves. Only the invalid and underaged remained within half a year after

The Harvard Crimson

VOL. LXXI. No. 68.

CAMBRIDGE, MASS. FRIDAY, APRIL 6, 1917.

PRICE, 5 CENTS.

PERCY HOCKEY CAPTAIN

LEADING GOAL GETTER OF THIS SEASON'S SEVEN WILL HEAD TEAM NEXT WINTER.

PREPARED AT EXETER

George Almy Percy '18, of Arlington, was yesterday elected captain of the University hockey team for the season of 1917-18. Percy prepared at Exeter, where he was captain of the hockey team and he was captain and right centre on the 1919 Freshman seven. For the past two years he has been a speedy and aggressive member of the University team during which time he filled the position of right centre in a most capable manner. In the course of each season he caged a total of nine goals, a number considerably larger than that of any other member of the team.

UNION CHOSE 1917-18 OFFICERS

D. M. Little, Jr., Elected Vice-President in Annual Balloting.

The light vote cast in the election of the officers and committeemen of the Union for the year 1917-18 held yesterday resulted as follows:

President, Major Henry Lee Higginson '55, of Boston.

Vice-president, David Mason Little, Jr., '18, of Salem.

Secretary, Lloyd Kirkham Garrison '19, of New York City.

Members of the Governing Board: Sewell Nightingale Dunton '18, of Circleville, Ohio; Malcolm Justin Logan uL, of South Boston; William Otho Morgan '18, of Highland Park, Ill.; Chester Samuel Nickerson '18, of Cliftondale; Hampton Robb '18, of Cleveland, Ohio; Edward Reese Roberts 1L, of Cape Girardeau, Mo.

Members of the Library Committee: Professor George Henry Chase '96, Professor Charles Townsend Copeland '82, Professor William Allan Neilson '94, Francis Barlow Bradley '19, of Convent, N.J.; Powell Mason Cabot '18, of Brookline; Richard Stockton Emmet '18, of South Salem, N. Y.; Aaron Davis Weld '18, of Boston.

Trained Chemists Needed

The American Association of Manufacturing Chemists is preparing to meet the increased demand for trained chemists which the war will cause by getting in touch with students in colleges and technical schools throughout the country. A great many men will soon be needed in the plants which receive Government contracts for war supplies, and in many other branches of military activity.

A committee has been formed in the University to gather statistics concerning students qualified to serve as chemists. Enrolment blanks, which do not in any way obligate the signer, but which will supply a list of University men who can be called on, may be had from the following committee: Prof. G. P. Baxter, Prof. E. P. Kohler, F. S. Bacon 2G, A. A. Cook '18, J. H. Hodges 2G, R. O. Hunneman '17 and M. L. Swanson '18.

RESOLUTION PASSED BY HOUSE

REPRESENTATIVES AFTER ALL NIGHT SESSION VOTED 373 TO 50 TO CONSIDER GERMANY AS BELLIGERENT OF UNITED STATES

PRESIDENT WILSON'S SIGNATURE AWAITED

STRONG MINORITY SHOWING DEFEATED BY EXHAUSTING POLICY OF ADMINISTRATION SUPPORTERS IN MOST HISTORIC SITTING OF NATIONAL CONGRESS.

Early this morning the House of Representatives brought to a close one of the greatest sessions of its history by passing the war resolution which the Senate accepted the day before yesterday. The final roll call showed 373 in favor of the measure and 50 opposed. By this action the United States has entered the great European war on the side of the Allies, determined to carry the struggle to a successful termination by every means at its disposal.

It was apparent since 10 o'clock yesterday morning when the House convened that it would follow the lead of the Senate and definitely commit the nation to conflict, and the greater part of the long discussion was taken up by the short speeches of various members who supported the measure, but wished to put themselves on record as reluctantly accepting war as the only course of honor. The one final step which will make the resolution complete is the signature of President Wilson, which will be affixed early this morning.

A somewhat unexpected opposition to the bill developed during the course of the afternoon and evening. It became evident that more than 40 members would vote "no" at the last roll call. Probably the greatest surprise of the evening was the shift of Congressman C. Kitchin, of North Carolina, to the side of the pacifists and with him what many weak-kneed followers. At the close of his protesting speech, however, Mr. Kitchin admitted that the measure he opposed would undoubtedly pass.

During the afternoon the House debate dragged, but at night the discussion became more lively. It was marked by several disturbances of a personal nature. Congressman Burnett, of Alabama, while attacking Kitchin, found occasion to direct a remark to Congressman Stedin, from his own state. The two Alabama members commenced such a furor that it was necessary for Sergeant-at-Arms Gordon to raise the mace to quiet the disorder.

The Senate adjourned Wednesday night to meet again at noon tomorrow. As the resolution must be returned to the Senate while that body is in session, President Wilson will not receive the historical document for approval until this afternoon. From the moment of his approval war will be on.

The Government is immediately putting into effect the plans which it has long been formulating for use as a moment as the present. An army of 1,797,- 946 men is provided for in the War Department's emergency military measure, under which the regular army is to be increased, the militia of the various states is to be drafted into Federal service, and an additional 1,000,000 men are to be raised by selective drafting. Telegraphic orders for the mobilization of 16,000 members of the Naval Militia and the Naval Reserve will be flashed throughout the land immediately upon the signing of the war resolution by President Wilson. Secretary of the Treasury McAdoo has asked that Congress appropriate immediately $3,500,-

(Continued on page six).

DEAN BRIGGS ISSUED STATEMENT UPON NOTICE OF ACTION BY CONGRESS THIS MORNING.

OPPONENTS INFORMED

DEAN BRIGGS' STATEMENT

"Because of the declaration of war the Harvard Committee on the Regulation of Athletic Sports has decided to give up all formal intercollegiate contests until further notice."

L. B. R. BRIGGS '75,
Chairman.

At a quarter past three this morning, less than 15 minutes after the passage of the war resolution by the House, Dean Briggs, acting with the power intrusted to him on March 24 by the Committee on the Regulation of Athletic Sports, issued the accompanying statement calling off all formal athletics at the University. The Dean has recently conferred with Professor Corwin of Yale and Dean McClenahan, of Princeton, who were acting in a similar capacity for their respective universities, and a joint decision to abolish intercollegiate athletics when war should be declared was reached. It is understood that they have already taken action on the matter. Mr. Fred W. Moore '98, the graduate treasurer of athletics, is this morning attending a meeting of delegates from Cornell, Columbia, Princeton, the University of Pennsylvania, and Yale, held in New York City at the Hotel Martinique, where the entire sport problem will be settled.

The following letter is to be sent today to each of the opponents of the University affected by Dean Briggs' announcement:

"Under present conditions it is almost or quite impossible to carry out schedules of games planned in times of peace. Our teams are broken up; the interest of our athletes is rightly transferred to other things than athletics; and there is here, as elsewhere, a general feeling that formal and important intercollegiate contests would be out of place at such a time as this. It is with great regret that we cancel our games. I have little doubt that your experience and your wishes are much like ours.

"Hoping that our teams may meet when the war is over, and that the interval will not be long, I am sincerely yours,

L. B. R. Briggs.

For the Harvard Committee on the Regulation of Athletic Sports."

What is Going on Today

5.00—Lowell Institute lecture. VI. "The 19th Century Composers." Dr. A. T. Davison '96, Huntington Hall, Boylston street, Boston.

8.00—Intercollegiate Fencing Association Championships, New York City.

The Weather

Forecast for Cambridge and vicinity: Today, rain; tomorrow fair. Strong westerly winds becoming southerly.

April, and the paper stumbled along with a changing staff. Turning out a daily sheet became a tougher proposition as Harvard shrank to 60 percent of its former enrollment.

The most important move of the postwar period was the decision to buy the *Harvard Illustrated Magazine*. *Life* was still 17 years in the future, and the term "photojournalism" had not yet been coined. But there was an increasing realization throughout the newspaper industry that photographs had become indispensable to a modern newspaper, and practically every Sunday paper in the country was groping its way toward the new age of photography with a rotogravure section. This particular phenomenon was more often than not an innocuous, somewhat bland showcase for less than brilliant photographs. The *Harvard Illustrated* was no exception. Since its beginning in 1899, it had given itself largely to posed, rather staid photographs of events at Harvard, group shots of teams and extracurricular activities, and portraits of important Harvard personages.

The absorption of the *Illustrated* by The Crimson provided the nucleus of what is now the Photographic Board. The *Illustrated* was issued biweekly, its photographic equipment became the property of The Crimson, and most of its editors became Crimson photographers. So, in the decade 1910–1920, The Crimson acquired its two youngest departments, the Editorial and Photographic Boards, and became essentially the modern Crimson.

Nineteen twenty was the year of the new linotype press. A gift of $1000 in the autumn of 1919 made the purchase possible, and finally The Crimson had a bigger paper. A column wider and five inches longer, the new sheet was ready to handle the news explosion which occurred at Harvard between the wars. The editorial page, which had gone from one to two columns before the War, used its extra ten inches to take up the cudgels of a slew of new causes undreamed of before the War.

By all appearances, no great social changes took place in The Crimson in the years between War and Depression. Things seem to have gone along as well (or poorly) as ever. The new press brought an expanded paper, and the new prosperity brought an expanded Business Board. A full-time accountant was put on to keep the Business Board's teeming profits in order.

The Crimson of the 1920s was respected, as we see from an article, quoted in the fiftieth-anniversary history, by Mr. John Palmer Gavit writing in the *New York Evening Post* of May 5, 1922:

> The Harvard Crimson — a very fine and high-grade expression of the best student sentiment — has great influence and deserves to have it. Twice, upon entering the dean's office early in the morning, I found that day's Crimson on his desk, with an editorial marked; each time the editorial made suggestions for bettering administrative methods, and each time the suggestion was complied with. I saw the editorials of The Crimson voicing the growing movement for reform in intercollegiate athletics pounding their way, day after day, by sheer sanity and force, into the public opinion of the college, both faculty and students.

More features — a regular graduate school column, more and more frequent reviews, a 1924 campaign series written by Faculty members — cropped up in the 1920s. Punches, elaborate initiation ceremonies, dances, dinners, and pranks on *The Lampoon* made the decade sparkle. The 23 to 2 victory over *Lampy* — in baseball, football, basketball, hockey and anything else — was already a tradition. Starting in 1925, the *Confidential Guide to Harvard* gave the students' view of courses, and the next year, the Vagabond, who is still wandering through Cambridge, meandered into the paper. Victor O. Jones '28, whose Notes From the Back of an Envelope graced the editorial page of *The Boston Globe* for decades, worked with Thomas H. Eliot '28, the former chancellor of Washington University, and George Anthony Weller '29, author of the Harvard novel *Not to Eat, Not for Love,* in making the last half of the decade the brightest period to date.

Time of Challenge: 1930–1940

The Crimson's first serious competition in decades hit the stands in the spring of 1934 — it was a newspaper founded and staffed by ex-Crimson editors. This civil war followed a period in which the Depression wiped out The Crimson's Business Board, and came at a time when no two editors seemed to be on speaking terms with each other. To the outsider, forty years away, it is a mild surprise that the paper got through the thirties.

As it headed into that decade, The Crimson seemed to be less and less a hard news paper. The (allegedly) weekly "Bookshelf" supplement added distinction to the tone of the paper, with articles by Lincoln Kirstein '30, Henry Murray, Theodore Spencer, and other noted figures in arts and letters. The pictorial supplement continued, as tame and proper as any Sunday rotogravure section, and photographs became a more important part of the paper itself. Football, in season and sometimes out, took up columns of front-page space, and Hu Flung Huey, The Crimson's prognosticator, would monopolize page one with his predictions for Saturday's games. Football extras rolled off the press with greater and greater frequency. Meanwhile, up front in the Business Office, things got worse and worse. Nineteen thirty gave way to 1931, and only some clever bookkeeping — the suspension of a debt owed one Crimson account by another — allowed the paper to show a profit. In 1932, not even that did the trick; the paper lost $500, even though it paid no editors' salaries.

Disaster was on the horizon, in more than one form. While the money had been evaporating, the news page had been deteriorating.

The first sign of the malaise appeared in the comment books. Whereas the comments of the 1920s had largely been restricted to the day's paper, and were usually impersonal and to the point, the editors of the 1930s began to digress, commenting on each other's character defects, stories the paper had missed, the ineptness of the candidates, and, more and more frequently, the number of mistakes the paper had made. Interviews, profiles, press handouts — anything but real news appeared on the front page, day after day. "For the University daily newspaper The Crimson is unchristly lousy," wrote one editor, and the sentiment was echoed by a growing minority of the News Board. In all fairness, running The

Crimson in those days was an almost impossible job. The executives, who should have had their full time to devote to news, were coordinating a drive to generate national advertising; everyone who could was on the streets drumming up business.

The academic year 1932–33 ended on a sour note, but September brought a new dedication to accuracy, and to excellence. Joseph J. Thorndike '34, John U. Monro '34, Osborne F. Ingram '35, and others, led a movement to restore The Crimson's credibility, a movement which seemed at first to be succeeding. But by winter, the paper was slipping back. "We are in grave danger of losing all the ground we have gained," Thorndike warned the staff. JESUS H. CHRIST IN THE FOOTHILLS was Ingram's comment on one particularly outrageous error. Some of the enthusiastic newshounds insisted that the paper be expanded; six pages, they said, was the minimum necessary to do justice to College *and* national news. The Business Board, barely rehabilitated, smelled disaster and giant losses in an enlarged paper, and rounded up enough votes in the winter executive elections to elect their candidates.

War was declared.

Some of The Crimson's best talent walked out of the Sanctum after the election, never to return. Tempers had run high, and the election had swung on a few key votes. Some of the Business Board's electors had not been seen on Plympton Street for months. After the decision, eleven editors departed to found their own paper.

The Harvard Journal gave The Crimson the only tough fight in its history. One *Journal*ist threw down the gauntlet in a defiant note to Crimson President John H. Morison '35:

> I will make a proposition to you. I'll be Crimson newsboy,
> if you'll be *Journal* newsboy — of course, you must realize
> you'll have much longer routes to cover.

The shock of secession galvanized The Crimson into action. Suddenly, all the things everyone insisted couldn't be done — the scoops, the big stories, even the six-page papers —

became everyday happenings. Osborne Ingram, the inveterate invoker of the Deity, became managing editor, and made a journalistic silk purse out of the sow's ear of a green and inexperienced young staff. Meanwhile, in the *Advocate* building behind Claverly, the *Journal* people were turning out a lively, inventive, readable paper. "Congratulations to the *Journal*ists," wrote one of Ingram's untrained minions one day. "Whatta Col. 5 scoop *they* got, oh boy oh boy." *The Journal* contracted for printing with a Cambridge paper, and came out regularly, six days a week, plus extras.

The Journal had the staff. The Crimson had the facilities, the business contacts, and the tradition. Since it did not begin publication until after the Easter vacation, *The Journal* was in a weak position to attract subscribers. In balance, The Crimson had the edge.

The battle was neck and neck for a few weeks. *The Journal*'s layout was original and intriguing, with plenty of five-column headlines and pictures. Eight *Journal* pages every day gave readers Harvard, national and international news, and even Radcliffe news — something always scandalously neglected in the old Crimson. *The Journal*'s Sunday edition — it omitted Mondays — scooped The Crimson often on weekend news. Through it all, the College maintained neutrality. Although Dean Hanford had tried to stop the split before it became public, he treated both papers impartially, giving official notices and news to both.

The end of the fight was predictable; when the year ended, so did *The Journal.* Its editors lost money, sleep, and study time in their struggle to set up and run a new paper. Commencement brought capitulation, and The Crimson once more had the field to itself. But The Crimson of June 1934 was inestimably better than its namesake of a few months before. The efforts of loyal staff had made it the kind of paper the *Journal* people had wanted in the first place, and the 1948 history tells us that the two groups buried the hatchet.

The waning of the thirties brought the last major structural change in the running of The Crimson. Under the old system, editors would climb a ladder of advancement, from assistant managing editor to managing editor to president, stepping in the first rung in their junior year and advancing one grade every semester. Under this plan, the first choice for president in every class was forced out of office after only a few months. In the thirties, with an expanded paper, a brace of supplements, and a *Confidential Guide* now issued as a separate magazine, the president had little time to do anything but learn the technicalities of his office before moving on. Thus, in 1937, the Constitution was overhauled, specifying that officers would be elected in the fall of their junior year, take office in February and leave office in January of their senior year. The first president elected under this system was Cleveland Amory '39.

By the late thirties one Crimson institution was firmly established. Arthur Hopkins, the linotypist for the Crimson Printing Company who served at 14 Plympton Street from 1929 to 1965, began his rise to immortality in the midthirties, when he became the chief of the shop. As Caspar Weinberger '37, president, wrote in 1964:

> Art Hopkins's contributions to The Crimson went far beyond his unparalleled technical skills. He was, I know, a personal friend of, and held in the highest esteem by, all of the members of all of the boards in all of the years I was there. I know, too, from conversations with other editors of earlier and later vintage, that everyone who ever had any association with him at all felt the same way. He was as much a part of the paper as the masthead, but much more. For it was as much a matter of the same personal pride to Art, as it was to every editor, to see that the paper appeared on time every morning and was presentable, accurate, complete, and maybe even interesting.

The editions of The Crimson marking the tercentenary of Harvard College were packed with ads. Among the biggest advertisers was the tutoring-school business. When the scholars from the greatest universities in the world gathered in 1936, they, along with the alumni, statesmen, and other dignitaries, read about their day's activities in stories that ran side by side with advertisements for Manter Hall, "Widow" Nolan's, and half a dozen other institutions of lesser fame dedicated to

making money from the laziness and lack of dedication of
Harvard students.

Time magazine began the fight against "tute" schools. E. O.
Tilton '36, who went to *Time* from The Crimson, published an
article in the fall of 1936 exposing the abuses of the schools,
and singling out Manter Hall. Manter Hall replied with a libel
suit, in which it won six cents worth of damages. In 1937, the
Student Council issued a report damning the tutoring schools,
and asking The Crimson to stop carrying their advertising.

As a matter of hard financial fact, The Crimson would have
been hard put to drop tutoring ads completely. They ac-
counted for upwards of $2000 a year in income — nothing to
be sniffed at. At the personal request of Dean Hanford,
though, "tute" ads were not included in the *Confidential Guide*
from 1937 on; thus freshmen were spared from corruption
until they could find their own way down to Mt. Auburn
Street.

Amory's board began the editorial campaign against tutoring schools, but was still unable to drop the advertising. Only
in March of 1939 were the ads done away with. A few weeks
later, an editorial decried the schools as "intellectual broth-
els," and a lead story of page one announced:

> By unanimous vote last night The Crimson Board decided
> to exclude all tutoring school advertising until such time
> as the tutoring schools are restricted to functions not in-
> consistent with sound educational practice.

Tutoring schools were defeated; but it took several months
of a Crimson campaign. When a Crimson poll revealed that
three-quarters of the senior class had made use of the schools,
the College instituted the regulation against tutoring schools,
which stands to this day. The schools went out of business,
sold their buildings, and disappeared. [It should be noted that
the present Manter Hall School is a legitimate college prep
school with no relation to the tutoring school of the same
name.]

In 1940, the specter of war could no longer be ignored. The
Crimson now realized that war was inevitable, and urged

preparations. The paper that announced the bombing of Pearl Harbor carried a 5:11 a.m. time slug. The Crimson had stayed open until the last possible minute, to get the latest bulletins.

The War and Its Aftermath: 1940–1950

UNIVERSITY DELAYS IMMEDIATE ACTION, screamed the Harvard-oriented headline on the Pearl Harbor story. And so, it seemed, the administration had actually done, if you compare the day to World War I, when The Crimson got Dean Briggs out of bed to cancel the athletic program. But the sneak attack took the country by surprise, and it was only in the coming weeks and months that the University would swing into a wartime stance. The University ran a summer term in 1942, and The Crimson ran a summer paper, on a three-times-a-week basis.

The Class of 1944 took over the paper in early summer to give '45 a chance to go to war. The Crimson seems to have run more smoothly than anything else in the country that year, even with depleted manpower. One series of editorials urged the national government to "Give Us the Blueprints" for the national defense. As its own contribution, The Crimson gave the nation its fence — to be melted down for ammunition.

The Crimson put on its uniform on Friday, May 14, 1943. The banner on the paper read "The Service News," and a box on either side of that title carried a large question mark and the plea, "Submit a Name." A few weeks later, a local clergyman won the paper's $25 War Bond by submitting "Harvard Service News."

The stories which ran in *The Service News* were of a kind The Crimson has never run: KHAKIS, NAVY BLUES TO MINGLE WITH CAPS AND GOWNS AT GRADUATION RITES, an early issue announced, summing up the entire mood of Harvard at the time. But would the civilian Crimson have ever called commencement "Graduation"?

The Graduate Board decided not to empower *The Service News* to editorialize. Instead, the paper was administered during the war by a board of David M. Little '18, master of Adams House and secretary of the University, Mrs. Anna

Hoke, the paper's accountant, Donald T. Field '31, and Thomas S. Kuhn '44. These four oversaw a rotating, uneven, erratic staff which sometimes amounted only to Mrs. Hoke and Art Hopkins, as they turned out first a weekly, and later a semiweekly, from The Crimson's quarters.

Dan H. Fenn Jr. '44 ('46), who took over the presidency in 1942, returned in 1946 as the last editor of *The Service News*, to supervise its demobilization. By the February registration, The Crimson announced its intention of reappearing, and shortly afterward, it did.

The financial rebirth of the paper was more difficult to achieve. The trustees had absorbed a *Service News* deficit, but the building needed extensive renovation, and a new heating system had been put in. When Mrs. Hoke decided to retire with *The Service News*, the future seemed even more bleak. But The Crimson pulled through, as it always has, and it always does, and it always will. To survive and to prosper, any community needs a newspaper. A community's newspaper will be its voice, and its conscience; it will prod, it will protest, it will expose, and it will complain; it will report, it will explain, and it will give praise when praise is due. It will not philosophize, and it will be read. The community will support it, and it will keep the community alive.

Harvard is just such a community.

CHAPTER 1

The University

JUST TO THINK of Harvard as a university, with roots going back to, say, the beginnings of medieval universities in Europe, is asking for a lot of trouble. In the first place, medieval universities were run on the sometimes sound assumption that teachers were employed by students, who could — and often did — discharge their mentors at will. Harvard, renowned for the scholarship and research of its professors, has difficulty, some will say, just getting the emphasis on teaching right, never mind the employment arrangements.

Still, the vast array of committees and departments dedicated to research and publication, and to teaching undergraduates, graduates, professionals, and more recently the continuingly educable, *is* called a "university." It follows that the university can be explained or at least intuitively understood, and that's what The Crimson has been trying to do for more than a century.

What will become clear to readers as they go on is that the University is often presented at its most dramatic or controversial moments, some of which did not always reflect well on Harvard. This quality may have something to do with the nature of news: conventional wisdom would say that "Harvard teaches student" is not news, but "student teaches Harvard" (or "takes over Harvard"), now that's news. The selections also reflect the editor's bias in assuming that Harvard, The Crimson, or any other university or newspaper show their true colors during moments of crisis. And one thing that may not be immediately obvious from reading the articles alone is that as a result of, or during each of, its many controversies

Harvard often grew as a university. That is why, it seems, The Crimson has often cast an independent, critical gaze at the University. Not because the University was incapable of the excellence it has striven for, but because it was always capable of more: its own standards and the very faculties it was developing in student editors were being applied.

Unfortunately the University's full range, and The Crimson's coverage of it, has been presented here in adumbrated form. Emphasis has been given to the College over the professional schools, graduate departments, and research-oriented institutions such as the Society of Fellows or the Radcliffe Institute. At least some of the issues covered — education of women, employment practices, academic freedom — may suggest what these other aspects of the complete University were, in The Crimson's eyes — or were meant to be.

What exactly a "university" is, well, that's something The Crimson, along with the rest of the world, is still working on.

*   *   *

One of the first issues of University education to confront The Crimson at its inception was that of the education of women. In his inaugural address of 1869, Harvard President Charles William Eliot, Class of 1853, commented briefly on the higher education of women, saying that Harvard wouldn't yet take on "the difficulties involved in a common residence of hundreds of young men and women of immature character and marriageable age." Eliot's attitude seemed to be shared by most Harvard students and alumni. Within the next decade, however, not only would Harvard prepare examinations for women, but some of its most distinguished professors would contribute to the foundation of a nameless institution for the higher education of women in 1879.

EDITORIAL

Higher Education of Women

May 16, 1873

At the meeting in Boston of the Social Science Association last Wednesday there was an exciting discussion concerning the Higher Education of Women, in which President Eliot was severely attacked for not opening Harvard College to women. The advocates of reform rely chiefly on theoretical and abstract reasons. They say that the College is endowed by the State, that women pay taxes, and that therefore it is legally wrong to refuse them the advantages of education that have been procured by their money; that girls in the public and private schools often display a great capacity for study, and often lead the boys; that it is absurd to demand from women great talent, or genius even, before they are allowed the privilege of the higher education.

The reasons of opponents are chiefly practical, such as their experience has taught them. Thus, President Eliot says that, having examined some 30 mixed colleges in the West, he has come to a conclusion hostile to them . . . Mr. Eliot says that both male and female physicians agree in declaring that women are physically unfit for study; Mr. Raymond, of Vassar, says that 400 healthier women can hardly be found than those at Poughkeepsie. In view of this confliction, our condition is much like that of jurors in a murder trial after listening to the testimony of chemical experts.

Colonel [Thomas Wentworth] Higginson quotes Voltaire: "Ideas and beards are alike, women and very young men have none." So we do not place much confidence in our opinion in this matter, which is as follows:

. . . If women come to Harvard, the true policy of the College will be teaching, pure and simple, without any laws to control the students outside the classroom. Then it will be expedient that the dormitory system will be entirely abolished, and instead students will room and board in private houses, as they do in German university towns. If so radical a change as this is really necessary, Mr. Eliot may well hesitate; for a well-endowed college for women could be established at hardly greater expense than the change would necessitate.

By 1882, as more and more professors gave courses to increasing numbers of women in a small house at 15 Appian Way, the three-year-old institution elected a president, Elizabeth Cary Agassiz, and took on a name: officially, the Society for the Collegiate Instruction of Women, and unofficially, the "Harvard Annex."

A Visit to the Annex
FROM AN OCCASIONAL CORRESPONDENT

April 28, 1885

"Where is the 'Annex'?" is a question whose frequency surprises the well-informed. That the inquirer speaks hesitatingly and adds, "I ought to know, but I don't," is a tribute to the unobtrusive life of this rigorous offshoot of Harvard. This ignorance of the location of the Annex is due, of course, to the fact that it has no buildings of its own, but occupies rooms in a small house on a side street. Its surroundings compare unfavorably with those enjoyed by the women students of every other eastern school of its rank. Four rooms in a private house are at the service of the students during the day. None board there, for, happily, the Annex is unencumbered by that "relic of the Middle Ages," the dormitory system.

The interested stranger will find nothing to attract his attention in the exterior of the house . . . there are few visitors; perhaps because the students hesitate to take their friends to the rooms, lest they intrude upon the privacy of the family whose home it is. If you enter, you find, on the left, a parlor which is used occasionally as a recitation room, and the rest of the time, as the sitting room of the family. Next to the parlor is a recitation room, and over these are the study and another recitation room. A laboratory is fitted up in a house across the way.

The study serves as reading-room, cloak, and lunch room for the 53 young women now enjoying the instruction of the Harvard Professors. The reading-room of the "Harvard Annex!" Your fancy, unbidden, suggests harmonious colors, inviting easy chairs, a few choice pictures; a happy blending of order and confusion in the details; a wooden mantel, framing a fire-place, and perhaps a bust of Minerva, or, at least, a stuffed owl presiding over it; book-cases filled with all that a student needs to have at hand, leaning in comfortable retirement against the walls; a study, with room enough for 50 people, and not too much for one.

Alas that the reality is so far from embodying your ideal! The 1200 books stand boldly out into the room. Simplicity, to speak moderately, reigns everywhere. She appears, in not her most attractive form, in the Franklin stove. She stares blankly at you from her BOOKS RETURNED, and BOOKS RECEIVED, which are pasted on the wall over the narrow mantel-piece, and which indicate that there is to be found the connection between the Annex and the Harvard Library. The dimity curtains and patch-covered window-seats cannot be offended at being dubbed "simple." But simplicity abdicates her sway when she approaches the study table, where confusion, I am told, too often reigns. The chairs, also, rebel against being confined to their primitive use, and offer their arms and backs to a heavy burden of Newmarkets, sacques and hats. The interested reader can obtain no adequate idea of the harmonious details I attempt to describe, until he realizes that this room has the ordinary proportions of a chamber. Order is, doubtless, a strong element in the character of the Annex students, but there are overruling circumstances.

No one doubts the wisdom of stating this experiment in the higher education of women, in an unobtrusive and moderate fashion. The success of the plan is its own justification. Now, the time for small beginnings and meager accommodations is past. The large and growing body of students demands suitable surroundings. The Annex is waiting, like the Bartholdi statue, for the public to realize its need of a substantial foundation.

Early in 1893 President Agassiz approached President Eliot with the idea of bringing the Society and Harvard closer together. The Society wanted to be self-governing, to award the bachelor's degree, and to have the diplomas countersigned by the president of Harvard attesting to the fact that "no instruction was provided of a lower grade than that given in Harvard College." The Harvard president and fellows would visit the Society and approve all teachers appointed. Before the Harvard Overseers voted on the matter, the Society renamed itself: Radcliffe.

In spite of heavy opposition, Radcliffe won approval from the Board of Overseers and went on to have the Radcliffe College Charter approved by the Massachusetts legislature in 1894. Throughout the period of Radcliffe's inception, The Crimson reported and editorialized sporadically on the debates over the higher education of women, the Society's growth, and the diploma controversy. From these articles we can observe what the undergraduates, the alumni, the press, and the public thought of what was still called an "experiment" as late as 1893 — 56 years after Mount Holyoke was founded.

To say that negative attitudes predominated throughout is to state the obvious. One can discern a pattern of thought toward women's education that vacillated between paternalistic support for cross-registration of "bluestocking" types, unequivocal support, and a noncommittal sense of compromise. ("Degrees to women direct from Harvard," said an editorial of January 13, 1894, is only a "question . . . of time." To understand what time means at traditional Harvard, one must remember that women undergraduates didn't receive degrees directly from Harvard until 1963.) Some pro–Radcliffe Charter petitioners to the Overseers — including Theodore Roosevelt, Class of 1880, and William Dean Howells — did actually think, in 1893, that Radcliffe students should receive their degrees directly from Harvard.

One attitude that never seemed to change in the history of Harvard-Radcliffe relations during the nineteenth century was the Victorian attitude toward sex expressed so succinctly by President Eliot in his inaugural address. When examining these attitudes, which appeared frequently in The Crimson, it's impossible to clearly draw the line between simple prudishness and a more calculated sense of sexual politics. ("We have too much respect for women to wish to have their association with us in our college course," an 1879 editorial stated.)

While a woman's physical attractiveness — all the nineteenth-century clichés: grace, pale complexion, frailty — would be a distraction to supposedly serious students (editorial, 1873), an education would make her liable to become, in most cases, "uninteresting," and even then "women ought not to receive the same salary as men . . . because they are personally weaker and cannot endure what men can" (editorial, 1889). In his inaugural address Eliot had added that Harvard's decision to shy away from co-education was "not influenced by any notions about the innate capacities of women. The world knows next to nothing about the natural mental capacities of the female sex." Such unknowingness was not without purpose.

EDITORIAL

Harvard and the "Annex"

December 7, 1893

. . . For years the Annex has followed the course of Harvard College, and all instruction has been given by professors and instructors of Harvard. The same plan will be pursued when the Annex changes its name to Radcliffe; and the only apparent difference will be in the degree. Hitherto the Society for the Collegiate Instruction of Women has been able to give nothing beyond a certificate stating that the graduate has performed the work required for the degree at Harvard. In the future, they will not only confer a degree of their own, but this degree will be made doubly valuable by bearing the seal of Harvard University.

The statements in the newspapers to the effect that students of the Annex under the new agreement will be admitted to the full privileges of the University are absolutely incorrect. They have already given outsiders the idea that something like coeducation is to be put into practice here, while in reality the distinction between the Annex and the College is to remain exactly as at present.

It is interesting to note the change of the official name to Radcliffe College. Investigations which have recently been made revealed the fact that the first woman who ever gave money to Harvard was, by her maiden name, Anne Radcliffe. Her bequest of £100 was made in the year 1640; and it seemed desirable to Mrs. Agassiz, the president of the present Society, that a college for the education of women should remember, in the days of its prosperity, the first woman who showed an active interest in educational institutions.

The year 1894 not only marked Radcliffe's receipt of a state charter but the twenty-fifth anniversary of President Eliot's administration. Eliot would continue as president until 1909, when after forty years of service to the University he would retire.

The following editorial gives a brief outline of Eliot's many accomplishments during the first 25 years, for the most part his most enduring advances. It should be said that Eliot's initiative was not always as warmly received as appeared in retrospect. In 1884 Eliot had spoken out on the need for changing the liberal arts education from the sixteenth-century emphases on Latin, Greek, mathematics, rhetoric, and exposition. These courses were then compulsory for freshmen; indeed, some background in them was required for admission, which limited the student body largely to eastern-private-school graduates. Eliot saw more need for science and modern languages. When he made a public speech on the matter, graduates from many universities, led by editors of The New York Times, *seriously questioned such an innovation as transforming a true liberal arts education into a course of overspecialized studies. Within the year, however, Eliot had set his plan in motion, also allowing freshmen to take some elective courses for the first time in Harvard's history.*

The Graduate School, about which you will read, was probably Eliot's finest moment. Created in 1872 as the "Graduate Department," it was renamed and reorganized as the Graduate School in 1890, and finally given its present name — Graduate School of Arts and Sciences (GSAS) — in 1905.

In addition to creating the Graduate School, reforming the curriculum, and making ties with Radcliffe, Eliot's other great — if not universally approved — achievement was the erection of Memorial Hall to commemorate Harvard's Civil War dead.

EDITORIAL

President Eliot's First Quarter Century

May 19, 1894

Today closes the twenty-fifth year during which President Eliot has been at the head of the University. It is a period of service remarkable alike for its length and for its importance in the University's development. The Harvard of 1894 is widely different from the Harvard of 1869. Then there were about 100 members of the teaching staff and 1000 students; now there are over 300 on the teaching staff and over 3000 students. To this growth, no other man has contributed so much as President Eliot.

Largely through his efforts, the funds of the University, the necessary condition to every expansion of its work, have been raised from about two millions of dollars to considerably more than eight millions of dollars, and, in addition, the value of the equipment of the University has been increased by over two millions. At the same time, every department of the University has been subjected to a rigorous supervision.

Weakness has not been tolerated. Some departments have been revolutionized; all have been strengthened.

The most important advances which he has directed have been the more complete introduction of the elective system and the establishment of large resources for higher learning. In 1869, out of the 128 courses of instruction offered in the academic department, 34 were prescribed; now out of 720 only 9 are prescribed. Weaknesses the elective system undoubtedly has, — weaknesses that are never to be overlooked, and yet the evil of the system is far less than its good. It places before every student the opportunity of enlarging himself where the fullest growth is possible, it tends to the economy of mental power, and is certainly the characteristic of the modern idea of education. It has added richly to Harvard's reputation that she has been the pioneer for this country in the introduction of the system.

At the time when President Eliot came into office other institutions than Harvard were beginning to provide means for the higher learning. It is obvious that, if Harvard had failed to keep abreast with this movement her prestige as the leading seat of learning in the land would have been gone. The up-building of the Graduate School has been, for this reason, the most important development of the University in which President Eliot has taken a leading part.

Such, in briefest outline, are the main services of President Eliot to the University. No man, unless he had the highest abilities, could have done such work. With keen sagacity, he has foreseen the action of educational forces; with unfailing resources of quick intelligence, adroit action, and steady will he has met these forces and maintained the position of Harvard in all circumstances. He is a man of action; always thoroughly acquainted with the matter in hand from its broadest aspects to its minutest details, always clear as to his own intention, always calm, swift and unhesitating in its realization. No university president in the country is his equal in executive ability, and it is safe to say that, when his administration closes, the executive of Harvard will have to be reorganized.

In his moments of deliberate respite, he is open, genial, and engaging; but he seldom is at leisure. At work, he seems an immense will, regulated by very powerful and very precise intellectuals. He is grave, austere, self-sufficing, reserved, and the embodiment of dignity. If only his point of view is taken, his position on every question is found to be supported by the soundest logic; but, under the necessity for much action, he seems at times to give the benefit of the doubt too easily in favor of his own point of view. On this account, he rouses such frequent and, as it seems to us, such needed opposition. Against him all who see truths which he underestimates need strenuously to contend. On such an occasion as the present, however, it is fitting that all thoughts of opposition should be laid aside and recognition given to the great service he has done the University. He is a magnificent force, that has given aboundingly to the life of Harvard.

When Abbott Lawrence Lowell, Class of 1877, assumed the presidency of Harvard in 1909 the foundations had already been laid for educational achievement. Lowell assumed the task of expanding upon the motifs composed by Eliot: elaborating the elective system, refining the concept of honors in academic achievement, and as a step forward, creating a system of "concentrations" in each field, along with tutorials. Tutorials were first introduced on a major scale with the general examination in 1917. Originally designed for honors students in a few, selected departments, tutorials were destined to expand to other departments under Lowell, and, eventually, under Conant, they would include a large number of sophomore and group tutorials for most students, as well as one-on-one tutorials for honors candidates.

Among Lowell's greatest achievements was his support for and expansion of the University's graduate and professional schools — the schools of Public Health (1913) and Business (1927) were founded during his tenure; and the Graduate School of Education was created in 1920 out of the old GSAS department. Along with these educational advancements came a sextupling of the endowment to $126 million in 1933, and the inevitable expansion of the University's facilities: Widener Library, Memorial Chapel, Paine Hall (music), Wolcott Gibbs and Coo-

lidge Laboratories (chemistry), the Indoor Athletic Building, the Larz Anderson Bridge, and Business and Medical School facilities were all built during Lowell's tenure, and countless additions were made to already existing buildings.

Seven new Houses and the House Plan that they represented were probably President Lowell's most visible and enduring contribution to Harvard. Of course, without the generous $10 million gift of Edward S. Harkness, Yale '97, it would not have gone forward, but it was Lowell who pushed the House Plan through, against heavy student opposition (more than half polled by The Crimson at the time were opposed to it) and some alumni pressure.

The Crimson played a key role at the very inception of the House Plan. The idea was not a new one. As Edward C. Aswell '26, former Crimson editorial chairman, has recalled, the House system, or "The English college system" had been "favored from time to time, in desultory fashion, ever since the turn of the century." What provided the impetus for the plan, in the end, was a student-led and student-oriented initiative. Aswell writes: "The idea of conducting a study of the Harvard system from the point of view of students — the beneficiaries of its virtues, the victims of its defects — was born in the Sanctum of The Crimson." Conducting the study alongside Aswell were William I. Nichols '26, then Crimson president, and seven other students. The year was 1926, and Nichols, writing in 1978, can recall the story well:

The "Lowell-Harkness Plan" was, actually, *'The Harvard Crimson Plan"! . . .* For strategic reasons we arranged for the idea to be formulated by a "Committee on Education" set up within the Student Council, of which we were both members. Aswell was Chairman of the Committee and the result of our deliberations was a "Student Council Report on Education." This was then published with enthusiasm in The Crimson and, via us, publicized nationally through the press associations.

The essence of the report was a detailed plan whereby the then big and faceless Harvard College could be broken down into human-scaled units ("Houses") after the Oxford and Cambridge models. It was this report which came to the attention of Edward S. Harkness, the philanthropist. As a loyal Yale man he first proposed the idea to Yale.

When they turned him down, he went to Cambridge at his own initiative, trudged up the granite steps of University Hall, and made his amazing $3,000,000 offer to President Lowell [subsequently increased by Harkness]. Later, of course, Yale changed its mind and launched its own house plan, but only long after the Crimson-initiated House Plan at Harvard was well under way.

Accounts vary as to the real input of The Crimson into the House Plan, some maintaining that, as it was true that Lowell had always been keeping such a House system in the back of his mind, the Crimson initiative merely came at the right time for Lowell to use it wisely.

Whatever the idea's origins may have been, it was clearly Harkness's independent act that set the present House Plan on its way.

Curiously enough, by the time blueprints were being drawn up for the seven new Houses, The Crimson was opposed to the House Plan as "undemocratic" and "a misdirection of wealth." This policy slowly changed to the point where, by 1932, students choosing their House could read in The Crimson about each one's weaknesses and strengths.

Theories Still Rampant as Harvard Prepares for Opening of New Houses — Camp Is Divided on Issue
One Group Afraid of Democracy, One Fears Club
June 17, 1930

Harvard's 295th year will see the beginning of the mooted House Plan. Although the black tower of Dunster House breaks the skyline on the Charles and the blue and gold of Lowell House rears itself above the masses of brick piled below Mt. Auburn Street to testify to the corporeal change which has already begun to take place in the University, both the aims and the eventual development of the new move toward the socialization of the undergraduate years in Cambridge remain indefinite.

While the House Plan may be said to have originated from the idea first nurtured by the erection of the freshman dormitories, which are soon to assume new functions as additional

House units, only the extremists are bold enough to advance startling theories concerning the future glories or defects of the scheme. Thus far the battle seems to have raged about two salient points advanced by prospective boosters and knockers. The first idea is that the House Plan will degenerate into a glorified club system and incorporate together with all that is English, dilettante, and emblazoned, a supreme disregard of the "individual." These epithets, which usually assume the opprobrious position of stigmas when hurled hot in undergraduate conversations, take their origin from two sources. The first of these is the method used for selecting men for the first two Houses, and the second is from the statement made by President Lowell to the effect that the men already in a House will have the major voice in saying who shall go in after them.

Fully as loud are the clamors of those who oppose the second possible development. They picture Harvard as a future real estate development with all the streets named "Main Street," all the suburban dwellers called "Babbits," and all the inmates of various races, creeds, economic standing, social pre-eminence, intellectual interests and oddities — in fact all kinds and characters forced into one big family, which is supposed, unlike most families, to be free from dissension. The great cry is aimed at the supposed sacrifice of "individuality." This point of view is that of the objectors who have seized upon "cross section" as a term of great significance, while, as a matter of fact, it may mean anything from something to nothing.

More moderate critics regard the House Plan as a move which will, by various checks and balances, avoid either of these extremes. Little is safe to predict other than that the housing quarters will be nearer than the present dormitories, the Yard will no longer be the center of domiciliary attraction, the restaurants on the Square will lose money, the Houses will supplant the classes in intramural rivalry, the members of the undergraduate body and the faculty will be in a more favorable position for the development of mutual understanding, and real estate prices on the Charles will rise.

But while the future students of Harvard under the new organization are experiencing qualms of apprehension, joy, or revolt, the physical aspect of the University is undoubtedly bewildering those graduates of War days, the students of the era of John the Orangeman, and especially the inhabitants of Harvard when the mauve decade was in full swing and Harvard had a philosophy department. For even the massed chimneys of Dunster House, both the useful and the purely aesthetic ones, are only a few of the outward signs of change. The towering bulk of the new gymnasium opposing the Georgian structure of Lowell House has meant that the small buildings below Mt. Auburn Street have given way before the forward march of mass education, that the rural aspect of the streets in the vicinity of the Freshman Dormitories [then situated by the river] has stiffened into the more canyonlike semblance of Wall Street. Already the walls of the Power Plant across from Weld Boathouse have fallen, and the foundation for the third unit [Eliot House] is about to be placed.

Standish and Gore will be merged into another unit [Winthrop House], while McKinlock and an addition across the way will make still another [Leverett House]. These with Smith, as a unit [Kirkland House], and the combined facilities of Russell, Randolph, and Westmorly with a dining room built on the present site of Russell Annex as still another [Adams House], will complete the Houses so far planned.

The promotion of racial harmony and equality was hardly one of President Lowell's concerns, even by the conservative standards of his times. When freshmen dormitories, requiring residence, were opened in 1914, blacks were not allowed to live there until the issue came to a head — largely in The Crimson — in 1923. Even then, blacks were admitted in segregated units, and would continue to live so in Harvard dormitories up until World War II. In 1922 Lowell had also blundered into the issue of imposing quotas on admissions, largely to restrict the disproportionate numbers of Jews, relative to the general population, who went to Harvard (this the result of Harvard's former tolerance, in relation to most other private colleges). The upshot of this controversy — during which The Crimson defended quotas on the grounds that Harvard should be representative of the general population — was that, while quotas were not instituted, the pol-

icy of "geographical distribution" was, with largely the same results. What follows is just a sample of the considerable limits to tolerance at Harvard in the thirties and beyond.

EDITORIAL

The College Negro

May 16, 1932

One thing, it seems, that many university officials imagine is a demand by the college Negro for social opportunities. This is a tragic delusion, for nothing is further from the intelligent Negro's mind. He has long ago become socially self-sufficient — and, especially in a city as large as Boston, social satisfaction is quite obtainable. What he does expect includes the practical advantages that his University can offer: the opportunity to learn by conversation, and, if necessary, by invitation. These are pitifully denied him at Harvard. Of the four Negro members of the Class of 1932, all of whom are candidates for honors, none was admitted to the House Plan, which, ironically enough, was to present a cross section of the University. President Lowell, in a letter to *Opportunity*, a Negro journal, readily states that there is no policy with regard to Negroes in the Houses. Yet none have been admitted.

Medical schools the country over look forward joyfully to the day when Negro schools will be able to offer a medical education which will be sufficiently attractive to Negroes graduating from white universities. If this question is put: "How may this Utopia be achieved?," the inevitable answer is that the best white medical schools must educate the better prepared Negroes to undertake the responsibility of raising the standards of Negro medical schools. Harvard [Medical School] has not admitted a Negro since 1927; as a leader in liberal education, it sets a bad example.

Memorial Church, first proposed to commemorate only the American dead of World War I (three German graduates died in the war) and also to be a place only for Christian services, met with strong opposition from The Crimson. The controversy caught the eye of The New York Times, *which ridiculed The Crimson in its editorial columns, saying "some of the children are bawling in the college newspapers."* The Nation, *on the other hand, defended the Crimson line, in rather eloquent terms:*

> Now these protesting young men, if we understand them, are not objecting to religion as such, however much they may be questioning some of its current manifestations. They do seem to object, however, to the assumption that God is Nordic, Protestant, capitalistic, and pro-Ally. And they do not believe that the universities have the right to use the millions they can so easily command for the uncritical propagation of accepted ideas and beliefs. The students seem to be doing honest and genuine thinking, and in their thought we see far more hope both for the universities and for the religion of the future than we can see in the action of a corporation that would build an unneeded chapel in the midst of a living university.

Memorial Church, once constructed, was destined to be the center of another controversy, presented later in this chapter.

EDITORIAL
_____

The Compulsory Chapel

March 10, 1931

News that plans are going ahead rapidly for the erection of a chapel as a memorial to the Harvard men who died in the World War is unwelcome. Although a majority of the alumni has passively favored the proposal there has been vigorous opposition from a minority of the graduates. And in Cambridge militant opposition to the War Memorial Chapel has been the one consistent feature of undergraduate opinion since the idea was first brought forward.

Much misinterpretation has been placed upon this antagonism. It has been said that the objection of undergraduates is to a memorial in itself. This is not true. The undergraduates feel that the proposed memorial is a poor one, and they desire a memorial which would have more meaning in future years. The suitability of a chapel as a memorial is already demonstrated in the colossal failure of Memorial Hall to mean anything to Harvard men of the past few generations, except as an eating place, an examination room, and a floor for the now defunct Junior Prom.

It is difficult to understand why the administration is in favor of the project . . . The answer seems to be that there is sufficient graduate finance. Eight hundred thousand dollars has been raised, and can be used only for a War Memorial. It is palpably undesirable to return this fund. But it is possible, with a little patience and foresight, for the administration to convince the alumni that a far more suitable memorial might be erected.

There will be opportunities in the next few years to contribute something at once beautiful and useful, as the center of University life becomes adjusted to the new position on the river. At other universities, such edifices as infirmaries, athletic centers, student unions, and even classroom buildings have not been considered too mundane to serve as fine expressions to the memory of war dead.

Any memorial to be a valid tribute must embody the united sentiment of those in whose name it is given. To railroad through the University a War Memorial Chapel that does not express the ideals of all Harvard men is to confine its significance to brick and steel.

James Bryant Conant '14 became president of Harvard in September 1933, at a time when, as The Crimson pointed out, "the physical development of Harvard is an accomplished fact . . . to a large extent the new president's work will consist of . . . minor adjustments, . . . rounding off the edges, . . . and reconciling the conflicts presented by the many innovations which have been implanted in the University in the last 50 years." Under Conant, who incidentally was a Crimson editor, the sciences were enormously expanded at Harvard; the School of Public Administration was established in 1939; the ideal of a liberal arts education was formalized into the concept of "General Education," by

Harvard President James B. Conant '14 rises as Harvard scores a touchdown against Colgate in 1952. Conant, a former Crimson editor, was Harvard's president from 1933 to 1953. October 20, 1952. (Photo by George A. Hermann '54)

which students would study at least a few broad, general, introductory courses in each of the fields of humanities, social sciences, and natural sciences; and the endowment grew from $126 million to $360 million.

Conant's presidency was not without its controversial moments, the foremost being academic freedom issues. The first test was the Walsh-Sweezy affair of 1937. The case resulted from one *of Conant's major "refinements": the new policy of requiring "up or out" decisions regarding junior faculty. (Either they were promoted to tenured positions within a set time limit, or they were given notice of termination; none would be kept on indefinitely in nontenured positions).*

J. Raymond Walsh and Alan R. Sweezy '29 were radical economists who, along with five other instructors in the Economics Department, were given notice that, under the new policy, only two would be kept on, the decision being based on prior publication of merit. Neither was retained (since both had been led to believe that publishing scholarly articles could wait), and charges were leveled by the Cambridge Union of University Teachers and two student groups that the Economics Department rejected Walsh and Sweezy because of their politics. The Crimson response follows.

Ironically, in the following year, 1938–39, then Communist Granville Hicks held a one-year tutoring post at Harvard, an appointment that met with criticism in the popular press and, from The Crimson, praise as "the most positive academic step that the University has taken forward this year."

EDITORIAL

Tempest in a Teapot

April 12, 1937

With the announcement by the University last week that Dr. Walsh and Dr. Sweezy had been given two-year "concluding reappointments" as instructors in Economics, the familiar outcry of academic intolerance of advanced views and interference with academic liberty was bound to arise. Considering their popularity and ability, some outcry is not surprising, but the tumult and shouting, and all the familiar paraphernalia of petitions, protest meetings, and probing committees designed to make them martyrs, can only work intense hardship on the two men.

Two things, in the main, are responsible for the tempest in the teapot. First is their well-known political views. But "concluding appointments" are given daily to men in all fields, when crowded departments hold out no chances for them to rise to professorial rank. There is no reflection on the abilities of Dr. Walsh and Dr. Sweezy. The Economics Department is unique in that the great percentage of its professorial chairs are held by comparatively young men, and, as professorships are permanent appointments, no future is held out for the large number of instructors now rising in the field.

It is definitely against University policy to keep a man on in a temporary position longer than six to eight years. The wisdom of this policy may be open to question. But it is certainly fairer to give the man two years in which to better his position elsewhere. The Economics Department, which has charge of promotions, has twice passed over these two instructors and promoted others, because it felt that, while Sweezy and Walsh were concededly popular and excellent teachers, they were likely, on the basis of their record of scholarship, to remain stationary in their academic standing. Whether the administration's theory of productive scholarship as the principal basis for judging a man is a wise and proper one presents an entirely different question. The only point at issue here is whether the two men were dismissed because of their political views, and it seems eminently clear that their political views did not have anything to do with the matter whatever. It is only because their views are known that the furor arose.

In this particular case, it is understood that the Economics Department, because it feared the adverse publicity that might result, went ahead and recommended Walsh and Sweezy for the regular three-year appointments. However, it is thought that the administration definitely opposed making a special case out of the two men merely because their views were known, and stepped in to request that the usual procedure, that of giving concluding appointments, be followed in this case as in all others.

The second reason that the matter has been kept in the public eye is because the University issued an ill-timed and impolitic statement declaring that the decision was reached solely on the grounds of "teaching capacity and scholarly ability." Although the University's record is practically perfect in placing men whose appointments have been concluded in other institutions this statement may very possibly make it hard for Walsh and Sweezy to obtain teaching positions in other institutions. Their appointments were ended because of the crowded Economics Department. "Teaching capacity" had little to do with the case.

It is well to remember that the worst possible thing for the two men in question is the all too familiar routing of petitions, and investigations, and martyr creation. Nothing could make it harder for Walsh and Sweezy than to have this storm of protest over a perfectly routine matter, and the sooner they put a quietus on the whole affair and the sooner the University issues a much needed clarification of its true position, the better it will be for all concerned.

During the war, the University necessarily shrank in scope and purpose. President Conant took a leave of absence to concern himself with the Interim Committee, the five-member panel advising President Roosevelt on the uses of the atomic bomb. When college deferments were no longer given in 1941, Harvard decided to issue three-year "conscription degrees." Many University members were involved in the war effort. Harvard scientists, for instance, left off the pursuit of truth in order to work on projects such as refining radio-jamming techniques and underwater sound-detection devices. Largely because of the efforts of Louis Fieser, professor of Chemistry, Harvard also helped develop napalm.

One noteworthy development during the war years was the opening in 1943 of Harvard courses to Radcliffe women. Up to that time Harvard professors had given their lectures to Harvard men and then walked up Garden Street to the Radcliffe Yard to repeat them to an exclusively female audience. Not all courses were made co-educational and seating was still segregated, as the measure was motivated by wartime expediency; it would not be made official until 1947. Even then, joint exams and mixed seating were subjects to be hotly debated, not realities. The following article from the postwar period captures the atmosphere of the times.

Joint Instruction Flourishes in First Year
Initiated During Wartime,
Female Invasion Is Here to Stay
BY CHARLES W. BAILEY '50

May 6, 1948

Nine months ago Harvard men came back to class to find that red and yellow leaves were not the only things descending on the Yard. Radcliffe, which for years existed by the courtesy of University teachers, had officially moved into the College.

The ensuing months have seen Joint Instruction, originally set up during the war, firmly installed as a regular practice. In spite of early squawks from this side of the Yard and seating complaints from the Annex, all has gone along pretty much as expected. More than 1300 Harvard students, by far the largest group in the College, are in group IV on the rank list — right where they usually are; and Radcliffe grades are much the same as ever, according to Karlene Madison, secretary to Dean Sherman. "We have just about the same number of girls going on probation as always . . ."

. . . Dean Bender has, as yet, found no rough spots on the student side of the question. "No student complaints have come through to me," he stated, "and I have had no reports of trouble through the Radcliffe office. Apparently there's been no bad feeling, and no funny business yet."

Dean Kerby-Miller of Radcliffe, in charge of the academic fortunes of the Annex girls, echoed Bender's remarks, adding that the 'Cliffe contingents seemed quite at ease in the Yard.

The arrival of the female scholars in College classrooms has posed a few educational questions, however. The old system of separate classes allowed the girls to have smaller sections; they were able to get better acquainted with their teachers than they are now, and have been in some cases unhappy about this. But Dean Kerby-Miller feels that this loss has been compensated for by the fact that the girls have had to learn to study in a different fashion — to organize their work over a longer period of time and a greater range of subject matter.

English 7 — this spring's largest course — contains approximately 50 Radcliffe students. If the course were given at Radcliffe, these 50 girls might be able to carry on a class discussion; but when several hundred Harvard students are added, this is impossible . . .

. . . The basic question of comparative study habits, excellence, and aptitude for reading and examinations has been shown in sharper light by this year's experience. Harvard students have traditionally maintained that 'Cliffe dwellers are grinds — that they study by rote, that they think little if at all, that they put the fishhooks on the end of every grading curve. Some of these contentions are apparently borne out by the first year of practical experience. The Radcliffe dean's office agrees that the new system is strange for the girls — "They feel a little lost in those big classes" — but claims that they are doing just as well as before the big switch.

As for the men, the student attitude is apparently mirrored in the mind of Dean Bender, who maintains that the 'Cliffe dweller of today is a better-looking number than her mother or aunt of 20 years ago. The inclusion of girls in lectures, while perhaps discomfiting the monitoring system, has produced no real complaints on this side of the Common. "It's just a case of the marginal student being sacrificed to the marginal Radcliffe girl," comments David Murray Jr. '47, a senior whose curriculum has included a fistful of joint courses.

With classrooms definitely under permanent joint regimes, thoughts of some have turned to co-educational exams. Backers of the plan argue that similar exam conditions would equalize results; opponents, on the other hand, are firm in maintaining the value of segregation.

"I don't know what I'd do without an hourly solitary cigarette in an exam," claims Mary Brant, Radcliffe '51, who opposes any merger. Harvard also has objections: "Girls are all right in classes, but in exams you have to concentrate," muttered an Eliot House sophomore recently.

The postwar period saw the Conant administration's greatest achievement: the 1946 report General Education in a Free Society. *It is said that the report, which had its beginnings as early as 1943, had far-reaching consequences for higher education throughout America, with many other universities adopting its recommendations. This may well be true, but it is one of the ironies of Harvard's General Education plan (as, no doubt, it will be with the 1979 Core Curriculum, which has supplanted it) that it was a marvel of precision planning betrayed by idiosyncratic execution. Nobody at Harvard ever had the power or, more likely, the inclination to create a highly disciplined and coordinated structure for the courses given in humanities, natural sciences, and social sciences. Professors whose disciplines fall within these three broad fields have always determined, in somewhat uncoordinated fashion, the rather individualistic contents of their courses. And students, who are supposed to learn the fundamental concepts and methodologies underpinning each field, have been more likely (lest they choose very carefully) to come away with a smorgasbord of basic facts, interesting but arcane minutiae, and disputed theories.*

When it comes to the subject of General Education, The Crimson files contain reports too numerous and tomes too wieldy to adequately summarize them. The only pattern that emerges is a consistent expression of discontent with General Education (often leading to valuable reforms) based on theories ranging from "high serious" considerations for GE's lofty intentions, to more mundane arguments against "force-feeding" education. Readers will have to be content with the initial, experimental introduction of General Education, which serves as a reminder that, however impracticable, and under any name, it is an ideal worth striving for.

Committee Organizes Seven General Education Courses to Start in Fall

Next Year's Freshmen and Sophomores to Get First Choice as Wright's Administrative Group Limits Enrollment to 410 in New Experimental Courses Prescribed by Report

May 14, 1946

Still expanding its central salient in the pedagogic battle over educational objectives, the Committee on General Education has organized seven area courses for 1946–47 open to next year's freshmen and sophomores, it was announced yesterday by Professor Benjamin F. Wright, chairman of the committee.

Instructed by a Faculty vote six months ago "to provide not less than two and not more than four" full courses in each of the three areas, the committee has scheduled three courses in the humanities and hopes by next fall to add one apiece to the two now being announced in each of the areas of social sciences and natural sciences.

Juniors and seniors will not be allowed to sign up and the total enrollment so far is restricted to 410 men since the initial program has been designed as an experiment through which the instructors in charge expect to evaluate the suitability of materials, topics, and methods.

Now in the process of publication, a pamphlet describing the seven courses should reach all of the present freshmen, by mail Thursday, according to Wright. Applications to enroll should be filled out at Holyoke House 20 from next Thursday until the following Thursday, May 23.

Applications submitted by present freshmen will comprise up to two-fifths of the total enrollment, with another two-fifths reserved for incoming freshmen and one-fifth for Radcliffe students. In case of oversubscription the committee proposes to select by chance rather than by grading, in order to get a fair average sampling of students.

In May 1949 The Crimson began what was to remain a long-standing tradition throughout the fifties: the Academic Freedom Report. The first such supplement — a representative sample — contained 21 articles and an editorial on a range of issues related to academic freedom: the firing and suspension of professors and instructors for their political beliefs, state legislative activities such as requiring professors to sign loyalty oaths, and the abrogation of student rights. It was apparent by 1949 that the Cold War was already affecting universities across the country, even before the advent of Joseph McCarthy and his kind.

President Conant, who resigned to become German high commissioner in 1953, had at least one moment in the fray, which set the tone for Harvard's response to McCarthyism. As late as 1951 Conant's policy toward Communists at Harvard — to be adopted by President Nathan M. Pusey '28 — was often misunderstood, as a 1951 Crimson headline illustrates: CONANT SAYS RED TEACHERS SHOULD BE REFUSED POST. *Harvard's position was almost that strong, but it was also tempered by certain conditions that, if understood, make clear that while Harvard reacted to the Cold War far better than most universities, it also failed to truly defend academic freedom. The following excerpted article, which places Communism at Harvard in its proper perspective, elucidates the administrative response to Communism.*

In the spring of 1953, when the Board of Overseers was searching for Harvard's new president, Frank B. Gilbert '52, a former Crimson managing editor and then a law student, solicited famous cartoonists' conceptions of the new president's appearance. A few are reproduced here.

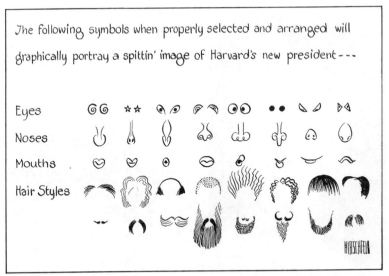

"Hope this fills the speculative vacuum created by President Conant's retirement to the knackwurst country," wrote Al Hirschfeld, drama cartoonist for *The New York Times.* March 9, 1953.

The new president and his family in "a sea of troubles" — as seen by Virgil Partch, cartoonist for *Collier's* magazine. May 11, 1953.

"I won't be surprised if the next president of Harvard looks like this. This is a man who can face up to the ills of the world with equanimity."

— Charles Addams

The New Yorker's R. Taylor explains his prediction for the new president: "Perhaps still younger. This is the Age of Youth. Whiskers are vanishing . . . the crew cut, now pretty well established in academic circles, especially with the young, will prevail . . . the nose seems to be shrinking . . . ditto ears . . . if Conant's is any indication of a trend, we may expect a broader grin . . . dress is, of course, becoming less and less formal. It may be that tielessness and collarlessness will be the order of the day." March 16, 1953.

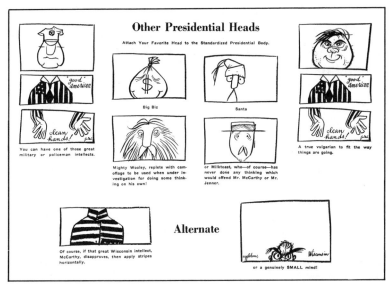

Robert Osborn, Yale '28, a freelance artist whose work has appeared in *Look, Life, Harper's,* and *Fortune,* supplied The Crimson with his own captions for the game "Pick Your President." Students were invited to place their favorite head on top of the standard 1953 presidential body. In suggesting the alternate (the head depicts McCarthy) Osborn facetiously noted that he was born in Oshkosh, Wisconsin — 11 miles from Senator McCarthy's birthplace. He had no idea that Nathan M. Pusey '28, also hailing from Wisconsin, would be selected Harvard's next president. March 26, 1953. (Copyright © 1953 Robert Osborn)

Stephen O. Saxe '51, Crimson staff artist, wrote that a few special features were included in his drawing of the new president: "the Countess Mara beard (Pat. Pend.) denoting wisdom and years; tweedy jacket with natural shoulders (conservatism); Harvard beanie (perennial youthfulness); and green bookbag for carrying lunch to Massachusetts Hall on rainy days (common touch)." April 16, 1953.

Communism: Its Effects on a Few
Have Produced a Harvard Myth
BY W. W. BARTLEY III '56

April 22, 1955

. . . The "Red Decade" [the thirties] that has been magnified and dramatized so much amounts ultimately to a number of liberals at the University sympathizing with Communism; to about 15 graduate students and teachers — from the lower academic grades — out of a faculty of approximately 1880 teachers actually joining the Party; and to perhaps a slightly larger number, from the College, temporarily banding together. According to all reports, most of these had quit the Party by 1940 . . . unfortunately, this is the period which created the only reputation which the University still has for a large segment of the population . . .

By 1948, the last openly Communist organization [at Harvard] — with the possible exception of the John Reed Club, which lingered on until 1950 — had disappeared.

World Communism was no longer either an academic theory, a plan for social progress, or a wartime ally, but a constant and belligerent threat to the nation's political and economic order. In the circumstances, many Americans began to drag the skeletons from their closets to see what Communism had been doing within. [FBI agent Herbert] Philbrick's testimony [before the House Committee on Un-American Activities], focusing its attention on Cambridge and Harvard, brought the University into the discussion from the very beginning, and administrative officers were faced with the problem of forging a policy which would meet the new situation practically while not infringing on traditional academic freedom.

Many observers of the University's resulting course of action have assumed that University policy actually did — as is sometimes claimed — simply reaffirm President Lowell's classic 1917 statement on academic freedom. [That statement relied on, in part, and used some of the same language of a Crimson editorial of 1914.] He had maintained that a professor "would cease to be a free citizen" were he to accept a chair under restrictive conditions. "Knowledge," Lowell had explained, "can advance only by means of an unfettered search for truth on the part of those who devote their lives to seeking it . . . and by complete freedom in imparting to their pupils the truth that they have found . . . in spite of the fact that a researcher may discover error instead of truth."

Closer examination, however, clearly shows that while the formula may be the same, its exegesis is different. As late as 1938, the administration was not opposed — at least officially — to retaining a Communist on the faculty . . .

. . . By 1949, however, things had changed. On June 8 of that year, Conant signed his name to a special report of the National Education Association's Educational Policies Commission, which stated that Communist Party members "should not be employed as teachers."

Conant's statement, surprising as it was, was generally accepted by the faculty. Postwar events had made Russia's aims and methods clearer. Intellectuals were ready to make a truce with the brute necessity of the future. Their principal concern was no longer change, but — in a new age of constant totalitarian threat from both sides of the Iron Curtain — preservation of that decade's freedom . . . Conant's stand seemed sensible. His reevaluation and reinterpretation of Lowell's stand presupposed a redefinition or better, reclarification, of academic freedom itself. Conant's position, which has been reaffirmed by Pusey, can, by joining some of their various statements, be formulated somewhat as follows. It retains emphasis on completely free inquiry, while limiting complete freedom in two nonessential respects. Academic freedom is protected from itself, so to speak, by banning from its domain any adherents to a philosophy which itself does not allow for the same freedom or is logically inconsistent with academic freedom. Also, the traditional principle that academic freedom does not entitle a scholar to disregard the law of the state was extended from the usual application to specific acts — such as murder or theft — to embrace a system of ideas — insofar as Communism was in fact such a system and insofar as it advocated overthrow of the American government.

Conant's stand, however, as he has repeatedly pointed out, is conditional. The University cannot, he insists, inquire into the political opinions or activities of its faculty members, lest any nonorthodox view tend to be branded as Communistic. Conant issued a special release following his signing of the 1949 Educational Policies Commission report, calling attention to one clause in the document: "We condemn the careless, incorrect and unjust use of such words as 'Red' and 'Communist' to attack teachers and other persons who in point of fact are not Communists, but who merely have views different from those of their accusers. The whole spirit of free American education will be subverted unless teachers are free to think for themselves . . .

"It is because members of the Communist Party are required to surrender this right as a consequence of becoming part of a movement characterized by conspiracy and calculated deceit, that they should be excluded from employment as teachers." Two weeks later, Grenville Clark '03, then senior member of the Corporation, elaborated on the president's statement. "There will be no harassment of professors," he said, "for engaging in open and legal meetings. There will be no apparatus of inquiry and closer watch. The harm done by the effort necessary to discover even a single clandestine Party member would outweigh any possible benefit."

The conduct of congressional investigations and the mild hysteria which they provoked made the importance of these conditions evident . . .

[The preceding article was awarded the Dana Reed Prize in 1956.]

As the previous article demonstrates, interpretations of the Harvard administration's actions during the McCarthy era were based largely on public statements. Clearly, all Communists would be fired. But what of former Communists? A few cases of individuals called before Senator William E. Jenner's Internal Security Subcommittee, Representative Harold Velde's House Committee on Un-American Activities, and Senator McCarthy's Permanent Subcommittee on Investigations gave a different substance to Harvard's words. In those cases, three faculty members, Wendell H. Furry, Leon J. Kamin, and Helen Deane Mark-

ham all invoked the Fifth Amendment when asked by the various committees about their alleged affiliations and actions in the Communist Party. On May 20, 1953, the Harvard Corporation's findings were released; Furry was found guilty of "grave misconduct" for having lied about a colleague's political affiliations when questioned by the FBI in 1944. "Grave misconduct" meant that Furry, a tenured associate professor of Physics, could have been removed; he wasn't because the Corporation thought the action had taken place too long ago, "in a very different climate of political opinion." Kamin and Markham were judged guilty of "misconduct," since, the Corporation claimed, the use of the Fifth Amendment by academics was hurting universities, which would be cleared if frank replies were given. "But more important," the Corporation reasoned, "the use of the Fifth Amendment is in our view entirely inconsistent with the candor expected of one devoted to the pursuit of truth. It is no excuse that the primary purpose of its use is to protect one's friends, or to express one's feelings that congressional committees are bypassing the constitutional safeguards of due process of law, or to avert a danger of prosecution for perjury in case one's testimony should later be contradicted by the false testimony of others."

Yet another controversy, this time within the Law School, arose when two students, twin brothers Jonathan W. and David L. Lubell, were called before the Jenner Committee in the spring of 1953. The Lubells also invoked the Fifth Amendment, although they apparently had little to hide. In the following weeks the Lubell brothers were pressured from the top two Law School Record *posts, Jonathan Lubell was forced to resign from the Law School Legal Aid Bureau, and both would have been thrown out of Law School altogether if an alumni group had had its way and were it not for Law School Dean Erwin N. Griswold, who defended their right to study there.*

Accounts published years after the McCarthy era was over (in Lipset and Riesman's Education and Politics at Harvard *and in* The New York Review of Books*) reveal that there was yet another level on which the Harvard administration took action toward former Communists who were never confronted with public charges. In one case, in the spring of 1954, a man promised the job of counselor for foreign students was denied that* *post when his past Communist activities were revealed to McGeorge Bundy, then dean of the Faculty of Arts and Sciences. Bundy has defended that action on the grounds that the post concerned was an administrative one, to which the criterion of academic freedom did not apply, and also, "In 1954 Harvard was indeed embattled with Senator McCarthy and because it was engaged in defending its academic freedoms it was under an obligation not to behave foolishly in its administrative appointments."*

In another case, in the spring of 1955, a man being considered for an instructorship, normally renewable and often the first step toward tenure, was refused that position because of his past Communist affiliations. In this case, one that clearly involves academic freedom, Bundy has revealed that the Corporation was responsible for the action, which Bundy says he himself "disagreed with" (the nature of Bundy's disagreement has yet to be revealed). The man in question had refused to give the FBI evidence on the activities of any former Communists except himself. As Bundy has explained, "The Corporation did publicly attach a negative weight to incomplete candor on the part of ex-Communists, even for teaching appointments; that weight lasted until about 1956."

Finally, a third case, about which the details remain sketchy, involves a person who was not given a recommendation for an outside job because he refused to cooperate with investigators seeking information on past Communist activities.

There may be many more such cases, particularly ones where an individual eventually consented, under penalty of losing his nontenured position, to give authorities information regarding the activities of former Communists, or even still-active Communists, who in those days were liable, at the extreme, to serve jail sentences of up to six years for their membership.

When reading the following summary of events at Harvard, readers should keep in mind that Harvard's actions were far from pristine. As a result of their courageous actions, Helen Deane Markham and Leon J. Kamin both were left with unrenewable contracts with the Corporation. Markham, who, as it turned out, was never a member of the Communist Party, was fortunate enough to receive a full professorship of Anatomy at Albert Einstein Medical College, but that was not until 1957 — for three years her future career was a matter of grave doubt. She served at Albert Einstein until her death in 1966. Kamin's graduate education was finished at Harvard, funded by a private research grant. He then "chose" to go to Canada — since there was little hope that he could find a teaching position in the United States — where he remained from 1954 until 1968, teaching at McGill, Queens, and McMaster universities. Since 1968, he has held a professorship in Psychology at Princeton University. The Lubells were drafted after law school, spent two years in the army, and then "delayed" their application to the New York State Bar Association, since, as Jonathan Lubell recently described it, they were "advised, because of the atmosphere" that they would not be found acceptable by the association's Character Committee. In 1958, the Lubells finally applied and were accepted into the bar. Since then they have practiced privately in New York, are now senior partners in the firm of Cohn, Glickstein, Lurie, Ostrin, Lubell, and Lubell, and Jonathan Lubell recently argued a case before the Supreme Court.

In all of these cases, it can be seen that careers were delayed and placed in jeopardy. It is sad, then, and ironic, to say that on the whole Harvard's actions may actually have been better than those of the vast majority of American universities. Harvard allowed Furry to stay on (he became a full professor of Physics in 1962, a position he held until retiring in 1977). And Harvard at least allowed contracts of nontenured teachers to expire, whereas many other universities summarily dismissed former Communists and those accused of being former Communists. Keep in mind, when you read the following summary, that Harvard's actions may have been better, and then ask yourself whether "better" was good enough, and whether Harvard deserves its high reputation for the defense of academic freedom during the McCarthy era.

The University in the McCarthy Era: A Brief Summary

BY BENJAMIN W. HEINEMAN JR. '65   June 17, 1965

The Principals

The Interrogators — Members of Congress

Senator Joseph R. McCarthy (R-Wis.), Chairman, Permanent Subcommittee on Investigations of the Senate Committee on Government Operations.

Senator William E. Jenner (R-Ind.), Chairman, Subcommittee to Investigate the Administration of the Internal Security Act and Other Internal Security Laws of the Senate Committee on the Judiciary.

Representative Harold H. Velde (R-Ill.), Chairman, House Committee on Un-American Activities.

The Interrogated — Members of the Harvard Faculty

Wendell H. Furry, associate professor of Physics (now a full professor).

Leon J. Kamin, teaching fellow in Social Relations.

Mrs. Helen Deane Markham, assistant professor of Anatomy.

*The Honored — Men Cited by the Faculty for Defending
Academic Freedom*

Paul H. Buck, Provost and Dean of the Faculty of Arts and Sciences; Chairman, Administrative Committee to Assume the President's Duties (from January to July, 1953).

Charles A. Coolidge '17, Fellow of Harvard College; member, the Administrative Committee.

Erwin N. Griswold, Dean of the Law School; member, Special Faculty Advisory Committee to the Corporation.

Charles A. Wyzanski '27, Federal District Judge; President of the Board of Overseers.

Nathan M. Pusey '28, President, Harvard University.

The Events

1917: President A. Lawrence Lowell's Annual Report defines academic freedom with reference to both scholarly and political activity.

1949: Alger Hiss put on trial in New York as a result of an investigation by the House Committee on Un-American Activities. The "subversive" issue becomes prominent in the national consciousness.

1950: Senator McCarthy, in a speech in Wheeling, W. Va., charges that the State Department is "full of Communists," launching the "McCarthy-era" investigations of subversive activity in the federal government and higher education.

1952: *November* — Senator Jenner's Senate Subcommittee on Internal Security announces plans to investigate Communists in the nation's colleges and universities.

1953: *January* — President James B. Conant resigns to become United States high commissioner of Germany. Provost Buck takes over his duties.

"Ah, now we're on the right track! What else did you tell those little lambs in Slavic 285B?" David Royce '53, '55½, '56 depicts the essential absurdity of the Jenner, Velde, and McCarthy hearings of 1952–53. Three Harvard teachers and two students were called before such hearings, all because of their alleged past connections with the Communist Party. There were no known Communists at Harvard at the time; and even those with past affiliation or loose connection had participated mainly on an intellectual, discussion-group level. March 27, 1953.

Colleges and universities around the country begin to fire or suspend professors who refuse to testify before congressional committees by invoking the Fifth Amendment.

February — Wendell Furry appears before a congressional committee for the first time. Testifying before the HUAC in Washington he refuses to answer questions, invoking the Fifth Amendment. The Harvard Corporation faces a crisis; what action should be taken regarding Furry?

March — The Corporation reviews the transcript of Furry's testimony before the Velde Committee (HUAC).

The Senate Internal Security Subcommittee arrives in Boston to question Leon Kamin and Helen Markham about alleged Communist affiliations and activities. They both take the Fifth.

April — Furry voluntarily sends an affidavit to Chairman Velde explaining his political activity in the past two years (1951–1953) and then appears for the second time before the HUAC in Washington to testify that he has not been a Communist since 1951. He invokes the Fifth Amendment in refusing to answer all other questions.

May — The Corporation announces that all three Faculty members will remain at Harvard although Furry was guilty of "grave misconduct" and Kamin and Markham of "misconduct."

June — Nathan Marsh Pusey is appointed president by the Corporation. McCarthy attacks the new president, calling him a "rabid, anti-anti-Communist."

November — Senator McCarthy calls Furry before his committee in New York. Furry, in his third appearance before a congressional hearing, refuses to answer questions under the protection of the Fifth Amendment. McCarthy threatens him with contempt of Congress proceedings.

McCarthy accuses Harvard and Pusey of spawning a "Red mess." Pusey defends Harvard and higher education, while criticizing the Wisconsin senator.

1954: *January* — Furry, testifying for the fourth time, changes tactics. He does not use the Fifth Amendment although he refuses to answer some questions. Kamin also refuses to answer questions relating to friends who had been Communists and, like Furry, doesn't take the Fifth. McCarthy again threatens proceedings for contempt.

1955: Furry and Kamin are arraigned in Boston in January on contempt charges. Kamin is acquitted and the contempt citation against Furry is dismissed on the Kamin precedent.

1957: McCarthy dies of hepatitis.

[With an accompanying article, the above was awarded a Dana Reed Prize "Honorable Mention" in 1966.]

In the January 8, 1958, Crimson, readers learned that on the previous day President Pusey had announced a 25 percent tuition increase: from $1000 to $1250, the fourth such increase within the previous decade and the fifth since 1929, when tuition for undergraduates was $400. Pusey also announced a salary increase for faculty, top salaries to full professors increasing 25 percent to $20,000, the average professor's salary going from $13,000 to $15,000.

The Crimson's editorial response is an eloquent summation of an age-old problem. (Tuition in 1979 was more than $5000.)

EDITORIAL

Professor, Can You . . .

January 10, 1958

"Young man, the salary increase is a gesture and a . . ."

"Professor, can you . . ."

"Tribute which is long overdue. I have dedicated my time . . ."

"Professor, can you . . ."

"And talent to the education of such . . ."

"Professor, can you . . ."

"Young men as yourself and if I am to continue and if . . ."

"Professor, can you . . ."

"Others of my intellectual achievement and ambition are . . ."

"Professor, can you . . ."

"To be found to replace me, then this salary increase was . . ."

"Professor, can you . . ."

"Both necessary and praiseworthy."

"Professor, can you spare a dime?"

President Pusey and the University have gone through more than one cruel April. Before 1969 there came the April of 1958, a time when religion, a supposedly unintended anti-Semitism, and Memorial Church all mixed together in a hot controversy sparked by news buried deep inside a reflective, philosophical feature. The key excerpt from that feature follows.

Religion at Harvard
BY W. W. BARTLEY III '56

March 28, 1958

. . . For years it had been a tradition at Memorial Church that any student might be married there, and many couples, including some Jewish ones, had sought out the church's Appleton Chapel to exchange their vows. The interfaith use of the building seemed only natural. Daily chapel services had been abandoned in 1886 and President Eliot and his successors had made clear their intention not to allow any particular religious group to gain dominant influence in the University . . .

In 1955, however, [the Rev. George A.] Buttrick [preacher to the University] refused to permit a Jewish student to be married in Memorial Church by a rabbi. This month he reaffirmed the "Protestant Christian" tradition of the church and his conviction that "it would be intellectually dishonest for Christian and Jewish marriages to be carried on beneath the same roof." Deploring the use of shifting altars at MIT's chapel, Buttrick praised Brandeis University's decision to build three separate chapels. Acknowledging that there should be some official place at Harvard where Jews might marry and worship, Buttrick suggested that a synagogue be built — "at the initiative of the Hebrew Community" — on University property in the Yard. As an indication of his own tolerant spirit he said he would ask to be allowed to contribute the "first $100" toward the building.

Buttrick is completely sincere in his conclusions, which follow from his Presbyterian premises . . .

. . . What a splendid place Memorial Church might have been for Harvard men to collaborate in articulating their shared religious aspirations. What a fine symbol for their reaffirmation of a concern for those religious creeds and ways which are, in President Pusey's own words, "records of human experience at its very deepest levels of meanings." Instead, the fiat of a Presbyterian preacher — which is held to have something to do with "intellectual honesty" — forbids 25 percent of the student body from marrying beneath the college chapel's roof . . .

To the Crimson feature and to an editorial saying that "the new sectarianism — whatever its pious motives — succeeds in cheapening the past and discrediting the present," Pusey responded with the following letter, which probably caused as much of a stir as the initial article. In the following week mail would come pouring in to The Crimson denouncing the new exclusionism; Crimson articles would gently point out that Mem Chapel, contrary to Pusey's ill-informed notion, had indeed been used for non-Christian services with authorization; newspapers and radio broadcasts would deliver the news around the country; forums on the place of religion in the University would be called together; and faculty members led by Perry Miller, Mark DeWolfe Howe, I. Bernard Cohen, John H. Finley '25, and Morton G. White would petition Pusey to open up Memorial Chapel to all denominations.

Finally, two weeks after the crisis began, the Corporation contradicted Pusey and reopened Memorial Chapel for use by non-

Christian groups, with the proviso that its essential "Christian character" not be altered.

The Christian Tradition

April 9, 1958

To the Editors of The Crimson:

The Crimson's recent article on Religion at Harvard and the subsequent editorial would lead your readers to believe that a fundamental change has been made in the role of the Memorial Church at Harvard and that this change has been brought about by the present preacher to the University. Such is not the case.

Harvard's historic tradition has been a Christian tradition, and although Memorial Church is not considered as affiliated with any one denomination it has always been thought of as a house of Christian worship. This was made explicit both in the architecture and symbolism of the present building and in Dean Sperry's words: "Wherefore unto the King Eternal, Immortal, Invisible, the only Wise God, we dedicate this Church in the service of Christ."

Occasionally in the past people of other faiths have requested the private use of the Chapel for non-Christian services, such as marriages or funerals. In all such cases the University preacher and his predecessors have made clear that the Corporation feels that the Memorial Church is a place of Christian worship. So far as I know the only isolated exceptions to this rule occurred without authorization, or when there was no Chairman of the Board of Preachers.

The Corporation has always felt that the many churches in the vicinity of the Square and other places of worship in the Boston area would be preferred by those who are firmly attached to one religious persuasion or another. For those who do not feel they want to use such places of worship and yet still prefer a non-Christian service, Harvard has always been willing to provide facilities in Phillips Brooks House or elsewhere in the University.

Nathan M. Pusey

*One of the more important aspects of any university is its stu-
dent composition, which in turn is defined by its admissions policy. Probably Harvard's penultimate great reform, one that almost made it a truly national university, was the changes made
in its admissions policy during the early sixties (the final reform
would be merger with Radcliffe and sex-blind admissions). The
reforms would at least attempt to diversify Harvard's student
population, making it representative of all classes and ethnic
groups, and lending support to the still-contentious idea that
here was the nation's leader in education.*

Bender's Final Report on Admissions Warns
Against "Elitism," Increasing Cost of College

Blasts "Top-One-Percent" Policy

BY MICHAEL S. LOTTMAN '61

September 30, 1961

The strong voice of former Dean of Admissions Wilbur J.
Bender '27, which guided the College's admissions policy
through eight significant years, returned today in his final
report to warn of the hazards facing the Harvard of the future.

In language ranging from bitter rhetoric to frequently beautiful prose, Bender's valedictory report expressed fears for a
future Harvard grown sterile with self-conscious intellectualism. Further, Bender predicted that a Harvard education
would cost $4000 to $5000 a year by 1970, and that the College's scholarship funds will be inadequate to their task.

The report to the dean of the Faculty of Arts and Sciences
for the academic year 1959–60, completed last spring, created
considerable excitement among official Harvard before its
eventual release today. It is accompanied by a University
News Office release that omits many of Bender's charges and
worries and concentrates on a statistical summary.

In 1960, with Harvard able to admit only 30 percent of its
candidates, Bender foresaw an end to the meteoric rise in
applications that marked his tenure, because of discouragement on the part of students, schools, and alumni workers.
Last spring his predictions came true.

Bender expressed great worry about the College's scholarship program in his report, pointing out that the "self-help" gap for scholarship students had grown from $450 in 1950 to $800 in 1960.

"Only a handful of American colleges have total endowments as large as our financial aid capital funds," he wrote. "Yet despite this extraordinary outpouring of funds, which can hardly be expected to continue at this pace indefinitely, no significant gains were made in lowering the economic barrier to a Harvard education."

The former dean warned against taking "the continuous-tuition-increase road," saying that "easy money is dangerous money, for institutions as well as individuals."

He devoted the major and final portion of his report to an eloquent attack on the "top-one-percent" policy — an attempt to admit only students who would stand, academically, in the upper one percent of the country's undergraduates.

Bender observed that high-school rank can be a false indicator of promise for the future: "The top high-school student is often, frankly, a pretty dull and bloodless, or peculiar, fellow."

Selection of a student body based solely on high-school grades, test data, and Predicted Rank List standings, Bender said, could turn the College into a collection of brittle, neurotic superintellectuals.

Finally, Bender made a plea for a Harvard with some students "who aren't brilliant or leaders, who are just plain, ordinary, decent, uncomplicated human beings . . . to provide a human scale in this community of supermen."

He asked for a College "with some snobs and some Scandinavian farm boys who can skate beautifully and some bright Bronx pre-meds, with some students who care passionately about editing The Crimson or beating Yale . . . Won't even our top-one-percent be better men and better scholars for being part of such a college?"

When historians look back at the sixties and Harvard's role in that decade, priority will probably be given to the University's still-expanding role as a research institution and its increasingly stronger links to the government. Depending on nuance, one is likely to hear about Vietnam War–related efforts, the University's role in increasing educational opportunity, or struggles to change an outdated curriculum (by, for instance, recognizing Visual and Environmental Studies and Afro-American Studies as legitimate disciplines).

The sixties will not be remembered as a decade generally kind to President Pusey (or, some might say, he was not kind to the decade). Early in the period the subject of parietals was still a raging issue, a carry-over from the fifties, and a perennial in The Crimson's pages; when Pusey decided to abolish the Latin diploma in 1961 The Crimson protested ("Latin Si, Pusey No") and students rioted in the streets ("Turn back," The Crimosn editorialized, "before the guillotine rises in Harvard Square."); and in 1962 his administration suffered a serious morale problem with both faculty and students, a fire to which The Crimson added fuel by publishing an unprecedented seven-part editorial series attacking Pusey's want of imagination, lack of understanding, and unawareness of the issues before the University (to add insult to injury, the series was awarded the Dana Reed Prize for the best undergraduate writing that year). Then there were the late sixties, and the Great Divide of Harvard (see Chapter 3).

Co-education at Harvard-Radcliffe during the sixties will probably only warrant a passing glance from historians, despite the fact that it caused such great tumult within. After all, co-education dated back to Oberlin in 1833 and it was a fact of life well before Harvard-Radcliffe got around to it. The unfortunate thing about this historical shortsightedness is that the merger was one of Pusey's relatively finer moments. He encouraged the proposal initiated by Radcliffe, then under the presidency of Mary I. Bunting, though his administration strived to maintain Harvard men's greater numbers.

It would not be until after several slow-going years during which alumni pressures and student demands were at odds that the administrations of Presidents Derek Bok and Matina Horner completed the so-called nonmerger merger by which Harvard became responsible for the education, discipline, and extracurricular activities of all Harvard-Radcliffe men and women, co-educational living would officially begin, and, in 1975, equal access admissions would finally be instituted.

The initial, Big News, however, had come out six years earlier in two-deck, five-column headline.

Radcliffe Makes Merger Proposal; Negotiations Will Begin March 3
BY CAROL R. STERNHELL '71

February 24, 1969

Radcliffe's governing board has finally proposed marriage to Harvard and the next move is up to the groom — the Harvard Corporation, scheduled to meet on March 3.

At a surprise meeting of the College Council on Saturday afternoon, Radcliffe declared her own demise as an autonomous institution and will propose merger to the Corporation before its March 3 meeting.

The council's vote followed a special meeting of the Radcliffe trustees, who requested the council to "initiate discussion with the president and fellows of Harvard College with a view to merging the two institutions." Radcliffe trustees have only advisory power.

Today Mary I. Bunting, president of Radcliffe, will send a letter to the Harvard Corporation proposing the merger.

Now the decision of whether or not to discuss merging the two schools rests with the Corporation, Mrs. Bunting said. She declined to predict the Corporation's decision, but said that President Pusey had attended Saturday's meeting and had seemed favorable toward the proposal.

President Pusey refused last night to comment on any aspect of the proposed merger.

Last week one member of the Corporation said that the general feeling among Corporation members seemed to favor merger. No members of the Corporation would comment last night.

Mrs. Bunting said at dinner last night in Holmes Hall that the Corporation will probably decide March 3 to send discussion of the whole issue to the Faculty and wait for their vote.

The College Council — Radcliffe's official decision-making body — was not scheduled to meet until March 3, but held an unexpected session immediately after the trustees' meeting. The council included Mrs. Bunting, Kathleen O. Elliott, vice president and dean of the college, and nine trustees, all of whom were already present for the trustees' meeting.

At the meeting, Pusey pointed out the importance of the Harvard Faculty's having full responsibility for the total education of Radcliffe students, Mrs. Bunting said. The Faculty presently has responsibility only for Radcliffe's academic instruction, not for the girls' social life or discipline.

"We of course don't know yet whether the Harvard Faculty is willing to assume this responsibility," Mrs. Bunting added.

Mrs. Bunting declined to reveal the exact vote of the all-day meeting, but said that the "great majority of trustees voted for the plan." "Merger does not necessarily mean co-ed dormitories," she emphasized. "But we all know that President Pusey has said there will be no co-education without merger."

After Saturday's meeting, Mrs. Bunting told the press that "it will take some time to bring about an actual merger." Last night at dinner in Holmes Hall she said that total merger would probably take about a year.

Although co-educational housing will not necessarily follow merger plans, Mrs. Bunting said, in view of the [Radcliffe Union of Students] poll on co-ed living "a change in housing will be seriously considered." The poll, taken earlier this year, revealed 95 percent support at Radcliffe for co-ed dorms.

It seems that the best way to close a chapter on the University is with a piece meant to make the several Harvards understandable to incoming freshmen. The article, which explains itself, is just as valuable to the indoctrinated as it is to the uninitiated, and probably presents all the best reasons why the articles that have preceded it won't satisfy everybody's idea of what Harvard University really is.

What Harvard Means
30 Theories to Help You Understand
BY NICHOLAS B. LEMANN '76

September 1975

You've probably heard the story about the three blind men and the elephant, the one where each blind man grabs a different part of the animal and each comes away with his own erroneous idea of what it is — the one who grabbed the elephant's tail thinks it's a rope, and so on.

It's like that with Harvard, too. The people here aren't quite so blind, to be sure, but they are intensely, incessantly analytical about themselves and their surroundings. There are few constants in Harvard's 339 years other than that, for all that time, people have thought they had the place figured out and disagreed violently on their interpretations.

So to help you understand, here are 30 different Harvards, each almost as real and true as all the others. It may all confuse you, but so, at first, will Harvard.

The Essential Harvard

1. Eliot Superlative Theory

Charles William Eliot, who was president of Harvard through the late 1800s, and the turn of the century, once called Harvard "the oldest, richest, and freest" university in the country. You can't dispute him on the first two points: founded in 1636, Harvard is unquestionably the oldest institution of higher education in America; and its endowment, about $1.4 billion, makes it still by far the richest (University of Texas is second, but it's all new money). As far as freedom goes, well, Eliot was speaking before the advent of experimental colleges where you can do whatever you want. The tremendous freedom still exists for faculty members but the rest of us would probably be a little less fettered elsewhere.

2. Faculty Get Down to Basics Theory

The august Harvard faculty, threatened some years ago by student radicals, was forced to state its principles. This is what it came up with: "The central functions of an academic community are learning, teaching, research, and scholarship."

3. What's All the Fuss About Theory

John Reed '10, the only American buried in the Kremlin, shortly before his graduation summed it up like this: "College is like the world; outside there is the same class of people, dull and sated and blind." Reed's theory probably has less currency than any other; all the rest depend on the notion that Harvard *is* different, and therefore worth puzzling over.

Harvard the Institution
4. Best Theory

Perhaps the most common of Harvard theories is that it's the Best, period, and everything else falls into place from there; no doubt you share that view. All sorts of American education councils are constantly trying to quantify this theory by rating various schools according to esoteric criteria, but for people here it's mostly a matter of whether you believe in your heart that Harvard is the best, or whether you don't. It certainly has bright students and topnotch faculty, but there are always naysayers.

The naysayers, though, are in their own way subscribers to the Best Theory. Their position is usually that Harvard is not the Best only because it has recently gone to the dogs. They assume that Harvard once occupied the state of grace from which it has fallen.

5. Forgotten Undergraduates Theory

Most undergraduates here feel generally that they're getting the short shrift; the conventional wisdom is that if it's just a good college education you're looking for, rather than the Harvard mystique, you should have gone elsewhere. You won't get much individual attention from faculty members, and you're mostly allowed to go your own way. Harvard leaves you alone.

A selling point of this theory is that Harvard College doesn't have the indisputably high ranking among colleges that, say, Harvard Law School or Harvard Medical School have among law schools and medical schools.

If asked to elaborate, a proponent of the Forgotten Undergraduates Theory would blame faculty members for his plight, explaining that they're all either trying to publish, or making pots of money doing consulting work, or off skiing in

Gstaad. The system for rising through the academic hierarchy here does not, after all, reward teaching ability.

6. Mother Theory

Harvard is like a womb, sheltering you for four years. As Samuel Pitts Duffield '92 put it in a Class Ode, "Fair Mother, we pray for the help ere we turn Toward the doubt and darkness ahead;/May the fires of thy beacons flash high as they burn/And illumine the path where we tread."

7. Lover Theory

Harvard is like a coquettish woman, always tempting you with its glories while holding them back. From another Class Ode, by Henry Copley Greene '94: "Fierce maiden, true life, whom we wooed with grim fight,/In Past dreams to thy conquest we woke."

A cruder version is the Whore Theory, which goes like this: "Harvard is like a whore, see, 'cause you pay to get screwed."

This is also probably a sexist theory.

8. Left-Wing Bastion Theory

The late Senator Joseph McCarthy used to refer to Harvard as "the Kremlin on the Charles" and "a smelly mess," and most of you will probably notice that people here are to the left of the people back home. It used to be that Harvard students — a lot of them anyway — were quite radical, and a few years ago there were building occupations and an active SDS chapter and so forth around here. Conservative alumni — one never hears about liberal alumni — are supposed to be in a constant froth about Harvard's extreme liberalism. In 1968 Harvard President Nathan M. Pusey '28 called Harvard students "Walter Mittys of the left," adding, "They play at being revolutionaries and fancy themselves rising to positions of command atop the debris as the structures of society come crashing down."

All that has died down a bit, but even people considered conservative at Harvard, like Pusey, have fought for causes generally considered liberal, like anti-McCarthyism.

9. *Right-Wing Bastion Theory*

This theory has two facets: first, that Harvard is conservative in its internal policies, even racist and sexist, and second, that Harvard is conservative by nature because it is an entrenched institution in a conservative nation. From the days of John Reed and W. E. B. DuBois, Class of 1890, who said he was always considered "a nigger on the team" here, people have complained about Harvard's white male ambience. And the University has also had an indirect role in political battles that could hardly be called liberal — from President A. Lawrence Lowell's call for Sacco and Vanzetti's execution to Henry Kissinger's departure from the Government Department to oversee the Vietnam War. For all its eccentricity Harvard has never been greatly at odds with mainstream, old-line American capitalism. (cf. Ruling Class Theory.)

10. *General Education Theory*

President James Bryant Conant '14 wrote in 1943, "Today, we are concerned with a general education — a liberal education — not for the relatively few, but for the multitude," and thus invented the prevailing optimistic theory about what Harvard College does. You will supposedly come here and become well-rounded and interested in the world around you, and opening your eyes in this fashion is Harvard's institutional purpose. General Education is still around, of course. Your proctor will tell you about it; mostly it means you have to take a science course here even if you don't want to, but the spirit still lingers.

11. *Business of Education Theory*

President Bok is known to complain from time to time about how administrative his job has become. It's understandable: his predecessors might have been simply educators, but Bok has to be head of a huge, labor-intensive, recession-plagued, hard-to-operate corporation. To make his job easier, Bok and his lieutenants have made Harvard a little more cost-effective, something that runs against the grain of the place and has stirred up some grumbling about how Bok's nothing but a bureaucrat. In any event, Harvard is huge, with a $200 million annual operating budget spread over hundreds of divisions that must each break even. So one could say that Harvard is just another corporation, except that it is in the business of educating people.

12. Philosopher-Kings Theory

Before Bok, at least, if you had asked a Harvard savant about who ran the place, he would tell you the faculty did — they were, you see, this group of brilliant, quarrelsome, egomaniacal men, primarily interested in advancing knowledge, who somewhat incidentally kept Harvard going as well. It was an appealing theory because it implied that as long as there were brains here the place would run itself. Now, though, the theory has faded a little. Everybody knows the faculty members think they run the place — but the administrators really do.

The Harvard Man

13. Manifest Destiny Theory

William Bentinck-Smith '37, who was President Pusey's assistant for years and should know, once wrote: "The really important difference between Harvard men and other men is that the former went to Harvard and the latter did not. Like it or not, any entering Harvard freshman is subject to what might be called college predestination."

If you want to concentrate on Harvard as a collection of people rather than as an institution, you have to go on the assumption that there's a sameness to people here; you can be specific about Harvard people, their personalities, backgrounds and fates, or like Bentinck-Smith you can be general: everybody at Harvard (even the women, he must have meant) becomes a Harvard Man, and that's that. No need to define it further.

14. Thirteen Varieties Theory

Before the admissions office went computerized a few years ago — now they are supposed to sit around and say to each other, "I've got a good boy here; he's sort of a 142" — they had a breakdown of all Harvard people into 13 types, designated by letters. There was W, for wheel, which meant an ambitious, driving type, and X, for cross-country, which meant a plodding but determined type, and so on. They were all Harvard men if they were admitted, you understand, but there were still slight variations.

15. Finley Two- and Six-Variety Theories

John H. Finley '25, a semiretired professor of Greek, is a veteran theorizer. In one well-known version of his Harvard Worldview, there are arrows (ambitious, motivated types) and teacups (those out to find themselves). In another there were six types — activists, scholars, and so on.

16. Yale Three-Variety Theory

The *Insider's Guide to the Colleges*, published by the editors of *The Yale Daily News*, says there are only three kinds of people at Harvard; wonks (who study a lot), jocks (who go out for sports and drink) and preppies (who join clubs). There are some hippies, the guide admits, but basically if you're not already one of the three classic types you'd best hang it up.

17. Hall Product Theory

Stephen S. J. Hall, vice president for administration, also takes a student-oriented view of the University. "I consider Harvard really one of the finest universities in the world as far as the product they turn out," Hall said last year, explaining why he came here from the Sheraton Corporation. "Basically, that's what we're here for — to turn out a product."

18. Fisher 10,000 Factory Men of Harvard Theory

Francis D. Fisher '49, who directs the Harvard office that counsels students on careers, thinks so many people are going to college these days that pretty soon college graduates — even Harvard graduates — will be forced into blue-collar jobs. Fisher's office publishes a book called *After Harvard What?* that predicts "that new and tougher competition will exist from the brightest Ph.D. on down, that many, no matter how well-educated, will end up doing work of a somewhat different kind than the work which someone similarly educated would have undertaken even a few years ago."

19. Fitzgerald Indoors Theory

From F. Scott Fitzgerald's *This Side of Paradise,* this is future Princeton man Amory Blaine reflecting on where to go to college: "I want to go to Princeton. I don't know why, but I think of all Harvard men as sissies like I used to be, and all Yale men as wearing big blue sweaters and smoking pipes . . . I think of Princeton as being lazy and goodlooking and aristocratic, like a spring day. Harvard seems sort of indoors . . ."

20. You Can't Tell Him Much Theory

Harvard men, this theory goes, are Harvard men because they're not — that is, the good thing about Harvard is that it doesn't turn out a prestamped, homogeneous product. William James said, "Our undisciplinables are our proudest product," and President Conant agreed: "Harvard was founded by dissenters. Before two generations had passed there was a general dissent from the first dissent. Heresy has long been in the air."

21. Stamped From the Mold Theory

On the other hand: there are those tho think Harvard turns out people, or should turn out people, who are similar, upper-middle-class bureaucrats. The New American Movement, for instance, a local leftist group, published a pamphlet called *Introducing Harvard* a few years ago that said: "That is what Harvard trains you for: surviving and rising in the bureaucracy of your choice." Even President Pusey, in his "Walter Mittys of the left" speech, saw his mission as bringing radical students into the fold, saying: "Bringing students of this persuasion back to reality presents a new kind of challenge to college education."

22. Harvarder-Than-Thou Theory

This is the popular image — Harvard men as snobs, outwardly cynical and blasé and self-assured (that's the part

Harvard taught them) and inwardly ambitious (that's the
part they came with). People have been talking about Harvard snobs for at least two hundred years and for two
hundred years it's been at least partly true. It will be strange,
because while at first it will seem more foreign than anything
in the world, after a couple years you'll notice — on a trip
home, maybe — that without even wanting to you've picked
up some of the Harvard manner, too.

23. Not Everyone Can Be One Theory

Dr. Chase N. Peterson '52, vice president for alumni affairs
and development, went on a local talk show a few years back
when he was Harvard's dean of admissions. He talked about
Harvard and truck drivers. "Truck driving is still an honorable and well-paid profession," Peterson said. "All youngsters
are not equipped to go to college . . . all of them have different aptitudes and attitudes." Harvard fit into things thusly:
"Harvard stands for excellence and high standards and there
is nothing wrong with that." *The Boston Globe* called Peterson
"outspoken" for all that, which is true in that a lot, maybe
most, of the people at Harvard probably agree with him but
almost none would say so on TV.

The Harvard Life
24. Sex Theory

There was a great '60s junk novel called *The Harrad Experiment* that was about a college in Cambridge, Mass. (Har-Rad,
get it?), where they put all freshmen in rooms with members
of the opposite sex, just so they could be fully educated. The
point is that if you were going to hint plausibly that any
American college is a sex haven, you'd hint that it's Harvard.
The old tabloid Hearst newspaper in Boston liked that Harvard the best: HARVARD BARES WILD PARTIES was its banner
headline one day.

On the surface, perhaps it's justified: there are co-ed dorms
here, even co-ed bathrooms, and everyone talks about sex all
the time. You will be able to tell your parents Harvard sex
stories that will shock them. But as always with such things,

the talk outweighs the action. Harvard's generally exotic image is what makes the sex-haven tag fit.

25. *Psychological Meat Grinder Theory*

You'll hear a lot of this one this year — in this issue of The Crimson, for instance. One self-acclaimed Harvard savant used to say, "The thing about Harvard is that if you're cool, it's cool. It's only if you've got some flaw, some weak point. Harvard will find it, and bring it out." People are always talking about how *intense* it is here, how they've changed, how high school seems long ago. Maybe people are happy at Harvard but they're hardly ever contented.

The reason this probably happens is that it's a tremendous shock for people who are used to being big shots to come here and have to adjust to being just like everyone else.

26. *Place of God Theory*

For much of its early existence Harvard's function was primarily to train young men for the Protestant ministry; the University was founded in piety, and, some say, that piety lives on (it's just a little harder to find these days, having become sort of secularized). On the surface Harvard is a fairly Godless place, and President Pusey used to attract a great deal of derision by saying things about "the present low estate of religion at Harvard." Someone once asked Pusey what the single most important quality for a Harvard president was, and he answered "a belief in God," but nobody says that sort of thing any more.

27. *Seat of Learning Theory*

The first thing written about Harvard that everyone has been able to dig up is a pamphlet called *New England's First Fruits*, apparently designed to entice people into emigrating here. It says the University was founded "to advance learning and perpetuate it to posterity." Years later Thomas Wolfe's fictional hero, Eugene Gant, came here and started reading books like crazy because "he simply wanted to know about everything on earth; he wanted to devour the earth and it drove him mad when he saw he could not do this." If there was anywhere you'd expect a modern Dr. Faustus to turn up it would be Widener Library, but these days, alas, people mostly talk about how they learned what they learned at Harvard outside of classrooms and libraries, how they had "learning experiences" here.

28. Paris on the Charles Theory

There are those who say the specialness of Harvard comes from its location in Cambridge, America's most suave and continental and sophisticated city. That's something of a chicken and egg problem, but people *do* sit around in coffeehouses in Cambridge a lot and there *are* a lot of bookstores and newsstands and people talking French in the street. Nobody seems to get up before noon. Where else are there block-long lines to see twenty-year-old Swedish-language films on weekday nights?

Harvard and the World

29. Ruling Class or Training Ground of the Elite Theory

Charles William Eliot said, "There is an aristocracy to which the sons of Harvard have belonged and, let us hope, will ever aspire to belong." Eliot should know; when he came to Harvard he was related by blood or marriage to a sizable chunk of the faculty and administration. It's not quite so close-knit now, but *Introducing Harvard* maintains, "No description of the educational process at Harvard could be complete without mentioning the college's historic function: educating the sons and daughters of the nation's elite."

The average parental income of students here is sky-high, and the University's Governing Boards, if not its faculty, are still populated by the heirs to America's oldest East Coast fortunes. In that sense Harvard's real function is to train the children of the powerful to take the power themselves, so as to keep it in the family. The reason Harvard graduates have had such a profound influence on America — five of them have been U.S. presidents, countless others presidents of corporations — is not so much their innate talent as their good luck at being born to the right parents. Harvard just added

the polish and gave the elites' children a chance to get acquainted with each other.

30. Meritocracy or Breeding Ground of the Elite Theory

The more current view of Harvard in American society is that
the University is the ultimate agent of upward socioeconomic
mobility; a perfect meritocracy, it culls the one or two best
kids from practically every high school in America. It's competitive and high-key, so much so that even staunch liberals
like David Riesman '31 are beginning to have doubts. In his
new book Riesman says the meritocratic atmosphere doesn't
do much for learning or finding yourself or that sort of thing.
Maybe you'll end up a part of the new antimeritocracy, slide
right through Harvard, and go back to Dubuque after you
graduate to work on the farm. By then you'll probably have a
few theories of your own.

CHAPTER 2

College Life

WHEN ONE THINKS of "college life" the phrase conjures up two different — and opposing — ideas. First is the essential sameness of the experience; certain things just don't change and these perennials seem to be associated with late adolescence and blossoming adulthood: students enjoy a certain amount of freedom at college, sex becomes important, society finally opens up to them. But another image "college life" produces is associated with the era in which one went to college. In the 1890s people became acquainted with the bicycle, they went to football games and drank beer from kegs, they wore straw hats in the spring; in the Roaring Twenties nobody drank — legally — so everybody drank from hidden flasks, a few college-aged men could take dates out in new Model T Fords and for the first time they had a private, enclosed environment away from parents, teachers, and peers; one mark of the thirties was the way in which many college students embraced Communism . . . and so on.

The following section captures both of these images, the sameness and the difference. Harvard from 1873 to 1973 didn't change much in some respects: students today are still concerned with their accommodations, they go through the trials and tribulations of various traditions, they still make (or endure) the same cafeteria banter. But Harvard also went through some very major changes, as will become apparent when you read this chapter. First, The Crimson came on the scene (in 1873, as The Magenta), and *The Lampoon* followed along just a little later. Living conditions were far different: lighting, horse and buggies . . . Harvard had far different traditions then, too. There was the early-morning bell, which theoretically arose the students for early-morning chapel; one was served by waiters at the Memorial Hall cafeteria, and one walked on footpaths through the Yard rather than on sidewalks. The following articles aren't meant to produce any sort of far-reaching, conclusive social history of Harvard over the past century. They're simply glimpses into the lives of students, chosen because they seemed to be interesting or insightful glimpses, and chosen with the hopes that readers would come away with an enlarged vision of Harvard's social history, of its college life.

*   *   *

Gas in the Entries

February 21, 1873

In calling attention once more to the subject of gas in the entries, we hope not to appear to cavil or to display a childish fretfulness. But it is a matter that greatly incommodes the students. The fact that the gas is allowed to burn till eleven o'clock is a tacit acknowledgment that the convenience of those who pass through the halls ought to be provided for. There is no reason that the gas should be put out at eleven, rather than at nine or ten; for few go to bed so early, and most find it natural to get their water and coal after everything else has been done. We do not lay much stress upon the danger that anyone may tumble down stairs and break his neck; but, from personal experience, we know that it is very exasperating to come down with a thump and a bite of the tongue, when we have miscalculated the number of steps. The possibility that one may be brought up full against the wall or dashed down a few steps into the stomach of another wayfarer makes locomotion in the winding halls of Matthews not a little exciting.

The worst of the matter is that the gas is turned off at the meters, so that it cannot be lit again during the night. A man's vexation when he finds himself in a black basement with only a match or two in his pockets is almost intolerable.

The present state of things is a marked change from what it was two years ago. Then, it is true, that gas burned in the entries till only half past ten; but a full blaze could be got at any part of the night in the basements. Now the brightest light in many of the buildings is only a glimmer, that hardly serves to make the darkness visible.

Thoughts on Returning to College

September 27, 1878

What a change it is to return from one's summer wanderings to the bustle and hurry of college life! Everything presents such a rude contrast to the things we had become accustomed to during the summer. In a week or two, to be sure, we have dropped into the old ruts, and are going along as smoothly as if we had never been away, but for the first few days everything seems strange.

In the morning, for instance, instead of enjoying a quiet sleep, and getting up at a reasonable hour, we are roused by the relentless Jones with his prayer-bell. There is no instrument of torture yet devised by man which can cause more misery than a loud bell rung early in the morning [7 a.m.]. It is especially disagreeable when one has been up late the night before at a political or temperance meeting. The pretext on which it is rung, too, is a frivolous one. If a man insists on going to prayers, he can surely be awakened without rousing all the victims of catarrh and general indisposition, who are unable to attend. Why should all of us be awakened at the same moment? John Stuart Mill says the uniformity is a bad thing. This prayer-bell must be given up; it crushes out all individuality, and is a barbarous relic of the past.

If it is unpleasant to be roused from a heavy sleep, how much more unpleasant is it to have to get up and go to prayers! Our own personal experience in this matter has not been very extensive, but we can easily imagine what it must be. We are happy to say that we made the acquaintance of a very gentlemanly physician this summer, who told us never to be out in the morning until after prayer-time. We promised to obey his instructions faithfully.

Memorial Hall is not like your table at home; there is no getting over that fact. The noise at first seems intolerable, but you soon get used to it and begin to make a good deal of it yourself. Instead of a neat maid to wait on you, a burly Negro slams down your plate before you, and hurries off again. It is hard to realize at first that it is necessary to wait a considerable time before getting anything to eat, but you soon learn that it is indeed so. The superannuated turkeys and hens will doubtless be as numerous and excellent as ever. It seems cruel, however, to kill an animal that is so near a natural death by old age . . .

— Henry S. Butler, Class of 1877

Give Us Gondolas

February 19, 1887

Great Jove! And can these things be? The Yard is a lake of raging water, whose billows roll over the unprotected sidewalks, and never a glimmer of light at night to act as light-house on the vasty deep! This particular editor of The Crimson fell in three feet of water, and wandered off the main channel of the sidewalk into deeper gulfs twice last evening in voyaging from Holworthy to Weld. There was water everywhere, and nothing to guide him in it. The president is away, we know, but we must appeal to the pity and humanity of the residuary powers. Let us either have light or raised sidewalks in the Yard until the spring floods are over, or else do please, kind masters, give us gondolas.

Classmate of Rinehart Tells
How Legend Actually Began

October 2, 1952

To the Editors of The Crimson:

If not too late for news value, I should like through your columns to meet a friend's request by recounting my own recollections and impressions of a once-friend who died a week ago, and of the manner in which his name came to adorn the Harvard Hall of Myth. I refer to J. B. Rinehart, whom I knew well some months before his first name was spelled "Oh." He was a member of my Class of 1900. He was also my table mate; for a year we ate mutton together at table 6 in Memorial Hall. Among other 1900 men at the table was Ralph Kent, of Concord, New Hampshire, who was as long as Rinehart was squat. They roamed the Yard together, a sort of Harvard "Mutt and Jeff."

Rinehart roomed upstairs in Grays Hall, at the south end of the Yard. Kent often sought him, but instead of walking up three flights, would stand below and issue forth his name. There was nothing unusual in this. Men frequently called up to their fellow students reposing in the open window seats during the hot June of 1900. But the extra frequency and high power and plaintive tone of this particular call, combined with the figure of a long, lank, loose-limbed son of the New Hampshire hills, gradually, from day to day, during that last exam-crammed fortnight of the year, began to pierce the subconscious stratum of the brain-sweating, window-seated public mind. Such was the highly charged psycho-electric atmosphere on one of the afternoons before an exam the next morning at 9:15 a.m.

I was not present in the Yard on the hour wherein the shout was heard around the world. But the account of it I obtained from Walter Prichard Eaton, 1900, who now lives in Sheffield, Mass., and who should properly tell this story. So I tell it subject to his correction, for the archives of an ever-to-be-corrected history.

Walter was hunched up in his window seat. It was in Matthews, or else in Weld, I have forgotten which. Both halls flank Grays. It was in the after-luncheon doldrum time of day, when mankind in its senses should be ossified and not prodded. Walter was tired out; "brain fag," the railroad men would call it. He was ripe to be keynoter at a convention on explosives. And all unconsciously, he was just that, for the convention sat in silence in a score of open windows.

Suddenly he was aroused. Something vaguely familiar was being said. Then said again — and in accent familiar. Eaton turned and looked. Sure enough, there he was! That long figure of a man in front of Grays. He watched it. It took a long breath, and then up rose neck and mouth; once more brayed forth that plaintive, and this time extra-powered cry — "Oh Rinehart!"

Something snapped in Eaton's cranium. But he did not jump out of the window. His soul jumped out instead. He leaned forward. Utterance of some sort there must be. Had Eaton satire only lent him utterance, he might have said, "When you call him that, smile." Had Eaton ire only lent him utterance, he might have told the gent whose son he was. But neither instinct came along; instead ire and satire met in one grand incandescence; and voicing this potent compound, as only Eaton can, he rasped forth the cry of Kent in one long lingering lunge — *"Oh Rinehart!"*

For an instant the convention held its silence. Each man suddenly leaned out. Something weird had happened in the Yard — which was their present world. Then from somewhere, from some window, Eaton knew not which, and it never will be known, there issued a second echo of Kent's lamentive strain . . . Then a third . . . Next a chorus . . . You know the rest in the talk you have heard. The chant has reverberated through the decades. At the time of the Harvard Tercentenary, in 1936, the headlines read RINEHART HIM-SELF IN TOWN.

I attended that occasion. I met Rinehart for the first time in 36 years. We spent much of the time together, for we were the only ones in sight from table 6. We went together to a little impromptu dinner of the Class of 1900. There several stories were told as contributions to the Rinehart saga. I think it was Arthur Drinkwater, our devoted Class Secretary, who told of a life being saved somewhere abroad (I think it was Cairo) by calling the magic words from a window. Also, of a man, broke in New York's Grand Central, being enabled to take his train . . . May the spirit of "Oh Rinehart" march on — saving lives and binding them as fellow culprits in our wicked world, secure within the legends concentric of table 6, of 1900, and of Harvard.

Benton MacKaye '00

Radcliffe Survives Years of Sneers
Annex Maidens Today Win Crimson Men
BY STEPHEN O. SAXE '51

September 1951

"We Radcliffe girls are a long-suffering group, but under the kind of persecution we have received at Harvard's hands, even a Griselda would revolt. It seems to me that the time has come to show that we have feelings and that they have been seriously injured."

So wrote Sophie Reagan, Radcliffe '41, in a letter to The Crimson back in 1940. She was troubled not only by Harvard's traditional scorn for Radcliffe, but also by a specific and undeniably inflammatory incident. A few days before a Crimson editor had escorted Miss Toni Sorel, contender for the title of

"Number One Oomph Girl of the Nation," into the Harvard Yard. Later, over a daiquiri, Miss Sorel had this to say to the press:

"Here I stood in the Harvard Yard, lousy with ivy and tradition, when the whole picture was ruined — a couple of strange creatures came waddling along. Radcliffe girls are horrible. They have hairy legs and fat fannies and shouldn't be allowed in the Yard."

Perhaps her words were true; perhaps they were not. At any rate, the Harvard of 1940 agreed wholeheartedly. Harvard likes Radcliffe now. Harvard holds hands with Radcliffe, marries Radcliffe, and has babies by Radcliffe. The reason is the remarkably retarded adolescence of the two institutions — otherwise known as Joint Education.

From the very start, Radcliffe was entirely dependent on Harvard. It had Harvard professors, Harvard standards, and Harvard assignments. It wasn't long before some Yardster of the '80s called the Society "The Harvard Annex." The girls on Garden Street could not very well object, since their institution was exactly that.

For a long, long time after its formal chartering of Radcliffe in 1894, Harvard was generally cordial but distant. The attitude of most men was not so much one of scorn, but of (and we blush to use the word) indifference. In 1908 *The Harvard Illustrated News* (which was edited by H. V. Kaltenborn '09) ran an article entitled "Radcliffe on Harvard," which indicates attitudes then prevalent on both sides of the Common. The article, by an anonymous Radcliffe undergraduate, said in part:

". . . once in the library (the Radcliffe girl) gets her books and sits penned off from the Harvard occupants of the history reading-room, her back discreetly turned toward them; all of this is done with an amused consciousness that, while such behavior satisfies her own sense of proprieties, it is quite unnecessary: Harvard is unconscious of her existence."

During the First World War relations between the two institutions began to change — for the worse. A stereotype grew in the Harvard mind, and assumed gigantic proportions. It was a picture of "the typical Radcliffe girl" — sloppily dressed, bespectacled, ugly as sin and not nearly so tempting. The trouble was that Harvard was going collegiate, and the col-

legiate attitude toward college was, above all else, uncomplimentary.

Leaving the realm of fancy for a moment let us take a look
at the facts. In October 1928, some obscure statistician, hard
at work under a green eyeshade in a dusty room, came up
with a monumental discovery. Fifty-three percent of all marrying Radcliffe girls had Harvard men for husbands! The
Crimson could do nothing but make a grimace that would
pass for a smile, and the day after the discovery, it stated
Crimson policy on Radcliffe in an editorial, called "The Mat-
ing Call."

"The legend surrounding Radcliffe's ivory towers and its
bespectacled inmates must yield to the pressure of figures,
cold, exact figures . . . If Radcliffe has overwhelmed the
sneers of a decade, and emerged from a chrysalis of contempt
as the most alluring fata morgana for several thousand potential bachelors, what use caution?"

The editorial continued:

"Fifty-three percent of marrying alumnae attract Harvard
husbands. But 5 percent of them reach out after MIT men.
This fact must be considered significant. Why should Harvard
men be favored in such preponderance? The obvious answer
is to be found in the superiority of the Coop and the Widener
Library as trysting places over the barren laboratories of the
Technological Institute."

"Oh I say, Rollins, about that hour exam . . ." Drawing by David
Royce '53, '55½, '56. April 12, 1954.

The result of Sophie Reagan's rebuttal to Miss Sorel was the formation of an organization of militant Radcliffe girls. It was called "The Committee to Take Radcliffe Seriously." Nobody took the committee seriously, much less Radcliffe.

The big change, when it came, was not the result of internal but external events. In 1942 the pressure of war and mobilization made financial troubles at Radcliffe bad. In 1943 Jerome D. Greene, Class of 1896, secretary to the Harvard Corporation, wrote in a report that "possible revision of the arrangements by which the instruction of members of the Harvard faculty is made available at Radcliffe College," in other words, "Joint Instruction," was contemplated.

And it came to pass. During the war years Harvard men gradually got used to seeing girls in their classes; their minds were elsewhere. They were annoyed by what they believed the girls' academic methods to be, and still are slightly. They believed Radcliffe girls learned everything by rote, spewed it forth at exams, and got A's. Or, rote learning failing, they would sidle up to an instructor, display a little leg, and get an A.

The Crimson reporter who covered the Phillips Brooks House tea in '47 brought back a different report from the ones by his predecessors. His story was headlined "No Lemons at Brooks House Tea." Apparently the rest of the College got the same idea. On February 11 Dean Mildred P. Sherman of Radcliffe announced dramatically that "the process of saying goodnight had degenerated."

Shocked, Radcliffe girls banded together and approved plans to keep men out of the dorms after 10 p.m. on weekdays. The Harvard reaction to that can be illustrated by reprinting a poem that was sent to The Crimson by three Harvard men, in spiritual collaboration with Andrew Marvell:

On Learning That Radcliffe
Votes Chaste Farewells

Had we but world enough and time,
This coyness, Radcliffe, were no crime.
We would sit down and think of ways
To spread our love o'er many days.

Thou should by sluggish Charles' side,
With New Directions as your guide,
The fate of men and books decide
And damn the old with comments snide.
But college days are all too short
And not too long may we cavort:
The dorm's a fine and private place,
But none henceforth shall there embrace,
Since at our back we always fear
The curfew hour drawing near.
For parting passions — time compressed —
Are crudely felt and ill-expressed;
And chilly as the good Dean's breast
Is Boston's winter at the best.
The cold stone steps outside the houses
Have not the atmosphere which rouses
The feeling waked by well-filled
    blouses,
(Line censored — Ed.)
If we can't make the clock stand still,
We'll go to Wheaton — Damn — we
    will!!

But they didn't mean it for a minute. Once more we must turn to fact over fancy; six out of ten Radcliffe girls marry Harvard men. Perhaps the Harvard attitude was no more than a cry of protest; now that cry is no more than a gasp. Harvard has almost completely succumbed to the charms of Radcliffe.

Goldfish Swallowing: College Fad Started Here, Spread Over World

Holworthy Resident Wins Bet as Mind Triumphs Over Matter, Tea

BY RICHARD A. BURGHEIM '55

May 6, 1952

When a Yale dean snidely called a recent Eli student stunt "a great deal better than face slapping or eating live goldfish," he revived an issue as dead as — one hopes — are the gold-fish.

The most-publicized college fad in history started on March 3, 1939, in the Harvard Union, when freshman Lothrop Withington Jr. '42, goaded by a bet with his roommates, downed a goldfish never to be upped again. Pocketing a wager of $10 in good 1939 currency for his efforts, the Yardling thus ushered in a two-month period, which *Time* magazine called "among the maddest in the annals of U.S. undergraduates."

As summed up by Withington, now a conservative business-man, "It was purely a case of mind over matter. I didn't mind, and the fish didn't matter." But the fish did matter to some. The Animal Rescue League was indignant about the sit-uation and, shortly thereafter, Massachusetts State Senator George Krapf filed a bill "to preserve the fish from cruel and wanton consumption."

Most of the reaction was favorable, however, and Withing-ton still has a "trunkful" of fan letters and newspaper clip-pings. Job offers poured in, and he was subsequently elected to his class Smoker Committee.

Among his correspondence Withington still cherishes a let-ter from a Kansas man who wrote, "If you ever want $10 that bad again, just let us know and we'll send it to keep you from becoming constipated."

But beneath the surface glamour, there was plenty of hard work and courage. Withington had practiced diligently at his Holworthy aquarium, starting with small fish and gradually working up to the four-incher he swallowed at the Friday night Union performance.

In swallowing, Withington followed a definite plan. The Yardling's experimentation proved the immediate mastica-tion process superior to the decisive gulp system, as the latter had to be followed instantly by a fish-killing beverage, like Union ice tea.

At this point, pioneer Withington dropped out of the busi-ness, although even today the incident follows him. He re-ports, "I've never been able to duck it, but I certainly don't regret it."

Taking over where Withington left off in March of '39 was

Lowell House sophomore Irving M. Clark Jr. '42. In ten minutes, on the evening of March 26, Clark, clad in a Crimson sweater, gulped down 23 of the aquatic animals, his weight climbing from 158 to 165 in the process. During the sprint Clark paused only long enough to suck on an orange between fish. Circus offers followed, but the sophomore was uninterested, preferring to retain his "amateur standing."

The Boston papers naturally leapt on the story as an example of the decadent ways of Our College Youth. In the *Boston Herald* one Eva Williams Raymond burst into poetry thusly:

> To end the paranoiac prank,
> O Harvard, how I wish
> You'd put the students in a tank
> And graduate the fish!

CIRCLING THE SQUARE

Threskiornis

November 30, 1956

There are very few places he hasn't visited. He has been seen on Boston's newspaper row, and mingling with the seagulls on the city waterfront; he has gotten a shave and a steambath at local establishments; he has been tête-à-tête with Miss Rosita Royce backstage at the Old Howard; he has visited the Russian delegation in New York City; and, in between, he has occasionally been found on top of the *Lampoon* building at 44 Bow Street.

But you won't find Threski (short for Threskiornis, which supposedly stands for *Ibis Aethiopia*) there now. For *The Lampoon*'s sacred bird-symbol is reportedly still recuperating from injuries received at the hands of The Crimson last spring. And besides that, the years have been tough on this venerable symbol of recent Crimson-*Lampoon* rivalry.

It all started, as far as most local historians can remember, sometime around the Second World War. Written records are scarce and biased, but the consensus seems to be that a Crim-

Threski, *The Lampoon*'s Sacred Ibis, gets a checkup at the University Health Services before taking one of his annual jaunts about town, puzzles his wise friend at the Museum of Science, and engages some fellow fish eaters in lucid conversation. The Ibis's disappearance from atop the Lampoon Castle always seemed to be blamed on The Crimson. May 11, 1956. (Photos by Robert M. Pringle '58)

son editor was badly injured by a fall from the *Lampoon* roof while either stealing the bird or attempting to return it after it had been stolen.

This had a sobering effect for a few years, but in 1951 The Crimson once more pirated the sacred Ibis, and started a minor war which has continued on down to the present. The bird had fallen down of its own accord during a storm and had been turned in at the University Lost and Found, where a Crimson editor claimed it under false pretenses.

For some reason *The Lampoon* thought David L. Ratner '52, the rather staid editorial chairman, had stolen its bird, so they kidnapped him and took him to an abandoned house in Ipswich. They took his clothes from him for a night, then gave them back and lashed him to a potbellied stove for a group picture. Shortly thereafter, Ratner escaped, and the *'Poon* soon recaptured its bird.

After a year of relative quiet on its perch at 44 Bow, the Ibis suddenly disappeared again in April of 1953. [See Chapter 4.]

In the spring of 1954 and 1956 Threski again disappeared mysteriously only to be photographed at various local points of interest. He was returned to the *'Poon* offices last June, but will probably not attain his former heights until the *'Poon*sters scrape up $45 to cover the cost of resoldering him to his perch. How long he will stay up thereafter is uncertain.

— Philip M. Boffey '58

EDITORIAL
_____

Equal Opportunity

October 5, 1960

Emily Post died the other day; the demise of this lady high executioner of the uncouth marks a final expiration — Victoria is dead, long live the twentieth century. The time has come to talk of Radcliffe women being allowed to have men in their rooms more often than the allotted and tea-soaked twice a year . . .

Three policemen beat Paul R. Rugo '55 onto the ground during the infamous "Pogo Riot" of May 15, 1952. Student "riots" — large rallies, often held in the Square, and during which students would catcall passers-by or shoot them with water pistols — were common occurrences in the 1950s. Rugo, according to eyewitness accounts reported in The Crimson, was walking along with his date when he was apprehended by the police for no reason at all. In all, 28 students were arrested, and a number of them were beaten by the police, who also stole another Crimson photographer's film and harassed Crimson reporters covering the action. In the end, students were allowed to plead nolo contendere and were set free, and several Cambridge police officers were given reprimands. May 16, 1952. (Copyright © 1952 Robert T. Root '54)

Faculty Approves Co-ed Living
For Three Houses Next Spring

BY DEBORAH B. JOHNSON '71

December 10, 1969

The Faculty yesterday approved three experimental co-ed housing exchanges for next semester, establishing the first official co-ed housing in the history of the College.

The proposals still need official approval by the Radcliffe Council and the Harvard Corporation before they can go into effect, but Presidents Pusey and Bunting said yesterday that approval is certain.

The exchanges — between Winthrop and North Houses, Adams and South, and Lowell and East — would involve 50 students from each House. The students in the exchanges will be chosen by processes decided upon in each House.

Jerome Kagan, professor of Developmental Psychology and head of the Faculty Committee on Residential Living, proposed the exchanges only ten minutes before the scheduled close of yesterday's meeting. After fewer than five minutes of debate, the motion passed overwhelmingly.

The proposed exchanges probably will continue only through spring. The Harvard-Radcliffe merger is scheduled for completion over the summer, and long-range co-ed housing will probably be instituted next fall.

Four major aspects of the exchanges approved yesterday are:

• No freshmen will take part;

• No one who does not wish to move from his present room will have to do so;

• Harvard Houses will be integrated by suite, and Radcliffe by floor;

• Academic and disciplinary responsibility for those in the exchanges will remain with the House of origin.

UHS to Offer Sex Counseling

November 6, 1971

After years of tactful silence, the University Health Services (UHS) has begun to deal openly with the question of sexual services. A new sex-counseling service will open Monday.

"It's a supplement to things that have been here but never explicitly organized," Margaret S. McKenna '70, assistant to the director of the UHS and coordinator of the service, said yesterday. "Many of these services were available last year but people didn't know how to get to them."

McKenna will be assisted by two students, a male and a female, from Soc Rel 1901, a field-work course in counseling. Many students prefer to talk to another student, McKenna said, because they find doctors too intimidating or too abrupt.

The program will facilitate referral to UHS doctors, but many students won't need to see a doctor, McKenna predicted. "Much of the information you don't need a doctor to tell you," she said.

. . . Students may come alone or in couples, and may walk in or call for an appointment. No records will be kept, and absolute confidentiality is assured . . .

McKenna and the students have been meeting with several UHS doctors and psychiatrists, including Dr. Warren E. C. Wacker, director of the UHS, to clarify procedures. Commenting on the results of an experimental sex-counseling program at Radcliffe last year, Wacker said, "I think there is a need for sex counseling. Sex is not one of the things you take SATs in. The possibility for ignorance in this area is quite good" . . .

McKenna said that the institution of this new service indicates a shifting attitude toward sex at Harvard. As recently as 1963, the dean of Harvard College was quoted in *Sex and the College Student* as saying that he was disturbed by the fact that many students felt that a student's room is his castle and that his sexual behavior is his private affair.

CHAPTER 3

Editorial and Politics

THE IMPORTANCE of Harvard in national and international affairs is often exaggerated and distorted; it seems inevitable that Harvard is constantly credited with more influence than it actually has. In the early part of the century, John S. Reed '10 and Upton Sinclair would associate Harvard with conservatism and Wall Street, while people like President Wilson's attorney general, A. Mitchell Palmer, the country's first big "Red Menace" witch-hunter, and (in 1922) then-Vice-President Coolidge would see Reds and sedition in the University. President Lowell's part in the Sacco-Vanzetti execution; President Conant's appointment of then Communist Granville Hicks '23 to a tutoring post; the rising interest in Communism among Harvard students in the 1930s; Harvard's ostensible lead in defending academic freedom against McCarthyism; President Kennedy's tap on Harvard resources; the government roles of Bundy, Kissinger, Schlesinger, Dunlop, Moynihan; Harvard student activism for civil rights in the early sixties and against the Vietnam War in the late sixties; all these phenomena have led to vastly differing and occasionally wildly distorted conclusions about Harvard's overall contribution to the political life of this country and of the world.

The task of evaluating the University's political role will have to be left to a scholarly tome. Looking briefly at the last century, however, it would seem that Harvard displayed a long tradition of political conservatism in both its official and unofficial capacities. The University's more recent strain of liberalism has proceeded cautiously, and even up to the present the University has rewarded and encouraged men (not the generic pronoun) in what can only be called traditional patterns of success, while it has rarely been in the vanguard in providing an atmosphere for progressive thought, or promoting egalitarian ideals. If Harvard isn't exactly Wall Street, it *does* invest its money in stocks (and not always the most conscionable stocks); if the University isn't synonymous with the government, it *has* worked closely with the government during wars, it *has* taken more and more money from the government, and it *has*, on occasion, given special dispensations to professors on extended leaves while they were working for the government.

One of the most fascinating aspects of Harvard's political role has been the contribution of Harvard professors and administrators to individual politicians, broad-based political movements, and the government. Again, it is difficult to assess the University's role as an institution. Leaves of absence are generally granted to all professors for whatever purposes they choose. The few instances, however, when the University has given extended leaves of absence for professors in high government positions — one was given to Henry Kissinger, for example — might arguably be said to represent an indirect form of political action.

Professors may also do consulting work for political purposes but, at least according to the University rules, only on their own time. The Corporation used to accept government contracts to do classified research, but since 1946 such contracts have been expressly forbidden. As McGeorge Bundy, then dean of the Faculty of Arts and Sciences, said in 1955, "It has been Harvard's historic policy to emphasize the importance to the nation of open research in basic subjects."

If Harvard as an institution has made few direct contributions to political activity, it has not discouraged University members from getting involved. In fact, Harvard has been rather proud of the public roles of its alumni and faculty members. When President Kennedy entertained the Corporation and the Board of Overseers at the White House in May 1963, a luncheon was held at which, naturally enough, a presentation was given on "The Role of Harvard Men in Government Over the Past Half Century."

In 1952 Adlai Stevenson consulted four Harvard professors

during the course of his campaign. Eisenhower tried to get some political mileage out of this fact by saying in a campaign speech, "It is high time we had real and positive policies in the words that we understand . . . we are tired of aristocratic explanations in Harvard words." Ironically, after his 1952 victory Eisenhower appointed more than a dozen Harvard men to the higher echelons of his administration, including President Conant as German high commissioner, Henry Cabot Lodge '24 as U.N. ambassador, and Sinclair Weeks '14 as secretary of commerce.

JFK consulted no less than 12 full professors during his campaign. Nevertheless, Kennedy was wary of the relationship between what he called "eggheads" and politicians. As he told a Harvard commencement audience in 1956, politicians like himself should consult intellectuals "to bathe us in the soothing waters of the scholastic pool." But Kennedy warned that politicians were more interested in "winning popular support . . . and only indirectly is truth the object of our controversy." Kennedy's statement notwithstanding, participation by Harvard men in government since the early sixties has been unusually high. In 1960 McGeorge Bundy left his position as dean of the Faculty of Arts and Sciences to become assistant to the president for national security affairs. In 1968, Nixon appointed Henry A. Kissinger '50, professor of Government, to the same position; he also appointed Daniel P. Moynihan, professor of Education and Urban Affairs, as assistant to the president for urban affairs. John T. Dunlop moved from his position as dean of the Faculty to become secretary of labor in 1975–76; James R. Schlesinger '50 moved from one position to another in high government, from being head of the Office of Management and Budget, to chairing the Atomic Energy Commission, to directing the CIA, to his appointment as Secretary of Defense, to his last position as Secretary of Energy.

To present all The Crimson's articles on Harvard men in government would make for an entire book in itself. But The Crimson's depiction of Harvard's role in national and world politics and its own editorial commentary on important events do provide fleeting glimpses of the changing world view in the University and among undergraduates. The picture is far from complete. That can only be expected from a paper that ran full force only nine months out of every year (led by a new group of executives each time), and which has always given University events and concerns priority over the outside world. But The Crimson is an important historical document to the extent that the University *did* become involved in broader political movements.

Before continuing any further, the process of Crimson editorial decision making should be explained. When the paper was founded all editors voted on editorials, and that is the procedure today. As early as 1878 the paper explained how it arrived at its editorial policy, and this same explanation was given throughout the first 50 years. But it appears that when The Crimson went daily, editorials became the prerogative of the president and this tradition continued until 1911, when an Editorial Board distinct from the News Board was created. Even then, the higher executives often had a great deal more to say about editorials. It was quite some time — not until the mid-1930s — before formal editorial meetings, open to the entire staff, were held regularly. In the early thirties, for instance, individual writers were usually assigned to put together an editorial column; not unpredictably, glaring inconsistencies resulted when two editors had different ideas on the same subject, and occasionally editors would write large, comprehensive essays on small, incomprehensible subjects.

If Crimson editorial positions have seldom been models of consistency, it was mostly because of the fast turnover of students on the paper. In a 1957 editorial the problem was summed up neatly: Crimson editorials, it went, "say something about the need for imagination (and realism) in foreign policy, boldness (and gradualism) in domestic policy, and House-ification (and money) in University policy." So it goes. News and editorials on political events often have reflected the particular interests of individual editors rather than considerations for the most comprehensive coverage (within The Crimson's resources) or the interests of the paper's readership. And The Crimson's unique, democratic form of editorializing oftentimes meant that the news peg on an event would be lost before an ed meeting could be called, and consequently no position would be taken.

All of which is to say that when one reads through The Crimson's pages, one is confronted with a curious and interesting amalgam of articles. One day's paper would have a column-five story on a national event, the next day the follow-up would be buried by University news, and the following day the story would disappear forever. Rather than simply mimic or cater to the interests of its readership, The Crimson sometimes took on an educational role by printing articles on issues outside the mainstream of American politics; but then the paper also sometimes ignored issues that were far more important (and closer to home) to its readers.

Of course, national events and out-of-the-way political subjects weren't major considerations when The Crimson began. For almost the entire first 50 years of its existence The Crimson wasn't the least bit concerned with politics or the outside world. If, several centuries hence, the paper were to remain the sole document of the period 1873–1923, historians studying that period would come away with the distinct impression that the United States was largely a nation of sporting gentlemen who were concerned with their inadequate dormitories, boardwalks in their poorly drained school yards, the latest developments in the progress of the football, track, and baseball teams, University teas, and the elegant abstractions of men named Eliot, Lowell, Norton, "Copey," and Kittredge. That is not to say that major political issues didn't get any coverage or editorial comment, only that it was rare indeed. In the paper's one major venture outside University-related affairs before the Great War — the Great Britain–Venezuela dispute — The Crimson printed letters by such dignitaries as Theodore Roosevelt, Class of 1880, and William James, Class of 1863. But then, either sensing a controversy beyond the scope of its understanding, or simply consciously deciding non-Harvard affairs were not in its purview, The Crimson published the following statement, which reflects its policy for most of the first 50 years: "The columns of The Crimson are suited only for those communications which confine themselves to the bearing of the question on university men and especially the Harvard man." This case extended to news stories and editorials as well as letters.

The editorial columns of the early Crimson weren't completely lacking in seriousness, as the numerous editorials on the University attest. But generally speaking, the editorials of Franklin Delano Roosevelt '04 on the importance of attending football games are the mark of those times. It was not until Americans took more interest in the European war that editorials, in 1915, began commenting on the world — specifically world peace — albeit in the context of proposals for students' summer military camps. In the fall of 1916 The Crimson began a conscious policy of commenting on major events outside the University.

President Lowell's active participation in the League to Enforce Peace, which began in 1915, might be said to mark the beginning of Harvard's — and The Crimson's — widening political horizons. By the time war was declared The Crimson had already expanded its single editorial column to two, and it reported on all important war developments. The war was probably the single most eye-opening experience for The Crimson, in terms of overcoming its isolationism. One dramatic editorial in February 1917 — virtually on the eve of Wilson's declaration of war — points this out. Entitled "A National Crisis," it referred to the undergraduate's lack of knowledge concerning U.S.–European relations and went on to say, in forthright terms: "The undergraduates of Harvard and all other American colleges must lead the way in the forming of a new, and what the future will proclaim, most valuable of all American habits, that of taking an intelligent, active interest in America's national problems . . . we . . . must regard the United States as a unit in the great group of world nations . . .

". . . one thing this crisis ought to bring home to all patriotic students in our colleges: the woeful ignorance of the national problems before this country today."

Another indication of The Crimson's broadening perspective was its extensive coverage of the 1916 presidential campaign and its willingness to break its theretofore neutral position on election campaigns by endorsing a candidate in 1920.

(A more extensive treatment of The Crimson's involvement in presidential campaigns appears at the end of this chapter introduction.)

Sports would still dominate the news and editorial columns, right through to the thirties, but less so than before. And by 1930, as one Crimson editor put it, "scarcely a week went by without some reference to outside news." So, sporadically through the twenties and continuously from 1930, choice of and emphasis upon outside subjects would be major considerations in the Crimson pages; that has been the case right up to the present.

One period is an exception to this general rule and that is the era of *The Harvard Service News*, which, as was explained earlier, was denied the right to editorial expression. The Crimson's postwar headline summary of *The Service News* places the paper's almost-impossible task in proper perspective: PARASOL IN HAND, SERVICE NEWS TEETERED DOWN EDITORIAL HIGH WIRE IN SEARCH FOR WILL O' THE WISP IMPARTIALITY. A story about *The News* throws this problem into stronger relief. F. O. Matthiessen, professor of English, had been asked to review a controversial novel, Lillian Smith's *Strange Fruit*, which was being banned in Boston. When Matthiessen's review was about to appear "various pressures" — as The Crimson's most recent history describes them — were opposed to printing portions that attacked the Boston censors. Only by printing Matthiessen's views in a letter to the editor was The Crimson allowed to run them at all. *The Service News* simply didn't print articles on controversial issues; it mainly confined itself to a lot of ink on what the navy boys were up to during R&R. Thus, it wasn't until The Crimson went back into service in 1946 that the paper resumed its serious coverage of national and international issues.

And it was in the postwar years that The Crimson really became something of a cause célèbre, when its impact reached far beyond the University community. In the late 1940s it began to print its yearly supplement on academic freedom (described in Chapter 1); in the fifties it was at the center of the McCarthyism storm; in the early sixties it covered the explosive issue of "mind-expanding" drugs and it sent reporters down South to report on civil rights marches; in the middle and late sixties The Crimson was on top of the antiwar movement, and eventually it would become widely known for its radical stand in support of the National Liberation Front (NLF) in 1969. Through the early seventies, The Crimson maintained, on and off, the same sort of radical stance first enunciated in 1969. At times its positions were completely out of touch with general student or public opinion, but the paper tried to formulate a credible leadership role in its editorial columns and in the types of news it covered (labor stories, for example).

The evolution of The Crimson from an entirely self-centered student publication to a newspaper that has assumed a commanding role in generating news and formulating opinions on important national and international questions will become self-evident as you read this chapter. It is an evolution that demands a certain amount of respect, even from those who may disagree strongly with the paper's emphasis on news or its editorial policy.

Presidential Elections

An interesting feature of The Crimson's history is the fact that for almost the first half century of its existence it chose not to make explicit endorsements of candidates in presidential campaigns. As early as 1883 the paper had already come to proselytize on the importance of becoming involved in elections. But the impression one receives from these early editorials is that a proper gentleman refrained from such ungentlemanly behavior, or if he did become involved in politics it certainly wasn't to be publicized. The Crimson never revealed the motives for its refusal to make endorsements. Probably the best indicator of the paper's attitude during the first 50 years comes from an editorial published in October 1900: "The amenities of College life and intercourse seem to require that The Crimson should not take a stand in the present political campaign."

Outright endorsement notwithstanding, The Crimson did occasionally jump into the fray. In 1883, for example, an editorial put forward an elitist position attacking the then rampant corruption in government: "It is only by the concerted action on the part of the well-educated that the country can be saved from the ignorant decisions and absolute tyranny of a class of low politicians who have obtained but too great a hold over the people . . ."

In the following year an editorial of June 6, commenting on the intelligence of the women at Wellesley College who held their own straw vote, contains a thinly veiled endorsement for Edmunds (the Republican candidate who eventually lost to Blaine at the party convention). The editorial is worth reproducing in its entirety because it also supports woman suffrage:

> We have been informed that a canvass was made recently among the students of Wellesley College to ascertain their choice for president, and that this canvass resulted in a majority of the votes for Edmunds. This is truly gratifying. The principal objection men seem to have now-a-days to women's suffrage is that if women were empowered to vote they might disagree with the "lords of creation" in political matters as, it is said, they have a habit of doing in many others; but the way in which Wellesley supports the views of Harvard, as expressed by the canvass made by the Union a few weeks ago, shows plainly that these sweet girl graduates and students are of one mind with us. As we remarked before, it is truly gratifying. Hereafter we are sure that Harvard may be counted as among those who are heartily in favor of giving women "equal rights" in voting.

After Blaine and Logan had won the Republican Party nomination, the College voted for them over Cleveland and Hendricks. The Crimson ran no editorial on the 1884 election itself, but in October it did advocate that every Harvard man march in the Republican torchlight parade since the University had elected Blaine in its straw vote.

No opinion was expressed in 1888, nor in 1892, and in 1896 only a short editorial appeared espousing active participation in the election. As was already mentioned, The Crimson took no position in 1900. In 1904, after Teddy Roosevelt was elected, The Crimson took the position that "Whatever our political stripe, we all have reason to be proud as Harvard men that the voice of the people has given to a Harvard man for four more years the highest honor and responsibility the nation can bestow."

Under the headline GOOD CITIZENS VOTE, The Crimson said, "Every man . . . should . . . cast his vote . . . in support of clean, intelligent politics" in 1908, apparently a veiled endorsement of reformer Roosevelt's hand-picked successor: William H. Taft. And in 1912, while Wilson won over Roosevelt in the University straw vote, The Crimson took no position.

Charles Evans Hughes, the Republican candidate, won a plurality over Wilson in the straw vote of 1916; The Crimson, as one of its historians would later write, "struggled manfully to maintain a neutrality which would support Hughes in the campaign." On election day an editorial tried to deemphasize the outcome, saying that "the important and most encouraging feature of the 1916 campaign has been the increased and active interest in American politics exhibited by the college men of this country."

Interest in politics certainly blossomed at The Crimson as the next four years saw the editorial page devoting more and more space to national and international affairs. By 1920 The Crimson was ready to speak forthrightly on its choice for president. If most readers haven't guessed already, The Crimson's choice in 1920 was Republican. With the one exception of the 1912 defection to Wilson, Harvard had been Republican ever since Lincoln (and before that the College was in the Federalist and Whig camps); it would remain solidly conservative, pro-GOP until the 1950s. (In ten University presidential polls over the 44 years previous to 1952, Harvard had cast 15,324 Republican votes to 9520 for the Democrats.)

The basis for The Crimson's pro-Republican stand in 1920 was threefold: Harding exhibited "principles" that would aid in the "solution of America's problems"; he could promote the "internal well-being of the country"; and he would be the best president in terms of the "lasting establishment of the

League of Nations." So the rhetoric went, at any rate; essentially The Crimson was bearish on Harding's probusiness attitude in that he brought "hopes of business prosperity, more nearly equitable tariff adjustments, trade stimulation and national economy . . ." He also had a tougher line on the League of Nations than the Democrats, who were "going in . . . without reservation." Predictably, The Crimson supported "Silent Cal" Coolidge in 1924.

In 1928 The Crimson seems to have missed its preelection endorsement but made up for it by saying afterward that "America has selected well" in choosing Hoover. The 1932 election posed something of a quandary for The Crimson; one of its own past presidents, Franklin Delano Roosevelt '04, was on the "other side." In November 1931 it came out wholeheartedly in favor of FDR, saying he would give the nation a "capable and intelligent leadership." But then in 1932 The Crimson wavered; an editorial explained that "neither the Republican Party nor the Democratic Party have shown themselves capable of recognizing the country's basic problems to say nothing of handling them." The dilemma of "favorite son" versus "favorite party" did not go away in 1936, however. The job of endorsement was made easier by the fact that The Crimson had a long tradition of pacifism: Landon thus seemed the logical choice. But a peculiarly rabid strain of Republicanism led The Crimson to attack Roosevelt as a "traitor to his fine education" in early 1936. This stand was modified later in the year by a predominantly pro–New Deal Editorial Board, although the paper as a whole still chose Landon (to the chagrin of even the loyal Republicans, one of whom commented, "Godhelpus what a hopeless cause it is to defend Landon").

Roosevelt apparently still hadn't redeemed his fine education by 1940, for in that year The Crimson went for Willkie. The decision, however, was based more in the fact that The Crimson was still strongly pacifist until late 1941. Four years later, *The Harvard Service News* failed to endorse a candidate; it wasn't allowed to take editorial stands. The consensus of contemporary editors agrees that the paper, by that time predominantly Democratic, would have supported Roosevelt. By

1946 The Crimson's move to the Democrats was evident in a series of editorials culminating in the position that electing "a mediocre Democrat is preferable to [electing] a mediocre Republican." And so, in 1948, it came as no surprise that The Crimson supported Truman, even though the University at large remained convincingly Republican (the College, for example, voted 2 to 1 in favor of Dewey).

Through the fifties The Crimson became something of a political leader, supporting Stevenson in both 1952 and 1956 while the College wavered to Stevenson in 1952 and went back to Eisenhower in 1956. It wasn't until 1960 that The Crimson and the University reached a consensus in favor of Kennedy, and through the decade the University and The Crimson voiced their support for the New Frontier and the Great Society. The 1968 election brought forth an unusual series of editorials on the presidential race. As early as December 1967 The Crimson voiced its support for Eugene McCarthy, which wasn't too surprising since the paper and the Minnesota senator shared similar views on Vietnam. But then, after Bobby Kennedy entered the race on the tail of McCarthy's early primary victories, an editorial in March 1968 advocated KENNEDY INSTEAD OF MCCARTHY. Kennedy's assassination and the eventual nomination of Hubert Humphrey didn't, as one might have expected, lead to support for HHH. Instead, The Crimson stood by the ideals it had expressed earlier and proclaimed in the ed column that there was "no choice" for president. "One could vote for Humphrey," the editorial said, "were the country still not reeling under the impact of the liberal Democratic administration, had Humphrey not allied himself in Chicago with the repressive chieftains of his party, had he not stood against the minority plank on Vietnam, and were he sometimes able to throw off the oppressive weight of his own rhetoric." Instead of Humphrey, readers were urged to register their "protest vote" by choosing a candidate of the left or by not voting for president.

McGovern in 1972 and Carter in 1976 were the obvious choices for a paper that had swung to the left in the late 1960s and early 1970s and then moved to more moderate ground as the decade wore on.

To Robert T Root — with thanks for this photo — which made me look like a candidate — almost!!

Adlai S. Stevenson

Adlai Stevenson in Boston during the 1952 presidential campaign. This photo was later picked up by the Democratic National Committee and used on one of the major Stevenson campaign posters in 1956. At that time the College was still backing Republicans; Harvard students wouldn't switch to majority Democratic support until the Kennedy campaign four years later. October 28, 1952. (Copyright © 1952 Robert T. Root '54)

Since the fifties, when a photo by Robert T. Root '54 depicting a smiling Adlai Stevenson waving to Boston crowds was used by the Democratic contender on his campaign posters, The Crimson has given extensive coverage to the presidential campaigns, especially in the New Hampshire primary, where the long grind began, and where fortunes were made and political careers ended.

*   *   *

Harvard indifference has always been a mainstay of Crimson editorial writing, not only because Crimson editors wished to see more constructive action on the part of their contemporaries, but also, no doubt, because they wanted something to write about (other than indifference).

EDITORIAL

Harvard's Political Indifference

February 16, 1884

The great lack in our national life of the present day is that of educated men who are willing to go into politics. This arises of course in large part from the fact that our public service has been almost entirely monopolized by men of exceedingly low principles, who have made it, in the language of the day, "too dirty a business for a gentleman to touch." But the original cause is that our young men while in the midst of their education are too much taken up by other things to give any attention to public affairs, and thus, at the very time when their attention and their interest would be of most service, both to themselves and to the nation, they acquire a distaste or an utter indifference for all matters of this nature. Nowhere is this tendency more seen than at Harvard. Here, beyond some courses in the abstract principles of public policy and one or two debates in the Union on political subjects, the University affords no opportunity for activity in thought or action on public matters . . . If even thirty men in each class become really interested in [a] matter [such as Civil Service reform], so that they would take some trouble to set forth their views in the different sections of the country to which they might go after graduation, we should soon hear from it. They would become the leaven which would leaven the whole loaf . . .

One of the more important foreign crises of the late nineteenth century was the Cleveland-Olney affair, sparked by the dispute between Venezuela and Great Britain's colony British Guiana. The Latin American country and the British colony were at odds over their boundaries, and the British prime minister, Lord Salisbury, refused to submit to international arbitration. On December 17, 1895, President Grover Cleveland sent Congress a message saying that, under the auspices of the Monroe Doctrine, he would settle the dispute himself. Earlier in the year, in July, Secretary of State Olney had sent a threatening message to Lord Salisbury. There was a panic on Wall Street over the possibility of war. But eventually the British signed a treaty submitting the dispute to international arbitration and war cries faded. Immediately after the president sent his message to Congress, however, The Crimson printed a letter attacking Cleveland's warlike stance. In the ensuing weeks Teddy Roosevelt and William James entered the debate in The Crimson's columns to make the Cleveland-Olney affair the first controversy over foreign affairs to enter into the otherwise isolationist pages of the paper. No such issue — aside from the Spanish-American War, which directly affected students — would again be considered fit for The Crimson's columns until the fall of 1916.

In April 1898, when war was declared against Spain in Cuba, Harvard undergraduates rushed to do battle, as many young men did throughout the country. Seeing the rush and perhaps rejecting the jingoism ("Remember the Maine") and the inane popular deprecations of Spain, The Crimson cautiously advised Harvard students not to enlist and to take a wait-and-see attitude.

Seven Harvard men would die in the Spanish-American War, most of them of diseases contracted in the tropical climate and not on the battlefield. The editorial dedicated to their memory displays a rare elegiac elegance, especially for a period in The Crimson's history generally marked by formal, stilted prose.

EDITORIAL

In Memoriam

October 10, 1898

As it was in '61, so in the early spring of '98, in fewer numbers perhaps, because the need was less, but with just such a strong spirit as before, the men of Harvard University enlisted in the forming regiments for the front. Some went as commissioned officers, some as privates; some were in the infantry, others in the cavalry, others wore sewed to the sleeve of their shirts the red cross of the hospital corps; everywhere throughout the vast extent of armies in Cuba, in Puerto Rico, or left behind to sweat and toil in weariness, men we had known and men we had heard of, men they placed in command of companies, or in the third relief of the guard, were doing what ought to be done.

One man, a senior, who enlisted as a private in the very beginning, was given a commission before there had been any fighting, and when the fighting began he was promoted. By a brave regiment he was called a brave man.

There are no more battles now. The men are returning, and we see them about the college as before, but of course, not all who went in the spring; for the work that these men had set out to do would not permit of that. And to those whom we shall not see here, either this year or the next, who fought as their teaching had told them, and did it well, to them full honor is owing, and to them is given in sadness the great love of this University of Harvard. Hollister, Furness, Sanders, Crapo, Adsit, Lahman, Henshaw — they are the men who have gone. They died in service, and, when they were buried, United States troops stood at attention.

The Crimson's most recent history best tells the story of the Great War's beginning:

The night of Thursday, April 15, 1917, will always stand out as one of the most exciting in Crimson history. After a long vigil into the small hours of the morning, word was received over the telephone from Washington that the House had passed the war resolution. Immediately the editors in charge routed the ever-patient Dean Briggs out of his bed and secured from him his statement suspending all formal athletics until further notice, which was printed in column four. A flaming two-column three-inch head of the one word, WAR, was built in old wooden type unearthed in some dusty recess of the printing shop. Serious as the occasion was, it was impossible to resist the temptation to run off a few copies with the letters transposed to read RAW, for private distribution to the president and managing editor. Various metropolitan newspapers in New York and Boston carried a reproduction of the front page on the next day.

The Crimson rushed through its war editorial for publication the following day. The sentiments expressed were commonplace opinions of the day; the headline, in typical Crimson fashion, was obscure: RAGNAROK, *which derives from Scandinavian mythology. Literally it means "the doom of the gods," and it refers to the end of the world followed by the rebirth of the just and righteous.*

While the war was in progress The Crimson continued publication, and during that time it covered and supported two liberty bond drives, a Red Cross campaign, and the war-works movement. For a short time, from October 4 to October 24, 1917, the paper suspended publication. When it resumed, it would remain a weekly until early 1919. More than 10,000 men of Harvard served in the Great War, including 15 Crimson editors who were killed in action or died in the service.

10,256 University Men Served in Great War

February 1, 1919

The War Records Office has just compiled statistics showing that 10,256 University men have been enrolled in the armed services of this country and the Allies, or in the various auxiliary branches such as Ambulance, Red Cross, or YMCA during the war. This total does not include those men in the SATC or other units who would not, under normal conditions, have been at the University. Forty-seven percent of the men were commissioned as officers in the branch of the service in which they served, and 284 appear to date on the Roll of Honor of men who gave their lives in the service. One hundred and sixteen were decorated for their heroic actions.

In a statistical comparison of war records, the University leads Yale throughout, excepting in the College Naval Unit, where Yale led by 115. Yale claims the only College Field Artillery School, the largest College Naval Unit, the first American Mobile Hospital, and the only Training School for Signal Corps Officers, Army Hospital Laboratory, and Chemical Warfare Service.

The University, on the other hand, was the only American college to have a mission of French Officers, and a Naval Radio School.

The statistical comparison between the University and Yale follows:

	UNIVERSITY	YALE
Total in Service	10,256	8000
Holding Commissions	4911	3500
Roll of Honor	284	163
Faculty Members	168	75
Men in SATC	1367	1309
Men in Naval Unit	441	556

Besides these men, there were 5000 Radio students at the Cambridge training station who were using the University buildings, and dormitories, and the Cambridge Common. There have been, in addition, 700 naval cadet officers, the majority of whom received commissions.

After the war and during the 1920s The Crimson was somewhat conservative in its editorial stance. It supported the League of Nations, but chose poorly when it decided that Harding would be the best president to push it through. And it supported President Lowell's call for student scabs in the 1919 Boston police strike (200 students participated). In the same decade, however, The Crimson would support the strike in Passaic, New Jersey, condemning the police treatment of Norman Thomas; give moderate approval of "industrial democracy" (as long as it wasn't "socialist"); and condemn the Ku Klux Klan, equating it with Italian fascism and describing it as a "bigoted and militant minority."

The highlight of that decade in terms of Harvard's contribution to American politics was President Lowell's service on a committee to advise the Massachusetts governor on the Sacco-Vanzetti case. The Lowell Committee, as it came to be known, found both men to be "guilty beyond a reasonable doubt," despite much evidence to the contrary. The Crimson gave this event minimal coverage at the time.

At Harvard during the thirties interest in socialism and Communism increased, as it did among many intellectuals around the country. Of course, as The Crimson was quick to point out in 1930, not many students were active in politics: "Here in America the student stays in Old World dormitories and lets the New World go by. The politicians and the press have been in the habit of terming college students radical, but nothing could be further from the truth. The Harvard undergraduate body has been completely stand-patter." Still some students were active: the Socialist Club, which had died during World War I and was revived with the La Follette and Thomas campaigns of 1924 and 1928, grew in the early 1930s. The group began publishing The Socialist *in 1930, a fortnightly paper, and occasionally — as in its stand against military and naval science at Harvard — The Crimson would find itself in agreement with the socialists. When Norman Thomas came to Harvard in 1932 The Crimson would hail him — albeit cautiously — as a "man who adds to trenchant criticism of the existing economic situation a complete plan to remedy it."*

Generally, The Crimson took a rather detached view toward leftists: "Harvard has her share of reds," it said in 1930, "of all shades — from a pinkish tint to a dark-blood red — and Harvard's rather fond of them in a very mild sort of way. They add to the variety of the college scene. The extreme radicals, with their clowning, are frequently amusing; while the more moderate radicals are usually more wide-awake, better-informed, and more stimulating company than their less liberal fellows."

As the "dark-blood red" description might indicate, The Crimson didn't approve of Communism. In 1931 an editorial did run questioning reports of atrocities in Siberia, calling them "blatant absurdities" (we now know how wrong this was; at the time it was a more tenable position). But by 1932 The Crimson was still Republican enough to disapprove of the Harvard Liberal Club's entry into the National Student League (NSL), which apparently held forth views similar to the Communists', views The Crimson described as "a mass of radical pottage."

Hitler caught The Crimson's eye — and its immediate disdain — in 1931, when an editorial attacked the Nazi party's rampant nationalism and anti-Semitism as products of "the rankest demagogism." In 1934 anti-Hitler feeling seemed to be increasing at Harvard. In May two students were arrested for participating in an anti–Nazi party demonstration focused on the presence of the German cruiser Karlsruhe, *in Boston Harbor. The "Anti-National Student League" ("the personnel chooses to remain anonymous" — i.e., The Crimson?) issued an unfortunate statement, quoted in the* Karlsruhe *story, saying that it would be "prepared actively to oppose any hostile demonstrations against countries with which we are on friendly relations."*

That same spring, The Crimson took a rather controversial stand on the "Putzi" Hanfstaengl donation. Ernst E. F. Hanfstaengl '09, Chancellor Hitler's foreign press secretary, had offered his alma mater a $1000 traveling fellowship to Germany. The Crimson not only advocated that Harvard accept the donation, but also that it give Hanfstaengl an honorary degree. President Conant didn't listen to The Crimson.

After almost a decade of antifascism (with a few occasional lapses such as the Hanfstaengl affair), The Crimson faced one of its most serious political crises with the German invasion of Poland. The high ideals of the past, pacifism not least among them, came into direct conflict with practical considerations that were as simple as they were horrific — Winston Churchill's statement of May 1940 sums up that pragmatism rather well: "Without victory there is no survival." The issue of intervention versus isolation divided The Crimson (as it did the College) and resulted in massive editorial meetings.

John C. Robbins '42, president in 1941, was caught up in the political debate, and, recalling the events in a recent letter, he writes: "From the fall of 1939 on, our central issue was external to the University: where to stand on the war . . . We all opposed the Nazis. But, at least until the summer of 1941, most of the Crimson board was concerned with keeping the United States out of the war . . . I suppose this seems remarkable . . . it now does to me, in hindsight. I can't remember the trains of thought that led me to believe we should stay out. I wasn't an 'America

Firster.' I guess an important element was hearing Norman Thomas give an eloquent address on the war just after it started, in September 1939 . . . we met as a board incessantly over the two-year period. Good Lord, how we shouted at each other! . . . Colleagues tell me that Jack Kennedy used to participate hotly in the debates . . ."

The most representative example of The Crimson's neutralist position comes out of the earlier part of the long debate: a two-part editorial entitled "Credimus" ("We Believe").

EDITORIAL

Credimus

May 17, 1940

Borne along on the tide of German victory in Holland, swelling ever larger as the marching hordes spread and grow, the spirit of intervention is upon us. "The Allies are faltering," it cries. "America must do something." Well, what shall we do? What can we do?

To answer those questions, we need first of all to weigh war and its consequences against peace and its possibilities.

We must recognize that, if the United States declares war, we will be adding millions of men to the present carnage; we will pour down the drain countless wealth and resources; we will devote all our strength and attention to an external struggle, and risk the consequences internally; we will be opening the doors to a fascism which, drawing on the unemployed and others in America who are not participating in the benefits of our democracy, and feeding on the new spirit of force which war brings with it, may destroy the very freedom which interventionists would have us to go abroad to defend. That is the war-side of the scales.

On the other hand, we can stay at peace. We can make that peace not a period of lethargy and waiting-for-the-wolf, but one of active progress; we can prevent the rise of a Fifth Column of dissatisfied citizens by extending democracy to every American, and by adapting our social and economic systems to meet the needs of a free industrial America as they have never yet been met; we can strengthen our defensive arms

. . . to defend this country and this hemisphere if at any future time that becomes necessary . . . [and with] no such militarization of our civil life as is entailed in preparing for offense . . . and we can cultivate and improve our relations with Latin America, making trade and friendship the watchwords, continuing to replace North American imperialism with Pan American cooperation. That is the peace-side of the balance.

Is that the whole picture? demand the interventionists. Granted that war is undesirable and peace desirable in the abstract, they say, is there not another more important consideration? What if Germany wins the war? Where will American be then? . . .

Given a choice between on the one hand the sure and immediate horrors and costs of war, to ourselves as individuals and to our nation as a social democracy, and on the other hand the possibility of a German victory and some future threat to the United States as a result, we choose the former alternative. And we think that here stands with us the vast army of Americans.

Soon after The Crimson ran its editorial favoring U.S. neutrality in Europe, President Conant gave a speech advocating further armament. Predictably The Crimson denounced Conant's position, and shortly thereafter, the following letter from John F. Kennedy '40 was printed. Earlier that same spring Kennedy had written his senior thesis on the problems England faced in fighting the Axis powers, problems stemming from slow armament. Kennedy's letter is taken almost word for word from the first chapter of that thesis, which was published in the fall of 1940 as the book Why England Slept.

Support for U.S. Armament

June 9, 1940

To the Editors of The Crimson:

In an editorial on May 31, attacking President Conant's speech, you stated that "There is no surer way to war, and a terribly destructive one, than to arm as we are doing." This point of view seems to overlook the very valuable lesson on England's experience during the last decade. In no other country was this idea that armaments are the prime cause of war more firmly held. Lord Grey's statement in 1914 — "the enormous growth of armaments in Europe, the sense of insecurity and fear caused by them, it was these that made war inevitable" — was quoted again and again by the successful opponents of British rearmament. Senator Borah expressed the equivalent American opinion in voting against the naval appropriations bill of 1938 when he said, "One nation putting out a program, another putting out a program to meet the program, and soon there is war."

If anyone should ask why Britain is so badly prepared for this war or why America's defenses were found to be in such shocking condition in the May investigations, this attitude toward armaments is a substantial answer. The failure to build up her armaments has not saved England from a war, and may cost her one.

Are we in America to let that lesson go unlearned?

John F. Kennedy '40

If The Crimson's neutralist position on the war was unacceptable to some of its own editors — JFK had been on the Business Board — it was appreciated even less by many faculty members, among them the noted historian Samuel Eliot Morison '08. In his letter Morison captures the sentiment prevailing among those of his own "generation," a sentiment The Crimson would not share until the following September.

Morison on the Wisdom of Ancient Gaffers

December 11, 1940

To the Editors of The Crimson:

I do not wish to trouble you or your readers with my own views on the war, but should like to say something about the attitude of the generation to which I belong, men forty to sixty years old who took part in the last war. It seems to be assumed by some of your undergraduate contributors that those of us who advocate intervention are either naively ignorant or grossly malicious. A number of your editorials and letters to the editor suggest that men in college are much better informed than we about propaganda and other roads to war; and that, having been brought up during the Depression, you have suffered more than we from the consequences of war. Not infrequently we are reminded that our age will entitle us to stay at home while the young men fight.

Now, what advantage have you young men over us ancient gaffers in knowing the evils of war? The books, documents and films that you have read and seen, we too have read and seen. The Depression that hit you in childhood or youth cost many of our friends their jobs, or wiped out their life work. Most of us who were in the armed forces of 1917–1919, as well as those who were not, have a strong personal and emotional bias against war. The last war was such a deception, seemed so futile even as early as 1919, and was followed by such moral slump, contempt for civil rights, reckless speculation and consequent depression, that most thinking men of my generation acquired a strong scepticism about the value of war, and a firm conviction that America must and should keep out of the next one.

If, then, one of your professors, parents, or others of our generation comes out in favor of the United States helping Great Britain, whether "short of war" or up to and including complete American belligerency, the chances are he has done so after due deliberation, with at least as full knowledge of wars present and past as you have, and after considerable soul-searching. The chances are that he has reached this harsh conclusion almost in spite of himself, and only because he believes war to be a lesser evil than the probable consequences of a Hitler-controlled world. In all probability, his own observations of the totalitarian state in action have caused him to throw overboard a vintage-of-1919 conviction that anything is better than war. As for the argument that we are not fighting age, I would ask you to consider that total war spares nobody of any age, and that most men of my generation have sons, nephews or pupils of fighting age.

Far be it from me to deny any student's right to argue and agitate in favor of American neutrality as I was doing in 1916–17. I only ask that when one of your elders, who has been through the last war, presents an argument for the United States entering this one, you at least credit him with sanity and sincerity, and abstain from offensive charges of ignorance, hysteria and sadism.

Samuel Eliot Morison '08

The Crimson finally supported intervention in the fall of 1941, but the war years were lean ones for the paper politically. The Service News *printed no editorials and, as one contemporary editor remarked, the* Service News *group "had been chafing at the bit at not being allowed an editorial expression." When The Crimson went back into service in March 1946 the liberal ideology was to predominate on the ed page.*

An interesting story by Robert Sturgis '44 ('47), president of The Crimson in 1946–47, reveals some of the inner workings of The Crimson during the shift away from its Republican past:

Nineteen forty-six was a congressional election year, the first after the war, the first occasion in some time when The Crimson could express itself politically, and the last time the Republicans came up with a majority in Congress.

One of our Graduate Board members was Frederick Ayer '11 of Wenham, a major contributor to the Republicans. In mid-October, Waldo Proffit '46 ('48) wrote an editorial stating The Crimson's position, which was that in an election with no very outstanding candidates, "we prefer a mediocre Democrat to a mediocre Republican." That same evening or the next one, I received a fat letter, special delivery, which included a rather long letter from Frederick Ayer Jr. '37, explaining in essence why a mediocre Democrat was not better than a mediocre Republican, and a covering letter from his father asking me to call him immediately and tell him what I proposed to do about publishing the letter.

I called him the next morning and said that we did not propose to publish and, besides, that it was too long. He of course resigned from the Graduate Board. Then cooler heads, principally that of Charles Moorfield Storey '12, prevailed, getting me together with Mr. Ayer at an amiable lunch at the City Club on India Wharf, agreeing on a shortened version of the letter, publishing it (a week or so after the election), and making a parting gift of $100 to The Crimson's building fund.

In 1947 the Truman Doctrine and the Marshall Plan both won strong Crimson support. The Marshall Plan was of special interest because it had been first revealed at the 1947 commencement. The following account, published in 1962, provides the details of that historic occasion. Marshall's address defined a new role for Harvard in the world of politics: from that day forward it would be considered a valuable platform for major political pronouncements.

Harvard Hears of the Marshall Plan

BY ROBERT E. SMITH '62

May 4, 1962

As the endless line of degree candidates and dignitaries formed in the Old Yard at Harvard's first fully formal commencement since the war, George C. Marshall chatted with Edmund M. Morgan '02, then Royall Professor of Law. Morgan, who was to escort the secretary of state in the procession to the steps of Memorial Church, mentioned that Marshall's apparent anxiety about his coming performance was unusual. "He assured me that he was expected to say something of importance," recalls Morgan. "Who expected it? He did not specify."

Even President Conant, who had entertained the old general at his house the evening before, was not led to expect a major address from Marshall. But word of Harvard's honorary degree to Marshall and his appearance at the University had leaked to the press 24 hours earlier. *The New York Times* that morning wrote, "He is expected to deliver a speech which perhaps will include an important pronouncement on foreign affairs."

In Cambridge, however, the capacity crowd of 15,000 showed up in the Yard not so much in expectation of seeing history made, as simply in awe of the man. Few public figures before or since have inspired such admiration among those in the Harvard community as George Catlett Marshall.

Behind the mace-bearer in the traditional procession to the Memorial Church steps, Morgan escorted Marshall before a group of 11 other distinguished honorary degree recipients. Among them that day were T. S. Eliot '10, James Wadsworth, I. A. Richards, J. Robert Oppenheimer, George Henry Chase (former dean of Harvard), W. Hodding Carter Jr. (editor of the *Greenville* (Miss.) *Delta Democrat-Times*), Frank L. Boyden and General Omar N. Bradley, the other afternoon speaker.

In the parade of caps and gowns, Marshall, dressed in a business suit and with hat in hand, slowly walked to the platform and acknowledged the appreciative applause along the way. A loud ovation greeted him as he reached the stage.

After conducting the traditional morning ceremonies and awarding the first 11 honoraries, Conant finally reached General Marshall, "an American to whom freedom owes an enduring debt of gratitude, a soldier and statesman whose ability and character brook only one comparison in the history of this nation."

As Marshall and the other dignitaries adjourned to the Twenty-Fifth Reunion Class Marshals luncheon, the crowd thought that it had seen most of the show. But Marshall's speech at the afternoon Alumni Association meeting was still to come . . .

The atmosphere was neither tense nor expectant as the program proceeded as usual at the afternoon Alumni Association meeting: the national anthem, the alumni president's talk, an address by the governor, and two scheduled addresses, and the Seventy-eighth Psalm. The Republican Governor Robert F. Bradford '23 of Massachusetts rose and announced, "Ladies and gentlemen — the secretary of state." After an appreciative ovation, Marshall stepped to the rostrum.

"President Dr. Conant, members of the Board of Overseers,

ladies and gentlemen," Marshall began. "I am grateful —
touched by the honor accorded me by the authorities at Harvard — overwhelmed as a matter of fact. These historic and
lovely surroundings, this perfect day . . . a wonderful as-
sembly," said the general, — "a tremendously impressive
thing for a person in my place."

From there, the secretary began his prepared text. "I need
not tell you gentlemen, that the world situation is very
serious." Fidgeting with his glasses, rarely looking up from
his notes, speaking undramatically and sometimes inaudibly,
George Marshall went into a somber description of Europe's
losses — "the visible destruction of cities . . . factories,
mines, roads . . . long-standing commercial ties, private institutions, banks, insurance companies, and shipping companies — in short, the dislocation of the entire fabric of European economy."

It was a simple, twenty-minute speech without oratorical
flourish or verbiage; it revolved around one unmistakable
fact: "It is logical that the United States should do whatever
it is able to do to assist in the return of normal economic
health in the world, without which there can be no political
stability and no assured peace."

This was undoubtedly not the first time, in public or private, that this thought had been expressed; but from that
point historians would date America's foreign aid to Europe
and America's policies on the Cold War. Historians would
treat that moment as a landmark in American foreign policy.
And from that point, Harvard University would come to expect — or at least hope for — a major political pronouncement from its commencement speakers. Upon invitation most
would-be speakers would be reminded of Marshall's history-
making address and many would allude to it in their own
speeches.

Marshall led to his main point by saying: "The remedy lies
in breaking the vicious circle and restoring the confidence of
the European people in the economic future of their own
countries and of Europe as a whole."

The audience and the press considered this the keynote of
Marshall's pronouncement. (MARSHALL PLEADS FOR EURO-

PEAN UNITY, said *The Times* the next day.) The general continued: "Our policy is directed not against any country or doctrine but against hunger, poverty, desperation, and chaos. Its purpose should be the revival of a working economy in the world so as to permit the emergence of political and social conditions in which free institutions can exist. Such assistance, I am convinced, must not be on a piecemeal basis as various crises develop. Any assistance that this government may render in the future should provide a cure rather than a mere palliative.

"Any government that is willing to assist in the task of recovery will find full cooperation, I am sure, on the part of the United States government. Any government which maneuvers to block the recovery of other countries cannot expect help from us. Furthermore, governments, political parties, or groups which seek to perpetuate human misery in order to profit therefrom politically or otherwise will encounter the opposition of the United States."

Here, and at the end of his talk, Marshall cut off the applause — lowered the impact by moving quickly to his next point. As the audience rose to applaud the end of his address, the secretary took off his glasses, leaned forward on the lectern, and reached into his pocket for some scribbled supplementary remarks. Then he reiterated his earlier point, "the vast importance that our people reach some general understanding of what the complications really are, rather than react from a passion or prejudice or an emotion of the moment." It was this gesture that led many members of the audience to believe to this day that the "Marshall Plan" was an impromptu stroke of genius that the general happened to toss out at the end of his prepared address.

"After the speech, the applause was tremendous and the distinguished guests crowded around the secretary," reports [Laird] Bell ['04, then president of the Alumni Association]. The audience surely grasped Marshall's plea for European unity, but few, if any, were aware that day of the significance of his plans for the United States' role in the European recovery.

"I was much impressed . . . as were many of the others I

talked to," says Conant. "However, I am frank to say I had no suspicion that the speech would turn out to be so epic making. That it was a major speech there could be no doubt, but since none of us knew that it would be immediately picked up by high-ranking officials of foreign countries, we could not anticipate the subsequent developments."

The immediate favorable response by foreign officials was not accidental. "Unbeknownst to Marshall, Undersecretary Acheson had called in key English correspondents, briefed them on the upcoming proposal and urged them to dispatch the full text of Marshall's remarks in their papers," according to a member of that year's senior class, Douglass Cater '47, now Washington editor of *The Reporter*.

"I am told that the British Embassy in Washington for economy reasons failed to cable the text. Thus it was that when Foreign Minister Ernest Bevin and others sought to find out more about what Marshall said they had to turn to the press." The speech evoked great enthusiasm from Bevin and it was he who later organized Europe's unified positive response . . .

Conant, in a letter to Marshall in 1951, said, "Your speech at the Harvard commencement of 1947 will always remain an honored memory at Harvard."

The Crimson's politics in the 1950s were characterized by liberal moderation. McCarthy stirred up much controversy (see Chapter 1). But aside from that, editorial positions were confined largely to mainstream politics — lengthy analyses of Eisenhower's various policies in the same vein as The New York Times.

There were a few exceptions to this general rule. For instance, in a two-part editorial in March 1955 The Crimson advocated that the United States extend diplomatic recognition to mainland China, including support for its admission to the United Nations. Castro's Cuba was the subject of many editorials in the latter part of the decade; it would be cast in an aura of sympathetic amusement until 1961.

By far the most important issue in the editorial columns of the late 1950s was desegregation. The Crimson recognized the

dangers and almost insurmountable barriers lying in the wake of
the Supreme Court decision on Brown v. Board of Education of
Topeka. Two years after that historic decision, The Crimson
seemed to be even more aware of the problem; it described "the
South covered like a battleground; murderers of Negroes acquit-
ted, Negroes severed from their jobs, liberal whites threatened
with ostracism, and violence sometimes just around the corner."
Its position, liberal and calling for a "pragmatic" approach, was
not original, but it was still controversial for its time. And talk
would be just that, talk, until 1960, when an editorial advocated
that northern students "sit in and be counted."

As The Crimson grew more liberal during the 1950s its "intol-
erance toward ideas of the right" grew stronger, or so some of
its critics alleged. Chief among the targets against whom The
Crimson would wing its eloquent rhetoric was William F.
Buckley, who, as a Yale man after all, deserved nothing better.

CABBAGES AND KINGS

The Conservative Mind

May 5, 1955

William F. Buckley made a speech down at Yale the other
night. Buckley, you might remember, is the author of *God and
Man at Yale* and of *McCarthy and His Enemies*, about the only
book favorable to McCarthy to have been reviewed in *The New
York Times*. His subject was "The Liberal Mind," of which he
probed three aspects: its inconsistency; its intolerance; and
its contempt for facts and evidence. This, he said, is the kind
of mind that dominates both political parties, from President
Eisenhower leftward.

To show the inconsistency of the liberal mind, he told a
story about Mrs. Roosevelt. In her regular question-and-
answer column in the *Woman's Home Companion*, she had
been asked whether she would shake the hand of either Senator McCarthy or Andrei Vyshinsky. She said she would shake
with both. The next week, she was asked whether she would
have shaken with Hitler. She would have, Mrs. Roosevelt answered, in Hitler's early years; but not after he had started his

The 1965 march on Montgomery, Alabama. Ten years earlier, the Rev. Martin Luther King Jr. had begun the civil rights movement by opposing segregation on Montgomery's buses, and The Crimson annually sent reporters down South to cover the events. Here, a marcher beaten by local law enforcement officials is hauled off. March 22, 1965. (Photos by Peter Cummings '66)

mass killings. Reminding his audience that Vyshinsky had been responsible for some mass killings himself, Buckley offered this as evidence of the inconsistency of the liberal mind.

This must have made an impression on the audience, for the hand-shaking subject dominated the question period. Asked whether he would have shaken hands with Vyshinsky, Buckley said most decidedly not. Nor Stalin. Any Communist? No, he said. Did that mean he favored ending diplomatic relations with Russia? Yes. And would he boycott any international conference with Communists, given that it might involve shaking hands as a preliminary? Yes. Buckley favored no conference of *that* kind.

Would he shake hands, asked one cynic, with anyone whom he knew had shaken hands with a Communist?

"I would," Buckley replied, "but I would feel quite differently about it."

After making it clear he would not have shaken hands with Hitler either, he tried to drop the subject. No luck. A student who had been to Europe on a Fulbright Scholarship asked him about Franco. Yes, said Buckley, he would shake hands with Franco. Franco and not Stalin? "The meaning of his life is different from that of Stalin's."

He elaborated:

"One who wanted to traipse through Madrid making speeches against Franco would find it much different from trying to traipse through Moscow making speeches against Stalin."

"As one who has traipsed through Madrid," said the Fulbright, "I don't think there would be any difference at all."

"Where are your scars?" asked Buckley.

"I didn't risk getting any."

As the evening wore on, Buckley's reception line lengthened. He would shake hands with Peron, though not Tito, and with British diplomats who had shaken with Communists — though he wouldn't feel good about it. Would he have shaken with FDR even though Buckley thought he had betrayed us into the Second World War and sold us out at Yalta? Yes, said Buckley, because there was a difference between "subjective" and "objective" treason.

As the audience left, Buckley probably felt as if he had developed a case of bursitis. Whatever other maladies the audience might have wished on him might better be left unsaid, since they are evidence of the liberal mind's intolerance toward ideas on the right.

— Milton S. Gwirtzman '54

Boston politics provided a bottomless wellspring of material for the vitriolic pens of Crimson editors. When, in 1966, the Boston School Committee made an unusual decision regarding race matters, The Crimson resorted to one of its favorite editorial weapons: the reductio ad absurdum.

EDITORIAL

Zap — You're White

October 24, 1966

The Boston School Committee has at long last taken a firm step to cut down the number of racially imbalanced schools in the city. In a unanimous decision last week, the committee boldly voted part of the problem out of existence.

The committee's method — like its thinking on so many aspects of the racial question — was serenely simple. Massachusetts under the state school desegregation law determines racial imbalance by the percentage of nonwhites in a school. The School Committee has now decided to count 671 Chinese students as white. So by the committee's figures, there are 36 imbalanced schools in the city, although state officials, using the now presumably outdated definitions of the U.S. Census Bureau, persist in counting 48.

There is nothing really wrong with the School Committee's facing the old problem in a new way. Humpty Dumpty did it all the time. "When I use a word," he told Alice, "it means just what I want it to mean, neither more nor less." Of course Alice protested: "The question is," said the egg, "which is to be master — that's all."

Since the School Committee has now seized the initiative in solving the problem of racial imbalance, it is something of a puzzle why the group didn't throw gradualism to the winds and go all the way. The committee members could, after all, have said that Negroes are whites, and ended racial imbalance in Boston altogether.

It can be properly said that the antiwar movement truly arrived at Harvard on a certain cloudy day in November 1966. On that day Secretary of Defense Robert Strange McNamara's presence at Harvard left the door of student unrest slightly ajar. It would open further as the decade came to a close.

McNamara Mobbed, Jeered by 800; Monro and Watson Are Appalled
BY STEPHEN D. LERNER '68

November 8, 1966

Secretary of Defense Robert S. McNamara was mobbed by some 800 demonstrators and forced from his car as he attempted to leave Quincy House late yesterday afternoon.

The University Police car in which the secretary rode was

Secretary of Defense Robert McNamara argues with SDS member Michael S. Ansara '68, and then reluctantly consents to clamber onto a car and take the microphone. Then the shouting began. November 8, 1966. (Copyright © 1980 Julian Levy '69)

blocked by over 100 SDS protesters sitting in front of and behind it as it tried to move down Mill Street. Finally, McNamara emerged from the car into the jeering crowd and was hoisted up on the hood of a convertible parked at the curb in front of McKinlock Hall.

McNamara had been visiting Quincy House to lunch and talk off-the-record with two small groups of undergraduates as part of the Kennedy Institute's Honorary Associates program.

On the car's hood he agreed to face questions from the crowd "for five minutes" about American involvement in the Vietnam War.

With his face visibly tightened and grim, he yelled into the SDS member's microphone, "I spent four of the happiest years at the Berkeley campus doing some of the same things you're doing here." But there was one important difference. "I was tougher and more courteous."

After some catcalls including "murderer" and "fascist," the secretary replied with vehemence, "And I was tougher then and I'm tougher now."

Addressing Harold B. Benenson '68, cochairman of SDS, McNamara said above the shouting, "Listen, you organize a meeting that will be nonviolent and I'll come. I have a meeting across the river now and can't stay." The unruly crowd continued to push forward.

At this point, the area around the car was so choked with demonstrators that it was impossible for McNamara to leave. "O.K. fellas, I'll answer one or two of your questions," he said. But, he shouted, "Remember two things: First, we're in a mob and someone might get hurt and I don't want anyone hurt — I also have an appointment on the other side of the river in five minutes."

Mill Street was now jammed from one end to the other behind Quincy House. The Harvard patrol wagon the secretary had abandoned was jostled by the screaming, pushing demonstrators and virtually helpless police. One of the Harvard policemen tried to join the secretary on top of the other car, yelling, "We have to stay near you." But McNamara shrugged him off and the policeman fell back into the mob.

Michael S. Ansara '68, cochairman of SDS, grabbed the microphone and called for two questions from the crowd. Ronald E. Yank 3L, a leader of the demonstration, asked why the administration kept on insisting that the war resulted from aggression by North Vietnam in 1957.

The secretary was now at home — these are the kind of questions he is used to facing. "The war didn't begin in '57, it started in '54, '55 when a million North Vietnamese flooded into South Vietnam," he replied.

"Yeah, and they were all Catholics," a demonstrator yelled back.

McNamara answered, "A report from the International Control Commission states that it was aggression. I didn't write it. All you have to do is read it. You haven't read it and if you have, you obviously didn't understand it."

"We've seen it," someone shouted from the mob.

Obviously angered, McNamara countered, "Why don't you guys get up here since you already seem to have all the answers?"

"How many South Vietnamese civilians have we killed and why doesn't the State Department disclose the figures?" Stephen L. Saltonstall '67 then asked McNamara.

"We don't know," McNamara said simply.

"Why don't you know, don't you care?" students screamed from all sides. The crowd got out of hand; questions and epithets were shouted from all sides; no one could have heard McNamara even if he tried to continue.

About ten Harvard and Cambridge policemen pushed their way through to the car he was standing on and formed a protective cordon around him. Then they whisked him into McKinlock Hall, part of Leverett House. Two policemen blocked the door as students, pushed from behind, pressed forward.

The crowd was a mélange of pros and cons, the critics vastly outnumbering McNamara's supporters. When the secretary finally made his break to the door, a number of students started pushing demonstrators around, blocking for the police, and acting as self-appointed bodyguards. No one was seriously hurt.

The intrigues surrounding the Mill Street incident would

thrill even a veteran James Bond fan. SDS placed its main troops outside the Quincy gates, but they remained in constant contact (by walkie-talkie) with other possible exits and McNamara's movements in Quincy House.

Around 4 p.m. word spread that McNamara would drive out of the Quincy House garage on DeWolfe Street and exit into Memorial Drive. Some 100 demonstrators anticipated the move and linked arms around the garage. A blue sedan, driven by an unidentified student, idled in a parking lot on DeWolfe Street, ready to pull out in front of McNamara's escape car and stall until the troops arrived.

When the garage doors sprung open, a few students broke the demonstrators' line, shoving them to the ground and dragging them out from under the wheels of the car.

But it was all a put-on. Sitting serenely in the back of the car was Stephen B. Young '67, a resident of Quincy House, who had voluntarily offered his assistance to Graham T. Allison Jr. '62, an Institute official who drove the car.

The decoy worked: several hundred students came running around to the back of Quincy House leaving Mill Street almost deserted.

Meanwhile, McNamara was being hustled to the Mill Street exit where Harvard police awaited him. A small contingent of demonstrators who had not abandoned their post in the excitement lay down in front of the car. Others quickly filed in behind the car, stopping it in its tracks.

After the "physical confrontation," which SDS had been aiming for ever since they heard officially that McNamara would not debate Robert Scheer, managing editor of *Ramparts* and articulate critic of the Vietnam War, McNamara was reported to have taken a safer route through the central kitchen tunnels. He emerged at Kirkland House.

A spokesman for SDS said that it was regrettable that McNamara was allowed to leave after answering only two questions instead of setting a time and place for a debate.

Quincy House had been decked out for McNamara's visit. Sheets hung out of the windows sporting a variety of slogans: Kill the Cong, Back Mac, Kill for Peace, Napalm SDS, More Pay for NROTC, Vietnam: Edsel of Foreign Policy, and Black

Day for Gordon Linen. A loudspeaker blared out "Mack the Knife" across the courtyard.

Harvard had a unique view of itself last night, as it watched television replays of the day's action.

Early in February 1969 the Faculty finally approved a Student-Faculty Advisory Committee resolution denying academic credit to ROTC. But near the end of March President Pusey revealed that the Corporation had decided to do everything possible to retain ROTC at Harvard — within the strictures laid down by the Faculty. Some members of the Faculty tried to impress upon Pusey the idea that its decision had been a moral and political one as well as simply a statement on academic procedures. But, Pusey replied, the Faculty had overwhelmingly defeated the SDS resolution based precisely on moral grounds, which indeed it had. The central problem, according to Pusey, was whether the Faculty would "take in as voting members people who haven't gone through the normal academic process. Already lawyers are working on a way to get around this." The choice of words (if accurately quoted) was not the best; that statement may have marked the beginning of the end of Nathan Marsh Pusey's administration. For neither the Faculty nor the students wanted to hear that they were being got around, not at that crucial juncture.

What happened next is well known: The march on Pusey's house and the occupation of University Hall on April 9, 1969. The Crimson published an extra that same day, reporting the occupation, but with one major error: it said that the rally held outside University Hall immediately preceding the occupation had voted 800 to 400 to occupy the building. In fact just the reverse was true — a large majority of students had voted not to occupy. A correction box appeared the next morning. But, amidst charges of Crimson bias throughout the ROTC uproar, an honest typographical error like that was not taken lightly. (It would not be lost upon the Alumni Bulletin, *when in the next month's issue there was an article advocating the creation of another student newspaper.)*

Details of the actual occupation are fairly well documented, as are the facts of the Bust. One viewpoint that is worth presenting here, however, is that of the building occupiers as the police descended upon them.

It is not easy to weigh the occupiers' disruption of the University, their forceful eviction of deans, their rifling of administration files, against the University's commitment to continue undisturbed in its search for truth, and the deans' rights to their workplace and their privacy. Not when the University's contribution to the Vietnam War — in which untold death and destruction was explained away by mistruth and distortion — hangs in the balance. It was probably not an easy decision for President Pusey to call in the police. But it may be easier to contrast Pusey's means and ends to those of the protesters. Consider the demonstrators' objectives and then consider this:

Inside, With Arms Linked, the Kids Awaited the End
BY JODY ADAMS '69

April 12, 1969

We finished our last formal discussion — about "sanitation" in the building and tactics in case of a police bust — at 1 a.m., Thursday morning. The big Harvard-red Faculty Room that was our discussion room/student lounge looked worn and tired. Bodies were scattered over the rug curled in tense sleep, stretched out for cigarettes, and hunched in drowsy conversation. Oil portraits of robed Harvard luminaries lined the walls and God only knows what they were thinking behind the steady, academic gazes that they kept fixed, unblinking, on the empty packages of Tip Top bread and bottles of diet grape soda.

Kids were sleeping in there and upstairs, in the row of small, square, white rooms that hold the files that hold our I.Q.'s and Predicted Rank Lists.

I knew that I wouldn't be able to sleep, so after a tour of the headquarters I stationed myself on the first floor, the only area that was keeping itself awake. It was harsh, and white, and very light. Some kids in the main receptionist's office reading old *Life* magazines and playing with the dead telephones. Down the hall, people looking busy at typewriters talked rapidly into the one winking telephone, and walked back and forth carrying pieces of paper with messages for each other. In plush reception rooms off the main hall people not looking busy played bridge, ate sandwiches, and laughed a lot. In one of the reception rooms, I found a fantastic blue armchair that rocked, and was quite happy from 2 to 3:30, reading the old yearbooks and freshman registers that were in the bookshelves.

At about 3:30 I heard the first rumor. Harvard had asked the Cambridge courts to stay open all night. A few minutes later I heard the second: the bust would be at about 4:30. After that they came more and more frequently, and with more and more variation, until, finally, at exactly 4:50, a voice, louder than any I had heard all evening said, "O.K., this is it, they're coming."

I had no doubt that this *was* it. I found the six people there that I knew the best and attached myself to them. We had been told to stand in line and link our arms together, to form a solid mass of bodies that would represent the peaceful resistance — the only resistance — we were going to offer to the cops. All of the people from upstairs were waking up and gathering with us in the hall. They were groggy, and had puffy, sleep-swollen faces.

When we were all there, the same loud voice told us that the gates had been opened, there were several patrol cars and paddy wagons driving up, and the cops were massing in the firehouse. I felt a dull sensation in my stomach at the sound of "paddy wagons" but I was really not afraid of them. I was too sure that nothing that bad could happen. It would obviously be incredibly stupid for Harvard to pull anything really dirty at that point — it took so little sensitivity or intelligence to see that. I never really considered the possibility of violence.

The leaders began passing out small pieces of cloth soaked in water to put over our noses and mouths in case of tear gas. We all began to sing "We Shall Not Be Moved," but all anyone knew was the first verse so we stopped. A voice told us that the cops had clubs and that a bust was almost certain. We sang the first verse of "We Shall Not Be Moved" again. The voice said that they had started to march from the firehouse to University Hall. We sang the first verse again and again until it wasn't funny anymore but only a little sickening.

I was standing toward the middle of the crowd near the window, but it never occurred to me to look through that window to see them coming. It was almost irrelevant. All I knew was in the hall and all I felt was the warm pressure of two arms linked in mine. There could be nothing to be afraid of. Somehow, childishly, inexplicably, and certainly unlike most of the people still in University Hall at 5:15 a.m., I *trusted* Harvard.

Then the same voice again, but out of breath and urgent: "They're really coming, and they're coming fast, look out." My eyes found the eyes of the girl next to me, and for a long moment, we seemed to pity each other.

All at once I heard a loud commotion outside on the steps. It sounded in the first flash like a newsreel of a riot. Men's voices were shouting and girls' voices were sighing loudly. I heard the movement of feet and material against the concrete. A new voice ran into our hall and screamed, "They're really getting violent out there." The word violent jumped from his mouth into my mind and became real and I was terrified. Jesus Christ. Not for this. I was there to *watch*. I was in University Hall because I was curious and because I like the idea of the night. I was not *this* committed to the [SDS's] Six Demands [against ROTC and Harvard's policies as landlord]. I hardly knew a God damned thing about Cambridge rent control or the Inner Belt. If I was going to be busted, I didn't want it to be for this night. It was a mistake. I was almost nauseous with fear, because I knew that if I was going to get hurt it wasn't going to mean anything.

We began to chant, and to sway back and forth, "Smash ROTC, No Expansion." The noise on the steps increased. Suddenly it swelled and I saw a surging tidal wave of baby blue helmets, and baby blue jackets crisscrossed wildly by thick brown clubs. Baby blue, I thought, how grotesque. It was the color of cheap plastic toys — and it turned into the color of the next few minutes. The cops were rushing into the landing way behind the steps, smashing their clubs down on the kids who were waiting, helpless. They weren't looking where they were hitting, just holding their clubs up and bringing them down as quickly and in as many directions as they could. I heard moans, and saw a boy run from two cops holding his bleeding head as they swung at him. A furious rage came into me and my mood changed with the crack of one of the monstrous clubs. The sight of this — the *fact* of this — I would protest and protest with my presence. I hated what they were doing — and I hated Harvard for allowing — or for asking — them to do it, as much as I could hate anything. I was still afraid, but it was a different, and much purer, kind of fear.

The cops turned from the kids on the landing to us in the hallway. They started to push us back down the narrowing hallway to the dead end of the locked door at the other entrance. They charged the crowd, swinging their clubs at the heads and middles of the kids up front. We fell back onto each other, but our arms were still linked tight. They kept beating at us, moving deeper into the crowd. I fell back on a black wooden Harvard chair, and about twenty people fell on top of me. The chair broke in half, and we all slammed onto the floor. I scrambled up, without the surrounding arms for the first time, and saw a boy run back into the part of the hall that was still empty, and turn off into a room I had not noticed before. Lots of people turned and ran after him. Just as I got to the door, the entire mass of people in the hall fell to the ground, unable to stand the force of the cops' clubs and bodies any longer. When they fell down the cops kept hitting them. I saw three girls on their backs shouting, "No, no, no, no," while the cops continued to hit them in the side with their clubs.

I turned and ran into the little room, where people were jumping out of an open window. I climbed onto the window ledge feeling an enormous press of bodies behind me, and hearing the clubs close behind them. I looked down the 10- or 12-foot drop and saw a circle of cops waiting for me. I stared at them, unable to move for several seconds. Then the press behind me got stronger. I made eye contact with one cop. "Will you catch me when I jump?" "Get off the God damned window." "I cannot get off, there are too many people behind me." "That's your problem honey, get the hell off of the window." "I can't get off and I'm going to jump down. Will you please catch me so I don't get hurt." "I'm not catching you, honey — just get the hell out of there."

Just then a boy who had jumped ahead of me ran out in front of the cop and stretched his arms up to me. With incredible joy I let myself drop from the building and into his arms. We embraced very quickly, and I ran past the cop who told me to "Get the hell out of the Yard" in a tone of voice that made it obvious that he couldn't stand the sight of me. I found two friends who had jumped just ahead of me and we walked quickly from University Hall out the Mass Ave gate. It was dawn and a hollow light was all around. The three of us clung to each other and wept and shivered and cursed all at once. The other two stayed there and I walked alone around the outside of the Yard to another gate. Mass Ave was already dirtying the dawn with buses and cabs and trucks. I felt a fear that turned to fury and a fury that turned to sorrow and a sorrow that turned to tears, and I started to cry, and cried and cried until I thought I would never stop.

Vietnam had been in The Crimson's pages as early as 1954 when — shortly before the fall of Dien Bien Phu — an editorial called for more technical and economic assistance to the Vietnamese and less military aid to the French. But Vietnam did not become an important issue in The Crimson until March 1962, when a three-part series on the country by Kathie Amatniek '64 triggered serious discussion. Editorials and news accounts would continue unabated for the next 15 years on the escalation of the war, its conduct, the negotiations, the so-called Peace Treaty (and the continuation of the war afterward), to the victory of the NLF and Vietnam's postwar conditions.

In April 1963 The Crimson called for the United States to "withdraw as gracefully as possible" from a Vietnam run by Diem's "nepotism . . . [detainment of] political prisoners, censorship of the press, and concentration camps." The editorial suggested that even a Communist Vietnam would be "better suited to the long-run interests of the U.S."

In February 1965 The Crimson made a stronger statement, saying the United States should "get out of Vietnam." It stated that

U.S. military policy had been a failure, that we were supporting dictatorships in Vietnam, and that the administration should cease all air attacks on North Vietnam and work for a "negotiation leading to withdrawal of American troops."

In October 1965, however, The Crimson revised its position, saying that American withdrawal "would now be more than an international embarrassment. The U.S. has repeated its commitment too often, in words too strong, for any of its promises to be considered genuine if it reneges on this one." Thus the fatal logic ran its course: commitment meant only further commitment. In addition, the notion that Vietnam would become Communist if the United States withdrew — a supposition leading to calls for withdrawal earlier — now meant that the United States must stay. Key to the new position was the belief that the Johnson administration was "not . . . responsible for the continuation of the war."

In February 1966 The Crimson shifted again: this time to the position that the administration's conduct of the war was wrong-headed, but that immediate and unconditional withdrawal should not be considered. Instead, deescalation of the war, and the establishment of military "enclaves" and further negotiations were called for. Withdrawal was ruled out on the grounds that such action would lead to a "bloodbath and chaos."

The "enclave" stance was to remain the Crimson line for some time, although criticism of the Johnson administration increased. In March 1968 The Crimson supported draft resisters. As the ROTC issue heated up, The Crimson pressed more and more strongly for the war's end. But no major changes in editorial policy were to occur until October 1969, when the following editorial stated support for the National Liberation Front.

The position was not a popular one, even on campus. Opposition to the war came from many different quarters at Harvard, but only a small minority tacitly supported the NLF. The editorial received widespread attention: mail poured into The Crimson, the Alumni Bulletin made note of it, Martin Ochs of The Chattanooga Times devoted an unfriendly column to it, and the French paper Le Monde referred to the editorial in its coverage of the antiwar Moratorium.

President Pusey (left) listens to a student during a Student-Faculty Advisory Council meeting in the Winthrop House Junior Common Room. The February 1968 meeting was held to discuss Harvard's investments in southern corporations with discriminatory hiring practices. Harvard's investment practices have continued to be a major political battleground. At that time Pusey said, "Our purpose is just to invest in places that are selfishly good for Harvard. We do not use our money for social purposes." Eleven years later, President Derek C. Bok would say of Harvard's $1.5 billion in investments: "As an investor, Harvard has declared its opposition to the South African regime and has pledged itself to vote on shareholder resolutions in the manner best calculated to overcome apartheid. I believe that these actions represent the most ethically responsible course for Harvard to take . . ." Sitting on the couch in the foreground are: Martin Peretz, who has since become editor of *The New Republic*, and professors Stanley H. Hoffmann, Erik Erikson, and Rogers Albritton. November 26, 1968. (Copyright © 1977 Diana Mara Henry '69)

End the War: Support the NLF

October 15, 1969

Today's Vietnam Moratorium will be the largest and probably the most important single protest against the American intervention in Vietnam since the war began. Whether or not such protests as these can ever by themselves succeed in forcing the administration to withdraw from Vietnam, a successful Moratorium will clearly indicate to President Nixon that the political costs of continuing the war into the months ahead will be far greater than they have been until now. Everyone who stands for an immediate withdrawal of American forces from Vietnam should support today's Moratorium, and should do whatever he or she can to make its impact as large and as visible as possible.

The main criticism being leveled against the Moratorium by defenders of U.S. policies in Vietnam is that such public demonstrations of dissent have the effect of encouraging the National Liberation Front and their North Vietnamese allies to wait out the United States at [the] Paris [Peace Talks] in the expectation that American public opinion will eventually force a withdrawal of American troops without prior concessions by the Vietnamese. Such criticisms must be troubling for many of the politicians and prominent citizens who have recently jumped on the Moratorium bandwagon, since it is undeniable that the existence of a strong antiwar movement in the United States does remove whatever incentive to "negotiate" the continued American presence might hold for the Vietnamese. Any doubt on this score was removed last week when spokesmen for the North Vietnamese and the new Provisional Revolutionary Government (a coalition of Communist and neutralist groups) publicly saluted the Moratorium and the antiwar initiatives of American politicians such as Charles Goodell of New York.

. . . The antiwar movement has reached the stage where it finally can and should declare that it opposes the war not only because of the loss of life in Vietnam, not solely because of the cost to America, but because the declared enemy of the American government in Vietnam is indeed not our enemy at all. It is time to declare that we reject not only the methods of the American intervention but the goals. The National Liberation Front whom we have been trying to exterminate has the support of the people of Vietnam. It deserves our support as well. And we can best support the NLF in exactly the same way that we can best support our own troops — by demanding that all American troops be withdrawn from Vietnam immediately.

The war in Vietnam is not, as many of its liberal critics would have it, a "quagmire." It is not a "morass." Americans are fond of viewing Asian wars as vast, unintelligible struggles involving numberless hordes of small, identical, machinelike fanatics. This view explains in a comforting way why the Vietnamese have been able to mount such an incredibly strong and tenacious resistance to American domination in South Vietnam.

But the Vietnamese who have fought against us are not machines . . . The bravery and devotion of these people can't be explained by racial stereotypes: to understand why they fight, one needs to understand what they are fighting for, and what they are fighting against.

The National Liberation Front could not have successfully gained and retained control of the South Vietnamese countryside without the support of the people who live there. The successes of the NLF, when contrasted with the inability of the Saigon regime even to hold its own during the four and a half years of American intervention, seem to establish beyond question that the NLF substantially represents the South Vietnamese people. A revolutionary movement like that of the Vietnamese cannot be sustained by terror, but depends ultimately on the allegiance of the mass of the population. The NLF has clearly won this allegiance, and the Provisional Revolutionary Government is the legitimate government of South Vietnam . . .

The American government has some solid reasons for not wanting to withdraw from Vietnam and admit defeat. An American withdrawal might have been possible in 1961, or in 1963, but once the decision to intervene on a massive scale was taken, the war took on a new character. American intervention has transformed the Vietnam conflict into a crucial test of American capacity to suppress movements of national liberation. Before Vietnam, it was not at all certain that even a substantially united people could defeat the concentrated power of the United States. The success of the Viet Cong and the North Vietnamese has shown that the United States does not have the strength to deliver on its promises of protection to the puppet regimes through which it manipulates internal politics in countries of the Third World. An American withdrawal would confirm this paramount lesson of Vietnam, and it is thus understandable that President Nixon and his advisers have "ruled out" the possibility of an abrupt, immediate withdrawal . . .

It is true that in supporting the Provisional Revolutionary Government in South Vietnam, the American antiwar movement will be inviting charges that it is betraying American soldiers in the field. The movement has survived these attacks in the past, and it will survive them again. The people of this country are not stupid, and they can see easily enough who is responsible for the fact that Americans are being shot at and killed in Vietnam. Government apologists have long tried to argue that the blame for the American deaths should be placed not on the men who sent Americans to die in Vietnam, but on the people who have urged that they be brought home again. This argument will not work much longer, if it ever did.

Not long ago it was widely held that opponents of the war had to limit their program to a demand for a bombing halt in Vietnam if they were to have any effect. The bombing was stopped, but the war goes on. Now we hear that the demand for immediate withdrawal has become permissible, but to argue for the Vietnamese revolution is a political dead end. The antiwar movement has never been well served by this sort of pessimism; it would not be well served now.

CHAPTER 4

Wit and Wisdom

Wit and Wisdom are born with man.
— John Selden

AS A CRIMSON EDITOR once remarked, the funniest event in *The Lampoon*'s history turned out to be a Crimson prank: lifting *The Lampoon*'s Sacred Ibis and giving it to the Russians to adorn a spire of Moscow University. It's a bit self-congratulatory to think such thoughts, and then again when you consider *The Lampoon*'s general drift of humor and its lack of imagination in *not* letting the Ibis go to the Kremlin . . .

That story, a couple of other pranks, and a number of funny parodies, spoofs, and "college humor" pieces represent part of the lighter side of The Crimson's past 100 years. Just about all the articles explain themselves. Only the HSA Birthday Cake Scandal requires some background. In a few other instances you just have to read on to get the point; if you don't get it, you probably never will.

*   *   *

Religion at Harvard

April 18, 1873

It has been remarked — by a graduate of Wesleyan and a schoolmaster — that Harvard men are distinguished by a materialistic and atheistic look. Like an iceberg, they can be discovered at a great distance by the chill that floats around and with them; for, after entering college, the religious feelings of most are quickly congealed into solid infidelity by the influence of the Cambridge school of theology.

Against the charge it is vain for us to plead that there is no Cambridge school of theology; that our instructors differ hardly more in the matter of their instruction than in their religious views (how then can there be an unbalanced effort to lead us from the strait way?); that Sears and Peabody were reared at Cambridge equally with Abbot, and now exert a more decided influence; that the average student bothers himself very little with doctrinal disputation, is careless concerning the opinions of Emerson and Hale, and graduates, as his father did before him, supposing that he believes the dogmas of the sect in which he was born; that it is as possible to express by a single word or sentence the religious characteristics of all the members of a great college as of all the people of Massachusetts; that there are men enough here, from most denominations, who live consistent with their principles, to give character to an ordinary sectarian "University"; that not a few leave college, as they entered it, with a firm belief in total depravity and the atonement; — must we not in candor admit that those who escape are exceptions to the rule, resist the tendency of the place? Such sophistry needs merely concise statement to be exposed in hideous nakedness.

Those of us who think must therefore admit that Harvard leans toward infidelity. The professors are much to blame for this. True, they do not directly inculcate bad principles. They are too wily to do that. They prefer to accomplish their end, in a safer and surer way, by the subtle teaching of manners and acts. Among the more abandoned students many a conspiracy is hatched; in cold blood they often settle on the best

RADCLIFFE'S NEXT CAN'T BE AN OLD MAN — HE WOULDN'T DIG ALL THAT YOUTH. AND IT CAN'T BE A WOMAN — SHE'D NEVER DIG ALL THAT SEX APPEAL. OBVIOUSLY, RADCLIFFE'S NEW PRESIDENT MUST BE A HARVARD UNDERGRADUATE.

In the spring of 1959 Radcliffe's search for a successor to President Wilbur K. Jordan led to more speculation by cartoonists in The Crimson's pages. This time *The New Yorker*'s Whitney Darrow Jr. contributed, as did Charles Schulz, who portrayed a dignified, bespectacled Snoopy sitting behind the president's desk. But only David Royce '53, '55½, '56 showed true genius in his clever nomination, reproduced here. The Radcliffe trustees, however, had other ideas, appointing Mary I. Bunting, who served as Radcliffe's president from 1960 to 1972. May 29, 1959.

plan of working the religious ruin of some fellow-student and ruthlessly execute it. All of us are familiar with the method of a young man's ruin. We know the lad who entered college a member of one of the strictest churches, well fortified by parental and pastoral advice. For a time all went well with him, and, having talent, he grew in culture and influence. At last, however, his strength failed, and he went down, carrying with him a host of less able men, —

"Thundering he fell, and loud his armor rang."

Such cases are common in every class, and are a sad commentary upon the culture of the institution. In fact, this is the present state of things, that no one but a man of iron will can hope to come here and resist the multitude of influences that quickly shall be set to work to lead him astray.

Perhaps, however, we may gain some consolation by reflecting that only half the assertion of the Wesleyan schoolmaster is well founded. Materialistic the students certainly are. But atheistic! — are they not rather idolaters; their own persons being the idols of the being whom they adore, and whose characteristics one may learn from the peculiarities of their worship? His shoulders are broad and his chest deep from much practice with the oar upon the placid Elysian streams; his eyes are quick and sure of sight, for he is skilled in foiling the adroit pitcher of the Olympian nine; his vest is spangled with charms and seals; his nails are pink with celestial henna; his cheeks flushed with ambrosia. Surely our young men are not atheists.

But bad as we are, we are not much worse than our brethren of the other great college, at New Haven. To be sure they are more punctilious, — do they not "retire" when we "go to bed"? — but this is a trifling matter. Here, then, are more Unitarians, there more Congregationalists; both parties are what they are rather from education and prejudice than from rational understanding and acceptance of doctrine. What choice, therefore, is there between them? The schoolmaster distinguished us from them by saying that while we have the look materialistic, they have the look of "gentlemen rowdies." 'Tis a rude expression, and I would not use it myself; but it shows the opinion of our Wesleyan friend to have been the same as mine, that Harvard is not much worse than Yale; while we are deficient in faith, they are deficient in works.

Therefore, parents of promising sons! who hope to see your boys developed by the wide and exhaustive culture of Harvard or Yale, beware that you do not offer them this apple of knowledge, for the death penalty is incurred by him who partakes thereof; choose you rather the quarries of Middletown, or the hills and trout-brooks of Williamstown, where the shadow of doubt has not yet fallen, and the infidel lifts not up his voice.

Jones's Diary

June 2, 1873

Oct. 1. *Whereas* it becometh a Sophomore to "lay aside childish things," and with his cane and beaver to assume a more manly and dignified character, not aping the manner of a street-car driver; *Resolved*, that I buy a copy of *The Science of a New Life* and a large diary, in order that I may daily live in accordance with the precepts of the one and enter the results in the other.

Oct. 2. Rose at 5 A.M., took a cold bath, and studied till Prayers. Squirted in Latin. Six hours at the Gymnasium. Bed at 9 P.M. How glorious is this new sensation of perfect health!

Oct. 3. Got up at 6 A.M. That seems early enough. In fact, I think Cowan is a litttle too strong in his statements. Burned my cigarette papers, gave away my pipes, and swore never to use tobacco again. Never! I am also going to Commons. I think the plain but nutritious food will be beneficial to me.

Oct. 4. Miserable headache all day. I had to take one little cigarette. They are very harmless; more than half paper. Deaded in Mathematics. I have always been more interested in Nature than Mathematics, and think I shall change to Nat Hist; besides it is easier. No Gymnasium.

Oct. 11. Given up my cold bath, as I find I can't get to Prayers if I take it. Lost six pounds, in weight.

· · ·

Oct. 15. Cowan must be wrong about tobacco. I have begun smoking again. I think it is immoral to swear off. Private for Prayers. Warning in Physics, — quite uncalled for, as I am sure I did half the paper.

· · ·

Oct. 23. Too sick to study, so cut all day, but went to see Lydia Thompson at night. She is splendid! I don't believe a word about her being over forty-five! Eliza Wethersby was charming! Seven of us took seats together and threw bouquets. She looked at us more than at any other part of the house. Must go again. Had a little supper at Parker's. For all Cowan says against late suppers, it isn't healthy to go to bed hungry, I believe.

Oct. 24. Headache all day. Have returned to my club-table. "Slum" may be cheap and healthy, but I lose too much flesh on it. Have given up Gymnasium. Walking is far healthier, even around a billiard-table.

Oct. 25. Went to the burlesque again to-night. More bouquets and melting glances from her languishing orbs in return. I applied at the stage door and sent in my card. She refused me an interview. Despair! Tried to drown sorrow after the most approved fashion. Missed the last car in consequence. Smith and Brown said they liked nothing better than walking out on a moonlit night, and watching the reflection of the lunar rays in the water as they crossed the bridge. I know it was raining hard, and the reflection was only that of the street-lamp shining on the wet bricks. As we came through the 'Port, Smith, after reflection, concluded that there were too many lights, and tried to put some of them out by tossing stones at them. I thought he succeeded, for I heard breaking glass, and it grew dark; but of course, as it was dark, I couldn't see certainly whether he had put the light out or not, and so climbed up to examine. Hearing a shout, I looked down and saw a policeman with hand on both Smith and Brown, also policeman's white bulldog sitting exactly in front of post and looking up into my face. He had such a yearning, beseeching look about his jaws that I decided to come down. Followed my friends down to the station. It would have been cowardly to have run away; besides the dog kept close to my heels. Expenses, $5 and costs; $10 to the reporter to keep my name out of his paper. I must write for more money. What if this should leak out? What would Cowan say?

.   .   .

Nov. 5. Father says I am spending too much money, — absurd! Of course, he wants his son to live like a gentleman, — and if I am going to be sick so much, it might be cheaper to retain a physician by the year, or leave college. How ridiculous! Summoned by the Dean for snowballing; suggested that an All-wise Providence had not given the ground its fleecy covering for nothing, had also given us hands to use; could it be possible that, if it was wrong to snowball, Providence would so tempt us? Result: public for snowballing, private for insolence. Truly, Justice is well represented in pictures with her handkerchief tied over her eyes!

.   .   .

Dec. 15. How deceptive are all human affairs! Cowan is a fraud; and this is my last entry in any diary. I don't like the business. It's unpleasant.

I write this in Concord, where I intend to pass the rest of the year. It seems that the reporter I bribed kept his promise, and did not put my name into his paper, but kindly furnished it, with full particulars, — drawing largely on his imagination — to all the other journals in the city. A few days after, the following letter brought sorrow to the parental roof-tree: —

                                     Carvard Hollege, Dec._____, 187___

— Jones, Sr.

    Dear Sir, — In accordance with a vote of the Faculty, it is my duty to inform you that your son, _____ Jones, of the _____ Class, is suspended from all college exercise until the beginning of the next academic year, for conduct unbecoming a gentleman.

    Yours, very truly,

                          _____ _____, Dean of Faculty

I intended to have the letter stereotyped to preserve the chirography.

There is nothing here to distract the attention; and where could one study better than in the birthplace of Emerson? I have given Cowan to the town library, and shall turn over a new leaf when I return to college.

The Crimson Breakfast

REPORTED BY OUR OWN CORRESPONDENT

February 6, 1880

In anticipation of the fifteenth birthday of The Crimson a breakfast was given by the Board at the Hotel Brunswick. It was not much of a breakfast, but that was what it was called. It began at noon and lasted until midnight, and it was the privilege of many dignitaries to be present. At the left hand of the presiding officer sat President and Mrs. Hayes, and at his right hand were the members of the Boston press, headed by the *Herald* man. But without lingering upon the guests or the *menu*, let us pass at once to the after-breakfast part — the intellectual feast.

At the close of the sumptuous repast the presiding officer rose with the assistance of his neighbors, and said, "Gentlemen, I give you as our first toast this evening, The Crimson. Long may she blush!"

This was considered inappropriate, inasmuch as The Crimson had never done anything to blush for; accordingly a new presiding officer was elected, and he who was deposed retired under the table in chagrin. The new President proposed the health of the newly elected Sophomore Board, and as none of them were considered able to reply to this toast, Mr. John G. Wh — t–r was called upon, and read the following ode:

The Sophomore

Blessings on thee, little man!
Sophomore, with cheek of tan,
With thy light-checked pantaloons,
And thy whistled opera-tunes.
With thy red lip, redder still,
Kissed by maids of Dana Hill.
O'er thy fair face broods immense
Harvard's proud indifference.
Faith, I love to see thee soar,
I was once a Sophomore.
Let the Senior strut and swell;
Thou hast more than he can tell.
He has calls and debts in store —
Blessings on thee, Sophomore!

Oh for Sophomoric joy!
Summonses without annoy.
Many useful kinds of knowledge
Never learned inside the College:
Of the tailor's tricky ways,
How the proud 'Port "peeler" slays;
Where the fire-ladders are;
How to catch a bad catarrh;
Feats of gymnasts wonderful;
How to pull a single scull;
How the hare and hounds is played;
How a tennis score is made;
How to walk like everything
With the famous Harvard swing;
How the tutor's life to vex,
How to flirt with the Annex;

How a cigarette is rolled,
How to grind up physics cold;
Where the swellest Seniors go,
Where the greenest Freshmen blow;
Of the Proctor's cunning way
On examination day.

Me all objects waited for
When I was a Sophomore.
For my sport the Freshman went
On my many errands bent.
For me each professor set
Just the hardest paper yet.
For my sake the postman brought
Bills from merchants of the 'Port.
Once a week came Connors up
To present me with a pup.
For my sake the President
Now and then a message sent.
For my sake the Bursar fair
Saved a splendid room in Thayer'
And the Janitor I kept
Smoked my meerschaum while I slept.
For my sake the man next door
Sang the whole of Pinafore;
And the athlete overhead
Trained when I had gone to bed.
I was monarch, — dun and bore
Waited on the Sophomore.

Happy, then, my little man,
Live and laugh while yet you can.
All too soon will come the drear
Aftermath of Junior year.
Soon it will be your vocation
To write theses in vacation.
Happy, happy, will you be
If you capture your degree.
Happy, if you can get through
Ere some tutor sits on you.

Mr. J. P. Tr–wbr–dge was next called upon, and sang the following

Song

White and blue is Columbia's Hue,
   And Dartmouth is very green;
And Yale becomes exceedingly blue
   When her boat in a race is seen.
White and red crowns Cornell's head,
   And Bowdoin blows in white,
And Harvard blushes a glowing red,
   Like Maud when I kissed her last night.

I love to see the white and blue,
   And Dartmouth's emerald green;
I love to see Yale's azure hue,
   When her boat in a race is seen;
I love old Cornell's red and white,
   And Bowdoin, and all the rest;
But I love, — I love my darling Maud,
   And The Harvard Crimson best.

This was considered rather too Anacreontic by some members of the Board, and one gentleman thought it was rough on Maud. It was voted to send the stanzas to *The Echo* as a college song. Mr. Francis Bret H–rte was then called upon, and responded with "Our Society . . ."

This was recognized at once as a gross plagiarism upon a dainty poem of the *Advocate*. Mr. H. was visited with scorn, and replied by throwing about the spoons. At this critical state of affairs Mr. Walt Wh–tm–n emerged from under the table, and delivered the following

Ode to The Crimson

O great, incomparable, and never-to-be-surpassed *Crimson*!
What have you done? What have you not done? What will you do?
You are a microcosm of the universe.

Essays, Satires, Editorials, Brevities, Jokes, Poems, Verses,
   Love-Stories, Tales, Critiques, Book Notices, Articles, Sen-
   tences, Words, swarm upon your pages.
You are read by Seniors, Juniors, Sophomores, Freshmen,
   Law-Pills, Janitors, Goodies, Pocos, Ladies of the Library,
   Car-Conductors, the Bursar, Jones, Waitt, Billy, the Faculty,
   the Corporation, the President, John, every one but proc-
   tors.
Crimson, I love you, and you love me. We love each other.
Hooray!
Likewise, Bravo! and I might add, Hoop-la!
You are the *Register* of college news, the *Advocate* of plank
   walks, the *Echo* of every noble College sentiment!

The effect of this production was overwhelming, until someone pointed out that Mr. W. had crowded puffs of The Crimson's three rivals into the last lines. He was prevailed upon to
return under the table, and the business proceeded with a
song by Mr. Edmund Clarence St–dm–n.

   Song

   Which is the paper that's famed for "Lies"?*
      The *Advocate*, Freshie; and Seniors say
   They always expect some witty surprise
      On every *Advocate* day.

   Which is the paper the Faculty love?
      The *Register*, Freshie, and I know why;
   Because in its pages they hope to shove
      Their pictures by and by.

   Which is the paper that likes to blow?
      The *Echo*, Freshie; and some men say
   That like all echoes, its echoes grow
      Much weaker, day by day.

   * This is a famous department of this paper, and the statement is intended
as a compliment.

Which is the paper by graduates run?
 The *Lampoon*, Freshie; and I should smile
At the cocky air of this graduate fun,
 It puts on so much style.

Which is the paper that's red as a rose?
 The Crimson, Freshie; it's always gay.
It dares all kinds of wrongs to expose,
 And gives them dead away.

The Board voted to have this song printed in all the college papers, after which Mr. John G. S–xe delivered an "Ode . . ."

This being received with groans, the President remarked that he thought it was time to hear from some of our friends across the water who were unable to be present, but had kindly sent over their little tributes. He then called upon Mr. James T. F–lds to read Mr. Algernon Charles Sw–nb–rne's

Ballad of Love Land

Wherever the spirit of light love wanders,
 To the last low edge of each long lone land;
Wherever his whispering sighs he squanders
 O'er a sweet, soft lip, or a dimpling hand;
Wheresoever a charming maid is,
 Whose sighs are tender, whose eyes are kind,
There are none to be found like the Cambridge ladies, —
 To talk you blind.

But among those beautiful blooming ladies,
 Who rule my heart with a rod of steel,
One bright particular starry maid is
 To whom I am plighted for woe or weal.
Shall I name her? The Crimson, whose charm encloses
 My heart in a soft and silky knot;
She's red as the reddest of all red roses, —
 In fact, red-hot.

Mr. F. delivered this with great feeling, and as much pride as if it had been his own, and the Board were all very much affected. Mr. F. was then requested to read another glowing tribute by Mr. Robert Br–wn–ng, entitled

The Proctor's Apology

Now!
Not now! I'll not subscribe unto thy wretched sheet.
What? You'll put an ear on me? I do not tumble.
Come, draw it mild, I am dead broke, my boy,
Else I would ante-up. I give myself away?
Am off my perch? You'll not bulldoze me thus
With all thy taffy. I will not weaken,
So fire away, old grind, you have the coldest cheek
Of any flunk in college. You're the boss snide —
   a tart piece on a tare,
And I will sit on you when next you try
To squirt in my elective, — that you call the soft.
When you have got it cold, and think'st to make a rush,
I'll get the bulge on you, — the dead wood,
And you shall slump and dead in spite of crib and cram, —
The section shall wood up, and you'll be tried.
What grow! You? Cut it short? Well, I should smile.
Come, but, you scrub, light out, walk off upon your ear,
Give us a rest, or I will fire you out.
You put on too much dog, too many lugs;
Come, hit her up, my Lippi, make a brace,
Or you'll get scooped, for such a boom as this
I ne'er was gagged by. You are too flush by half.
What, hire a hall? that's old, you bummer!
Come, strike; go gull some other duffer.
Would like a smile? Well, seeing it's you,
I don't care if I do. Beer's good enough for me.
   The proctor crawls.
Aha! my boy, that's into me! Thy paper's glorious;
It takes the belt, it yanks the bun,
It carries off the immortal cake.

The President next declared that he had reserved something choice from the Poet Laureate, Mr. Alfred T–nnys–n. It was called "A Fragment . . ."

This was discovered, however, to be a poem which The Crimson had rejected, and the President thought that home talent had better be encouraged in future. He therefore called upon Dr. Oliver Wendell H–lm–s for one of the poems of his boyhood. The Doctor gave

The Subscription Man

There are three frauds at college here
   Who help to drain one's purse;
Though two of them are bad enough
   The third is somewhat worse;
And if you'll lend your ear to me,
   Their tales I will rehearse.

You're grinding Greek some afternoon,
   A knock upon the door;
In walks the patent book-rack fiend,
   Who talks till you are sore;
You buy just to get rid of him
   What you have bought before.

Perchance you're dozing by the fire;
   A wretch drags in a book,
To come in parts, and twice a month,
   And begs you'll take a look;
You see he is too big to kick,
   And so you bite the hook.

You're smoking your last cigarette;
   A classmate "just drops in,"
And makes some foul old joke about
   Relieving you of tin;
Then takes out his subscription book
   To bleed you, with a grin.

No! pay the Poco if he'll take
   Your last old coat away;
And pay your board bill, though you know
   You're starving day by day;
And pay the scot when chum has not
   The wherewithal to pay.

But if you are a muscle-man
  Of goodly size to view,
And classmate is collecting for
  The Nine or for the Crew,
Just say you're training for the same,
  And hope that he'll train too.

Or if you are a little man,
  And that would be too thin,
Say you have other channels for
  The flowing of your tin;
And as for the athletic sports,
  You think them all a sin.

But if he is an editor,
  Who dabbles in *belles-lettres*,
And says, unto the *Advocate*
  He wants to make you debtor,
Pray tell him with your blandest smile
  You like The Crimson better.

This was considered uncomplimentary to the editors of the *Advocate,* and the Doctor was accordingly promptly admonished. Letters were then read [and] . . . it was moved that the remaining letters, including many from prominent college officials, be laid on the table. The Board then adjourned in confusion to the Cambridge horse-car, where a business meeting was held, and it was voted to use the funds, which the paper would accumulate during the coming year, for another breakfast one year from date.

      — Charles Wesley Bradley, Class of 1880

EDITORIAL
___

Owen Wister Still Survives

           October 16, 1911

The well-known reply of Mark Twain after reading his own obituary might well be repeated by Owen Wister. In truth both reports "were grossly exaggerated." Also the fact that the noted author is a former member of the Crimson board made the "story" of his death in Saturday's issue partake somewhat of the humorous. However, we leave it to our valued contemporary (with which Mr. Wister was, we are told, "affiliated") to smooth out the crumpled galley sheets and draw thereon a lively cartoon. We would suggest some appropriate scene from that best of Harvard College tales, "Philosophy 4." Nothing would convince us more surely that Wister is still, fortunately, very much alive.

The Student Vagabond

April 21, 1932

"What is spring?" she asked. "Spring," he answered, "why spring is when men sit on the front steps in the twilight smoking, when their wives sit with them, when all music is a waltz, when little girls tie blue ribbons in their pigtails and older sisters walk together laughing in the darkness. It's when young boys go shouting up the street and older brothers hang up their trousers at night to keep the press, when the man in G-32 borrows a car and goes to Wellesley, when the debutante reads poetry, when the moon is a soft golden cartwheel, and every breeze a zephyr. It's when every man is sick of four walls and a ceiling; the time when the last Victorian wrote that "man he must go with a woman which woman cannot understand," and Tennyson asked, "Ah, why should life all labor be, why should we only toil, the roof and crown of things?" Spring is when seniors try to get worried about Divisionals and can't, but only about studying for them; when juniors feel that there is nothing quite like a Chrysler and a bottle of Rye, when sophomores first realize they must have studied before, because they need a rest now, when freshmen write five-page letters to Dobbs Ferry. You know, my dear, that spring is here when all the College pages Rinehart, when the Pops begin, when there are people on the streets, when you don't have to go to a movie to prove to yourself that it's bad, when Scotch doesn't taste as good as Port and Sherry.

"When you feel different than you've ever felt before or ever will feel again, when you almost decide to call up the girl you met at the Somerset in December, when the world goes round, and birds sing, and girls laugh, and colors are bright, and the earth steams, and bands play, and life seems full and gay and ecstatic and you feel empty, and dull, and sodden, why then," he said, "it's spring."

"Oh yes, I see," she said. "Why — why spring is here, isn't it?"

Crime Prexy Abducted; Bird Spurns 'Poon
Nationwide Search for Duo

April 18, 1953

Two top Crimson executives, victims of a double kidnapping, were being sought by State Police last night. Michael Maccoby '54 and George S. Abrams '54 disappeared from the University late yesterday afternoon after successfully foiling an initial snatching attempt by members of *The Lampoon*.

Abrams is short, stocky, and has curly brown hair. Maccoby is short, stocky, and has curly black hair.

Maccoby's absence was reported shortly after lunch by his roommate, Anthony C. Beilenson '54, who noticed signs of a struggle in his room. Two hours later, The Crimson received an anonymous telephone call saying *The Lampoon* was holding Maccoby until its Ibis was returned. After an emergency full board meeting had voted 23 to 2 to "elect the Ibis and call it a fair trade," *The Lampoon* called again to say Maccoby had been rescued by Abrams and the two were returning to Cambridge.

They have not been seen since, but John Updike '54, *Lampoon* president, declared last night that his mob had recaptured both men, and were giving them "an extensive brain washing treatment in a dungeon at Old Westbury, Long Island."

Updike also warned that "no Crimson editor can rest safe in his bed. We promise, within a week, to depopulate Cambridge totally of this unfortunate element. After that, we will publish a daily newspaper ourselves."

In the absence of the two, Crimson affairs are being handled by a triumvirate of executives, headed by Editorial Chairman Milton S. Gwirtzman '54.

An intensive search by the Federal Bureau of Missing Birds last night located John H. Ibis '54 calmly tippling in a local saloon. Ibis was reported missing Thursday morning.

Ibis heatedly denied charges by his former associates, The Harvard Lampoon, Inc., of 1 Bird Street, that he had been abducted.

"I'm through," he said. "Finished. Fed up. I flew the coop myself. I say it's incredibis and I say the hell with it."

Looking haggard, unshaven, and green around the axillarys, Ibis went on to charge his society brothers with "mental cruelty, sadism, and neglect . . . All they did was laugh, laugh, laugh," he said. "And drink martinis — dry martinis."

"All that was almost bearable," he continued. "But when they told me they were going to roast me for their annual dinner, that was the last straw. 'Roast Ibis.' Ugh," he shuddered. "Imagine it — eaten like an ordinary bird. For soup, they were planning to have 'Ibis bisque.'"

Asked what he thought of *The Lampoon* as a publication, Ibis sighed and brought forth an image: "It's like chamber music with a bawdy brass choir interrupting all the time." But his distaste was tinged with a shade of admiration.

"Those guys," he said, "sure are colossal brasses."

Moscow University Gets Sacred Ibis
Russian Deputy Takes Bird From Crimeds

April 21, 1953

Threski, *The Lampoon*'s Sacred Ibis, now rests in Russian territory.

Semyon K. Tsarapkin, Deputy Representative of the USSR in the United Nations, accepted the Ibis on behalf of the Russian government yesterday at Russian Delegation Headquarters, 680 Park Avenue, New York City.

Michael Maccoby and George S. Abrams, Crimson president and managing editor who made the presentation on behalf of *The Lampoon*, expressed the hope that *The Lampoon*'s Ibis would find its final resting place on one of the spires of the new Moscow University, to be opened next fall.

Mr. Tsarapkin and Mr. Svirin, first secretary of the delega-

Crimson managing editor George S. Abrams '54 presents *The Lampoon*'s Sacred Ibis to Semyon K. Tsarapkin, chief deputy delegate of the USSR to the United Nations, at the Russian headquarters in New York City. Crimson President Michael Maccoby '54 (left) smiles approvingly. The two Crimson editors presented the Ibis to the Russians in April 1953 in the name of *The Lampoon* and for the express purpose of having it placed on the new Moscow University building. "They were assured," the original story said, "that their wish would be followed . . . The Russians expressed great interest in college studies and in student extracurricular activities, especially student pranks." April 21, 1953. (Photo by John B. Loengard '56)

tion, who acted as interpreter, indicated they would send the bird to Moscow immediately and voiced thanks from the USSR for the gift.

The Russians apologized for the absence of Andrei Vyshinsky, first permanent delegate, who was unable to get away from his U.N. duties for the presentation.

The Russians were cordial and showed a great interest in college curricula and student activities, especially American student pranks.

Abrams and Maccoby, who had been incorrectly reported kidnapped by *The Lampoon* over the weekend, returned to Cambridge late last night after spending three days in New York preparing the presentation.

"The Russians were extremely nice about the whole thing. It seemed to us they were going out of their way to implement their new peace offensive. We expect to get pictures from them of the Ibis's new resting place on a University of Moscow spire almost any day now," they said.

They commented that Tsarapkin was a bit puzzled as to what the bird represented. First he thought it was a stork, but was assured when he was informed it was "a sort of American peace dove."

The two editors, who were accompanied by Crimson photographer John B. Loengard '56, were astonished by the ease with which the arrangements for the presentation were made. "There were no hitches or hesitations in the entire affair," they said.

EDITORIAL

Bird of Freedom

April 21, 1953

There are many ways of show international friendship and understanding. One of the most usual is an exchange of monuments. France gave America the Statue of Liberty; America gave Britain a treasured statue of Lincoln; and so on. That is why the recent gift of *The Lampoon* to the Soviet government of one of its most treasured possessions is a firm step forward

in the path to peace. We thank *The Lampoon* for letting us do
the official honors, knowing full well that if they could have
made the trip, they would have done it themselves. World
peace deserves no less.

'Poonsters Demand Russians Return Ibis
Fail to See Humor of Ibis Sitting on Spire of
Red University

April 22, 1953

Harvard and Radcliffe students rose in protest last night
against *The Lampoon*'s attempt to take Threski, the Sacred
Ibis, away from the Russian people and the University of Moscow.

Over 300 girls from the Annex last night signed a petition
demanding "that the Ibis be left with the Russians, to whom
it now belongs by right of courtesy." Similar petitions were
being circulated in the Yard last night and will be available
in the Houses at noon. The petitions will be presented to both
the State Department and *The Lampoon* some time tomorrow.

"The spectacle of the Sacred Ibis anywhere except on the
Lampoon tower is not a subject for humor," funnyman John
H. Updike stated last night. "The Crimson pranksters seem to
have forgotten the rights of property. It's deplorable that
they've carried college jokes into the arena of international
relations," comic Updike added.

At New York, Semyon Tsarapkin, first deputy USSR delegate to the U.N., could not be reached for comment, but another member of the delegation told the Associated Press: "I
heard about it, but I think it is being taken up with Mr. Vyshinsky." Vyshinsky heads the Soviet delegation.

Meanwhile, telegrams from all over the country flooded
into Crimson offices at 14 Plympton Street. "You have done
much to ease the tensions of the Cold War with your straightforward humor," one from Chicago read.

Many have remarked about the curious inability on the part
of *The Lampoon* to picture the touching scene over Red
Square. The Ibis, with the graceful arch of its beak thrust into
the Moscow snow, would probably overlook the tomb of John

Reed, a former Communist *Lampoon* editor and one of four men to be buried in the Kremlin.

But the *Lampoon* was in no mood for either nostalgia or humor yesterday. A series of phone calls to Russian head-quarters at 680 Park Avenue, in New York City, succeeded in completely confusing the hapless Russians. According to *The Lampoon*, however, arrangements have been almost com-pleted for the return of its Ibis. A carload of editors is ex-pected to drive to New York today to take Threski from the center table on Tsarapkin's second-floor office, where it now rests.

Comment around the University was varied. Some thought it a "great gag." Others refused to believe the stunt had actu-ally happened.

Michael Maccoby and George S. Abrams, Crimson president and managing editor, have a series of 16 pictures taken within the Soviet headquarters by photographer John B. Loengard, Monday. Copies of these were loaned to *Life* magazine yester-day.

Maccoby and Abrams stated last night: "We are sorry that the supposed funnymen of *The Lampoon* do not realize that humor is a great panacea for the world's ills and a strategic weapon in the present fight against Communism. It is sad, in-deed, that such a petty sense of property has caused *The Lam-poon* to crawl sniveling and whining to the State Department. It is a move that can only sour the nation's laughter. For the State Department to take a hand in returning the bird would be nothing short of appeasement."

Nothing Very Interesting Takes Place at University

May 22, 1961

Nothing worth noting happened in the University yesterday. Or the day before, for that matter.

Nothing of interest was reported from the College, the Busi-ness School, the Law School, the Education School, the Divin-ity School, the Medical School, the Dental School, the Design School, the School of Public Health, the School of Public Ad-ministration, or the Graduate School of Arts and Sciences.

For a moment, it seemed that the day's first news story

might develop at Radcliffe, when Elvira R. Squirm '63 ran down the hall of her dormitory screaming, "Help! There's a man in my bed!" But it was a false alarm; Miss Squirm, whose eyes were watering from swallowing too much Listerine, had walked into someone else's room.

Some people studied; some didn't. Some played tennis; some didn't. Bartley J. Crum '64 slept all day.

Elsewhere, things proceeded apace. Howard J. Phillips '62 didn't attack anybody, and no one attacked him. The new Health Center remained 15 days behind schedule. Dean Monro reported that Peace Corps plans were "beginning to jell."

Meanwhile, it was announced that Homer J. Fonque '62, of Eliot House and Chicken Springs, Wyo., has been awarded the Hi Flung Hooey Memorial Prize for the best essay written during the year in the back room of a Chinese laundry. The prize is the income from two shares of Planters Peanuts common stock.

The Sparse Grey Hackie Award, for the best essay telling in 25 words or less "Why I Like Halvah," was not given this year. It was awarded last in 1825.

That's the kind of day it was.

Commented President Pusey, "No comment."

CABBAGES AND KINGS
___

Chicken Little

January 16, 1962

One day while Chicken Little was cultivating his garden, a piece of sky fell down and hit him in the head. "Oh dear, oh dear," Chicken Little exclaimed. "The sky is falling; I must go and tell the King." And so off he went to the palace.

Henny Penny

On the way he met Henny Penny, noted neurotic and intellectual. Henny Penny had been concerned for some time about the possibility of the sky falling. "I have been concerned for some time about the possibility of the sky falling," Henny

Penny said. "It is a sad commentary on our civilization that the sky falls, because we are conformists. And because not enough people write letters to government officials. And because there are hidden powers that seek to bring on destruction. I hate government officials. I hate."

Henny Penny was now screaming. She calmed herself and continued: "But I love the people of this country. I love the newspaper boy on the corner, the fishmonger with his song, the little child eating popcorn. Ah, people of this kingdom, I love you!"

Foxy Moxy

Just then Foxy Moxy sidled up. Henny Penny hated Foxy Moxy, who was a successful storm window salesman, stock speculator, and pillar of the community of long standing. Foxy Moxy had a proposition to make: "Friends, and you are my friends," he said, "suppose that the sky falls — and of course it won't. But if it does, what will we all need? Shelter, that's what. Shelter for ourselves, shelter for our possessions, shelter for our loved ones. And I just happen to have here with me contracts for the latest thing in shelters — Fox Holes, Patent Applied For. My own invention with a lifetime guarantee, easy credit, and plenty of closet space. Also: optional patio, Ping-Pong table, garbage dispose-all and . . ."

"I hate dispose-alls," shrieked Henny Penny. "I hate loved ones. I hate shelters, and patios and fox holes. Hate. Hate. Hate. And besides, they won't work. Because, when the sky falls, that will be the end. People may get momentary security from your Fox Holes. But finally they will rot or decompose or die of starvation or horrible disease. Women and children and pet parakeets — all will die." This prediction gave Henny Penny considerable satisfaction.

Foxy Moxy, on the other hand, was noticeably annoyed. "Look here, friends," he growled, addressing Chicken Little. "I certainly hope Henny Penny is not insulting my integrity. I wouldn't sell people something they couldn't use. Fox Holes may not be perfect, but 'they're better than nothing.' That's our company motto. Henny Penny seeks to soften us for destruction. I'm getting to think Henny Penny should be put out of the way." The fox bared his fangs and advanced toward the hen.

Owly Vowly

"Vait!" The voice was that of Owly Vowly, renowned scholar and analyst of contemporary affairs. "There must be no violence on this issue until vee have time to analyze it." Foxy Moxy slinked back submissively, for Owly Vowly spoke very distinctly, authoritatively, and with a slight German accent.

"The situation," the owl revealed, "iss very complex. Luckily, of the twelve forces affecting the problem the first six are irrelevant, the seventh, eighth and ninth are canceled out by the tenth, and the eleventh is untranslatable from the German, leaving the twelfth force — namely, the most important one — which I shall now proceed to simplify by game-theory analysis." Owly Vowly blinked calmly to acknowledge the gasps of admiration from his audience.

"The kvestion," he continued, "reduces to a zimple two-person-zero-sum catastrophe, in which there are three possibilities, X, Y, and Z:

(X) The sky falls — a catastrophe.

(Y) The sky doesn't fall — not a catastrophe.

(Z) The sky falls a little bit — maybe a catastrophe.

"In case Z — which is the relevant one — vat vould vee do in the sky's position? We might fall and we might not, depending on whether we wanted to or not. The solution to the problem, therefore, is to make the sky not want to fall. And this is done by a policy of . . ."

"Fox Holes," shouted Foxy Moxy.

"By a policy of deterrence," sneered the owl. "The problem is as yet theoretical and not practical."

"I hate deterrence," clucked Henny Penny.

"In any case," Owly Vowly concluded unruffled, "vat I have said supports rather than not supporting the suggestion of Chicken Little that we tell the King and I myself shall go along to clarify the problem."

Chicken Little heaved a sigh of relief. "Well," he said, encouraged by so impressive an endorsement, "let us go and tell the King." And so the animals went off to the palace.

At the Palace

When they arrived they were greeted by the King's press secretary, who announced: "The King reads books at a prodigious rate and therefore has a lightning grasp of the weather conditions in his kingdom and of all the statistical, economic, political, social, and philosophical factors of the situation. Since this is a constitutional monarchy, however, he has graciously consented to address his subjects."

A cheer went up from the assembled multitude, for at that moment the King walked out on his balcony. King Chipmunk III cut a handsome figure; his paunchy cheeks and tiny nose gave character to his noble chipmunk face; his rich coat of light brown hair was universally admired; and his high-pitched, squeaky voice sent chills down the spines of all his subjects.

"This is a time of crisis," King Chipmunk squeaked grandly. "The sky is falling. It is satisfied but not stratified. And will get lower before it gets higher. Yet higher it will get, if freedom can make it so. What is needed is courage, vigor, and self-sacrifice. My loyal subjects, I give you these words of advice: Ask not what the sky can do to you, ask rather what you can do against the sky. And as for shelter, do not fear to build but do not build from fear. And remember throughout that the weather is not negotiable."

"Hooray," yelled Chicken Little, and the other animals joined in, for the King was very popular. Then the press secretary added:

"The address of King Chipmunk III should clear all doubts from the minds of his subjects. Any apparent ambiguities in his speech should be interpreted as exhortations to his people to go home and work for the coming congressional elections. This is, after all, a constitutional monarchy."

Home Again

And so the animals went home, Owly Vowly to his books, Foxy Moxy to developing a new Fox Hole "with deterrent action," Henny Penny to writing perfectly frantic letters to government officials.

And Chicken Little went back to cultivating his garden. "Oh dear," he exclaimed, as another chunk of sky hit him on the head. But then he caught himself patriotically, remembering that one must, after all, accept such things in times of crisis and congressional elections.

— Josiah Lee Auspitz '63

When the Great HSA Birthday Cake Delivery Scandal hit Harvard, The Crimson ran big page-one stories on three successive days and then the following, inspired piece appeared. It all started when the HSA head, Dustin M. Burke '52, the University's "Director of Student Employment," tried to defend the HSA Birthday Cake Agency against a tough competitor, University Birthday Cake Agency, a private concern. Their line of business (if you can call it that) was to send letters to Harvard students' parents, soliciting orders for cakes to be delivered to the dorm on the appropriate happy day. Burke's tactic was to create a monopoly for the unusual HSA business, by warning parents that his *was the* only *agency authorized by the University to deliver cakes; any other agency was in violation of trespassing laws and subject to arrest. That wasn't quite true, as the University police chief repeated many, many times. Burke persisted, however, insisting it was an obscure regulation concocted by the University Solicitations Committee. Such an august body, The Crimson learned, actually did exist, but it hadn't met in more than a year. To cap off a great series of stories, one of the Solicitation Committee's reputed members, Dean Watson, insisted (wished?) that he was no longer a member of the committee, to which another member, Assistant Dean of the Faculty Trotenberg replied, "Dean Watson is just a little bit confused."*

CABBAGES AND KINGS

Happy Birthday

March 23, 1963

Why did Serb Bulgar die? And did he die in vain? Most Harvard men celebrate their coming of age with quiet joy; Serb marked his twenty-first birthday by jumping off the Larz An-

This photograph appeared in a Crimson of 1955, but only as a head shot of President Pusey. Comments Robert M. Pringle '58: "I was called in to take the place of the regular University photographer to take a picture of the deans of the University . . . In those days News Office photography was pretty dull stuff, even for deans. Single flash on camera, line them up, wham. But on this occasion one man was missing — Dean Horton of the Divinity School, who was sick. His colleagues decided it would be a great gag to send him a cheer-up photo of themselves, the assembled divinities of the University, begging for alms, pens and plates outstretched. I obliged. That's McGeorge Bundy, second from left, bottom row. Since I was developing the pictures at the Crimson darkroom I was given stern warnings to make sure that the negatives and all prints were returned to the News Office. I had every intention of keeping my word, but when I developed the photo — lo and behold: a *human*-appearing photo of President Pusey with a warm smile, quite a change from the usual leaden expression. We had nothing nearly as good at The Crimson. I decided it would not violate my pledge to blow up just Pusey's head and returned the negative and "all prints" to the nervous William Pinkerton, then the head of the Harvard News Office. A couple of months later The Crimson needed a stock shot of Pusey. My masterpiece was pulled — it so happened that it was the *reversed* version, so that it faced the story — and used for the first time. Pinkerton instantly spotted the picture. He was rabid. I was called into the News derson Bridge. (His body was recovered a week later by the Harvard Student Agencies Dredging Service, and condolences were sent to his grieving parents through the HSA Condolence Agency in a rhyming telegram: "We have bad news for you/ Your son's short life is through/ To manhood he had grew/ But himself in the river he threw.")

For Croat and Slovene Bulgar, Serb's hard-working immigrant parents, the tidings of their son's premature death — bitter as they were — came as no surprise. "Mr. Dirk told us not to meddle, Slovene," said Croat. "Serb's blood is on our hands." Only two weeks before, the Bulgars had received a letter from the HSA Birthday Cake Agency, warning them not to forget their parental obligations:

> Dear Hard-Working Immigrant Harvard Parents:
> Your son will be 21 years old next week. REAL American parents send their children cakes on this occasion. Do you want to be forced to return to the old country? Better send us five dollars for a real American cake.
>
> > Cordially,
> > Rusty Dirk
>
> P.S. Don't try any funny business. OUR Birthday Cake Agency is the only organization permitted to deliver cakes to your son!

"Poor Serb," Slovene had moaned, "he would choke to death on a real American cake. My cousin at the Window Shop can make him something nice."

Office and chewed to within an inch of my life for breaking my word. He was convinced and nothing would unconvince him that the picture had been reversed as a deliberate attempt to deceive him. Once again I swore that *all* prints of this terribly dangerous document had been turned over to the News Office, *all* linotype engravings destroyed, etc. Well, that wasn't quite true. One eight-by-ten survived; I just couldn't bear to let it go . . . I spent the rest of my undergraduate career taking pictures for the *Alumni Bulletin* — when not at The Crimson — a far more satisfactory arrangement all around."

"But Slovene," said Croat, "the letter."

"No buts," said Slovene, and the Bulgars sent their life savings to the Window Shop for a magnificent birthday cake. Slovene's cousin, Pfannkuchen, picked out the most elegant variety: a *Geburtstagfestspieltorte* — five rich layers, drenched in Viennese chocolate and smothered with whipped cream and hazelnuts.

It took two employees of the restaurant to carry the cake to Serb's room in Claverly, and by the time they reached the dormitory, they were visibly tired. Two men in black trenchcoats stood in the doorway.

"What have you got in the box, boys?" asked one of them. "Could it be birthday cake?"

"What if it is?" one of the cake bearers replied. "Who are you?"

"Committee on Solicitations," the man in black growled, and without any warning the two inspectors lunged for the box. The Window Shop employees did their best to save Serb's cake, but they were no match for fighters who had trained at the HSA Karate Institute. In a matter of seconds, the carton containing the *Geburtstagfestspieltorte* had rolled down the steps of Claverly into Mt. Auburn Street, where it was crushed flat by the wheels of an HSA Ollie Orbit Ice Cream Truck that careened around the corner of Holyoke Street.

So Serb never got his cake, and as he sat alone in his room on his twenty-first birthday, he despaired that his parents had not cared enough to remember his coming of age. His spirits brightened when he saw an envelope pushed under his door, for he was sure it contained a cheering message from his mother and father. Inside, however, was a mimeographed note:

Dear Harvard Student:
    A birthday is a time for celebration. Have some of that cake your immigrant parents were too cheap to send by calling the HSA Snack Agency and ordering several portions of our "Red-White-&-Blue Special" birthday cake.

Cordially,
Rusty Dirk

It was the final blow. Serb left his lonely room in Claverly and walked grimly to the river.

— Andrew T. Weil '63
— Anthony Hiss '63

CIVILIZATION IN CAMBRIDGE

Their Love of Equality
BY ALEXIS DE TOKEVILLE

April 18, 1973

I would first like to say how much I love your city. I have been to Leverett House, I have eaten at your Tommy's Lunch. This is truly God's country; it is only too bad you are not God's people.

When I first came to Cambridge my friend Ramon told me, "The bricks are very pretty, the ivy is very green, but the people, well Alexis, they are very strange." Only the next day I said to my friend Ramon, "Ramon, you are right, the students of Cambridge are certainly strange, and perhaps more than that." The night before I had gone to one of their local parties where a girl told me I should not wear my good suit but dungarees and a workingman's shirt. "God made me ugly enough," I told her. "If He had wanted me to look like a cow I would have been born in Texas." The students of Adams House are very smelly. At one of their parties you do not have to be a weatherman to know which way the wind is blowing.

The greatest passion of the Cambridge students is their love of equality. The cause of equality has been advocated by many great men in many eras, most of which were before I was born. Jean Jacques Rousseau said that society was not equal to the sum of its parts. Henry Ford made parts interchangeable. Voltaire said that "we must cultivate our own garden." Thomas Jefferson owned a large plantation. John Locke told us that when we are born our minds are like a *tabula rasa*, or a "blank slate." John Dewey thought we should keep it that way. History has taught us many lessons, few of which anyone remembers.

In the American Democracy there are a number of poor citizens who are known as the underprivileged. The privilege they do not have is money. Since some people are underprivileged it is understood that others are overprivileged. The children of the families in this second group all go to Harvard, or else to Radcliffe, its sister college. Of course, in the United States of America there is no explicit "privilege," but the children of those who are affluent and educated have an enormous range of opportunities early in life that guarantees their later success. They live in a literate environment, with books all around. The average overprivileged child of three or four will pull a volume down from the shelf of the family library and read as fast as he can slit open the pages. In the evening his parents will sip martinis or discuss the editorials of *The New York Times*, either way providing a stimulating environment for their schoolchild. By listening in on the parental conversations — "Bill and Mary are getting divorced" or "the market slumped twenty points in late afternoon profit taking" — he is unconsciously being prepared for his verbal aptitude tests. The exceptionally overprivileged child has an opportunity to mingle with adults, passing hors d'oeuvres on the evenings when his parents stay home, at which time they might pat him on the head or say hello.

These overprivileged Americans have had tremendous advantages. By the time they arrive in Cambridge they have been class presidents and National Merit finalists, and secretly wonder whether or not Jesus of Nazareth is their half brother. But they prefer to look like Indians and smell like buffalo.

It is not all so bad as that with the people of Harvard. Some are light-hearted and charming. In the spring they throw the Frisbee! To each other, back and forth. They want to have the good times. Today is the first day of the rest of their life! Yet they can also be a serious people. I have seen them at work in the laboratories of the twentieth chemistry course.

On one of the spring evenings I was walking across the footbridge across the Charles; the sun was setting with a few last rays lighting the green-covered walls and white spires of Cambridge. The cars rushed along on the highway with their headlights going and on the river a few last boats of crew raced. Monet and Raphael are right, I think, the world is beautiful.

The equality movement offers many real advantages. Everybody will have a great deal in common, so that it will be easier to make conversation. But, at the same time, there is not room enough for everyone on the botton rungs of society.

As everyone knows, the poor are the salt of the earth. The students of Cambridge think it is virtuous to imitate them, so they wear dungarees and dirty hair and tell "dudes" not to "jive" them. Actually there are many rich people who are quite salty. The behavior of the students might seem phony, but that is not what is so important. The truth is that virtue cannot be impersonated, and exists in people's hearts and minds rather than in their wallets and affectations. But this problem of equality is hard to solve. Perhaps the students of Cambridge are right that everyone should come together and join hands, but I think they should wash them first.

Some people might want to criticize what I say, but I hope they notice my funny accent and keep in mind that I am a third-world person.

— J. Whitney Stillman '73

CHAPTER 5

Sports

BECAUSE SPORTS at Harvard — as anywhere else — is very much a matter of record, and because there are thorough record books available elsewhere, as well as a complete history (the two-volume *H-Book of Harvard Athletics*), this chapter serves merely as a miscellany of some few interesting or great moments in Harvard sports and as an assemblage of the various forms of Crimson sports coverage down through the decades. So what you will read here are, for instance, examples of the gentlemanly manner of old-time sports writing ("A splendid game, indeed!"), an account of the greatest Harvard-Yale baseball game, or curios such as an editorial written by Franklin Delano Roosevelt '04.

Roosevelt's editorial indicates just how important sports once were to undergraduates; while he was using the paper's most prominent column to encourage a capacity-crowd rally in support of the football team, another section of The Crimson ran a tiny notice saying that President Eliot, poor man, would be giving a lecture that same night, at a conflicting time. (No wonder Eliot would say just two years later that football was unhealthy, immoral, and too rough, and raise such a stir that the Faculty would ban football and the controversy would reach the White House, where Teddy Roosevelt conferred with the Harvard coach to help settle the matter.)

Contrast FDR's editorial to the 1969 article "The Thrill of Defeat," and you'll understand how much attitudes toward sports changed at Harvard. The Crimson reflected this change accurately, since it was founded about the same time as organized intercollegiate sports began, and devoted most of its copy to the subject until the 1930s. It was during the thirties that colleges began working together to set limitations on recruiting, out-of-season practices, and the use of academically unqualified players. Similar reforms were proposed by The Crimson as early as 1925 when an editorial railed against "The Evil That Is Football," which caught the fancy of the national press and the comment from the *Chicago Tribune* that Harvard had become "merely an institution of learning." After the war, sports (at least at Harvard) wouldn't mean as much to students as they once did.

During that first Golden Half Century of Intercollegiate Sports, however, The Crimson had tremendous influence over sports, and not just at Harvard. First, you have to understand that, in the beginning, intercollegiate athletics were mostly student-organized, student-run affairs. At Harvard, faculty influence began to creep in with the creation in 1882 of the Committee on the Regulation of Athletic Sports, but students were included in its membership and student opinion still held sway. Even after the Harvard Athletic Association, founded by students in 1874, was taken over by the administration in 1893, the move was mainly an organizational one. It was President Eliot's big 1905 movement against football that began to turn the tide, and with the phenomenon of sports for the sake of alumni, President Lowell's creation of the Office of Director of Athletics in 1926, and the elimination of student representation on the Faculty sports committee in 1951, Harvard sports came to look like the efficient institution it is today — promoting competitive amateur sports and encouraging the "scholar-athlete." In the beginning, though, there were only students getting together for what we'd call "pickup" games.

It was just such a ragtag game between Harvard and McGill in 1874 that resulted in a rules squabble with other American colleges, and the first truly American football game in 1875. (That's the Harvard version, anyway, complicated by the fact that Harvard men played a funny rugbylike "Boston game" as early as 1871. So when the NCAA based the centennial of football on an 1869 Princeton-Rutgers rugby game, Harvard wouldn't have it. And Harvard must have been right:

after all, it was the only team in the country that had enough courage to run around on the field in 1971 with stickers on their helmets proclaiming the *true* centennial of football.) The Crimson of the period — then The Magenta — gives a fairly understandable account of the origins of American football: the essential thing to remember is that all the other colleges were playing a "football" that was like soccer, at least on a formal basis, and that it was Harvard that pressed for the American-like changes. The Crimson gave its support to these efforts, so it's fair to say that it contributed to the beginnings of American football, and that's why an article on the subject appears here.

Most of the other selections included here from The Crimson's first half century reflect the great student interest in and concern for sports. Whether there would be a well-represented football team, or the question of student "subscriptions" (subsidies for the teams, *all* of which came from students), or raising a sport to the status of a "major" sport, were all Matters of Great Importance. From the second half century there appear a few highlights: the revival of the Football Weekend as the social center of life after the war; the revival of football itself, which went through some shaky times in the late forties; and some memorable meetings with Yale (all victories for Harvard, of course) or rivalry-sparked commentaries thereon.

A lot is missing from this collection, mainly because most sports writing concentrates on the play-by-play, which is what readers need and want; few stories can be easily reread years later. A number of traditional Harvard sports aren't even mentioned: track, tennis, golf, soccer, fencing, wrestling, cross-country, squash, sailing, basketball, rugby, and skiing. There are still other sports at Harvard that you never hear much about, but at one time or another they had some enthusiastic adherents — shooting, boxing, judo, figure skating, polo, and even tiddlywinks are just a few that come to mind. In many of Harvard's sports — whether mentioned in this chapter or not — there have been some truly exceptional teams and individuals of Olympic and National Champion caliber. Often enough such excellence has been the result of

Ed Blodnick '54 (in back) and Bill Dennis '54 are shown here with a Navy player, as the ball seems out of their control, during a game with Navy in December 1952. (Photo by Marlowe A. Sigal '52)

some of the best coaching around. (One example proves the point: the hockey team of the midfifties. Members of the 1956–57 squad won every spot on the first All–Ivy-League team that year — a feat never accomplished before or since by any Ivy League team in any sport. Bob Cleary '58 was among this group and both he and brother Billy Cleary '56, who was a record-breaking national scoring leader while at Harvard, went on to star in the 1960 Olympics; and Billy Cleary has since become an outstanding Harvard hockey coach.) All of which is to say that Harvard can boast of a tradition in athletic competition so rich and The Crimson portrayed that accomplishment so well that you could spend years going through the Crimson files reading just the highlights; and even then you'd have to remember that The Crimson, though it has maintained a fine tradition of sports coverage, just couldn't cover it all.

That The Crimson does have an exceptional sports-writing

tradition is borne out by glancing at the bylines on some of America's better-known sports pages: Francis J. "Franny" Rosa '49 and John L. Powers '70 write sports for *The Boston Globe*; Stephen N. Cady '48 covers America's pastimes for *The New York Times*; and Andy Beyer '65 provides the *Washington Star* with the best horse-racing coverage in the country. A little-known fact is that David Halberstam '55 wrote numerous sports stories for The Crimson before moving on to cover the Vietnamese conflict and the Great Arena of politics. And there are handfuls of Crimeds writing on sports in magazines and in lesser-known but respected papers across the country.

One note about this chapter's format: all the articles explain themselves; there are no introductory remarks, but a few bracketed editor's notes help explain what are presumed to be obscure minutiae.

*   *   *

EDITORIAL

Foot-Ball

November 12, 1875

Our late successes on the foot-ball field, together with the near prospect of a game with Yale, has awakened a lively interest in foot-ball throughout the College. It is well known that Harvard declined to join the Association of Colleges, owing to the radical difference of our rules from those of the various other colleges. Though in so doing we laid ourselves open to criticism, yet an impartial observer must assent on consideration to the expediency of our decision. We did not in the least assert that our rules were the best; nor, as a Yale paper unjustly remarked at the time, did we think them so strictly scientific as to prevent us from contending with other colleges. The adoption of the rugby game is a sufficient proof that we gladly recognize the superiority of other rules, even at the cost of giving up our own. We have played under these rules with good success, and we do not hesitate to recommend their adoption to the Foot-Ball Association.

After many useless attempts to arrange games with several of the colleges of the Association, we have at last succeeded in arranging a game with Yale by means of a compromise between the two sets of rules. It is clear to everyone that rules resulting from such concessions as have to be made *cannot* be entirely satisfactory. Though much ingenuity was shown by the delegates at Springfield [where a conference to effect a compromise was held], yet there remain many points, trivial as they may seem at first, which need explanation and remedying. We lose one of our best rules; for though touchdowns count something, we have not the right to try for a goal after the ball has been brought in. We are allowed, as before, to run with the ball after having caught it on the bounce or fly; but with this exception we seem to have gained nothing of importance. The fault does not rest with our delegates. As before remarked, it is utterly impossible to make up rules by compromise that will suit all. Some one particular game, and that the best game that can be found, should be adopted, and every college should conform strictly to its rules. In giving up our so-called "Harvard Games," we worked a complete revolution in our system, and allowed the ball to be carried whenever caught. The suggestion that the game is for the feet alone, and not for the hands, is a mere quibble; for all sensible observers will agree that the use of the hands makes the game much more exciting and interesting. Again, we do not hesitate to claim the superiority of the leather ball over the rubber one. The former, besides retaining the air better, can be kicked both farther and straighter, and will last a much longer time. In setting forth the advantages of the rugby rules and ball, we only ask a fair, impartial hearing from the [Foot-Ball] Association. The fact that Harvard has played the game for the last year or so should be no obstacle to its adoption. The rules themselves, not the College, should be criticized. If the other colleges could witness a good game played according to the rugby rules, such as the late match between Harvard and Tufts, we are sure that they would be favorably impressed with the merits of the game.

As regards the coming match with Yale, it is much to be hoped that our team will meet with the success due to their late meritorious efforts; and it is quite probable that, notwithstanding a few peculiarities in the new rules, an exciting and interesting game will be seen on Saturday.

Baseball at Soldiers Field. (Photo by John B. Loengard '56)

EDITORIAL
The Devotion of Us All

November 18, 1903

During the next few days the thoughts of most of us will center on little besides football. It may be objected that athletics play too prominent a part in college life, but the fact remains that their position is such throughout the country that if we engage in intercollegiate contests at all the enthusiasm and importance attached to these contests is necessarily very great. Harvard men, both graduates and undergraduates, feel an all-absorbing interest in their team which finds an expression at this season on every occasion that any number of us come together.

In the Union tonight will be held the last mass meeting before the game. Even the great Living Room will be too small to hold all those who come to show the team their loyalty and interest. Such occasions, when entirely spontaneous, are not merely demonstrations over one team: they express in a wider sense the devotion of us all to the University.

> [Above editorial attributed to Franklin Delano Roosevelt '04, then Crimson president.]

Fourteenth-Inning Victory
Hard Drive by Hardwick Wins Exciting and Well-Played Contest

June 19, 1913

Harvard defeated Yale in the greatest game in the baseball history of the two universities yesterday afternoon in 14 innings by the score of 4 to 3. [Only one other 14-inning game, the longest recorded, has been played against Yale since. That was also a Harvard victory, in 1942.] The game was a thriller throughout and, as the length indicates, it was anybody's game for the entire 14 innings.

Harvard showed a faculty yesterday which has been lacking in many of the preliminary games, that of hitting in the pinches. Only 1 or 2 of the entire 11 hits were wasted yesterday and the men clearly proved by tieing the score in the last inning that this year's team is a fighting combination from start to finish. With the score 3 to 2 in Yale's favor in the ninth [Russell R.] Ayres ['15] tripled and [Robert T.] Gannett ['15] drove him in by a beautiful single between first and second, thus tieing the score. The next five innings were nip and tuck until, with one out in the fourteenth, Gannett doubled and crossed the plate when [Huntington R.] Hardwick ['15] smashed the cover off the ball by a terrific drive whose eventual destination was the freshman bleachers. The hit was the longest seen here in many seasons and would have been good for the winning run itself had Gannett not been on second. It was indeed a fitting climax to a 14-inning game with Yale.

Great Showing at Henley
Second University Eight Took First in
Classic English Event

September 25, 1914

By defeating the Boston Union Boat Club crew in the final round of the English Henley regatta on July 4, the University second crew scored the first American victory since the start of the annual competitions for the Grand Challenge Cup in 1839. The two entries from the United States nearly equaled the course record and outclassed their foreign rivals in every race.

The drawings for the opening round on July 2 threw the four English boats against the four outside entries. All the British crews were defeated, the most unexpected feature being Harvard's victory over Leander, a picked crew made up of the best Oxford and Cambridge oarsmen. A common characteristic marked the work of the foreigners, their rapid getaway, slow recover, and short stroke showing more power than the perfect body work and long stroke of the English.

The semifinal round, rowed on July 3 under ideal conditions, brought out the most spectacular work of the regatta. The Winnipeg Rowing Club of Canada, setting a stroke of 42, jumped ahead of the University second crew at the start. At the half-mile post the two boats were even, and from then on the University crept ahead persistently, and led at the finish by less than a length. In the other semifinal race the ex-

Harvard oarsmen composing the Union Boat Club crew defeated the Mainzer Ruder Verein of Germany, in a hard-fought race. The time for both races, seven minutes, very nearly equaled the course record, and proved that the two American boats qualified for the finals were among the fastest that had ever competed at Henley.

The Union Boat Club started splendidly in the final race on July 4. The graduates led by several feet for a quarter of a mile. At this point the undergraduates started to close up the lead, and were even at the half-mile. Then, as in the race with Leander, our second crew drew ahead, rowing perfectly. Union appeared to lack the drive which had marked the previous work, while the University boat traveled fast and smoothly. From the halfway station it was evident that the seconds would win, and eventually they crossed the finish with open water separating the boats.

The American victory, only the fifth time the Grand Challenge Cup has left England, closed a brilliant season for the University second crew.

Yale Swamped by Record-Breaking Score

Harvard Celebrated 41st Year of Football With Yale by Rolling Up Total of 41 Points Administering to Elis Worst Defeat Ever Given Them in History of Sport

Four Touchdowns by Mahan Closed Brilliant Football Career

HARTE HAD HONOR OF CARRYING BALL OVER FOR FIRST TOUCHDOWN EVER SCORED AGAINST BLUE IN STADIUM AND KING SCORED AFTER SPECTACULAR BROKEN-FIELD RUN OF 55 YARDS — WATSON EXHIBITED FAULTLESS GENERALSHIP THROUGHOUT — HARVARD LINE SMOTHERED YALE DEFENSE

November 22, 1915

Saturday, the twentieth of November, 1915, was the greatest day in the history of Harvard football. On that date was recorded a 41 to 0 victory over Yale — a victory gained by a splendid Crimson eleven that showed both impregnable defense and an offense that has startled the greatest gridiron critics by its bewildering versatility and its brilliant strategy.

Forty-one to nothing! In the scoring of those six touchdowns — four by Captain [Edward W.] Mahan ['16], one by [Richard S. C.] King ['16], and by [Richard] Harte ['17] — Harvard set several records. In the first place, it was the largest margin by which Harvard has ever beaten Yale [and remains so to the present day], the Saturday score lacking only 11 points of equaling the record set by Yale's 52 to 0 victory in 1884. Forty-one to nothing is also the most humiliating defeat ever suffered by Yale. The first touchdowns of the 41 to 0 victory, scored by Harte on his 35-yard run, was the first time Harvard has scored a touchdown on Yale in the [new] Stadium. The victory, furthermore, completed the last football season to be witnessed by the present senior class as undergraduates; and none of 1916, since entering College, has seen the University defeated on the gridiron by either Yale or Princeton. During the last four seasons Harvard has made 114 to Yale's 5 points in the series.

Perhaps the most noteworthy result of Saturday's contest was the glorious triumph of Coach [Percy D.] Haughton's ['99] football instruction. "Mr. Haughton," says *The New York Times* in an editorial entitled "Haughton's Harvard," "is a great coach, perhaps the greatest in the annals of the American college game."

As Coach Haughton points out, the Harvard team and the substitutes cannot be lauded too highly. Captain Mahan yesterday stated to a Crimson representative that he considered the 1915 Harvard eleven as the greatest football machine on which he ever played, and that the Yale eleven of this year was a more powerful set of individuals than was last year's Blue team.

Raccoons, Crowds, Bottles Feature
Lushest Yale Gathering of Decade

BY ANTHONY LEWIS '48

November 25, 1946

It was Yale weekend madness Saturday — madness that must have seemed more familiar to many of the alumni back in the end zones than it did to war-bred undergraduates on both sides of the field. From raccoon coats to built-in thermos jugs, Cambridge was a scene lifted out of the twenties.

Cars blocking streets half a mile up Massachusetts Avenue . . . crowds jamming every restaurant, bar, cafeteria and drugstore around the square . . . flags flapping in the breeze up Mt. Auburn Street, winding themselves around the flagpoles . . . masses of human beings seething over Larz Anderson Bridge before the game — eager, hopeful, warm and equally happy; then afterward — just a little tighter, a little colder, most of them a little less happy . . . all of these added up to the first really big weekend of the year.

The battle of the bands sort of blew away in the Stadium gale . . . the Yale tooters looked blue all the way through as the wind whipped through their loose-fitting uniforms . . . the Harvard Band started out with the temporary advantage of a lull in the storm, but the Crimson stands burst into a consternated hum when their drum major failed in two attempts to catch his baton after throwing it over the goal posts.

No one was quite sure how the battle of the brass drum began . . . but it ended with a three-wheeled drum carriage and a bruised Blue . . . quick action saved the day for the drum, and it rolled on the field again just in time to join the half-time serenade of the Elis . . . a slightly besotted tuba player performed on his instrument and around it . . . and the Wintergreen medley once again brought down the house.

The Yale stands started out with some vigorous pregame cheers, but five minutes later they had subsided to a morbid despondency . . . after the first quarter the cheering volumes gradually switched, with the sound of Brekekekek attaining eventual superiority . . . the goal posts went swiftly and cleanly — not with a whimper but with a bang . . . Richard Corcoran '46 was dangerous with his heels as he hung from the north bars . . .

THE SPORTING SCENE

Drumbeater's Holiday
BY DAVID L. HALBERSTAM '55

August 5, 1954

HARTFORD, CONN., July 27 — Bill Lee, the *Hartford Courant's* personable sports editor, crossed over the city room tonight, grinned at this reporter, and said:

"Guess what college was the first to send out its preseason football brochure?"

It is July — the temperature is 95, the college is Harvard.

Sure enough, sitting on the cover, looking as determined and formidable as he ever did during that goal line stand in New Haven is Captain Tim Anderson ['55].

Inside, in the same HAA cut which has graced this booklet for five years, is a wildly grinning sports publicity director, W. Henry Johnston. But for once there may be something behind the grin: for it is quite obvious to any seasoned Soldiers Field reporter that Johnston is optimistic.

Never in the past years would Johnston have dared let sports editors have some of July and all of August and September to think and read about Harvard football. It could be a pretty depressing thought in those days.

But as the company line in Cambridge goes Harvard was only two touchdowns — and thereby two games — away from an undefeated season in 1953.

As any reader will notice, however, the most frequently mentioned name in this book belongs to someone who won't play football this year. It is [halfback and third-team All-American] Richard J. Clasby '53 ("rhymes with touchdown"). All the sophomores and high-school captains whose names compose this brochure can't make up for Clasby.

Outside of its value for reminiscence' sake, and the tip-off on which lettermen flunked out, the booklet has limited use . . .

There are odds and ends of information which may come in handy during the course of the season. For instance, Harvard beat Andover 86 to 0 in 1886.

But the most disturbing thing about this booklet is not the

lack of concern the old-timers showed for prep schools, but its release date. The recurrent rumors about professionalism in Harvard athletics — which started the day the Crimson lost to Princeton [in 1953] by only one touchdown — have obviously been confirmed.

Any bids to take the sports pages away from Notre Dame, Maryland, and Southern Cal must start from the beginning. Even before all the "pro" football teams have started, Harvard is publicizing.

Where is the subtlety of past seasons — when the 1–8 records and discouraging preseason list of candidates necessitated a booklet marked primarily by fuzzy predictions and late delivery?

They are gone, evaporated in a world of [guard William M.] Meigs ['56], [wingback Robert R.] Cowles ['55], and Anderson. The days of hesitation have joined the Valpey full back spinner and Valpey [a Harvard coach for only two seasons] himself. Harvard can't wait for its opening game. Bring on the University of Massachusetts . . .

Crimson Swimmers Edge Elis 48–47
To Shatter 24-Year Bulldog Streak

By Rudolf V. Ganz Jr. '63

March 5, 1962

Versatile junior John Pringle ['63] piled up 13 points to lead the Crimson swimming team to a thrilling 48–47 upset victory over Yale Saturday in New Haven. It was Harvard's first win over the Elis since 1938, and only the second time the Bulldog squad has been beaten in 220 consecutive dual meets.

Snapping Yale's 24-year domination of EISL swimming took everything the Crimson had, including superhuman performances by Captain Bob Kaufmann ['62], senior freestyler Bill Zentgraf ['62], and Pringle. In the course of the meet Kaufmann tied his own University record in the 50; Zentgraf lowered his University mark in the 220 and set a new varsity time in the 440; and Pringle first won the individual medley, then came back to set a new Harvard record in the backstroke.

But none of these record-shattering performances were enough to win the meet. The Harvard varsity had used all its stars before the freestyle relay, leaving the squad no chance for a victory in the final event. Going into the 200-yard breast stroke, the score stood Harvard 40, Yale 39. And Yale had another seven points to come.

In the breast stroke, sophomore Bill Chadsey ['64] ranked a clear favorite over Yale senior Jerry Yurow, but the Crimson's other likely entries lacked experience and could hardly hope to squeeze out the essential points for second place. Two thousand cheering sons of Eli thought the meet was over, their undefeated record safe. Only a Crimson sweep in the breast stroke could send the trophy to Cambridge, and the Yalies were certain only Princeton great Gardiner Green could beat Yurow over 200 yards.

But the Bulldogs still got a shock when Pringle stepped up to the starting block. Pringle had not swum breast stroke all season, and only seven minutes before had climbed from the pool after a narrow backstroke victory over Eli star Bob Boni. Before that he had swum to a hard-fought first-place finish in the individual medley. After two exhaustive races, no one in the crowd thought he would be a serious threat to Yurow, who had over an hour's rest since Yale's leisurely victory in the medley relay. Everyone expected Pringle to finish far behind the leaders.

After 150 yards Pringle was solidly in possession of second place, some two yards behind Chadsey and four or five feet ahead of Yurow. Then Yurow started to move up. In the last length Pringle's exhaustion began to tell; with ten yards to go he led Yurow only by inches, and those inches were fast disappearing. Yet Pringle kept his slight edge to touch out Yurow by a tenth of a second, and complete Harvard's first Yale meet triumph in 24 years. The victory leaves the Crimson in sole possession of the EISL swimming crown.

In all, the Crimson won eight events, five of them in record time. The hapless Bulldogs claimed only the relays and the 100-yard freestyle.

And Then We Won; Big Hole Was Dead

By Thomas P. Southwick '71

June 1969

After the 1968 Harvard football season, the Harvard Club of Boston gave a dinner for the first undefeated Crimson team in 50 years. George Lalich '69 was asked to speak and he told the story of how he became the starting varsity quarterback.

"When we came to early practice the Boston-area papers didn't even mention me as a prospect," George said. "The only guy they seemed to think had a chance was someone named Big Hole. The columns read, 'And at quarterback the Crimson will have a Big Hole.' Well, I didn't know this guy Big Hole, so I decided to show up for practice and try my luck."

George won the starting position at quarterback, but for the preseason games it looked almost as if Big Hole might have done better. With raw rookies trying to fill the voids left by injured veterans like John Tyson and Dan Wilson, the Crimson first unit bumbled through a 16–7 [preseason game] loss to a weak New Hampshire team.

The pundits were ready with their criticism, and still they placed Big Hole at quarterback. The first half of the Holy Cross game made the most pessimistic forecasts look right. Those who had predicted losing seasons sat back and puffed half-time cigars confidently.

But something happened in the locker room at half time, something which changed that team from a loser to a winner. It didn't look it as the Cross came out in the third quarter to run the score up to 20–12, but those who know Harvard football could sense the comeback. We found some new heroes to replace those lost to graduation and injury. Most important, the new faces had the poise and the confidence to come back, and keep coming back all year. Lalich found a couple of sophomore ends, Pete Varney '71 and Bruce Freeman '71, and a defense that decided to dig in. Two fourth-quarter touchdowns provided the margin as Harvard won its most important victory of the year 27–20.

After the Holy Cross game the Crimson began to roll. Week after week the victories piled in, each more surprising than

In the 1968 Harvard–Yale football game Harvard was down by 16 points with only 45 seconds remaining in the game. What was to become the first undefeated Harvard team in over fifty years scored two touchdowns in those last precious seconds, and, with two two-point conversions, they tied up the game. The Crimson pronounced in a banner headline: HARVARD BEATS YALE, 29–29. But that was not the first exciting comeback in Harvard football history. In the 1954 game, Harvard was down, 9–0, going into the fourth quarter. After Harvard had scored one touchdown to make it 9–7, the big play of the game came on a reverse pass from Frank White '55 to Bob Cochran '55 (number 80), who is shown reaching for the toss, juggling it, and then gaining control and evading the Yale tackler. Cochran ran in for the score, the Harvard team won 13–9 and took the Big Three championship that year, the first time since 1941. November 22, 1954. (Photos by John B. Loengard '56)

the last. The key to any undefeated season is not to think about it. Take each game as it comes and play your best football. For the Harvard eleven this was easy. Each Saturday they were faced with a challenge, and no defeat could have been considered an upset . . . [First Bucknell fell, then Columbia, Cornell, Dartmouth, and Pennsylvania.]

Princeton stretched the Crimson heart to its limit. The defense, magnificent throughout the year, held the Tiger squad to only one tally. Again and again, as it appeared the Tiger tide might sweep past the tiny nine points the offense had amassed, the defense came up with a play to plug up the dam. A goal-line stand, a key interception by Tommy Wynne '69, and a come-from-behind, chase-down tackle by Mick Georges '69 were the highlights. But the Princeton game gave the pessimists something to talk about. "George Lalich can't pass," was the new phrase. But at least mention of Big Hole had disappeared.

And so the stage was set. Until the final whistle sounded at Princeton, the Crimson eleven hadn't really been thinking about Yale. It was too big, too powerful, too far removed. And always there had been a more immediate task at hand. And yet, after an easy rout of Brown, here they were. A Cinderella team facing the mighty Eli. Somehow it was impossible, and in the euphoric week before The Game people seemed to float from place to place. Harvard sophomores got rich with tickets going for $200 each. The pundits were almost too numb to write about the biggest college game in decades. The old grads were in their finest hour.

And it all centered around a group of about 40 guys.

Every obnoxious Yalie I know came up to me in the week before The Game to tell me tales of the fabulous Brian Dowling and Calvin Hill. They moved the clouds and made the sun shine. They walked on water. They lived like Gods.

And all I could tell them about was a group. A group of about 40 guys, none of whom, not even Vic Gatto '69, was a superstar, but all of whom wanted to win. It doesn't look like much on paper, and it didn't sound like much to the Yalies, but for anyone who saw the Harvard-Yale football game it was the margin of victory.

It was the most perfect ending to a perfect season. It was the Red Sox winning the pennant, or the [Eugene McCarthy 1968 near-upset] New Hampshire primary. It was a victory of the unknowns. Sophomore Bill Kelly '71, a reserve defensive back, and ends Pete Varney and Bruce Freeman became overnight heroes. And for Frank Champi '70, the moon-faced second-string quarterback, it was a dream — not the dream he says he had of the night before — but the dream he lived on the field.

By the third quarter it was over. For the pundits, the Yalies, the old grads, and those who had never seen the Crimson play before, and even for the coach. But for a few hopelessly naive romantics in the stands and about 20 players on the field it was not.

I was one of those romantics. I had seats on the 15-yard line toward the open end of the field. It was the second Harvard touchdown that did it for me. Crying and hoarse I turned to the guy sitting next to me and babbled, "We're going to do it. We're going to do it." Then Yale scored again and the skeptics relaxed. The score was 29–13 and Harvard couldn't possibly come back.

Forty-five seconds to go. Harvard down by 16. The Crimson on the Eli 38-yard line. A penalty. A run by tackle Fritz Reed '70. Bingo. A score from Champi to Freeman who beat the Eli hands down to the end zone. We could tie. I could barely see.

The kickoff. Everyone knew it was going to be onsides. Everyone except the Yale coaches who had set their usual blocks of flesh up on the front line of the receiving team. Miracle. Billy Kelly came up with the ball. Impossible. A draw. No Frank, it takes too much time. But it worked. Dowling watching from the bench. Carm Cozza stunned.

Three seconds to go. I was down near the field. "Hit the Big Fella!" But it went to the little man instead. The bumbling Elis had Big Hole on their squad now. He was defending Gatto. Six points and delirium.

People were on the field. Not me. I remembered the Dartmouth game a year before where a penalty on an extra point try had cost us the ball game. But that was a different team. Nothing could be denied our darlings. And the daintiest, the sweetest of those darlings did the job. The Big Fella, 240-point tight end Pete Varney. When Varney moves there's no denying him. He jumped high in the air after the catch with the ball held high. The Yalie had him in his arms, but there wasn't anything he could do.

I was on the field, drunk with joy. From the Yalies only silence. We carried tackle Steve Ranere '69 off the field and as he passed the Yale bench he raised his hands. We had won, 29–29. [The Crimson banner headline the following Monday said: HARVARD BEATS YALE, 29–29.]

Harvard for me will never be the same again as it was on that day. There will never be another team for me like that team. I may never go see another football game.

The Thrill of Defeat
BY BENNETT H. BEACH '71

November 13, 1969

Nowhere, at any time, has losing ever been quite so much fun — at least for me. Princeton was leading, 51–14. Rex Blankenship '72 and the inspired second team were diving deep in Tiger territory with 30 seconds left, and the Harvard Band was playing a mellow version of "Mickey Mouse." You just had to love it. Those of us left in section 35 were going wild. We had sat bored through the middle of the game, but now, in the last quarter, we were excited. We wanted Rex and his boys to score, and the sooner the better, so that Princeton could try for 57 points.

I've always appreciated being at Harvard, but never as much as I appreciated it Saturday, when I saw how much we could enjoy losing. Winning can be equally exciting, but it's boring in large quantities. I can sort of see them shaking their heads now at UCLA, Alabama, Michigan State, and other basics. They just wouldn't understand such irrational thoughts.

Shea Stadium fans would almost be able to empathize, but even they persisted in rooting for the Mets no matter how far they were behind. And I'm sure a winner like our vice president would scent Communism on the loose in section 35 and in other Harvard sections where Princeton had become the favorite. But it was nice to know that at Harvard, our happiness did not depend upon the success of the football team. It was similarly nice to know that the parties that night were not contingent upon a Crimson win.

We can certainly credit the band with helping us not to be blinded in our outlook. At one point they advised us, "Football isn't everything." Actually, that was shouted over to the Princeton side when we were behind, 45–7. Later, the band pointed out, "You may be winning, but you go to Princeton," which we all agreed was a wonderful observation.

But as I stood there singing the Mickey Mouse Club theme with visions of Annette dancing through my head, I thought of Tricia Nixon, wherever she was sitting. Was she, too, singing Mickey Mouse or was losing proving to be a bad experience for her? Perhaps she was accustomed to winning, and could it have been that she was at Harvard without her father's knowledge? She might have picked up some pretty dangerous thoughts around here. Yet she must still be safe, for I hear she gave a crewel embroidery of the Harvard seal to her date after he got into graduate school here. So I stopped worrying about Tricia.

And I started yelling again for more action on the field. The heroics, or whatever, of Rex were sort of filling a hole in my life, for I had not the misfortune to leave last year's Yale game five minutes before its completion. So Blankenship was fulfilling the Frank Champi role, and Denis Sullivan '72 was Pete Varney. Six seconds were left, and the tension was unbearable. Interference had just been called in the end zone, and we had new life. A buck into the line failed, but as the clock ticked on Blankenship refused to fold, and got the final touchdown with four seconds left. Princeton was fired up, and it was able to block the point after.

I was a bit shocked, to say the least, by Yovicsin's post-touchdown strategy. The situation called for an onside kick so that we could get the ball back and score in the final second. But Billy Kelly stayed on the bench and Richard Szaro '71 kicked a regular old kickoff and it ended. Yovicsin, though clearly disappointed, seemed to be taking it in stride after the game. "I have a lot of fun coaching," he said.

CABBAGES AND KINGMAN

The Greening of Yale

November 21, 1970

The game ended abruptly as the ball was pushed over a locked fence, and Mr. Capiello, with older campus policemen, quickly deflated it and drove it away in a pick-up truck.

"Pigs! Pigs! Pigs!" the students shouted benignly. "Free the bladderball!"

— the revolution at Yale, as captured in *The New York Times*, November 2, 1970

Cheap vituperation and petty chauvinism are rarely more appropriate than on Harvard-Yale weekend. Traditionally, most of it comes from the other side. We could laugh off their peculiar taunts of "Yale Reject!," knowing the opposite to be almost exclusively the case. Down in New Haven, one could assume they had nothing better to do than buy blue and white scarves (the Official Yale Scarf, incidentally, is manufactured in Harvard Square), carve their initials into the tables down at Mory's, and import girls for football weekends. Harvard was more worldly than that, initiating academic, political and social trends which Yale could only sniff at or copy (or both).

Suddenly things are different. Yale now wears the bell-bottoms in the Ivy League family. Their president gets attacked by Spiro Agnew. Their Classics Professor Erich Segal writes a "novel" about Youth Romance Today ("Jen . . . what would you say if I told you . . . I think . . . I'm in love with you." "I would say . . . you were full of shit." The ellipses are his.) which clings moistly at the top of the best-seller lists, bringing *lumpen* to the throats of the proletariat (because, a baker's daughter *can* marry a banker's son, even if she dies forthwith) while Harvard classicists are still back in the Middle Ages translating Greek. Then there's Yale Law Professor Charles A. Reich (all of whose students, the *Times* exclaims, call him "Charley"), who reports in his book, *The Greening of America* (currently churning off the Random House presses at a rate of 15,000 per week), that the machinery of Corporate America is destroying itself and that we should all await with him the inevitable emergence — like grass through the cracks in the sidewalk — of a new Consciousness of love, blue jeans and rock music, a Consciousness III. Says the *Times*: "Youth culture has gotten its very own Norman Vincent Peale." They were not referring to William Sloan Coffin, Yale's famous Radical Chaplain.

(Have you noticed this *Times* obsession with Yale of late? Their second front page talks of little else. I've read that Yale has girls now. They even live in the same dormitories, though in different entryways. There aren't very many, but as Kingman Brewster so aptly put it, Yale has a responsibility to produce "100 male leaders" every year. What with Consciousness III around the corner and Yale so hip, I guess they figure this is as good a time as any to begin attempting to fulfill that responsibility. Yale Admissions Director Inslee Clark — students call him Inky! — said Yale was going co-ed to improve the education of her men. I've also read in *The Times* that many Yale students are against the war in Vietnam and some are even working for liberal senators. Obviously *The Times* knows where it's at.)

The cynical here might take comfort in the knowledge that both Segal and Brewster were educated at Harvard, and that most of Reich's analysis is really Galbraith without the economics (a concept, admittedly, some might find as ludicrous as Galbraith without the modesty). They can snort to each other — and rightly so — that each Brewster speech, each Segal movie, each Reich pronouncement, each flattering Israel Shenker *Times* profile is a triumph of style over content, content still residing exclusively somewhere north of the Charles. But it's a triumph nonetheless. And can we ignore it? More than we suspect. Harvard's future may be truly affected by the greening of Yale.

For one thing, there's the presidency. Last spring, I asked Brewster for an interview for The Crimson. He protested shyly that "what with Harvard looking around for a new president, perhaps it's not the best time for *my* name to be splashed all over The Crimson." But like it or not, Brewster's name had been mentioned (if not splashed) practically everywhere else. With the possible exception of S. I. Hayakawa, he is the best-known college president in America. With dozens of colleges looking for male leaders, his national reputation has followed three of the four steps traditionally ascribed to the rise and fall of a movie star: I. "Who's Kingman Brewster?" II. "Get me Kingman Brewster." III. "Get me a Kingman Brewster type." IV. "Who's Kingman Brewster?" A Kingman Brewster type can be all things to all people. Most important, to alumni, he will keep things quiet. At a dinner last month the directors of the Associated Harvard Alumni — slavering in anticipation — asked student politicos from Faculty Committees, "Would Harvard students fall for a Kingman Brewster?"

Would they? Would Harvard students be taken in by a grinning hypocrite who came glad-handing his way down to Lowell House to pacify the natives whenever they got restless? Some of Brewster's stunts seem so obvious as to insult the intelligence even of Yale. A year ago, for example, Brewster spoke in front of the Yale Political Union, an apolitical student forum, and gained national publicity for his proposal that any Yale president's term be "reviewed" by the Yale Corporation every seven years. Whatever that meant — since no president has tenure and can be fired at any time — Brewster's first seven years just happened to be coming to a close and to no one's surprise he was allowed — nay, *encouraged* — to remain at his post. In that same speech, however, he dismissed unilaterally the growing pressure for student representation in university decisions. Students don't want power, Brewster revealed, they really want *responsiveness* (whatever that meant) from the administration. And he planned to supply them with all the responsiveness they could eat. Do Yale students want responsiveness? "Yes!" editorialized *The Yalie Daily*. Responsiveness is exactly what we want!

Sometimes they got responsiveness beyond their wildest dreams, most notably last May. Students announced a strike against Yale in support of the Black Panthers who were on trial in New Haven. Brewster announced he supported the strike. Or did he? At any rate, he didn't mind in the least if students and faculty members skipped classes. And Yale would supply food and lodging to all those coming down to support the Panthers. He never said, of course, that *he* supported the Panthers. He never said he didn't, either. He did say he doubted the ability of black revolutionaries to receive a fair trial anywhere in the United States. Whatever that means.

A little revolution can be a dangerous thing. Especially when it comes without cost. An elegant critique of the American Corporate State means little if you follow it up by saying that everything will be okay because, "No one can take himself altogether seriously in bell-bottoms." And moral outrage — however correct — summoned up upon convenience for its publicity value produces atrocities like the U.S. government's current prosecution of the son of a blue-collar family for murdering civilians in Vietnam.

So team, when you get out there on the field today, look straight through the purple shades and into the eyes of that Yale fullback in the paisley helmet. Think of him and Erich Segal and good ol' Charley Reich tossing flowers at each other in the Pierson College dining hall as Kingman Brewster broadcasts the Fugs out of his office window. Think of jean-and-workshirt-bedecked Yalies pouring out of Skull and Bones to spend their GM dividend checks on grass and antiwar ads in *The New York Times*. And win this one for Consciousness II.

— Michael E. Kinsley '72

The Non-Rivalry Rivalry

BY JOHN L. POWERS '70

June 5, 1972

Gentlemen, you are about to play football for Yale against Harvard. Never in your lives will you ever do anything as important.

— T. A. D. Jones, Yale football coach, circa 1920

Harvard is the only place people at Yale — from the administration to the players — are ever concerned with. I can't for the life of me figure out what's so great about it.

— Carmen Cozza, Yale football coach, 1970

It would appear that there has been a reshuffling of priorities around New Haven during the last half century. In the old days, for God's sake, no man ever had to sit down and figure out why there was a rivalry between Harvard and Yale. He felt it, right in his gut, in every fiber of his being. It was an instinctive thing.

So now it has come to this. Carmen Cozza, a man whom Delaney Kiphuth deemed fit to sit on the right hand of Jones, Walter Camp and Jordan Olivar in Yale football heaven, can't for the life of him figure out what's so great about Harvard. Ted Coy, Chub Peabody, I hope you're not listening.

The bloody cheek of it all! Next he'll be asking what's so big about the Big Three!

Actually, Cozza is not the only one who has been trying to figure out the reason for the sanctity of the Harvard-Yale rivalry.

A week from Saturday, nine men from Yale will row quietly to the starting line on the Thames River in New London. If all goes as it has for the past nine years, they will hand over their sweat-soaked shirts to their Harvard counterparts 20 minutes later, and ask themselves the same question. Why?

Why do the Harvard swimmers look forward to the Yale race, a meet they've won once since 1938?

Why does the Yale squash team consider it a moral victory if it takes home even one point in the Harvard match?

Why do the Yale track and cross-country runners lace on their Adidas year after year, just to follow Bill McCurdy's men to the finish line?

Actually, the Yale runners don't always. Last week, they decided that it wasn't worth their time to come to Cambridge after exams and race Harvard, even though it was their best chance to win the annual meet since 1968.

And therein lies the key to the whole attitude that was hinted at in Cozza's statement. How can a rivalry continue that in most cases is so one-sided, no matter how much gut feeling there was to begin with?

Of course, when it finally does happen, when the Yale crew, any Yale crew, beats Harvard, when the Crimson finally edges Yale in golf, it is a moment to remember. But is it worth coming to the Yale swimming meet for 34 consecutive years just to see Harvard win once? Probably not.

That's why the observation train was discontinued at New London. That's why they'll be giving away the Regatta program a week from Saturday. The same interest isn't there anymore, even among alumni. How many Yalies want to watch their varsity boat get hit with a wet mop nine straight times? How many Harvard graduates are sadistic enough to pay $9 a shot to watch it, either? Not enough, obviously.

And not only is the equality of competition dying: a lot of the sportsmanship has disappeared, too. After the hockey game at New Haven last February, Harvard coach Bill Cleary wouldn't allow his players to shake hands with their Yale opponents because he feared another outbreak of the fighting that had marred the entire contest.

A week later, in Boston, both benches emptied during a late-game brawl. More than 100 minutes of penalties were assessed in both matches.

And last fall, two Harvard freshmen left the Yale football game because of facial injuries caused by punches. Not exactly what T. A. D. Jones or Percy Haughton had in mind. The old spirit seems to have vanished. Maybe it's true what they say at New Haven: "The alumni would rather beat Harvard, the coaches would rather beat Dartmouth, and the players would rather beat Princeton."

CHAPTER 6

The Mail

THE CRIMSON has received too many letters from too many strange, irate, urbane, or clever readers to let them go by. The following is just a small sampling of what the files contain. Only the infamous "Drunken Legion" letters need some explaining, as you will see.

*   *   *

A Protest

April 23, 1875

To the Editors of The Magenta:

Gentlemen, — I trust you will give room in your columns to a few words in the interest of aesthetics, which would probably be excluded by the prejudices of a less enlightened periodical. My subject arises from the murders which have been committed recently in this neighborhood, and as I have already used the word "aesthetics" in regard to it, it is therefore needless to say that I am a disciple of [Thomas] De Quincey [who wrote *On Murder as One of the Fine Arts* (1847)]. I lay no claim to originality; my sole ambition is to raise a warning voice in defense of that art which derives its dignity, nay, its very birth, from my great master. Surely you will sympathize with me in this protest; you must agree with me that the fine art of murder was never more coarsely, more wantonly, more clumsily practiced than now. Other times have been unfortunate, some in the conception, some in the execution, of murderous designs; it would seem to have been reserved for this age to be thoroughly bad both in conception and execution. The causes of this lamentable degeneracy lie deep, and therefore should be all the more objects of solicitude to the artist. Murder, like architecture, like painting, and like poetry, is simply the expression of national feeling, colored by the peculiarities of the individual. Murder among the Greeks was, like the Parthenon and the *Iliad*, simple, objective, severe in style, regular, and graceful. So the highest forms of murder to be found in Teutonic nations resemble the Gothic architecture and the poetry of Shakespeare in their wilder style, their higher emotion, their deep and solemn mystery. Coming to our own time, is it surprising that our architecture, our painting, our poetry, our murders, all betray a miserable want of purpose, of sincerity, of well-trained effort?

At left: "Latin Si, Pusey No!" Students protesting Pusey's change of Harvard diplomas, from Latin to English. See page 81 and, in this chapter, "Ad Praesidem Harvardianae Dedicatur." April 28, 1961. (Illustration by Robert R. Copaken '61)

The age is shifting, unsettled, and insincere; can we expect that its art should not be so too? Men of today are confused by the magnitude and the number of the questions which Religion, Science, Literature, and Philosophy put to them so sharply and so remorselessly. Is it strange, then, that they are without convictions and therefore fail in art? . . .

. . . Gentlemen of The Magenta, you must grant me another audience at some future time; at present I will only add that I have on hand two finished designs, which I shall be happy to communicate to any worthy person. The first is for the killing of a venerable gentleman, high in position, universally respected and disliked. The other has in view the murder of a flute player. The first is, I fear (like Dickens's caricature of Leigh Hunt), somewhat disfigured by vindictiveness and personal feeling; the second, I make bold to say, is a very dainty piece of work.

H.C.M.

Our Pet Beast

November 14, 1922

To the Editors of The Crimson:

"Yearling," The Crimson's pet word for "Freshman," is defined by Stormonth as "a beast in the second year of its age."

LeBaron Russell Briggs
Professor of Creative Writing

Don't Forget the Players!

December 1, 1930

To the Editors of The Crimson:

I wish to express publicly my admiration for the woman who went out on the football field in the Yale-Harvard game Saturday and rescued the squirrel and one other animal let loose by some misguided person. I hope collegiate public opinion will condemn the letting loose of dumb animals on the field. This is the second instance I have witnessed of a dumb animal on the field.

This woman had courage and a kind heart.

Henry H. Wells, Yale '00

In the late twenties and early thirties The Crimson, consciously attempting to imitate The Times *(on both sides of the Atlantic), usually carried three types of editorials common to those august publications: "Ed 1" on local (Harvard) issues, "Ed 2" on "the rest of the universe, in a grave, instructive tone," as one contemporary put it, and "Ed 3," in a humorous vein. One day in October 1930 the editorial column ran a couple of routine Ed 1's — one on overemphasis upon football and another on the elective system — and sandwiched in between, a short, five-inch Ed 2 on the American Legion's convention stay in Boston.*

Editors didn't think much of the editorial at the time. But it was probably a bit too grave and instructive for the Legion and its boosters; for the editorial sparked off a heated debate in the letters column. In fact, more letters were received on this one issue than on any other in the first 75 years of The Crimson's history. Even the Alumni Bulletin *commented on the affair in its editorial columns.*

The subject quickly became Ed 1 material, with The Crimson itself providing the Harvard focus. The rest is self-explanatory.

Letters on the Legion
"We May Be Personally Defeated,
But Our Principles Never"

To the Editors of The Crimson:

I wish to be counted among those who stand with unqualified approval behind the editorial position of The Crimson in relation to the conduct of the American Legion during their week of convention in Boston. That The Crimson should be the only publication to break the conspiracy of silence on the part of local journals must be a cause of satisfaction to a multitude of Harvard men. The simple speaking of truth about the existing state of anarchy during the Legion week was an act of courage under the circumstances, and upholds the best tradition of Massachusetts. That the truth should be unpalatable to the class of critics who would attempt to muzzle the press is, of course, what might have been expected and quite in the natural order of events.

With a sense of grateful appreciation to the individual editors who possessed the journalistic instinct and fearlessness to deal with the disgraceful facts of this occasion as they deserved, I am

William Lloyd Garrison Jr.
Class of 1897   Boston

Listen to Reason

To the Editors of The Crimson:

So! The Harvard Crimson did call the American Legion Convention a "wholesale brawl etc." Well! "deah!" me! Let's give three long rahs for Harvard and The Crimson only don't make them too loud, it might annoy the "deah" old "Harvard Ladies"!! Of course, the scenes of disorder were caused by Cambridge and Boston hoodlums, amongst whom were probably some students, too young to have been "over there" in 1918, and who wouldn't have been there if they could have, but anyway do you "deah old things" really think the Legion (900,000 MEN NOT children) care what The Crimson thinks?

A. P. Knapp, Legionnaire
Washington, D.C.

Light Horse Harry!

To the Editors of The Crimson:

If they do put you in jail, you know the truth will make you free. LONG LIVE THE CRIMSON!

Henry Lee '02
Valparaiso, Ind.

FDR Asks Leadership by Press

The President's Message to The Crimson for its Seventieth Anniversary Issue Was Delayed Two Weeks by His Absence From Washington

February 8, 1942

The observance of noteworthy anniversaries can play a valuable part in our thought and action. The year 1873, which saw the establishment of The Harvard Crimson, carries the mind back to the early days of Dr. Eliot's long and notable administration and brings it forward, decade by decade, through all the changes in the life of Harvard which seventy eventful years have witnessed.

As an old Crimson man I am sure that I shall be pardoned a personal word — and I am sure, also, that I voice the sentiments of all that company of happy men when I say that none of them would exchange his Crimson training for any other experience or association in college days.

An examination of the files of The Crimson would be interesting to the extent that such a study would reveal whether the paper had run with the herd or been in the forefront in the formulation of campus opinion. My message for the seventieth anniversary is that The Crimson always should lead in the expression of honest opinion.

Very sincerely yours,
(signed) Franklin D. Roosevelt '04

An Instructor Responds to the Confidential Guide

Freshman Issue, September 1946

To the Editors of The Crimson:

It will not come to you as a surprise to be told that your *Confidential Guide* is no more confidential than you intended it to be. We teachers have the morbid curiosity the flesh is heir to. By now you may be sure your pamphlet has driven its little wedge into the brain.

If you had labeled my performance "scintillating," or "nervously exciting," or "intrepid," I could write to you without misgiving. But you have blasted me with "dull." Already I see next fall's "dull" and "truculent" blotting the page.

Dear friends, have you considered the consequence of your epithet? How can I explain it to my wife? "But dear, The Crimson called you dull." How can I explain it to my children? "Daddy, The Crimson called you dull." How can I explain it to my literary executors? "The painful fact is that, in spite of his eminence, The Harvard Crimson called him dull."

And suppose I were not married: "Oh, sir. No, sir. The Crimson called you dull."

My humiliation would be less if you had spared the scrap of respect you could so easily have spared. I have just reckoned that in the past year I have corrected papers for 225 students. Was there really not one who said, "Well, not exactly dull . . . that is . . ."? Or didn't you leave a single one unpolled, so that in your largeness of heart you could have made clear the partiality of your judgment? Think how different the impression if you had given the statistics: Glazier, 225 students: polled, 224 — dull. Then I could always have said, "Ah, but if they had inquired of Heartbalm, the result would have been different."

In short, sirs, I suspect you are a fraud.

Lyle Glazier
Instructor in English

In a special interview yesterday, Heartbalm was quoted as saying: "Well, not exactly dull — that is . . . but." — Ed.

Denies Rape Charge

March 2, 1951

To the Editors of The Crimson:

I am hurriedly writing to you with reference to the last sentence of the caption appearing beneath your rehearsal photo of *Dark of the Moon*. The sentence reads, "In the scene preceding the one above, Miss Northrup is raped on stage."

Let me hasten to assure the family and friends of Miss Northrup that (to the best of our knowledge) her chastity shall be when the play has run its final performance as it was before rehearsals began.

To be sure, in the scene to which you refer, Barbara Allen (played by Miss Northrup) does find herself in a rather compromising position. However, if technical arrangements proceed as they should, the climax shall be left to the imagination of the audience.

Warren Brody '52
President Harvard Dramatic Club

Circling the Trays

March 21, 1951

To the Editors of The Crimson:

The long-awaited circular tray has at last arrived in the House dining halls. Unfortunately, it is utterly inadequate for several reasons.

1. The three sizes of compartment around the center make it necessary to plan out ahead all the items desired so that the right size can be tendered for each, and the proper foods placed adjacent one another to minimize the number of rotations during the eating process.

2. The compartments are too shallow. My salad was placed in one compartment and ended up in three. The potato spewed over into the central milk-glass division, and the gravy required a skilled juggling act to keep it from flowing over the side. Also there was insufficient height in the ridges to aid in getting the last mouthfuls of applesauce on the spoon (the same will certainly hold true for peas, stewed tomatoes, etc.).

3. The tray spins like a Lazy Susan, particularly when one tries to cut "tenderized" steak (a hard enough job on the old trays), and the gravy then assails the knife-wielder and occasionally his neighbors.

4. It is difficult to pick up the tray, since there is no border or space to wedge the fingers between the tray and the table.

5. The color is not harmonious with the interiors of the dining halls, and the circular shape fights with the predominantly rectangular character of the halls and their furnishings (not to mention Leverett's trapeziform phenomenon).

6. I fear, furthermore, that the new tray may also serve in intramural "flying saucer" experiments, and perhaps even in postprandial roulette games.

In an age when "Functionalism!" is the war cry, the circular tray has certainly fallen early on the battlefield. Let us give it a quick burial.

Caldwell Titcomb '47

Vintage Critic

February 11, 1952

To the Editors of The Crimson:

In your article on Rene Peroy, Harvard's fencing coach, the statement appears, "Peroy in action is proof that a fencer, like a good bottle of Moselle, can improve with age." This careless simile should not go uncorrected. Any member of the Tastevin can tell you that a good bottle of Moselle will only improve with a little age, say up to five or six years at most. There may be rare exceptions, when a Moselle has been found to improve in bottle for as many as 15 or 20 years, but this is strictly the limit, and cannot be compared to the improvement and age of M. Peroy. Most connoisseurs would open their Moselles before three years. Andre Simon believes that the best Moselle is a very young Moselle; Maurice Healey, following Professor Saintsbury, will drink a four-year Moselle, but none older. It is possible that the writer of your article was thinking of a Hock, or Rhine wine, grown somewhat to the east of the Moselles, which does have a somewhat greater staying power; but it must be remembered that no white wine, not even a Montrachet, can really be said to improve with age. It is only the great red wines that do this.

Harvey A. Leve 3L

The Grapes of Wrath

February 20, 1952

To the Editors of The Crimson:

It was not without considerable interest that I read Mr. Leve's recent letter to you regarding Moselle and other wines. Leve is a man of well-known connoisseurship and erudition, and I venture to suggest that he could not possibly have made some of the sweeping assertions therein attributed to him. It is difficult for me to conceive, much less believe, that a man of his caliber would willingly lend his name to such troglodytic and heretical statements as "no white wine . . . can really be said to improve with age," and "most connoisseurs would open their Moselles before three years." I feel sure Professor Saintsbury has been mis-cited; such statements might not be strictly untrue as generalizations, but most members of the Tastevin would agree that they are gross over-simplifications. Why, it is like saying that all wines of the Medoc have intellectual bouquets — a statement that totally ignores the near bluffness of the Brainaire Ducru and the sincerity of the Pichon Longueville (doubtless due to its being a Pauillac). But to return to the Moselles: I have but recently enjoyed, in company with Mr. Leve, an Auslese Berncastler Doktor, a prince among Moselles, that was 17 years old and still displayed its fine breeding and sprightly elegance; and few indeed are they who would deny that the 1921 Piesporter Goldtropfchen was brilliant as late as 1939. As for the author's patronizing dismissal of Montrachet, I will restrain myself from protracted disputation, except to ask if he has had the good fortune in recent years to have tasted the 1908 vintage, which I daresay he would concede a wine of truly celestial delicacy. Nonetheless, I should like in conclusion to commend the author, whoever he may be, for bringing these matters to the public forum, since it is only by discussion that tolerance and truth can be achieved in these matters.

T. B. Lemann '49

Through Wind and Rain . . .

May 5, 1955

To the Editors of The Crimson:

Mr. William W. Bartley III, in his story on "Communism at Harvard" in The Crimson of April 22, 1955, said a letter addressed simply "Kremlin-on-the-Charles, Cambridge 38, Mass." was delivered without question to Eliot House by the United States Post Office.

This letter was not delivered by the Post Office to Eliot House or to any other place at Harvard University, but was endorsed "not found" and returned to the sender . . .

Louis F. Geiffrion
Postman in Harvard Yard

Flown the Coop

May 8, 1956

To the Editors of The Crimson:

Perhaps the least prominent of our Bow Street headquarters' many splendid accoutrements is a bird which surveys all the hearty fun both within and without.

We do not wish to suggest that we have become laconic since its lamentable disappearance early Saturday morning, for we are steadfast in our belief that we are the oldest college comics in America. But it has, you see, taken just a bit of the edge off our carefree spirits.

Spring seems to return every spring, and our Ibis has been known to fly away to New York and almost Moscow and even other places at this time of year. There were House parties last weekend, and we were all away from home at a House party, and hence unable to be sure that it wouldn't do so again this season.

We have appealed to the ASPCA and allied groups for assistance, but so far our search has been utterly fruitless. May I ask through the medium of your columns that everyone be on the watch-out for our lost brother. He is generally corroded and has feathers. Our phone number is EL4-8445.

Howard Corni '57
President, *Harvard Lampoon*

La Danse Macabre

September 28, 1956

To the Editors of The Crimson:

This is to thank whom it may concern for the H-R Mixer. I enjoyed it immensely and love all Harvard men dearly — especially the drunken football player who thickly asks you "Ain't they got no rock and roll in this here town?"; the prep school boy who arrives with more money than manners and will no doubt leave with more of the former and even less of the latter; the Big Man from Texas who tells you how to remember his name by shortening it to A. Wolf, and then with a great little gleam in his eye, continues the impression by drawling, "Where I come from a guy's a guy and a girl's a girl — "; the typical Ivy League character who came to Harvard to raise hell even as his grandfather Cabot before him; the intellectual who studies you as you dance and looks as if he eats T. S. Eliot for breakfast and makes you feel some odd sensation akin to indigestion in your intellectual stomach simply because you've been eating lollipops all your life. The evening is made complete by a junior from MIT who climbed in the window and is — sad to say — NORMAL. I mean of course, IN COMPARISON.

I thank you for the Mixer. It was lovely. I regret to say, however, I felt like an olive in a cocktail shaker. I am, in fact, thoroughly "shook up" and will probably hate all men for the rest of my life and get a complex on top of it all. Thank you again.

A Prospective Old Maid '60

Ad Praesidem Harvardianae Dedicatur

May 4, 1961

To the Editors of The Crimson:

He banished himself from the pedagogues' graces
By using, they said, inappropriate cases.

He gave to instructors abiding offense
With what they averred was contemptible tense.

As one, they declared he was bound to encumber
All of his syntax with errors in number.

They scornfully called him an arrant offender
For always ascribing inaccurate gender.

Aghast at his singular usage of "ut,"
They ribaldly made of him ridicule's butt.

And never their irony suffered abatement
As vainly he juggled the indirect statement.

His genitive style, which he sullied with "quod,"
Made 'em recoil as they would from a goad.

Their opinion of him was extremely deflative
Whenever they viewed his disdain for the dative.

None of them ever would take any stock
In his curious ways with the voc. and the loc.

Often, in flouting his wayward accusative,
Some of them got to be downright abusive.

From classical halls he was given the boot
For making the ablative too absolute.

His critics' avowals were hyperemphatic
That ever his Latin continued erratic.

They naturally knew there was no avail
In dispatching such a dunce to Yale.

So at last they gave him a demi-diploma,
But not, you bet, in the Language of Roma.

E. DuPont Lamont III

Another Philosopher King?

November 13, 1961

To the Editors of The Crimson:

Each morning I get out of bed,
And thank the Lord I am not dead,
Then, turning to The Crimson's letters,
(Words of wisdom from my betters),
I find a newly dreamed up theory,
Of why the world must be so dreary.
The reason is not the lower classes,
But the yelling, screaming Harvard masses.

I only regret that I have but five minutes in which to read
The Crimson but the rest of the time is occupied in studying,
sleeping or working on my bomb shelter. Harvard students
seem to have such a talent for knowing what will happen in
the next few years that it is a shame not to be able to read all
their theories. They are so, so cute!!!

Marx says that socialism will ultimately prevail if history
takes its course. Why should Russia make man begin again
when he has passed so far along the turbulent road to socialism? I cannot picture X and Y fighting. Nor do I know of a so-

ciety destroying itself intentionally. Wherein lies the advantage of a nuclear holocaust? Most people want peace . . . yet there is always the possibility of a fanatic touching off a nuclear war (for that matter the new health services building might dissolve in the next rain storm . . . or even become an efficient medical center) and this uncertainty is what makes life interesting. Who wants to live assured of the future?

Think how dull life would be if there were no possibility of nuclear war. No funny articles in The Crimson. No bomb shelters to build. No Civil Defense practices in the middle of Haydn's fifth concerto. Why, we'd have to return to the outer space scares, or perhaps invent something new.

As Ezra N. Suleim says, we should have "no illusions as to our predicament." But that predicament is not one of definite nuclear war, nor of limited conventional war. It is a predicament of uncertainty as to what will happen. Why do we insist upon bomb scares . . . all we do is increase the tension and stubbornness in the world. Unwillingness to compromise is the one thing which will lead us into war.

"For sooth, Alcibiades, the Philosopher King has come. Which one, you say? How should I know? There are so many." The only thing proponents of nuclear war have in common is a fear that the atomic bomb will become obsolete and so they give it good press as the quickest way to salvation. I suppose their ultimate goal is to have it included in the Lord's Prayer.

To believe in nuclear holocaust is pessimistic; to believe in conventional warfare or peace, optimistic; to say what will happen, stupidity.

Perez C. Ehrich '64

Limes and Lemons*

March 20, 1963

To the Editors of The Crimson:
  Re: Radcliffe
  What about the lemons?

James DeW. Perry '63
Jefferson Hill '63
John Payne '63

* See in Chapter 8: "The Three Flavors of Radcliffe."

Galbraith on Parietals

November 2, 1963

To the Editors of The Crimson:

I can't tell you how depressing it is to find Harvard having another discussion of these so-called parietal rules. For forty years, undergraduates with a special talent for banal controversy, and no doubt a secondary interest in sex, have known that this subject could be counted on to arouse a certain frustrated maternalism which lurks, however unhappily, in the interstices of any academic administration. The resulting debate has invariably combined exceptional dreariness with a crushing misinterpretation of the nature of a university.

The responsibility of the University to its students is to provide the best teaching that can be associated with the scientific, literary, artistic or other scholarly preoccupations of the faculty. Additionally, it provides libraries, laboratories and, though less indispensably, places of residence. Once when Harvard College was in part a privileged academy for the socially visible, it needed to assure parents that their more retarded offspring would have the supervision of men of the scoutmaster type who, however ineffectually, would try to protect them from the natural penalties of indolence, alcohol or lust. Otherwise needed and prestigious clients would be committed to other institutions. All this, happily, is now over. Thousands of men and women clamor for admission for the serious purposes of the University. It can be part of our bargain that they look after themselves.

Accordingly, rules need only reflect the special requirements of the academic community — the quiet, good order and opportunity for undisturbed sleep that facilitate reflection and study. No effort need be made or should be made to protect individuals from the consequences of their own errors, indiscretions or passion. Parents of Harvard and Radcliffe applicants who feel their children need a more protective environment should, no doubt, be put firmly on notice so that they may send them elsewhere.

It is clear that from among those who accept this bargain we will have all the students we can accommodate and presumably they will be more mature. We will need waste no energy or money in providing the surrogates of parenthood beyond the appointed time. There will be misfortunes but it will be recognized that these are inherent in personality and not the result of failure of efforts to control it. Our deans will be able to turn gratefully to the more welcome tasks of teaching and scholarship. Above all, no moral or biological issue being involved, we will be spared, praise God, any further discussion of these rules. Those who (one hopes on the basis of some special competence) are fascinated by the question of whether undergraduates are improved or damaged by fornication can organize private discussion groups or, if married, talk about it with their wives.

John Kenneth Galbraith
Paul M. Warburg Professor of Economics

War Opposition Congratulated

January 30, 1967

To the Editors of The Crimson:

May I, an old soldier and veteran of both World Wars, now retired, use a small amount of your space to congratulate the student leaders of the colleges and universities in your area for their active and open opposition to the Johnson administration war against the Vietnamese people. This is a brutal, cruel and disgraceful war the Executive Branch of the U.S. government is fighting halfway around the world.

Naturally, I cannot advise any young man to refuse to serve when drafted, because I cannot serve his sentence for him if and when convicted for refusing to serve. But I can, and each of us can, oppose the military draft and use all possible legal powers to have the draft abolished instead of revised as is currently proposed.

The security of the people of the United States is in no manner whatever endangered by the peasant people of Vietnam. The Johnson administration can arrange a cease-fire any day it chooses to accept the terms of the 1954 Geneva Agreement. If President Johnson would do this, he would raise the prestige of this nation and his own to the highest point in history.

Hugh B. Hester
Brigadier General U.S. Army (Ret.)

(The writer served in the U.S. Regular Army for more than 30 years. He served in WWI as a combat officer and was decorated by the French and U.S. governments for gallantry in action. As a staff officer in WWII, he was awarded the U.S. Distinguished Service Medal and the French Legion of Honor for this service.— Ed.)

Help Needed

March 4, 1969
[One month before the occupation of University Hall]

To the Editors of The Crimson:

For a research paper this term in high school, I am writing on the student demonstrations and I would appreciate it very much if you or your readers could give me some information.

Why hasn't Harvard had any publicized demonstrations? Are the problems being solved in other ways? If so, how? What was the reaction on campus to the riots [against ROTC] at Columbia and San Francisco State? Will there be more demonstrations in the future? How good, how sound is the present-day educational system?

Please feel free to write anything you like: these questions are just for suggestions. If you can refer me to someone else who is more involved I would appreciate it. Thank you so much.

Best of luck on the rest of the year!

Debbie Stranges
Owings Mills, Maryland

CHAPTER 7

Arts and Criticism

WHEN THE CRIMSON first began as the fortnightly Magenta it was essentially a small, writerly magazine containing some news and many essays, stories, and poems. Few of these earliest contributions are worth preserving for their literary merits. Despite its more literary orientation, the early Crimson rarely gave much attention to the arts either at Harvard or in Boston. While new books and dramatic productions would run in notice columns, literary and dramatic critiques, as The Crimson's fiftieth-anniversary history points out, "were destined to have checkered careers."

When The Crimson went to a daily format in 1883 the emphasis was placed on news and still fewer articles on the arts would appear. Then, in 1885 a new monthly supplement was published "to be filled with matter furnished by the English instructors, taken from the best themes and specimens of composition done in the regular College work." Here finally was an outlet for writers on the arts, at least for a few years.

In the fall of 1904 The Crimson began running an irregular, fortnightly column on "books by Harvard Men," with capsule reviews. The emphasis in the column was placed more on *who* wrote than on *what* was written. Despite the chauvinism — or because of it — the columns still make for interesting reading. For instance, in one column of February 23, 1905, there were reviews of books by President Eliot, George Lyman Kittredge, LeBaron Russell Briggs, William James Rolfe, and Josiah Royce.

On October 10, 1911, there appeared in the paper what was to be the first serious attempt to cover the arts: a weekly column of reviews of "New Plays in Boston." Previously there had been only a small notice column listing plays shown "At the Theatres." The new column got off to an auspicious start, with reviews of plays by William Butler Yeats's Irish Players including Synge's *The Playboy of the Western World*, on the American stage for the first time. The theater column faded out as a regular feature within a few years.

Although the arts received light treatment in The Crimson during its first 50 years, a few highlights of Harvard arts still stand out in the paper's files. In May 1881, for instance, some members of the University staged the first production of an ancient Greek play in this country: Sophocles's *Oedipus Tyrannus*. The first Latin play, at least at Harvard if not the country, was produced in 1894 — Terence's *Phormio*. The production of ancient drama at Harvard probably reached its peak in 1906, when very elaborate, year-long preparations led up to the presentation of Aeschylus's *Agamemnon*. The play was the first to be produced outdoors, in a stadium before a crowd of 3500, and included accurate reproductions of scenery, costumes, and stage accessories based on such scholarly sources as Greek vase paintings, the friezes of the Parthenon, and the Sarcophagus of Alexander at Constantinople.

In the field of letters two notable writers — Matthew Arnold and Henry James — were recorded as having presented lectures at Harvard. When Arnold came to Harvard in 1883, he appeared at the invitation of students, not the faculty. As The Crimson said of the "apostle of sweetness and light" at the time, "Few men with minds open to ideas have escaped the influence of Matthew Arnold . . . Few, especially, are the undergraduates who have not directly or indirectly felt his influence."

The tenor of The Crimson's book reviews, however, was more along the lines of one 1884 review of "Two Harvard Novelists" and this excerpt from a "Book Review" of 1887: "The Crimson board has received a very prettily-gotten-up copy of *Jack the Fisherman*, Miss Elizabeth Stuart Phelps' new story. Although it is a tale with a moral, it is one of the most powerful and interesting stories ever written . . . No story would be more sad and pathetic . . . the influence of a good woman . . . the effects of that terrible curse, rum . . ." etc., etc.

Of course reviews of the *Advocate* and *The Lampoon* appeared regularly, many times written by faculty members. But the reviews were usually workmanlike and rarely did they center on the writing. Considering the quality of college writing — at Harvard or anywhere else — it may have been wise not to concentrate on it too strongly. But such reviews lacked the notion that *Advocate* writers of today may become the nation's writers tomorrow. So, when The Crimson reviewed the *Advocate* of November 1909 much space was devoted to the question of the debating union and other University-wide issues the *Advocate* was then wont to address; this was followed by mention of the "pages of lighter tone"; and finally, almost as an afterthought, the reviewer says, "while the contributions of verse are from T. S. Eliot ['10] and C. P. Aiken ['11]." To be fair, later reviews singled out Eliot's poem "Spleen," saying "it might repay long study" (it doesn't) and praised Conrad Aiken for his "imagination" and "technique."

Crimson coverage of the arts did not make any advances until January 1920, when "The Crimson Bookshelf" appeared for the first time. The reviews went beyond the theretofore simple capsulizing and prettily gotten-up prose and began to consider books in terms of an American literary tradition that had something to say about American life. Commentaries that were thoughtful and engaging — if not brilliant and lucid — discussed such works as Sinclair Lewis's *Main Street* and F. Scott Fitzgerald's *This Side of Paradise* and *The Great Gatsby*. The Bookshelf was so successful that in November 1924 it was expanded to a monthly magazine supplement. Also appearing in 1920 was "The Crimson Playgoer." While their formats would change over the years, these two innovations marked the beginning of a continuing tradition at The Crimson of thoughtful and sometimes masterful essays on books and plays written for a highly literate and avid theatergoing audience.

As with so many other elements of Harvard, the arts at the University have collectively constituted a "world unto itself" right up to the present. The Fogg Art Museum, the Busch Reisinger, the Loeb Drama Center, and the various dramatic productions, concerts, exhibits, and publications sponsored by libraries, Houses, and independent student groups all represented a unique diversity of interests, but they had little impact outside the University community. The Crimson took notice of these activities in short stories on its news pages in its early history. It was not until the 1930s and 1940s that the paper would consider treating arts in the University in a more substantive manner, with full-length reviews. In the 1950s such treatment became a regular feature of the paper. Back in 1932, on the other hand, one assistant managing editor wrote that "the Bookshelf is properly high-class filler and should be available when there is room for it, rather than saved for a full page in one issue . . . I think it would be very foolish to make either the Playgoer or the Bookshelf a daily feature with space reserved for it."

Eventually these reviews *would* become more than just high-class fillers, as would music reviews, which represented some of the best arts writing of the 1940s. Among these music commentaries was a series by Martin Mayer '47 ('49) that lambasted Serge Koussevitzky and the Boston Symphony Orchestra.

In the 1950s, as The Crimson expanded in size, so did the arts coverage widen in scope and depth. Playwriting once again flourished at postwar Harvard, with student-written plays produced on campus. The Crimson took note of these plays as serious efforts by serious writers — a giant step from the earlier, cursory examinations of student writing. So, in March 1951 one can read Daniel Ellsberg '52 on plays by such noted writers as John Ashberry '49, Frank O'Hara '50, and Richard Eberhart (then a teacher at Harvard). Ellsberg wrote consistently on books and drama. While no single piece of his Crimson writing is extraordinary — all were very good — one excerpt seems important, in retrospect. Commenting on Jean Paul Sartre's novel *Troubled Sleep*, Ellsberg made special note of Sartre's intellectual characters and of their "failure to act — the vote they did not cast, the protest they did not speak . . ." The comment is revealing of the person who — no doubt struggling with his own failure to act — released the Pentagon Papers on the Vietnam War.

In addition to seriously reviewing Harvard arts the paper also continued to offer appraisals of movies, pre-Broadway productions in Boston theaters, exhibits at the Museum of Fine Arts, concerts by the Boston Symphony Orchestra, performances by dance and opera companies, and jazz and rock and roll concerts. With the exception of the pieces on jazz and rock, few of the reviews stand out today as landmark treatments of American culture. The reason for this might be that while long-standing art forms all had their well-known professional reviewers writing in standard review formats (which Crimson editors attempted to emulate), jazz and rock and roll were new phenomena that attracted livelier and more original kinds of writing.

Notices of "moving pictures" showing around Harvard appeared in The Crimson as early as the decade of the Great War. But reviews of "pictures" did not appear until the early 1930s. In the early 1940s "The Moviegoer" became a regular feature on page two. Film reviews in The Crimson of the fifties were generally of a high caliber. Although no single review can be said to have reflected outstanding writing, film reviewers were so well versed that they could give foreign films the recognition they deserved, with Truffaut's *400 Blows* and Resnais's *Hiroshima Mon Amour*, for example, receiving high praises. (The appearance of such reviews was as much a reflection of the Cambridge scene as it was a reflection of the editors' good judgment.)

The sixties marked the apotheosis of rock, which inspired most of the interesting writing on arts during that decade. All the other performing arts fell in submission to the Great God Rock, at least in The Crimson's pages. Near the end of the 1960s, however, film reviewing attracted an esprit de corps of Editorial Board writers, who, inspired by reviewers of the past, such as James Agee '32, and contemporary reviewers — Pauline Kael and Stanley Kaufmann — forged ahead with the newly recognized craft. Rock also never managed to completely displace drama from center stage, thanks to the literate reviews of Broadway and Stratford productions by Caldwell Titcomb '47, a traditional contributor to The Crimson's columns, and The Expert on the history of dramatic arts at Harvard.

In addition to its high seriousness, The Crimson also devoted review space to books and films about Harvard. It may be mistaken to say that reviews of Harvard books and movies constituted writing on the arts, but that was one area where Crimson writers shone. Harvard, after all, was The Crimson's turf, and editors who had hung out there for three or four years were well equipped to appraise the University as it was seen by writers, myth makers, and romance fakers.

A note on this chapter's format: many of the earlier articles require a bit of background, but from the 1950s on, the articles stand by themselves.

*   *   *

Charles Schulz predicts the 1959 choice for a new Radcliffe president: Snoopy. May 1959. (Copyright © 1958 United Feature Snydicate, Inc.).

In its earliest, more literary stages *The Crimson* regularly published poems, essays, and short stories. As contributions to American literature few of these efforts would rank very high. Still, some relatively famous writers and scholars were honing their skills in *The Crimson's* columns. Frederic Jessup Stimson, Class of *1876*, who became a lawyer and diplomat, also wrote many romances, among them the popular Guerndale (*1882*), which depicted the manners and mores of nineteenth-century Harvard. Barrett Wendell, Class of *1877*, went on to become a popular and highly respected professor of English at Harvard. William Roscoe Thayer, Class of *1881*, was a well-known writer and editor in his day, and was responsible for an award-winning biography of Theodore Roosevelt. *The Crimson* also produced a number of newspaper and magazine editors now long forgotten but influential in their own times.

Probably the only writer from the early Crimson days who is still remembered is Owen Wister, Class of *1882*, author of The Virginian (*1902*) and a lesser-known but very amusing tale of Harvard examsmanship, Philosophy 4 (*1903*). Wister's writings in *The Crimson* were confined mostly to poetry and a few wry jibes at Harvard's food and accommodations. The poems — with titles like "Adonis" and "Rondel" — were among the best to appear in *The Crimson*, but that's not saying much when one considers the High Victorian standards that then prevailed. Below is one of Wister's better poems; it should give readers a feeling for the often lofty literary pretensions and sentimental themes of early Crimson writing, which — it should be kept in mind — were not far different from the literary pretensions and themes of most contemporaneous American writers.

In the Title-Page of a Shakespeare

September 27, 1878

If thou dost read this book with but thine eye,
Seeing alone the printed pages turn
In dry succession, little shalt thou learn;

Save that it hath no lesson there for thee,
The thing unmeaning to thy mind will be;
If with thy heart and brain, then thou'lt discern
The flaming truths which in these pages burn,
Shedding a light on human history;
Read with thy heart and brain, then, read and know
The knowledge that one man had of mankind,
And thou'lt possess a precious gift indeed;
If thou canst not, — then do not try to read,
But fling the book unto the boisterous wind, —
'T will turn each page as well, when the light breezes blow.

o.w.
[Owen Wister, Class of 1882]

In the mid-1880s The Crimson would occasionally publish a supplement containing a collection of outstanding undergraduate essays. One of these supplements included an essay on free will by a junior, a young man who had come to Boston from Spain at the age of eight, gone to Boston Latin and inevitably to Harvard. This man would later write that "as an undergraduate at Harvard I was already alive to the fundamental questions, and even had a certain dialectical nimbleness, due to familiarity with the fine points of theology: the arguments for and against free will . . . were warm and clear in my mind."

The man's name is George Santayana, Class of 1886, philosopher and Harvard professor from 1889 to 1912. In addition to printing Santayana's exposition on free will, The Crimson published a simpler piece of prose, which displays the philosopher's equally nimble use of language.

King Lear as a Type of the Gothic Drama
A Junior Theme

March 26, 1885

King Lear may or may not be the greatest of Shakspere's [*sic*] plays, but of his great plays it is undoubtedly the most Shaksperian. For if we separate as much as is possible the qualities of Shakspere, and inquire by which of them he is most to be distinguished from other dramatists, I think we shall find it to be that gift of presenting a multitude of scenes and characters, a jumble of styles and incidents, within the limits of one connected drama. Other poets have written exquisite and sublime verse, others have known how to depict passion and unfold character: but no one else has given us these transverse sections of the world, where we see the prince and the beggar side by side, each thinking his own thoughts and speaking his own language; where we see the various intrigues and passions jostling one another as they hurry along the highway of life.

This wonderful spectacle is nowhere seen to more advantage than in *King Lear*. For here we have a central figure too great and awe-inspiring to be lost in the confusion of the scene. Lear's voice, whether in rage, madness, or contrition, is so powerful that all the whisperings and wranglings around him seem but its tumultuous echoes. The accompaniment of incidental action does not drown the voice of his supreme passion; and thus is avoided that fault which appears in some of Shakspere's historical plays, where the medley of sentiments and incidents is such that we are bewildered as by a rumbling and unintelligible noise. In the great tragedies, except *Lear*, this element, although constantly appearing as a living background for the principal figures, is kept distinctly subordinate: *Othello* is almost classic in its unity and continuity; *Macbeth*, although less compact, still turns on a single event; while *Hamlet* draws its variety and intricacy from the character of the hero, and not from any great admixture of foreign matter. But in *King Lear* we have two distinct plots and a large number of indispensable personages. It is noticeable, however, that there are no purely comic scenes in the play, — as if the poet felt that the subject was too harrowing to admit such episodes.

These peculiarities of *King Lear* have been thought to make it unfit for the stage. Lamb, in the midst of scathing remarks about one who had mutilated the plot and aspired to improve on Shakspere, asserts that *Lear* cannot be acted. Such a judgment may be regarded as a bolder impeachment of Shakspere than the mere alteration of a plot, since it condemns, not a part, but the whole, for the purpose for which it was written. For I take it that closet tragedies are not produced until authors get to be more in love with themselves than with nature. Undoubtedly it is hard to put *King Lear* on the stage; for it requires a great actor of the heroic school such as is seldom found out of Italy, and calls for an elaboration and perfection of detail which cannot be secured so long as the lavishness of the public does not equal its critical sense. But if it be said that the sublimity and complexity of *King Lear* render any representation of it necessarily inadequate, it follows that there is a fatal flaw and self-contradiction at the foundation of Shakspere's art. For if his living pictures cannot be made to move across the stage in all the telling truth of their contrast and variety, — Shakspere missed his vocation. He should have written poems or novels, not plays.

So great a paradox may well induce us to think better on this subject. Indeed, it seems to me that no play can gain more by being seen than such a play as *King Lear.* Who has ever realized, without the aid of the senses, all the horror and pathos of such a scene as that in which Lear speaks with Edgar and the fool? The majestic madness of the King, the bitter jests and incoherent ditties of the fool, the hideous gibberish of Edgar, each in its peculiar tone telling a story of great and unmerited woe, — what a marvelous harmony of discords! When we have seen this play, we do not, it is true, carry away a single definite impression, or a moral expressed in words; but we do feel in our hearts a dumb sense of the hideousness of wrong and of the sanctity of suffering: we feel the weight of the mysteries of this life, and we are made ready for high thoughts. For the office of the Gothic drama is not to give us merely the chiseled image of some heroic man agitated by one mighty passion, but rather to display the forces that are struggling in all men; to overawe us with the ghost of our own past and our own future, so that we may truly say: The world is passing in review!

— George Santayana, Class of 1886

A rather special treat came to Crimson readers in 1894 when Charles Eliot Norton furnished the paper with previously un-

*published fragments from the lectures of James Russell Lowell,
Class of 1838. These were published in six special supplements.
Lowell had been Smith Professor of the French and Spanish Languages and Professor of Belles Lettres from 1855 to 1872. Apparently neither his facility for languages nor his* Fable for
Critics *or the* Biglow Papers, *works for which we remember
Lowell, led to his appointment as Smith Professor; rather it was
precisely what has been presented in The Crimson — Lowell's
ability to give sweeping, image-filled lectures — which secured
him the position.*

*"A poetic, fanciful, eclectic garnerer in the field of letters,"
wrote Samuel Eliot Morison '08 of Lowell, he had "a mind original and richly furnished." All these qualities appear in the two
fragments below; they give one the feeling of being set loose —
unfettered by the rigors of academia — in a fantastical world. As
Lowell's biographer Martin Duberman says, the following selections are "learned but not pedantic, leading the student into the
Literature, not into scholarly irrelevancies."*

The Study of Literature

March 23, 1894

I confess that it is with more and more diffidence that I rise
every year to have my little talk with you about books and the
men that have written them. If I remember my terrestrial
globe rightly, one gets into his temperate zone after passing
the parallel of 40 and arrives at, what shall I call it, Sheltered
Haven of Middle Age, when, in proportion as one is more
careful of the conclusions he arrives at, he is less zealous in
his desire that all mankind should agree with him. Moreover,
the longer one studies, the more thoroughly does one persuade himself that till he knows everything, he knows nothing, — that after twenty years of criticism one is still a mere
weigher and gauger: — skilled only to judge what he may
chance to have been in the habit of inspecting at his own little
provincial customhouse. And as one gets older he is apt to
allow more for personal idiosyncrasy, and to have less cer-
tainty that the truth he has reached is not a one-sided one,
and that there are not 50 others equally important, and (per-

haps) equally unsatisfactory. Every bait is not for every fish. We begin by admitting the old Doctor's apothegm that Art is long; we gradually become persuaded that it is like the Irishman's rope, the other end of which was cut off. So different is Art, whose concern is with the ideal and potential, from Science, which is limited by the actual and positive.

Life is so short that it may be fairly doubted whether any man has a right to take an hour, and I have learned at least so much — that I hope less to teach than to suggest.

•   •   •

Whether [historian] Mr. [Henry Thomas] Buckle be right or wrong in affirming that the progress of the race has been purely intellectual and not moral, it is certain that the imagination and conscience of men are stronger motives of action, and lead to greater results than any mere intellectual convictions. The lever of the great English Rebellion was the Conscience of England, and though Lord Bacon has said that all revolutions begin in the belly, this is in no wise true of such as bring about enduring political changes. So during our own Revolution, though the quarrel certainly began about a point of law, yet the enthusiasm which carried it through disaster and privation to success was kindled and kept alive by the few pregnant abstractions into which the genius of Jefferson had condensed the principles of Bodin and Sidney and the eloquence of Rousseau. No wiser man, according to the wisdom of the world, ever lived than Goethe, and he said, "Woe to the man who has trampled on the dreams of his youth"; that is, the power of surrendering himself to a purely abstract enthusiasm. The imagination always asserts its place in history, for it is inseparable from the nature of man, and the story of Colonel Goffe at Deerfield is but a modern version of the Dioscuri and of St. James of Compostella. In my walk the other day, I saw a man sitting in the sun in front of a little cottage which commanded a pretty landscape. "You have a charming view here," said I. "Yes," he answered, "I take a great deal of pleasure in it though I cannot see it. I have long ago lost my sight, but I love to sit here and recall it, and think that it is all there." It lies in our own choice with what pictures we may fill our minds, whether our inward eye shall command noble prospects over the whole domain of human thoughts, or shall be bounded by the narrow alley of a merely utilitarian training.

I believe that the study of imaginative literature tends to sanity of mind, and to keep the Caliban Common Sense, a very useful monster in his proper place, from making himself King over us. It is the study of order, proportion, arrangement, of the highest and purest Reason. It teaches that chance has less to do with success than forethought, will and work.

In a lower sense it is also practically useful. For it is also a study of style. We win from it the secret of expression, we learn how shallow artifice is and how wearisome it becomes, we learn also how profound is Art, and how it is able to eternize the thought, the fancy, the feeling of some man who has been dust for centuries.

.   .   .

There is something in the bearing of the men of two centuries ago which marks them as different from ourselves, nay, as superior to us. It was simply that they were used to better society and have the air of the great world, of the world, that is, which makes fashions and is not made by them. They opened their Homer, their Sophocles, their Tacitus, their Horace, where we take up our newspaper or our novel. What an old Gascon prig would Montaigne have been but for the ancients, especially Plutarch. Yet his library did not swamp him, and though his essays are pockmarked all over with quotations, his temper is essentially modern, indeed, he is the first of the properly modern writers. It is not as ladders to the languages in which they are written that I would commend these books, but the languages as ladders to them, whereby we may climb to a larger outlook over men and things, to a retreat lifted above the noises of the world. It is not the scholarship I look at, but the sympathy with their higher mood, with that sweetness that comes with age to good books as to good men. Mere scholarship is as useless as the collecting of old postage stamps. Kant used to say that there was nothing in the world so dreary as the company of mere scholars. With nothing but Lemprire's Dictionary and Chapman's Homer, Keats at 20 was more imbued with the spirit of antiquity than Swinburne with all his Greek. And why? Because he read, not to become Greek, but drawn by a passion for the same ideal beauty that made the Greeks themselves Greek. The advice of Cato, *cum bonis ambula*, holds as good as books as of men. If the mind, like the dyer's hand, becomes insensibly subdued to what it works in, so also may it steep itself in a noble and victorious mood, may sweeten itself with a refinement that feels a vulgar thought like a stain, and store up sunshine against darker days. It is the books which heighten and clarify the character, whose society I would bid you seek. I think they tend to keep us pure. They disinfect the imagination; they fill the memory with light and fragrance. Whatever a man's station, whatever his other opportunities, there is one Company from which he can never be excluded, and it is that of the master spirits of all the centuries. When one reads Boswell, he cannot help thinking what a privilege it would have been to belong to Johnson's set, but only consider of what a Club every scholar may be admitted a member. "Study," said Montesquieu, "has been for me a sovereign remedy against the disgusts of life, and I have never had a vexation that an hour's reading has not dissipated." But a man could not say that, who should choose Paul de Kock for his bosom friend rather than Milton or prefer Miss Braddon's society to that of Vittoria Colonna. [Mary Elizabeth Braddon was a nineteenth-century sensationalist English novelist; Vittoria Colonna was a sixteenth-century Italian writer of religious verse.]

· · ·

The students of physical geography, as the horizon of observation and comparison gradually widens, are enabled to settle certain principles which are immutable in their relations; those, for example, of the distribution of mountain ranges, and of the climatic diversity of the eastern and western sides of continents. In just the same way, as the range of our study of literature widens, and the *terra incognita* diminishes to a few obscure points here and there, we are enabled to construct a tolerably perfect map of the globe of intellectual achievement and adventure and to color its boundaries, if only theoretically, yet with some approach to accuracy in the distinction of certain primary characteristics. In these lectures, it has been my desire, however inadequately in the nature of things I have been able to fulfill it, to keep these lines of psychical and aesthetic distinction more or less clearly in view; to grasp as well as I could and to illustrate such laws of criticism as seemed to me perennial in their application, and to leave aside as rubbish that dead leafage of deciduous facts which is swept rustling to and fro in the avenues of thought by the shifting breath of opinion.

[From lectures by James Russell Lowell]

Poetry in Homely Lines

April 27, 1894

I have known people who had to go to Europe to see a sunset, who could never find out how beautiful snow was till they saw it on the Alps. The familiar miracles of nature at home were too cheap, and there could be nothing wonderful in what they had only to look out of their back-windows to see. It seems incredible to them that God should come down in all his pomp and glory upon the hills that clasp the homely land-scape of their native village, — that he should work his wonders with the paltry material of their everyday life, that he should hang as fair diamonds of dew on Cambridge grass-blades as on their famous cousins of Mount Hermon. These autumn trees of ours that seem to have caught and kept the sunset in their branches till it looks as if a western evening-cloud had stretched itself in Fresh Pond meadows are too ordinary for marvel.

Thus it is that the beautiful fades gradually out of nature and life becomes dull and prosaic to dull and prosaic men.

[From lectures by James Russell Lowell]

Alumni Authors Have Long Tradition of Writing Novels About Harvard Life

December 5, 1959

Since the earliest days Harvard has been a blazing torch in the world of letters. Beginning in the midnineteenth century, however, some of her sons turned backward their thoughts to write about life at the College, whereupon the light in the dust lay dead.

The first, and unquestionably the worst, nineteenth-century

novel about Harvard life was *Fair Harvard*, by William T. Washburn [Class of 1862]. The book purports to describe the college experiences of young Wentworth Saulsbury and his companions, but according to the 1869 *Advocate* it is more reminiscent of the Arabian Nights.

As a record of social structure and practices at the College during that period *Fair Harvard* may have some value; as a novel it is without a prayer. The next issue of the *Advocate* went so far as to lament that it should have been published in English, giving our British cousins a false impression at a time when they were first recognizing our existence.

A comparatively better Harvard novel appeared seven years later in *Student Life at Harvard*, by George H. Tripp [Class of 1867].

There is a little emotional interest in *Student Life* — pathos or bathos, depending upon one's standards of criticism — when a desperately poor student named Cole dies in Divinity Hall during the noisy merriment of Class Day. This alone, declared the *Advocate* reviewer, is "enough to make it sacrilegious to compare the book with *Fair Harvard*."

The approbation from abroad that was despaired of with Washburn's novel came to *Student Life*. "It is full of life and spirit, contains wonderful specimens of American university slang, and will be read with special interest by English rowing men," noted the *Athenaeum*.

Better than *Fair Harvard* is not necessarily very good, however, and the public ignored both these volumes in significant numbers. It remained for *Hammersmith, His Harvard Days*, by Mark S. Severance [Class of 1869], to be the first popular Harvard novel. Much of the favor which it received can be ascribed to the fact that it is patterned after the very successful *Tom Brown at Oxford*. As might be expected, the weakest parts are those devoted to romance — the element of travesty is not wholly absent when:

> . . . a gas light showed him a pair of very bright little eyes without a particle of sadness in them now, and peachy round cheeks which ought never to wet with tears, and small red lips that looked exceedingly inviting . . . why

hasn't she asked him to call on her though? Why had she torn herself away so suddenly? Ah, my dear Tom! you are propounding riddles too deep for Delphi . . . Why is a woman a sphinx? Why are we pensive at Twilight? Where is the odor of last year's roses?

It is in the crew passages where the book comes to what life it may be said to possess —

> "Harvard, Harvard, Harvard! There she is! Harvard!" as the Varsity suddenly appeared hugging the very shores of the headland, and so concealed, until now, from the sight of the crowds below. Yale was in the centre of the lake, pulling beautifully.

In 1897 there appeared the last of the nineteenth-century fiction concerning life at Harvard. It was not a novel at all, but a collection of short stories entitled *Harvard Episodes* by Charles M. Flandrau [Class of 1895].

Episodes adds a new dimension to this type of collegiate writing. According to Flandrau it is the first such book that "did scarcely any shrinking either thematically or verbally, and, in a perfectly decorous fashion of course, there was hell to pay at once." The unidealized picture rankled, although it was well executed.

Probably the most significant story in the book is that of "Wolcott the Magnificent." Young Sears Wolcott II of the sophomore class is a man who has it made in the shade. He did not "make" the first ten elected to the Institute; he simply belonged there. Into his pleasant, if aimless, existence is suddenly thrust a gross intruder named McGaw. Ungainly, starving, and scholarly, McGaw is a strange contrast to Wolcott, who has been persuaded to aid him by engaging him as a tutor.

Having made McGaw thoroughly despise him, Wolcott somehow remains above it all and engineers his mentor's election to the Signet Society. McGaw then enjoys the luxury of blackballing his benefactor. But everything comes out nicely in the end.

All three College publications expressed sadness at the tone of Flandrau's book. Most acerbic was the *Advocate*, which dwelt upon nothing else. "Books of college stories that are merely pleasant accumulations of harmless lies," it declared, "college men are willing to let pass without comment. But a book like *Episodes*, with too much truth to be pleasant and not enough to be just, cannot be allowed to pass."

Flandrau himself was a 'Poonie, and *Lampy* took several bows for his success but was also a bit unhappy at the product. . . . "Even though he was a brother wit(?), we cannot help thinking that had he led his wit into more pleasant and more trodden paths, his light would have been clearer, and more far-reaching. *Harvard Episodes* are clever. They are well written and they catch a certain atmosphere exactly. But, on the other hand, very few of us know that atmosphere, or even admire the rumors of it which often come to us . . . Why publish such unpleasant things which glare so horribly in black and white?"

In his dedication, Flandrau had answered this question — "I have written about a very little corner of a great place, but one that we knew well."

The Harvard novel has not died out in the twentieth century; it has expanded and become more diversified and, occasionally, better. In 1903 Owen Wister [Class of 1882] published a lyrical book entitled *Philosophy 4*. For once this was not a first novel; he had already established his fame with *The Virginian*.

There are also problem novels — the problems of adolescents developing into men such as [William Clyde] Fitch's *None So Blind* and [George Anthony] Weller ['29]'s *Not to Eat, Not for Love*, which is considered by many the finest book ever to appear about Harvard. Robert L. Wolf ['15]'s *Springboard*, and *Ambition* by Arthur Train [Class of 1896], concern a social topic which needs no elaboration. There are books for teenagers such as John R. Tunis ['11]'s *Iron Duke* and there is even a mystery story in Timothy Fuller ['36]'s *Harvard Has a Homicide*.

With the exception of Wister, however, no major writer has written a novel about Harvard. The closest things to it are pages from John P. Marquand ['15]'s *H. M. Pulham Esq.* and Thomas Wolfe's *Of Time and the River.* One could argue that the subject is too limited, and undoubtedly a Tolstoi would find himself restricted by the College. But great novels have been written about far narrower worlds than Harvard and if it is narrow there is a compensating intricacy.

Architectural Harvard
BY RUSSELL B. ROBERTS '64

May 23, 1963

One of Harvard's finest collections, its most often seen but most frequently overlooked, is the body of artifacts in which the University lives — its museum of architecture.

Extant Harvard structures cover a time of 243 years and include at least one piece from virtually every important period of American architecture. In this respect the University is very fortunate: there are remarkably few communities in the United States with architectural quality and diversity matching Harvard's.

The best and most nearly complete set in the Harvard architecture collection is the earliest, that of the colonial period. The University owns eight eighteenth-century structures, half of them built especially for academic duties and half of them acquired after long service as private Cambridge residences.

Of these earliest buildings, the real masterpieces are Massachusetts Hall, Holden Chapel, and Apthorp House. Massachusetts Hall, one of Harvard's truly prize possessions, is the oldest College building, constructed in 1720. Few University buildings of equal merit have been erected since. The classic simplicity of its Georgian lines, the excellence of its brickwork, and its immaculate proportions are impossible to better. Holden Chapel, designed by an unknown Englishman, is a very beautiful little building, which manages to look modest and aristocratic at the same time. Its symmetrical simplicity is much like that of Massachusetts Hall, the only flourish being its ornately carved pediments which bear the arms of Samuel Holden, a London merchant and donor of the chapel. The interior of the building has undergone several thorough remodelings and lacks the elegance of the original plan but the Georgian proportions of the Chapel are still noticeable and still attractive.

The first bit of marked domestic affluence to appear in colonial Cambridge was Apthorp House, a grand-scale dwelling of 1760. It was built as a home for East Apthorp, an Anglican missionary, and its haughty grandeur infuriated the Congregationalists who then populated most of Cambridge and all of Harvard. They had worried for some time about the prospects of an Anglican bishopric being established in their midst and concluded that Apthorp's mansion was to be the "Bishop's Palace" and Apthorp the first bishop.

The house was easily imposing enough to induce such speculation. It stood at the top of a crest overlooking the Charles River with a large expanse of ground stretching before it and somehow had a way of appearing inordinately pompous whenever a Congregationalist should happen by. The neat rows of Ionic pilasters and windows, the classical doorway and the stately scale of the house, contributed to its attractiveness. Now the Master's Residence at Adams House, the building has lost its view of the river and most of its ground but its handsome interior and façade remain intact.

The design of Apthorp House was probably the work of Charles Ward Apthorp, the minister's brother and a relatively competent gentleman builder. Like most educated men of his time, Apthorp considered a knowledge of the orders of architecture an essential part of learning and had mastered the subject well. He was part of the tradition of gentleman architects, who provided Harvard with the schemes for all its earliest buildings.

Elmwood, a majestic wooden house which is now the official home of the [president], is an achievement of another good but unknown eighteenth-century amateur and it is almost as fine a place as Apthorp House. Harvard Hall was built in 1766 after plans sketched by Sir Francis Bernard, the colonial governor of Massachusetts who fancied himself a most proper builder. He was rather successful with his Harvard construction, which, until it was badly altered in the nineteenth century, had been a pleasantly attractive edifice; it could be attractive again, and ought to be restored.

Wadsworth House and Hicks House, the other two colonial domestic structures belonging to the University, are typical works of gentlemen designers and are very representative of the eighteenth century. Only one Harvard building of this period, Hollis Hall, has been attributed to a professional builder and even that is uncertain. Hollis was designed with polish and excellently constructed but still might be the handiwork of a well-versed amateur.

Charles Bulfinch, eventually to become one of America's most honored architects, was a gentleman builder before he was a professional. He came from a respectable Boston family which had cultivated in him an interest in all the proper disciplines and especially in architecture. He attended to this interest as an undergraduate at Harvard, Class of 1781, and on a trip to Europe after leaving college. His eminence as an architect came surprisingly early in his career, due mostly to the greatness of his design for the Massachusetts State House, one of his first commissions.

Bulfinch's work for Harvard included the original plan for arrangement of buildings in the Yard, Stoughton Hall (which he designed as a mate for Hollis), and University Hall, one of Bulfinch's best and one of Harvard's best. This is a building which commands the Yard with authority and flair, is dignified and also very handsome.

When University Hall was first erected, a large and ungainly portico was constructed across the front, apparently Harvard's addition to Bulfinch's original plan, but this was later removed and the exterior elevations seem to be now as the architect intended. Gone also is "University Minor," a row of outhouses which stood behind the main structure for many years.

The inside of the Chelmsford granite building has been drastically rebuilt on several occasions and only a small part of the original finish remains. The dining rooms and two kitchens included at the start are gone, leaving only the circular ports through which food was once passed from room to room. The one place in the building which still retains a solid Bulfinch flavor is the old second-floor chapel, probably Harvard's most impressive room, now the setting for meetings of the Faculty and the Board of Overseers.

It is possible that the University owns a third and "lost" Bulfinch, one of the large number of buildings which were designed by the architect but never credited to him. Fay House at Radcliffe, built during the time when Bulfinch was particularly interested in houses, possesses the characteristics of Bulfinch's style but unfortunately has lost the credentials of its origin.

After Bulfinch, Harvard erected no important buildings until the late nineteenth century, a time of professional architects and gaudy edifices. Among the most prominent extravaganzas of this time were Matthews, Weld, and Grays in the Yard and Claverly and Randolph on the Gold Coast. The excesses of these combinations of Gothic and Jacobean design, if unpleasant to see, are reminiscent of the age.

Only Memorial Hall *surpasses* the standard garishness of Victorian taste. Guides on one of the sightseeing tours now conducted through Cambridge claim that Harvard wanted so much to erect a great and lasting tribute to its Civil War dead that University officials asked every leading architect in America to contribute one detail to such a monument, put them all together and erected Memorial Hall.

But there was one great architect of this period who designed for Harvard a building which can justly be considered among the most important in the United States.

Henry Hobson Richardson's Sever Hall, finished in 1880, was a great influence on the changing styles of the time and eventually became a major step toward the twentieth century and modern architecture. This was the building in which Richardson reached the ultimate maturity of his art, in general design, in construction, and in the minute details of ornamentation. Preserving the massive boldness which was characteristic of Richardson and his Romanesque school, Sever achieved a new simplicity which was to be widely copied. The deep Syrian archway of the front side gave the building a remarkable sense of security; the brick carving in the cornices, the chimneys, and the friezes is some of the best ever done in this country; and the inclination of the building to harmonize with the older works in the Yard without sacrificing a distinct style of its own is something few architects of the late nineteenth century ever understood.

Richardson also designed Austin Hall, a building more characteristic of his work but neither as important nor as good as Sever.

In the nineteenth century, Harvard builders had followed contemporary trends on some occasions and completely reshaped them on others. In the first major period of construction in the twentieth century, both of these practices were abandoned in favor of an outright return to classical forms. This apparently was done chiefly to suit the wishes of President A. Lawrence Lowell, a man of reactionary tastes, who selected a Georgian style for the buildings of his House System in the 1930s. In making such a choice, Lowell was following the theories of gentleman architect Thomas Jefferson, who had advocated the use of classic styles for the official buildings of the new American republic, to give the government a look of stability and purpose, a transfer of aged nobility to the institutions of a young nation. Lowell wanted that same established look for his new Houses and it was natural that he and the University's architects selected a sturdy New England design.

The pseudo-Georgian look, however, was not restricted to the Houses. Virtually everything built in the Lowell years, including the Indoor Athletic Building, surely the world's largest Georgian cube, was designed in this style. Coolidge, Shepley, Bulfinch, and Abbott, then the regular University architects, pandered to their ancestors more than to art; but if not creative, at least their buildings are comfortable and outwardly attractive.

The twentieth century is leaving the University another legacy which is neither comfortable nor attractive. Leverett Towers, the still growing Holyoke Center, and the projected married students' housing complex [Peabody Terrace] are part of this legacy; they may be personally hideous but in the future they will be an important part of Harvard's architectural museum. They represent the New Victoriana, a school based on bald gimmickry, loud primary colors, starkness and bigness, which is responsible for a good measure of contemporary American buildings.

Fortunately, Harvard also has some highly original pieces of sensible modern design. Walter Gropius's Harkness Commons (1950) is regarded as one of his best works. In it his design gained a more fluid appearance than ever before and it became a great influence on the building of its decade. The new Geology Laboratory, designed by Gropius's firm, The Architects Collaborative, is another splendid, original building and Hugh Stubbins's Loeb Drama Center is a third.

The Visual Arts Center, a good work by a great artist [Le Corbusier], brings to Harvard and to the United States the results of some of the best experimentation in the history of architecture. A living dramatization of the creative arts, for all its functional flaws, it is a good and suitable home for the study of vision and creation. There are quirks of design which are nervous and unappealing, of course, and there are people who don't like it — for example, the Classics professor who compared it to two grand pianos copulating. But there is no bolder building at Harvard; no other can grab a man's attention and hold it for so long a time as the Arts Center does. It serves its special purpose as few other buildings can: it excites a new interest in the creative arts.

Sometimes the University builders have been more concerned with the accumulation of indoor space than with the creation of beauty and too often economics or tastelessness have blotched the landscape with ugly piles; but the University has been generally fortunate in its assemblage of edifices. A path extended in an easterly direction from Johnston Gate passes Massachusetts Hall, University Hall, Sever Hall, and the Visual Arts Center, Harvard's best buildings representing the most interesting periods in American architecture. Such a path wanders through the middle of a huge and amusing collection of buildings.

Besides architectural quality and diversity, those buildings have places in history and personalities of their own. The people who lived in them and the character the buildings managed to develop for themselves add a great deal to Harvard architecture. The community of buildings at Harvard have always meant more to the community of men than mere roofs and walls.

The King Revealed
The Elvis Presley TV Special

December 5, 1968

An Elvis special coming on the tube. Far out. But they better not put him in a tuxedo.

They sure didn't. From the instant that smooth face, the curled lip, the incredible hair with that well-groomed gas-station-attendant sheen, the leather — *leather!* — and his first words:

> If you're looking for trouble,
> You've come to the right place,
> If you're looking for trouble,
> Just look right in my face.

there was absolutely no doubt; this promised to be the bossest hour of television in a very long time. Cherry, man. Cool. Like his guitar-man said, "What a gig!"

From "I'm Evil," all of a sudden Elvis is in the middle of this tiny stage, surrounded by an audience of girls. Real live human being girls, with whitened hair and Montgomery Ward dresses and the belligerently Okie appearance that is associated with California dragstrips and jerkwater high schools. He's holding his own ax — "I didn't know Elvis could play the guitar."

"He can't."

"Look. *Look.* He is!"

He's smiling now, digging it. "It's been a long time, baby," he says, then in the tone that you'd expect of a man who's been around, done the whole trip, the tone that John Mayall tries to get into his music, he adds, "Real long time."

FLASH! *Elvis is back!* Oh wow! Yank those beers out of the mother icebox. The man, the MAN, the whole cause of everything. He's on the tube, can you believe, singing in a torrent of sweat in a black leather suit — no, wait, it's a high-roll collar dealie, and can you dig his pants? Heartbreak Hotel? Raunchy as ever? Hound Dog? It's too good to be true! That quiver that makes girls moan from their stomachs made me shriek at the top of my lungs: "Elvis, *Elvis*, you son of a bitch, you are the KING!"

Every minute of that show was like the last three seconds of the Harvard-Yale game. Or whatever moment in your life has ever turned you on to the point of shouting. As a rock and roll expatriate, I can remember many such moments: hearing Bill Haley screaming "Rock Around the Clock," in a movie theater; hearing Ray Charles, live at El Monte Legion Stadium, after singing ten minutes of "What'd I Say" in 1956 say:

"Hold it, hold it." Complete silence. Then:

"Hey — *yu'uh!*"

"Hey — yu-uh!"

"Ho-wo-oh." "Ho-wo-oh!"

"Huh!" "Huh!"

"HEY HEY HOOH HOOH HEY HEY HOH BABY THAT'S ALL RIGHT!"

Then there was the first time I saw Elvis on Ed Sullivan, the old man, that old dead man walking around with his hands up shouting "Silence! Silence, please!" and that incredible screaming of everyone in the nation, even if they were afraid to do it in front of their parents: "We did it! We did it!"

Well, I like a lot of the new groups. The Beatles, the Beards, whatever. The musicians are better — Mike Bloomfield, Eric Clapton, Butterfield, Jimi Hendrix. "The studios are better": 12–72 track, incredible microphones, stereo. *Stereo wasn't even invented when Elvis first came out.* "The engineers are better": Shadow Martin, Phil Spector, Jimmy Miller, George Martin.

This is Elvis surveying his domain, complimenting his children. You done good, chillun. I'm the king, though.

"You know, our music, rocknrollmusic, you know, s'got its roots in gospel, rhythm and blues. That's where it all sprang from." And then the Blossoms — remember the Blossoms? Hullabaloo? — come out and they do "Sometimes I Feel Like a Motherless Chile," while this incredible black dancer does a dance that everyone in the room likes. They liked a dancer on a TV special. *No one* likes dancers on TV. They always prance around and mince. These guys were studs; they had the moves. Then the Lieber-Stoller classic "I'm Saved," with Elvis leading the way:

"I used to smoke!" *"Smoke!"*
"I used to drink!" *"Drink!"*
"And dance the hootchie-coo!"
At that point I was so turned on I grabbed my girl and asked her: "C'mon, baby, let's go cruising!" Complete insanity. She pushes me away. I put my head next to hers: "Hey, baby, let's *make out!*"

Oh, who really remembers the good old days? Bicycle-chain fights? Beating up the teacher? Ducktail haircuts? The days before everyone walked around alienated, and after that, the days that everyone walked around stoned? Who remembers what it was like to not worry about getting busted? Who can tell me, who can think back and tell me about the days before acid was invented? I know, for a fact, that every single American boy has at one time rolled up the sleeves of his tee shirt to look studlier as he walked downtown; that every chick has snuck up her hems in junior high school so somebody can take a good peek. America! You dumb ass stupid brutal beast! Why did you abandon us? We loved you, we really did, we might even fight in your stupid wars if you hadn't forbidden Elvis. Why didn't you let us have friends with greasy hair? *Why?* Why couldn't we go meet our friends at the drive-in? Why couldn't we go to Union Hall to see Donny Dix. Why did you wrench us away from the turned-down transistors in our bedroom? Why? *Why?* Don't you see what you've done. America you *made drugs.* You *made* SDS. You *made* us follow Leary and Ginsberg and Marcuse. *You* created Haight-Ashbury, *you* gave us Dylan, you big creep. *Why didn't you let us love you?*

"Warden threw a party in the county jail." Lieber-Stoller, Mike and Jerry. They practically made Elvis. So many songs: "Hound Dog," "Heartbreak Hotel," "Little Egypt," on and on and on. "Jailhouse Rock," according to Peter Hayes, who anyone who is at all hip in Cambridge should know, or at least have *heard* of, says: " 'Jailhouse Rock' is the greatest song ever written." It's true:

> Number Forty-Seven say to Number Three
> Sure am pleased to make your company,

> You're the cutest jailbird I ever did see,
> Come on and do the jailhouse rock with me.

And that's the whole trip right there. We were prisoners. Elvis released us. Frank Sinatra said that Elvis's sound was the "martial music of every juvenile delinquent in the country." He was righter than he knew. We were *all* juvenile delinquents. These boots are made for walking, Frankie baby?

Then Elvis is back and sings "Love Me Tender," on that tiny stage in front of all those Okies. Remember? That was the song that your mother said it was all right to listen to. "Why can't he sing like that all the time?" It's pretty easy to see why. He *moves*, pacing up and down, holding it all back, looking at the ground, he's got it in him, let it out Elvis, *let it out*. And he falls to his knees and throws his head back and sweats and yells. "He's doing it! Right now!" For us! Ah, Elvis, for us!

Then "Big Boss Man," the blues, that's a long time ago, when that record came out. Eric Clapton was fifteen when that came out.

Then a schmaltzy song that tones things down a little. Elvis begins to slip away from us — ten more years, Elvis? As you play with your model airplanes in Graceland and sip Pepsis, while we're off somewhere, thirty or so? The last few minutes of the program are a rerun of the first few. "I'm Evil" again. You started it, Elvis. The liberator. The martyr to our increased sophistication. Grand old man. He's exactly the same as he was ten years ago, exactly. He started it. We love you, Elvis.

> Don't you mess with me,
> Cause I'm evil
> Whoa-oh, I'm as evil as could be.
> Just let me go my way man
> Cause I'm gonna get home free.

— John Leone '70

Harvard and the Novel

Not to Eat, Not for Love
By George Anthony Weller '29
Quinn and Boden; 1933; 421 pp.

Remember Me to God
By Myron S. Kaufman '43
Lippincott; 1957; 640 pp.

Faithful Are the Wounds
By May Sarton
Rinehart; 1955; 281 pp.

Windsong
By Nicholas Gagarin '70
Morrow; 1970; 275 pp.

Love Story
By Erich Segal '58
Harper & Row; 1970; 131 pp.

By Nicholas B. Lemann '76

October 21, 1975

By any logic Harvard should be producing a steady flow of great fiction. It seems to have both the raw material of which novels are made and an abundance of talented people eager to set it all down. Harvard is, after all, richly traditional, both historically and intellectually, offering much for novelists to draw on; the American Mind, people here will tell you, has sprung in large measure from those Harvard traditions. And if it's the sociology of a place that determines whether it produces fiction, Harvard fills the requirements. Where else is there a comparably intellectual hothouse atmosphere, where life's great questions are asked with so much frequency and insight? Where else is there such a heavy concentration of people in whose minds the first rogue glimmerings of fiction have burned?

None of the logic, unfortunately, seems to apply. To be sure, people at Harvard have been cranking out novels about Harvard for more than 50 years, but never very memorable ones. It's not that some of the greatest of twentieth-century fiction hasn't had scenes at Harvard — *Absalom, Absalom!* and *The Sound and the Fury* certainly did — but the good fiction that mentions Harvard is mainly concerned with something else altogether . . . Harvard may be useful as a setting in which to contemplate non-Harvard things, or as a symbol of intellectualism and the Puritan tradition. But it doesn't seem to be very good at providing novelists with the setting, action and main creative energy of their work.

The novels discussed here all fulfill the primary requirement of true Harvard fiction — most of their action takes place here, and most of their characters have some official connection with the University. They all rely on a fully drawn picture of the University at some particular time. They are not Harvard essays, or short stories, or journalism, or poetry, or diaries, all of which abound, and neither are they more than a rather large fraction of all legitimate Harvard fiction. Together they cover the university life of a period stretching roughly from 1925 to 1970, and because they share many of the same flaws, those flaws may speak more for the spiritual shortcomings of Harvard than for those of the particular novelists.

Windsong, a product of the strike era written by Nicholas Gagarin when he was an undergraduate, has problems in greater abundance than any of the other Harvard novels, so it may be a good place to start. It's a strange, disjointed book, told in parts that in their interaction manage to produce only confusion. There are three heroes, all of whom may actually be the same person — Gagarin himself, a rebellious preppie; Hal, a screwed-up preppie; and "The boy," a preppie who gets it all together at the Esalen Institute. All three float through Harvard, unhappy without really understanding why, although Gagarin comes closest to defining their anomie when he complains that Harvard cuts people off from their own bodies by overemphasizing the mind.

In the parts of *Windsong* when he's speaking in his voice Gagarin calls for sweeping educational changes: "The whole idea of intellectual validity has to be thrown out the window . . . Why, there should be courses in birds and animals and trees . . . courses probing into the ritual and mystery of life itself." As this implies, Gagarin is no radical; he acknowledges that "many of the radicals are beautiful people" but is generally baffled by their dogmatism. The occupation of University Hall is mostly an emotional experience for him, and he cares less about the issues involved than that "we were very beautiful in University Hall, we were very human, and we were very together."

The same lack of substance and vague emphasis on peak emotional experiences pervades the conventionally fictional parts of *Windsong*, the parts about how Hal graduates first in his class from St. Paul's, comes to Harvard, vacations in Europe, goes to parties in New York, and falls in love with a girl preppie named Flo whose attractiveness to him is always expressed solely in physical terms. Every time he sees Flo, Hal notices her beautiful (an oft-used word in *Windsong*) auburn hair and understated clothing, and not much more, and for her part Flo actually says very little beyond cryptic, off-putting remarks. The Hal-Flo affair endures crises, to be sure — she refuses to go skiing in Austria with him for Christmas, for example — but never gets very far off the ground. It's purely an adolescent obsession on Hal's part, hardly enough to sustain a whole novel, completely lacking in emotional depth or complexity.

All in all Gagarin's world is a bland one where very little happens and people's problems are so tied to their wealth that they don't arouse much sympathy. And Gagarin is inept at basic narrative skills, so that every section designed primarily to advance the action of the book is shot through with tedium:

> Francis lived on the twelfth floor of a huge apartment building on Third Avenue. Barry and Hal took the elevator up, and then rang the bell. Francis came to the door. 'Hi,' he said, 'come in.' Hal and Barry went in. It was a little after nine. Barry was wearing a gray suit. Hal was in corduroy pants and a dark jacket. Inside sitting on the floor were Peter, Hopie, Sara and Janet. Janet from the boat, Janet whose face was as pale white as ever. 'Nobody else has come yet,' Francis said.

Perhaps Gagarin's problem was that he was too ambitious, for although *Windsong* is modest in length it attempts to show all-consuming love, and what's wrong with Harvard, and what's wrong with the modern world, and to propose some tentative solutions (Esalen and the rediscovery of the body) to all three. George Anthony Weller, writing almost 40 years earlier, manages to be charming and unpretentious in *Not to Eat, Not for Love* by setting his sights far lower. His concern is with Harvard itself, not Harvard as it sheds light on the great problems facing mankind. He places few value judgments, and raises few complex situations. *Not to Eat* is a journalistic novel aimed at showing the mood and manners of undergraduate life here in the late twenties and early thirties, which it does quite well, and not much more.

Not to Eat must have been a conscious imitation of John Dos Passos' *U.S.A.* trilogy, which, in conveying the flavor of America, had few Harvard scenes itself. It's full of vignettes and characters that appear again and again, at "odd" times in the overall narrative. There's no plot, exactly — what binds the book together is a general progression from early morning to late night, from September to June, and from freshman year to senior year. The first scene, then, has a green freshman seeing the Square for the first time in the October dawn, and the last a jaded delivery boy dropping off stacks of Crimsons in Tercentenary Theatre late on commencement eve.

In between Weller devotes a lot of time to undergraduate activities, focusing particularly and perceptively on their hierarchical nature; people move from the J.V. football team to the varsity, get elected to The Crimson and punched for clubs, learn to write well, and move from social ineptitude to fairly mature love affairs. There are all sorts of writing tricks within Weller's thick social texture of Harvard — like Dos Passos, he plays around with point of view a great deal and uses interior monologues and neologistic runtogether words. Still, for all its considerable appeal, *Not to Eat* is not a real novel. Weller seems to be making a case for Harvard as a microcosm of life — thus the telescoping of youth, maturity and old age into four years — but his characters are still young, his institutions those of young people, and his dilemmas and relationships largely superficial.

So perhaps the problem is undergraduates, not the best raw

material for depth and profundity. Professors, maybe, and their convoluted, agonizing world of brilliant insight and petty infighting, would be more fertile ground. But that case is not particularly well made by *Faithful Are the Wounds*, the major Harvard faculty novel by May Sarton. *Faithful* is a roman à clef about the 1950 suicide of F. O. Matthiessen and the way people reacted to it; it's full of thinly disguised Harvard professors whose names the libel lawyers are keeping out of this review, and one gets the feeling that real cognoscenti would get a great deal more out of the novel than people who don't actually know the characters involved.

The Matthiessen character (by the way, *Faithful* does not begin with an "any resemblance" clause) is Edward Cavan, a brilliant (everyone in *Faithful* is brilliant) and radical English professor. Cavan, already something of an outcast from Harvard life, becomes unbearably depressed and lonely when the Massachusetts Civil Liberties Union agrees to affirm to the national ACLU board that it has no Communist members. With even the left-liberals backing down to the gathering forces of McCarthyism, Cavan feels as if nothing he does is worthwhile. His friends, sensing his depression, try to reach out to him; he, in turn, is surly and demanding, and one night he throws himself in front of an elevated train.

Faithful is a novel where only one thing really happens — Cavan's suicide — and the rest of the book is spent providing a plausible lead-in for it and, later, examining its effect on Cavan's friends. Sarton is concerned more with people's perceptions of events, the way events reverberate beyond their immediate importance, than with events themselves. So *Faithful* is hardly an action novel. It's clearly the product of someone well acquainted with academia, not only because of its characters but because of its lit-crit approach to writing as well. It's more an exercise than a novel; there is, for instance, a series of chapters in which one by one each of Cavan's friends assesses his death, and the chapters seem written mostly out of Sarton's desire to show she could handle such a difficult trick successfully. Similarly, deep emotions are forced into bland situations, banal dialogue used in complex relationships, and violent reactions matched with innocuous actions. Sarton certainly knows what a good novel is and to what depths of meaning it should aspire, but in *Faithful* there is always the sense of meager material being stretched farther than it will go. One woman reminisces about Cavan like this:

> He was here in this room, gentle and quiet at first, smiling at Damon's oldest jokes brought out nervously for the occasion; his suit needed pressing; he had praised the French peas; he had all that time been carrying his death around inside him like a secret; and they had not been able to get through to him, to hold him back. "Why isn't love enough?" she asked the walls again . . .

Sarton's world is a bloodless, blurry one, one where a general air of profundity wraps itself around the skimpiest of substance.

By comparison Myron Kaufmann's *Remember Me to God* is fraught with real dilemmas. Its Harvard is an institution of American society, not of the mind, and its characters' problems grow out of real social crises. *Remember Me to God* is about an upwardly mobile Jewish family, recently moved from Roxbury to Brookline and going through all sorts of status anxieties. The son, Richard, comes to Harvard and gradually gets more and more wrapped up in the New England aristocratic subculture here, with disastrous consequences.

Richard is a totally unsympathetic character, thoroughly despicable in every way. He joins *The Lampoon*, becoming its only Jewish member, and comes to lust after membership in the Hasty Pudding and the affections of preppie women, all of which means to him that he has to tone down his Jewishness. Toward that end, and for the edification of others, Richard begins to compile a little handbook full of pithy instructions for Jews on how to seem like Gentiles.

The whole issue overwhelms him; aristocratic Christians uniformly awe him and he is willing to do anything — even convert — to gain the total acceptance from them that will never, of course, be his. The feeling that emerges from all this is that Kaufmann wanted to make Richard at least an understandably confused if not good character. But he gets carried away, and Richard's feelings are so patently barren and objectionable that he loses some of his reality. Sure, all this is taking place in the early forties, the era of the Jewish quota, but it still stretches the imagination to think that a Jew would actually say, defending anti-Semitism in the State Department:

> Well, you have to be smooth in the State Department, for Christ sake! What do you expect them to do? Take a fat, baldheaded little guy in a fourteen-dollar suit, with gold teeth, and spits all over you when he talks, and send him over to London to make a curtsy to the King? I mean, after all, some Yankee prejudices are pretty understandable. So don't accuse people of anti-Semitism just because they expect decent manners.

Or muse, gazing longingly at the Hasty Pudding after he joins it:

> Do you realize how far I've come, what this proves? The necktie itself is an empty symbol, just snobbery. But the point is, that I'm proving these empty symbols don't mean anything . . . It's little incidents like this that are really milestones. It's sort of a one-man campaign against prejudice that I'm waging.

The clear message is that Richard has gotten in over his head, that the effect of Harvard on him has been wholly bad. He is constantly running into reminders that he is neither intelligent nor upper class, the two characteristics that you have to have in Kaufmann's Harvard to be a real part of the place. But this being Harvard, Richard is seduced by what the University promises; he longs for a world that he can never join and therefore would have been better off never having ever seen, and he slinks off to war at the end a shattered man. Harvard has destroyed his old identity, tempted him with a new one, and then held it away from him.

A gloomy world, this fictional Harvard, full of neurosis and small-scale tragedy, a hard place, for whatever reason, to be happy. Except, that is, in *Love Story*, where tragedy politely waits until after graduation. The great achievement of *Love Story* is that it doesn't get all bollixed up in trying to explain Harvard. Almost alone among Harvard novels, it's not written with a Harvard audience secretly in the mind and therefore suffers no qualms about using the University in its crudest symbolic form. Sure, Erich Segal knows the local vernacular and institutions, but his Harvard is really a very simple thing, exactly what most Americans associate with the name: wealth, status, prestige, freedom, success, loose morals. As a nationwide cultural symbol Harvard is quite rich, and Segal milks it as much as he can. People don't want to hear that Harvard is a seething bed of inner torment, and neither do they want a closely accurate picture of the various strata of life here. Harvard is class, a little obnoxious perhaps, and as such it does yeoman service in lending appeal to a hackneyed little narrative.

The problem with most Harvard novelists is their inability to see the Harvard Segal saw — and Faulkner and Wolfe, too, for that matter. Harvard novelists wrote mediocre novels, by and large, because they tried too hard to portray life here deeply and accurately. The novels, as a result, are filled with petty concerns, vague misery and characters just groping their way toward completeness. Theirs is a closely scrutinized and faithfully recorded university that is in no shape to bear up under that particular kind of scrutiny.

CHAPTER 8

I Will Be Read

THE CRIMSON'S MOTTO, from Byron, is "I won't philos-ophize, I will be read." This chapter is dedicated to that proposition. And it is hoped that the articles contained in it will reflect that motto, representing to readers some of The Crimson's best, longer writing.

There are a few interesting features about the following articles. It will become apparent that all of them are taken from The Crimson's last quarter century. It was not until after the war that feature-length articles were published on a fairly regular basis. And generally speaking, it was not until the late 1940s that The Crimson became a publication dedicated to extensive, in-depth coverage.

Many of the pieces in this chapter are self-explanatory; thus the omission of headnotes. All that is really important to remember is that the writers all shared one concern: using language and the medium of the newspaper to their utmost, occasionally extending them beyond their theretofore known limits. It is hard to convey this idea adequately. To be sure, some of the genres employed in this chapter's articles are matter-of-fact, everyday affairs: interviews, profiles, features. Some of the articles do not always meet today's standards and expectations, just as, say, a Rauschenberg montage seems passé to a gallerygoer unaware of its originality 25 years ago when it was first conceived and created. It should be remembered also that, to the extent that some of these pieces are only of historical interest, they may suffer upon rereading.

One more point of explanation: a number of the articles included in "I Will Be Read" (and in some of the earlier chapters) have been awarded the Dana Reed Prize. The prize, given since 1948 in memory of Dana Reed, who died in the Second World War, is offered to the best piece of Harvard-Radcliffe undergraduate writing to appear in an undergraduate publication. Each year the Dana Reed Prize committee — consisting of college alumni/ae — chooses a panel of three judges, who then review the articles nominated by the various publications and select the best article. The judges have included such notable writers and journalists as Norman Mailer, J. P. Marquand, Bernard DeVoto, Elizabeth Janeway, Anthony Lewis, John Updike, Adrienne Rich, Donald Barthelme, Maxine Kumin, V. S. Pritchett, Roger Angell, Joan Didion, Frances FitzGerald, Seymour Hersh, and Gloria Emerson.

Not all of The Crimson's Dana Reed Prize winners and honorable mentions appear in this book. Those not included deserve mention: the 1950 Academic Freedom Report by David E. Lilienthal Jr. '49, Burton S. Glinn '46('49), and John G. Simon '50; a 1951 report on the College's admissions by Douglas M. Fouquet '51 and Bayley F. Mason '51; a 1953 profile of James Bryant Conant written by Michael J. Halberstam '53; a 1959 article on Harvard's final clubs by Kenneth Auchincloss '59; a 1960 series on C. P. Snow by Joseph L. Featherstone '62; a 1962 four-part article on integration in a Maryland town by Paul S. Cowan '62; a 1962 series of articles and editorials on the dismissal of Richard Alpert by Joseph M. Russin '64, Andrew T. Weil '63, Josiah Lee Auspitz '63, and Michael W. Schwartz '63; a 1969 series on poverty in Alabama by James M. Fallows '70; a 1969 series of articles on the Esalen Institute by the late Nicholas Gagarin '70; a 1970 piece on 12 antiwar professors' visit to Capitol Hill by Michael E. Kinsley '72; a 1971 series on Henry Kissinger (later to be expanded into a book) by M. David Landau '72; and coverage of George Wallace's 1972 primary campaign by Lewis F. Patton '74.

The articles that are included here are placed in chronological order so that readers may understand the progression over the years of subjects and genres that have moved Crimson editors to write well.

*   *   *

CABBAGES AND KINGS

Beating the System

June 14, 1950

The Harvard examination system is designed, according to its promulgators, to test two specific things, knowledge of trends and knowledge of detail. Men approaching the examination problem have three choices: 1. flunking out, 2. doing work, or 3. working out some system of fooling the grader. The first choice of solution is too permanent, and the second takes too long.

This article is designed to explain how to achieve the third answer to this perplexing problem by the use of the vague generality, the artful equivocation, and the overpowering assumption.

It seems pretty obvious that in any discussion of the various methods whereby the crafty student attempts to show the grader that he knows a lot more than he actually does, the vague generality is the key device. A generality is a vague statement which means nothing by itself, but when placed in an essay on a specific subject might very well mean something to a grader. The true master of the generality is the man who can write a ten-page essay, which means nothing at all to him, and have it mean a great deal to anyone who reads it. The generality writer banks on the knowledge possessed by the grader, hoping the marker will read things into his essay.

Every nonmathematical field in the University has its own set of vague generalities. For instance:

"Hume brought empiricism to its logical extreme." (Philosophy)

"The whole thing boils down to human rights versus property rights." (Government)

"*Moby-Dick* is written on three levels." (English)

"The Holy Roman Empire was neither holy, nor Roman, nor an empire." (History)

"Locke is a transitional figure." (Philosophy)

"Marx turned Hegel upside down." (Gen. Ed.)

"Any theory of underconsumption and purchasing power must be grounded in the psychology of the people." (Economics)

"Berlioz is the founder of modern orchestration." (Music)

"Shaw's heroes are men of moral passion." (English 160)

"Differentiation and integration are fundamental to the dynamic maturation of the human organism." (Social Relations)

To check the operation of a vague generality under fire, take the typical example. "Hume brought empiricism to its logical extreme." The question is asked, "Did the philosophical beliefs of Hume represent the spirit of the age in which he lived?" Our hero replies by opening his essay with "David Hume, the great Scottish philosopher, brought empiricism to its logical extreme. If this be the spirit of the age in which he lived, then he was representative of it." This generality expert has already taken his position for the essay. Actually he has not the vaguest idea what Hume really said, or in fact what he said it in, or in fact if he ever said anything. But by never bothering to define empiricism, he may write indefinitely on the issue, virtually without contradiction.

Of course, some people are naturally conservative; they prefer to avoid taking a position wherever possible. They just don't believe in going out on a limb, when they don't even know the genus of the tree. For these people, the vague generality must be partially junked and replaced by the artful equivocation, or the art of talking around the point.

The artful equivocation is an almost impossible concept to explain, but it is easy to demonstrate. Let us take our earlier typical examination question, "Did the philosophical beliefs of Hume represent the spirit of the age in which he lived?" The equivocator would answer it this way: "Some people believe that David Hume was not necessarily a great philosopher because his thought was merely a reflection of conditions around him, colored by his own personality. Others, however, strongly support Hume's greatness on the ground that the force of his personality definitely affected the age in which he lived. It is not a question of the cart before the horse in either case, merely the old problem of which came first, the chicken or the egg. In any case, there is much to be said on both sides."

Just exactly what our equivocator's answer has to do with the original question is hard to say. The equivocator writes an essay about the point, but never on it. Consequently the grader often mentally assumes the right answer is known by the equivocator and marks the essay as an extension of the point rather than a complete irrelevance. The artful equivocation must imply the writer knows the right answer, but it must never get definite enough to eliminate any possibilities.

There is a third method of dealing with examination questions — that is by the use of the overpowering assumption, an assumption so cosmic that it is sometimes accepted. For example, we wrote that it is pretty obvious that the vague generality was the key device in any discussion of examination writing. Why is it obvious? As a matter of fact it isn't obvious at all, but just an arbitrary point from which to start. That is an example of an unwarranted assumption.

In the long run the expert in the use of unwarranted assumptions comes off better than the equivocator. He would deal with our question of Hume not by baffling the grader or fencing with him but like this: "It is absurd to discuss whether Hume is representative of the age in which he lived unless we first note the progress of that age on all intellectual fronts. After all, Hume did not live in a vacuum."

At this point our assumption expert proceeds to discuss anything which strikes his fancy at the moment. If he can sneak the first assumption past the grader, then the rest is clear sailing. If he fails, he still gets a certain amount of credit for his irrelevant but fact-filled discussion of scientific progress in the eighteenth century. And it is amazing what some graders will swallow in the name of intellectual freedom.

— Donald Carswell '50
[Awarded the Dana Reed Prize in 1951]

The Crimson proudly reprinted Donald Carswell's "Beating the System" in virtually every exam period from 1950 onward, presumably in the interest of its readers. That is, until the following devastating reply from "A Grader" was submitted for publication in 1962.

THE SYSTEM

The Grader Replies

January 26, 1962

Gentlemen:

I have, I must confess, serious doubts about the efficacy — or even the integrity — of the "classic" exam-period editorial, "Beating the System," you reprinted recently. I almost suspect this so-called "Donald Carswell '50" of being rather one of Us — The Bad Guys — than one of You. If your readers have been following Mr. Carswell's advice for the last eleven years, then your readers have been going down the tubes. It is time to dis-illusion.

He is right, of course, about the third alternative, and a very sensible one it is — working out some system of fooling the grader; although I think I should prefer the word "impressing." We admit to being impressionable, but *not* hypercredu-

WEDNESDAY, JUNE 2, 1954

thus, we see the decline of the Protestant ethic in Germany . . . //

Note to Grader
You are probably a nice guy and you don't deserve having to spend a whole afternoon trying to figure out my handwriting, but I can't help it, never having mastered Palmer

method. Besides I have to write fast on exams and the faster I write the sloppier my writing gets. It would be a lot easier for everybody, even graders, if there were a room in which people who wanted to type their exams could sign up for in advance and type like hell — hard, fast, and coherent. #

"The regular editorials on the need to use typewriters for final examinations," writes Claude E. Welch '61, former president of The Crimson, "had no effect at all on the administration (we Crimeds had an obvious incentive, given our training in finger dexterity and rapid bullshitting)."

lous simps. His first two tactics for system beating, his Vague Generalities and Artful Equivocations, seem to presume the latter, and are only going to convince Crimson-reading graders (there are a few, and we tell our friends) that the time has come to tighten the screws just a bit more.

Think, Mr. Carswell (wherever you are), think, all of you: imagine the situation of your grader. (Unless, of course, he is of the Wheatstone Bridge–double differential $CH_3C_6H_2(NO_2)_3$ set. These people are mere cogs; automata; they simply feel to make sure you've punched the right holes. As they cannot think, they cannot be impressed; they are clods. The only way to beat *their* system is to cheat.) In the humanities and social sciences, it is well to remember, there is a man (occasionally a woman), a human type filling out your picture postcard. What does he want to read? How, in a word, can he be snowed?

Not, let me insist and insist again, by Vague Generalities. We *abhor* V.G.'s, we skim right past them, we start wondering what kind of a C to give from the first V.G. we encounter; and as they pile up, we decide: C− (Harvard being Harvard, one does not give D's. Consider C− a failure.). Why? Not because they are a sign the student doesn't know the material, or hasn't thought carefully, or any of that folly. They simply make tedious reading. "Locke is a transitional figure." "The whole thing boils down to human rights." Now I ask you. I have 92 bluebooks to read this week, and all I ask, really, is that you keep me awake. Talk to me. Is that so much?

Artful Equivocations are even worse; lynx-eyed sly little rascals that we are, we see right through them. (Up to Exam #40. Then our lynx eyelids droop, and grading habits relax. Try to get on the bottom of the pile.) Again, it is not that A.E.'s are vicious or ludicrous as such: but in quantity they become sheer madness. Or induce it. "The twentieth century has never recovered from the effects of Marx and Freud" (V.G.); "but whether this is a good thing or a bad is difficult to say" (A.E.). Now, *one* such might be droll enough. But by the dozen? This, the quantitative aspect of grading — we are, after all, getting five dollars a head for you dolts and therefore pile up as many of you apiece as we can get — this is what too many of you seem to forget. "Coleridge may be said to be both a classic *and* a romantic, but then, so may Dryden, depending on your point of view. In some respects, this statement is unquestionably true; but in others . . ." On through the night.

I hope my inference is clear. The A's go to people who wake us up, who talk to us, who are sparkling and different and bright. (The B's go to Radcliffe girls who memorize the text and quote it verbatim, in perfectly looped letters with circles over the o's.) *Not,* I remind you, necessarily to people who have locked themselves in Lamont for a week and seminared and outlined and underlined and typed their notes and argued out all of Leibniz's fallacies with their mothers. They often get A's too, but, as Mr. Carswell sagely observed, this takes too long. There are other ways.

His third suggestion, the Overpowering Assumption, I think is the best: but not for the reasons he suggests — that the assumption is so cosmic it may sometimes be accepted. It is rarely "accepted"; we aren't here to accept or reject, we're here to be amused. The more dazzling, personal, unorthodox, paradoxic your assumptions (paradoxes are *not* equivocations), the more interesting an essay is likely to be. (If you have a chance to confer with the assistant in advance, of course — and we liked to be called "assistants," not "graders" — you may be able to ferret out one or two cosmic assumptions of his own; seeing them in your bluebook, he can only applaud your uncommon perception. For example, while most graders are politically unconcerned, not *all* are agnostic. This is an older generation, recall. Some may be tired of seeing St. Augustine flattened by a phrase, or reading about the "Xian myth.")

Carswell's further discussion of the O.A. is quite to the point — he himself realizes its superiority to any E., however A. His illustration includes one of the key "Wake Up the Grader" phrases — "It is absurd." What force! What gall! What fun! "Ridiculous," "hopeless," "nonsense," on the one hand; "doubtless," "obvious," "unquestionable" on the other, will have the same effect. A hint of nostalgic, antiacademic languor at this stage as well may well match the grader's own mood: "It seems more than obvious to one entangled in the petty quibbles of contemporary Medievalists — at times, indeed, approaching the ludicrous — that, smile as we may at its follies, or denounce its barbarities, the truly monumental achievements of the Middle Ages have become too vast for us to cope with, or even understand: we are too small, and too afraid." Let me offer this as an ideal opening sentence to *any* question even tangentially nudging on the Middle Ages. And now, you see, having dazzled me, won me by your personal, involved, independently minded assertion, your only job is to *keep* me awake. When I sleep I give C's.

How? By FACTS. *Any* kind, but *do* get them in. *They* are what we look for — a name, a place, an allusion, an object, a brand of deodorant, the titles of six poems in a row, even an occasional date. This, son, makes for interesting (if effortless) reading: and that is what gets A's. Underline them, capitalize them, inset them in outline form: be *sure* we don't miss them. Why do you think all exams insist at the top, "Illustrate"; "Be Specific"; etc.? They *mean* it. The illustrations needn't, of course, be singularly relevant; but they must be there. If Vague Generalities are anathema, sparkling chips of concrete scattered through your bluebook will have you up for sainthood. Or at least Dean's List. Name at least the titles of every other book Hume ever wrote; don't say just "Medieval cathedrals" — name nine. Think of a few specific *examples* of "contemporary decadence," like Natalie Wood. If you can't come up with titles, try a few sharp metaphors of your own; they have at least the solid clink of pseudofacts.

That's the secret, really. Don't write out "TIME!!" in inch-high scrawls — it only brings out the sadist in us. Don't (Cliffies) write offers to come over and read aloud to us your illegible remarks — we can (officially) read anything, and we may be married. Write on both sides of the page — single-bluebook finals look like less work to grade, and win points. This chic, shaded calligraphic script so many are affecting lately *is* handsome, and is probably worth a good five extra points if you can hack it.

But above all, keep us entertained, keep us awake. Be bold, be personal, be witty, be chock-full-of-facts. I'm sure you can do it without studying if you try. We did.

Best wishes,
A Grader

Sex and Society: Coming of Age at Harvard

September 1, 1957

(The editors wish to state that the views of the author do not necessarily represent those of The Crimson. However, as the editorial staff is engaged in private research, the results of which will not be released until July, the more readily available analysis of Mr. Royce must be accepted. The author is presently engaged in a study entitled "I Was an Undercover Agent at Lake Waban.")

BY DAVID ROYCE '53, '55½, '56

(The help of numerous Radcliffe girls in this project is acknowledged, without whose sporadic help the ways of women would probably have remained a mystery anyway. Investigating sex at Radcliffe is like making Tom Collinses out of warm water and lemon peels, but they're girls — you can't take that away from them.)

Nobody ever writes about the mental side of sex — doctors are bored with it, psychologists are scared of it, and philosophers are too smart to pit their neat little thoughts against such a monster issue. The undergraduate who investigates the subject is more often than not groping in the dark. If you're feeling ontological, you can go to the library and find lots of company. But if you feel like a big black tomcat at dusk, all you can do is yowl.

After you've yowled awhile, your roommates ask you to go try Radcliffe, where you proceed to spot a cute thing in a very stylish dress. Meeting her will be tough, but with ingenuity and incredible self-confidence it can be pulled off. The main trouble in meeting girls is that your selection is based at first on good looks, which actually mean nothing except that we feel they're necessary, which is actually pretty significant. After introductions, you'll both snow each other so well that, after you dig yourselves out months later, nobody will know who snowed whom, whether being snowed-in together is worth it, or when the thaw is coming.

But before you despair of the blundering guesswork your girl hunt must involve, remember that it was a hunch that made Edison invent the incandescent light. It was a hunch that made Napoleon march on Moscow. (If you want to know how the 100,000 who walked back to France felt, try walking down Garden Street at 1:10 some winter night after an unsuccessful date.)

The process of meeting the girl you have chosen is easier than it feels. First you catch her eye, and she draws her upper lip away from her teeth to show she notices you. Then you ask a girl nearby who that "girl in the corner" is. She smiles and says in a loud contralto:

"THAT'S MARCIA McGLINCHEY! WHY?" In the corner of your eye MARCIA is scuttling behind a sofa. "DO YOU WANT A DATE WITH HER?" cries your new friend, warming to her role. "SHE'S REALLY A LOT OF FUN!"

You never have much trouble getting a date. All girls are fascinated by telephone voices, as long as you take a nap before calling so your voice will be low. The first phone call must be done from notes, to be really effective. You must be just a little enigmatic, and give the impression of strength of character behind your taciturnity, amazing ability behind your boastful façade.

You must use all the latest predicate adjectives: "lunch," "shoe," "the most." You should show your sense of humor by giggling when you say something cute. And above all, you lose the game if you confess calling her because you think she's your type. You should appear at least to want to give her fun and laughs — dates, not tête-à-têtes.

Where to go and what to do is simple. You show her an amazingly good time on the first date, unless you're me, in which case you don't spend a red cent because you don't have it to spare. The flat-broke ploy is good because she'll know then that your daddy isn't sending you through, and you're either a self-made man or a scholarship boy — attractive in either case.

But if you want to show her the town, start by eating in a good restaurant, preferably one with a headwaiter whom you tip, and a dance floor. Then you drive out to some inaccessible-except-by-car foreign movie you've seen before, and discuss it intelligently over St. Clair's coffee. The second date, of course, you study together in your room. Make sure it isn't a time when either of you actually *has* to get some work done.

On the third date, you go to the University Theater for a

pleasant double feature. The U.T. on weekends is packed with Harvard, which makes collegiate noises and laughs at corny staging, and you'll feel at home. Don't buy reserved seats — they're slippery and you keep falling on the floor.

If you're giving her the flat-broke treatment, the U.T. date will let her know you really care; if you've shown her Boston's bright spots the previous time, it'll show her you're adaptable, not addicted to splendor, and not afraid she is. After the U.T., you adjourn to a sofa or car to see whether she was bluffing when she kissed you goodnight.

Sex, like any game, has its rationale. Most girls are tremendously relieved and deeply offended when you finally close in. Your girl friend's response, if she still approves of you, will be to express both feelings in a superb six-or-eight-word sentence, and let you go ahead. After all the rationalizations are on the table, the only really pleasant part of the whole business ensues.

According to the rules of the game, the boy makes the decisions. A girl never says "Don't," because she knows anyone from Harvard will considerately quit and apologize on the spot if she does. She says "Oh, please!" Another smoke screen in a series of little murmurs which could be either pure despair, pure pleasure, or any mixture thereof.

This delicious ambiguity, designed to keep the boy in continual tension, is one of the refinements we collegians have added to what was once a pretty straightforward game. Trying to be honest for once, you let escape a blissful sigh. There went *that* date, daddy-o. "You beast! You're *enjoying* it!" She recoils like a snake. Remember the rules: you decide what to do, but she decides how.

Love cannot be safely defined except as a "will to believe" in each other, but you're sure to leap at the most popular working definition among us intellectuals: "What is love? *This* is love!" When you've said that, since you're in the intertwined state wherein thoughts flow freely, she'll start wondering if it isn't just sex. Then you'll wonder if sex isn't enough (better not say it aloud).

Soon you'll both be wondering whether this is the "right person"; whether for such mixed up minds anybody could be

the "right one"; whether perhaps romance is hokum and anybody could be the "right one"; whether today's confused
Youth can make sane decisions about the appropriateness of
love, of sex, of marriage (pause for breath); whether all this
decision stuff isn't a negation of the basically inspirational
quality of Perfect Love; or whether maybe sex isn't everything
but it's a hell of a lot easier than all this stuff; and so on
around again.

Whatever you do about girls this fall, remember that it will
end badly. There's really no sense in going out at all. The advice above is for those who can't help themselves.

In the first place, you fool, you have to know what you
want. And you don't and probably never will. This puts you at
a distinct disadvantage with the ladies, who know exactly
what they want: lots of fun, lots of laughs, a bachelor's degree, and an intelligent, strong, pliable husband. Secondly,
you have to know how to get what you're after (if anything) —
which is the most difficult part. Every victory turns to defeat,
and the spoils of victory vanish without a trace. They'll tromp
on you, boy, they'll pluck your heart out and crack it like an
egg. But they mean well, and the fault is yours — you asked
for a date.

The Quest at Princeton for the Cocktail Soul
By John E. McNees '60

February 21, 1958

*"Now I know you guys at Harvard put an emphasis on individ-
ualism and that's fine," he said, refusing to acknowledge my
deprecatory gesture and attempt to interrupt. "But down here we
like a less impersonal way of living so you like and can be with
who you want for your friends and choose the guys you eat
with."*

*A cold wind swept over the thick dark grass outside, whistled
through the moonlit Gothic stonework, the parapets, battle-
ments, and pinnacles intricately crowning the buildings with
medieval bulk and solemnity.*

And through the windows glaring orange out of a hundred ma-

jestic black bastions, the committees are seen as they come call-
ing, catching sophomores just accidentally attired from top to
toe in immaculate tweeds, and Exeter yearbooks displayed with
casual prominence.
"Hello, we're from Cottage."
"Come right on in," and an inchoate cordial babble of wel-
come as they all heartily seat themselves, and suddenly find a ter-
rifying silence left standing.
"Uh, that looks like an old Currier and Ives you've got up
there" (the walls, they always start with what you've got hanging
on the walls, or with what you're majoring in or what you did
last summer or where you're from — but avoid that one, there's
danger there.)
And so it goes for ten or fifteen minutes. Total strangers con-
fronting total strangers, making nervous small talk with artificial
poise, watching through narrow eyes for the wrong color of
socks, a grammatical slip or affectation, a pun or wisecrack in
questionable taste. Then:
"Well, we really must be running along. A lot of men to see to-
night you know."
"Well, we've certainly enjoyed chatting with you."
Smiling and nodding and handshaking them out the door,
then turning to roommates with dread or accusations; and out-
side in the hall, the committees rating personalities on a grading
system from one to seven (except for Ivy, the top, which needs
only a plus or minus) — one even reporting the decision, incredi-
bly enough, on a walkie-talkie:
"This is Pete calling in for Cottage. Negative on wonks in Pat-
ton 96. Dirty story, grubby room. That's right: negative."

It's a two-dollar, one-hour train ride from Princeton, New
Jersey, to either Philadelphia or New York City. The nearest
thing to a girl's college for miles around is the public high
school, and there are only three theaters in the entire town.
When seeking relief from the academic life, therefore, the
average Princeton man invariably turns to his club. There he
not only takes all his meals, but forms friendships, watches
television, plays squash or bridge or Ping-Pong, drinks, parties, holds bull sessions, and even studies. Unless he's on a
varsity team, its intramural program is his only athletic out-

let, and when he becomes an alumnus, its activities will form the foci for fond memories, homecoming weekends, and pleas for financial support. More than any other part of the campus, it is the center of his life at Princeton.

"Bicker" is the annual ·process by which sophomores are chosen for election to the unproctored, privately owned and operated eating clubs. The college newspaper calls it "the most important single value-forming experience of the average undergraduate's career at Princeton."

The object of Bicker, according to a booklet published by the clubs themselves ("Now That You Are Eligible"), is to discover "personableness in the individual" and "congeniality of the total section." It is a method for assuring each club that any student to whom it offers a bid is of the "club type."

Immediately after finals — this year on Thursday, January 30, the Bicker committees of the clubs start to make their calls. These calls continue for ten days. Classes resume not long after Bicker has started, but they are largely ignored, sophomores finding it "hard to read anything more advanced than *Peyton Place*."

The committees call between the hours of four and six in the afternoon at first, then between seven-thirty in the evening and midnight. On the basis of a few minutes of stereotyped small talk the committees rate the eligibles, and the clubs immediately begin cutting their lists, most "from the top" as well as "from the bottom." Each night fewer clubs come calling at a given room. If, on the last night of the Bicker period, a sophomore is still receiving a committee, he has probably procured a "first-list bid." If not, and he has good friends whom a certain club is anxious to have, he may receive a "second-list bid" that will get him in if they accept their first-list bids, or if not enough first-list men accept that club's bids to fill its "section." Some sophomores receive bids from a number of clubs. Others receive none at all.

Individual sophomores are associated together in complexes of friends known as "preferentials," all of whose members desire to remain together with varying degrees of zeal. The exigencies of Bicker force most of these preferentials into greater or less states of disintegration, a process which widely subjects old friendships to severe strains and some-times even shatters them. A sophomore's preferential group may also be used by the clubs to appraise and manipulate him throughout the Bicker procedure.

Saturday afternoon at Holder Court, club representatives and hundreds of sophomores shivering in the icy wind stand with hands thrust into pockets or holding frigid beer cans, grouping and regrouping, talking in fast desperate undertones, trying to bargain friends into the same group, unload undesirables else-where, bid a sad good-by (as if parting forever) to classmates joining other clubs:

"Well, best of luck, Chuck" (wet eyed and swallowing hard). "I'm sure sorry you and George won't be going with me into Cannon."

"Ted's in trouble. He hasn't a bid yet. If you'd only turn down Tiger, Eldon, the two of us could get him into Charter."

"Hell, I hope Braddock does go to Key; I always thought he was a bastard anyhow."

Holder tower looms high above the thick mud that clogs the cordovans and white sneakers. "Named in honor of Christopher Holder," the plaque reads, "a member of the Society of Friends in America in the seventeenth century, devout, loyal to duty, pa-tient in suffering." Gargoyles leer down at the spectacle over the cloister arcade and from a phonograph stuck out the second-floor window of four entry the voice of a rock and roll singer blares fortissimo:

"Ain't That a Sha-a-a-ame!"

There is a definite hierarchy among the clubs at Princeton which is universally acknowledged, though the caste ob-viously implied by it is widely denied to exist. The highest echelon consists of "the big five." Ivy Club (wryly called "The Vine") is at the absolute summit; then follow, in no particular order, Tiger Inn, Colonial ("The Pillars"), Cap and Gown ("The Cap"), and Cottage ("The Cheese") — among whose former members have been both F. Scott Fitzgerald and John Foster Dulles. Graduates of the most famous Eastern prep schools, the scions of stock hallowed by generations of fame and money, and other individuals who can sell themselves well in 15 minutes or so, are nearly assured admission to one of these. To make Ivy is social apotheosis.

Then follow the host of "middle clubs," subject to gradation among themselves no doubt, though here any explicit ranking would be less objective and not generally conceded: Campus, Cannon, Charter, Cloister, Court, Dial, Elm, Key and Seal, Quadrangle, Terrace, and Tower. Dial took this year's only Negro.

Certain stereotypes are associated with some of the clubs which, like all stereotypes, fail in many individual instances. They are, however, more reliable, on the whole, than the images connected with the respective Harvard Houses. Thus, the campus "doers" or activity men are apt to be found in Cap and Gown or Quadrangle, and athletes tend to turn up, according to their inmost natures, either in Tiger Inn, the lair of "the gentlemen jocks," or in Cannon, home of "the sweaty ones." The captain of this year's football team, however, is in Ivy, which always has its pick of the entire class.

Sharing the bottom of the social scale with Prospect Club — though ranking if possible, even further down — is Woodrow Wilson Lodge, or, as it is commonly called, "the facility." Wilson Lodge was founded last year by the university and supposedly provides "an alternative to the club system" for those who want neither to renounce all social activity for three years of college life nor to pass through the indignity of Bicker and accept membership in one of the 17 eating clubs. But any one in the university, with the possible exception of the administration, will freely admit that the three-room facility in no sense provides a satisfactory alternative.

Last year, in an attempt to raise Wilson's prestige, Sophomore Vice President Robert Hillier dramatically announced that he would accept no bids from any club, but would join the Lodge and bring "sixty or seventy of the good men in the class" along with him. "Everyone's afraid that the facility will become a dumping ground," he stated. "Someone has to make the move to destroy the stigma that will result." Today, Hillier has become a junior member of Quadrangle Club; there are only 21 people in the facility, and it, along with Prospect, is a dumping ground.

The youngest, the cheapest, and the shabbiest of the clubs is Prospect. It is also the most democratically governed. Founded ten years ago, Prospect is unique in demanding neither undergraduate nor alumni dues, and its term rate is $80 less than that of Tower and $130 less than Ivy, which otherwise represent the two extremes. More important, Prospect is unlike the other organizations on Prospect Street in that its policies are not determined privately by a small clique of officers and a powerful graduate board. Alone among the clubs, Prospect can hold the sort of Bicker its members actually want.

This year Prospect announced that any sophomore who wished to join might do so by simply dropping in and signing the books, until either its capacity had been reached or the official deadline arrived. Isolated idealism of this sort, however, was naive in a situation so inherently unprincipled at its roots. The thousand and one vices and foibles of the system have long been concealed by the democratic boast that "everyone who wants to, makes a club." Jim Ridgeway, chairman of *The Daily Princetonian*, published an editorial warning Prospect that its policy would prove disastrous, that one club would be used as a scapegoat and dumping ground by the irresponsible other 16, who could then continue the old boast without themselves doing a thing to achieve it. As a result, the Interclub Committee summoned Ridgeway and his managing editor to their meeting place in the library of Ivy Club, hotly denounced them both for "incompetence," failure to "cooperate," a "negative" and "critical" attitude, and formally broke off all relations with *The Princetonian*.

Without once making specific criticisms of what had been written or charging factual inaccuracies, the ICC banned the press from all further Bicker events and information. Every one of Bicker's key decisions was made in personal anonymity and behind closed doors. The demands of the newspaper for an account of what was going on were flatly rejected, and the all-powerful ICC operated throughout without being responsible to anyone, least of all to either the administration or the student body of the Princeton community.

Bicker reaches its colorful climax during Open House.

Seven-thirty that Saturday evening and the entire class, bathed, brushed, shined, combed, and shivering, hurries through the dark night and biting wind across the campus to Prospect Street, where the grounds of 16 plush clubhouses — and the not-

so-plush Prospect Cooperative Club — stretch before them. The luckiest ones have received several bids and join one of the big five:

You stroll with anxious expectation across the broad lawn up to the great white columns of Colonial's porch. The door swings open and you and your group (throughout Bicker, you move in a group of three or four — you are judged, accepted, and perhaps rejected collectively) are swept into the dazzling warm uproar inside. You feel the soft depth of the rug beneath your feet and can see a bright, glittering, well-groomed haze all around you. Up the grand stairway, lined with upperclassmen clapping and cheering, until you reach the top where beaming and blushing abashedly you sign your name and receive the dark blue and red and yellow and green striped club tie from the president. A final huzzah, then you and the rest turn with relish to the serious business of the evening, consuming as much alcohol as possible. Everyone is shaking hands and slapping each other on the back. It is a bacchanalian love-feast and you drink freely. You are in.

Others, the majority, must accept bids to lesser clubs, and others still must go through the agonizing process of rushing from house to house, hoping to be accepted from the second list after all their more desirable classmates have signed the books. When at last these too are in, they drink still more freely and shout more loudly — trying to forget, though they are in, how it was they got there.

And finally there are the Others — those who are "in trouble," as the euphemism goes, who must somehow be fitted in somewhere by somebody so the clubs can again point with pride to the precious statistic 100 percent — 100 percent of those wishing to join a club did so" — the number by which alone the system can be justified. It must be able to claim the fact of 100 percent no matter how often or how strangely 100 percent must be redefined.

A council of the club presidents, the ICC, directs all 100 percenters to report to the back porch of Ivy at 9:30 sharp (oh heavy irony here, on the back porch of Ivy, entering not the front door or being admitted to the parlor, but stumbling through the dark around the carousing house, and coming through the servants' entry.)

At first they joke about their predicament (but actual tears will be shed before many hours have passed) — "I'd feel pretty bad if I didn't see so many of my friends here." Kind soft-spoken Ivy men take them aside and counsel them. Join Prospect, they gently urge (each adjusting his identical green and yellow striped tie). Join the poverty-stricken cooperative where you'll take turns waiting on your own tables and mopping the floor and be looked down upon for three years by the members of the real clubs. Join the wonk club, join the club for leftovers, and (ever so gently) hurry up about it, so we can show 100 percent and go back to the party. Resistance is firm, but in many cases gives way. Something in you resists being classified a wonk, but something deeper cries out against exile.

What constitutes the Princeton definition of "wonk" at Bickertime? The traits of a varied species can be most clearly grasped when combined into an extreme, idealized archetype, whose full obnoxious character each empirical individual but partially manifests and only for a brief time. To apprehend the Platonic essence, then, of the utter antithesis to the approved club type, imagine an inarticulate, introverted, morbidly shy sophomore from a small town in the provinces. He wears outlandish ties, dirty sweaters, and baggy pants. Not only lacking a crew cut, he is in bad need of a barber nearly all the time and obviously shaves but rarely. Until he arrived at the university he was educated in mediocre public schools, the whole of life to him lies in doodling with mathematics, and his idea of kicks is playing the violin. He is too undersized for athletics, has a horror, in fact, both of sports and drunken manly roughhousing, and his table manners, to put it kindly, are naive. The girls he dates when he dates at all are dogs, his conversation, when he talks at all, is incessantly intellectual and hardly what *The New Yorker* calls "sophisticated." Besides being childishly ignorant of his own inadequacies and ineptitudes, moreover, he wears thick glasses, has a large nose, and is flagrantly Jewish. None of the 100 percenters on Ivy's back porch were in so repugnant a state as this; even the sorriest of them participated in only a few of the characteristics of such an ideal form, and then in an attenuated degree. But one can clearly see why a social club would only be sensible in excluding such an individual, whatever the wisdom might be of admitting him to the university, and most of the officers on Prospect Street would agree that this precisely describes the sort of man who must at all costs be kept out. It is also a fairly accurate portrait of Einstein.

Here is the stigmata, the brand, the taint, clearly seen; the error of wearing white bucks for so solemn an evening, the misdemeanor of a soft, stammering voice, the felony of too loud and sure a one, the atrocity of a blue suit, here sitting a couple of silent boys with slanted eyes and yellow skin, from here the man who was academically first in the class leaving in discouragement to join Prospect, and here, recurring nearly two times out of every three, Israel's immemorial face is seen; the class has 16 Merit Scholars, 10 were in trouble on Thursday night, and 5 of them, too, are here.

And when they're sure you're not an unctuous agitator for Prospect Club, they are willing to talk to you freely, gather, gather around and tell you calmly about the fist fight at the meeting when Court Club decided to cut its Jewish quota in half because an unintentional influx one year was causing its prestige to flag; about what an ICC president told one of them privately and with a certain sadness one day, that "anti-Semitism in the clubs is something that can neither be exposed, nor proved, nor cured"; about the tacit and explicit demands of club alumni through the graduate boards that, though a few Jews may be admitted to every club, "they must be kept down to reasonable numbers" and that is why Prospect has so many Jews; about what a club representative had just told one of them quite frankly, "we'd like to take you but our quota on you people is filled up"; about —

The other heads abruptly part and there is suddenly only one single scowling face. The president of the sophomore class.

"Are you from the Harvard Crimson?"

"Yes."

"The ICC has voted the press completely barred here tonight. I'll have to ask you to leave."

"I'm not from The Princetonian, *you know. I have nothing to do with the university."*

"I know that. But you'll have to leave."

"Why?"

"I'm not at liberty to tell you."

"Why not?"

"Get out."

Someone standing nearby begins about:

"If it weren't for you damn newspaper guys, we wouldn't have this mess. These people wouldn't even be here tonight."

He has on a green and yellow striped tie. Ivy man. He's right: they'd be in Prospect.

A gust of cold air, the door slams, locks, and back out again in the 12-degree biting night wind.

"Shortly after that incident," The Princetonian *reported, "the central headquarters committee decided that too many people were on the proch without legitimate reason. They closed the doors and kept a careful tab on who went in and out. This immediately gave rise to the idea that the porch was a 'cage.' Even the men not in clubs began referring to themselves as 'cagers.' "*

Around midnight, the clubs run out of liquor and every door on Prospect Street spews forth a jubilant stream of staggering sophomores, juniors, and seniors. Leaning on each other, singing, shouting, a few pausing at the gutter to retch quietly for a moment then loudly rejoining the buoyant inebriated throng, they totter off toward the campus or a café where they can calm down with a cup of coffee. The fraternal transport is now at its beatific height. Arm in arm they reel indifferent to traffic or the piercing cold; one lifts his hands to the frigid heavens and races down the street backward, his scarf and topcoat wildly flapping in the wind, crying out in ecstasy, "Lord, Lord, Lord, Lord, Lord!" The unbroken tension of weeks — of a year and a half for some, has ended. Bicker is over at last, for them.

But on Ivy's back porch, for 42 remaining sophomores, the suspense has reached its most pitiless climax. Since almost everyone who was inside has gone home now and the porch has long been growing chilly, the 100 percenters are permitted to move into the Ivy dining room. They can see the silver candelabras now and the rows of empty bottles. Prospect had electric lights and beer tonight. Somehow the number dwindles to 35 as the discouraging hours pass, then 6 give way and trudge toward Prospect, and another 6 are placed as a few clubs each make the sacrifice and each consent to admit 1 lone 100 percenter (there to be pariah or sycophant for who knows how long). Above, in the library, like secret Teutonic Norns, the ICC meets in constant absolutely closed session, omnipotently spinning fate. Below them, 23 100 percenters remain, half of them Jewish. In Valhalla's lofty and concealed recesses, the list is gone over name by name: where are these to be placed?

An outsider observing Bicker finds it difficult to take the whole thing seriously. The enormous anxieties generated in every member of the sophomore class, the superficiality and downright silliness of its standards and ceremonies, the blatant injustices of the values and principles the system inculcates — all would seem ludicrous in any civilized community, but they are doubly comic when set in one of the nation's greatest universities and practiced by what is supposed to be a substantial segment of this generation's intellectual elite.

At the heart of the system, unquestioned by even the 100 percenters themselves, lies the principle of selectivity. As a member of Key and Seal expressed it, "In a democracy we are supposedly free to become as exclusive or as gregarious as we like, and if in a club situation we choose to be exclusive, this is our privilege." From that bit of casuistry — more often expressed as an innocent belief that "you've got a right to choose your friends and the guys you're going to eat with" — the code of values can be relentlessly deduced which summarily condemns certain personality traits, ethnic groups, and even scholarship, intellectualism, and originality themselves per se.

As David Riesman has pointed out, apologetics as a reaction to this kind of attack is inappropriate: "It surrenders the ethical initiative, for it permits the anti-Semite to frame the issue of debate and the norms of criticism." For to deny the fact that a Jew or a grind can't come up to country-club standards is to concede the validity of those standards.

A truly liberal education should neither teach bigotry and prejudice nor try to persuade students of the opposite lie that there are no significant differences between men in terms of personality, conventional social charm, race, or religious conviction. Its task is rather to show that these factors have nothing to do with one's ethical worth or human dignity — to help the student remold his system of values so that none of these traits are the controlling factor in evaluating another human being — to deepen and expand his vision to the point, in fact, where he rejoices in human diversity and creative individuality and actively seeks it out. Social insulation, a striving for comfortable homogeneous groups, the frank institutionalism of arbitrary and unreflective prejudices — these do not contribute to that aim. Even if the racial criterion were eliminated, the general principle of an ill-founded sort of discrimination would remain as an axiom of Princeton's entire social structure.

Deeper insight than anyone has yet applied might reveal that the most unfortunate victims of Princeton's vicious Bicker process are not necessarily those scores of students who are dumped in undesirable organizations or left altogether out in the cold. Rather it is the hundreds who happily make the respectable and especially the most desirable clubs on the street. It is they who have consented without apparent compunctions to build their prestige, success, and social contentment on the hypocrisy, mendacity, inhumanity, servility, pettiness and sheer unreason upon which Princeton's club system and Bicker procedure are obviously reared. It's the oldest truth in creation that there is evil in the universe and it is as a realistic schooling in the world's folly and wickedness that Bicker is usually defended. In letting her students, after months of reading Plato and Kant, Milton and Thoreau, pass complacently through the two weeks of Bicker, Princeton may well be defeating her own highest efforts at cultivating an operative system of values, and inducing in her sons the refined sort of ethical blindness which tactfully refrains from seriously applying standards of what is right in adjusting to the realities of what merely is.

Harvard, however, has no grounds for a holier-than-thou attitude toward her younger sister in New Jersey. Woodrow Wilson, the first and greatest opponent of Princeton's club system, scribbled the following among his notes for an address in 1906: "What is the future of the Upper Class Clubs? More and more expense and only social aims or University aims? Danger that we will develop socially as Harvard did and as Yale is tending to do."

Harvard's freedom today from the pestilence that still possesses Princeton should in no wise be interpreted as evidence for the stouter moral fiber of her undergraduate body compared to that encamped around Nassau Hall. It was only the House system which redeemed her — and a philosophy of education which viewed the student social structure as a primary concern and area of legitimate jurisdiction for a great university and which sought to rebuild that structure on a principle which was the inverse of selectivity: the principle of distribution within the House, geographical, academic, economic, and intellectual, with diversity of race and religion being considered relevant only insofar as they are eagerly sought after, never forming a basis for exclusion.

It was just such a goal that Wilson campaigned for, decades before President Lowell was to demand it in Cambridge. And the same elements which finally defeated him in 1908 would be sure to oppose vigorously any similar move by President Goheen to abolish the clubs 50 years later.

The alumni organized meetings of protest. One of the leading graduates of Princeton wrote to the *Alumni Weekly* denouncing the idea that students should be compelled to mix with their inferiors — "no one can make a gentleman associate with a mucker." In the pages of *The New York Sun*, an indignant letter signed "Ivy" appeared, demanding to know, "Is it possible that the doctrines of the confiscation of property and the superior wisdom of those in high places which have recently been so characteristic of our political life are to be received with favor in one of the most historic and conservative of our institutions of learning?"

Then — as now — the overwhelming majority of the faculty favored the substitution of "the college plan" for the club system, and the great masses of western alumni also supported Wilson's efforts.

But the eastern alumni, through the board of trustees and the financial pressures they brought to bear upon him, defeated Princeton's greatest president and the founder of her celebrated preceptorial system in what he regarded as "nothing less than the most critical work of my whole administration, the work upon which its whole vitality and success depends." It was Wilson's first great defeat and led to his first neuritic breakdown. He considered resigning and sailing to Bermuda, an island which, he wrote to his wife, "is certainly the best place in the world to forget Princeton, at least Princeton as an organization and a problem."

Flurries of protest have arisen subsequently on the Princeton campus. In 1918 and again in 1949, it was the demands of the students themselves which forced the clubs to consider the necessity of 100 percent, and finally compelled them to adopt it over strong alumni opposition. The principle has long since, however, degenerated from the intent of its founders, and this year was openly exposed as a patent farce.

At 2:10 in the morning, the meeting above at last breaks up and the decision descends. The sophomores in Ivy's dining room are hushed as they hear the verdict:

". . . The ICC will take no responsibility for those who have refused to take bids to Prospect. They consider any reasons for refusing as invalid . . ."

And so the sophistry predicted by The Princetonian *is made complete. Prospect held an open Bicker. Therefore in effect every sophomore got a bid from Prospect. Therefore any sophomore wanting to join a club could have gone to Prospect. Therefore 100 percent.*

". . . The ICC can determine no valid reason for distinguishing between Prospect Cooperative Club and the other 16 upper-class eating clubs, and holds that a bid to Prospect is as good as a bid to any other club. Nor can the ICC determine any valid reason for refusing an opportunity to join Prospect Club . . ."

They word the statement as firmly as possible, for they already know that no one, no one — least of all themselves — believes a single word of it. But the lie sustains the system for another year.

After a Bicker that took five extra nights of haggling to get a bid for everyone in 1955, *The Daily Princetonian* and other university organizations demanded the provision of an alternative to the club system. The result was the creation of the now discredited Wilson Lodge. It is in the rapid physical improvement of the Lodge plant, however, and the dim hope that it may eventually evolve into something akin to a Harvard

House, that *The Princetonian* and most of the other critics of the clubs still look for salvation. Just such a project was placed before Woodrow Wilson as a suggested compromise with his demand that the clubs be abolished altogether and the "Quad Plan," as he called it, be made universal. Wilson rejected it. He thought such a "sample quad" would be doomed from the start since only men not in the clubs would join it. The proposal merely dodged the issue, left selectivity untouched, prolonged the evils of exclusion for both those who were in and those who were out — availed nothing, in short, toward the solution of the problem that tormented Wilson at Princeton: "the blighting of the intellectual interests of many of her best minds and finest spirits."

A petition passes among the 100 percenters (100 percenters, whatever other name illogic may give them). It objects that racial and religious discrimination has been exercised in excluding them from the clubs, and pleads for a reply, a public review, a denial or an explanation.

Fifteen sign it.

The ICC flatly refuses to recognize it.

If history and circumstances show anything, therefore, they clearly demonstrate that the evils of the club system will be effectively eliminated only if: 1) the reforms well up directly from the students themselves; and, 2) they strike at the central doctrine of the present system, the basic axiom of selectivity. Compared with all previous reformers, this year's freshman class could usher in the millennium immediately by unanimously signing a petition which would declare they will not join a club unless Bicker is abolished and the university administration is given unqualified authority to assign sophomores to the various clubs by applying the distribution principle to the applications submitted, just as is done in the case of the Houses and the "colleges" at Harvard and at Yale.

But the Princeton conscience, both official and actual, has long grown jaded.

A few hours pass and despite going late to bed and the throb of stubborn hangovers, hundreds of undergraduates drag themselves to chapel Sunday morning, signing little white cards at the door to prove they've been there to get credit.

"The university is vitally concerned with all aspects of Bicker" — William D'O. Lippincott, dean of students, Princeton University — "but it has been, and still is, the policy to leave the conduct of club elections completely up to the undergraduates. We do not plan to use pressure to have these men integrated."

. . . Clouds without shift the shade of the light as it filters majestically down through the great blue stained-glass windows. (Twenty-three sophomores still without a club, 15 of these Jewish, 5 Merit Scholars.)

"The unfortunate allegations of religious discrimination . . . obscure the plain facts that there are today members of the three major faiths in this country in each of the seventeen eating clubs and that every one of the sophomores who has not joined a club in 1958 was offered club membership." — Robert F. Goheen, president, Princeton University — "It is fair to say that the seriousness of these allegations has been exaggerated by several individuals who sought to impose their wishes on the clubs . . ."

The voice of the organ echoes down the mighty, Gothic nave as the congregation rises to sing the Doxology —

"Praise God from whom all blessings flow . . ."

"The ICC recognizes the right of every club to be selective. Selectivity implies the right of a club to impose a religious quota, if it so desires." — text of a statement released by the Interclub Committee, Princeton University, February 10, 1958 — "The ICC does not approve of religious and racial discrimination, but has no power to control the Bicker policy of individual clubs. Ultimate responsibility for religious and racial discrimination rests with the individual members of the individual clubs."

And on the edge of the minister's solemn dark surplice as he sweeps up into the pulpit and the choir and organ thunder the last amen can be seen the orange and black seal of the university, and below it Princeton's motto:

(According to all present indications, Bicker will be back next year.)

"Dei Sub Numine Viget."

The Three Flavors of Radcliffe
BY FAYE LEVINE '65

March 12, 1963

Ask any Cliffie to tell you what type of girl goes to her school, and she will back away nervously, stammering "individuality . . . no stereotypes whatsoever . . . leave me alone," and things like that. The poor girl is afraid you are trying to squeeze her and her friends into a single mold; the stringy brunette mold perhaps, or worse, the intense, amoral, Bohemian mold. *Life, Holiday, The New York Times, Sports Illustrated,* and Leonie St. John became her eternal enemies as soon as they suggested one-word summaries.

Nevertheless, she knows that some things can be said about types of girls, and styles of doing Radcliffe. The whole experience, from background and preparation to dress, dating, courses, and even attitudes, comes in three different flavors.

Radcliffe may be done first of all in peach. This flavor appeals most naturally to girls who have been made aware of social life and social obligations throughout their lives. Perhaps their parents are of the administrative upper class, presiding over businesses or government offices. They probably applied only to Radcliffe and one or two other schools in "The Heavenly Seven" (as they would call it). And very likely they are from New England or the mid-Atlantic seaboard.

But not necessarily. Anyone can like the flavor. The style of dress is consistently tasteful. Girls often wear high heels and stockings. Coats with fur collars, small pins and wrist watches, camel's-hair anythings, gloves, jackets with print linings, and pretty colored sweater sets are common. This style approves highly of boys with vests, pipes, and woolen scarves around their necks; and likes to dress up on dates.

And peachy friendships are firm ones. Their cliques of four or five are as Final as anything institutionalized. Not that they are unfriendly to people outside their clique — if anything, a constant friendliness is inherent to the style. They are cordial to the point of exuberance, sometimes to the point of bedlam. If male they would be shouting at football games; as it is, they can discuss a hockey game vivaciously throughout a dinner. When asked what adjective they would use if they wanted to give another girl the highest compliment possible, they unanimously answer "charming" or "feminine."

Of course a flavor alone doesn't absolutely determine anything as objective as courses or extracurricular activities. Yet the composition of Fine Arts 13 somehow *feels* different. There seems to be more flirting, joking, and talking, more girls with careful makeup and shiny clean hair than in most lower-level survey courses. And majors like Soc Rel, Fine Arts, History, English, and History and Lit somehow have a peachiness about them.

Many girls who exemplify the style relax and enjoy social life in the popular sense of the word, dating a great deal, discussing boys and other girls more than their fellow Cliffies, and participating gaily in drama. Others, however, participate seriously in administrative organizations such as Radcliffe and dormitory government, in service organizations (like their mothers) and in choral societies. Where rules are to be tended, this group tends them. Briggs, the stronghold of the peach flavor, was the most vehement supporter of an orderly and extensive system of sign-outs in last year's debate.

And to them the Harvard-Radcliffe experience is most significant for its social milieu. What do you like best about this place? The most peach-flavored answer is "the people."

If girls don't fit into this style, however, they can do Radcliffe in chocolate. Perhaps they come from public high schools, where they started in conventional ways — as valedictorian or student council president or cheerleader. Perhaps they come from large cities in the South and West, or from the metropolitan area outside Manhattan. And perhaps their parents are middle class: high-school teachers, doctors, clergymen, some lawyers, some scientists. They are often the first in some group they know, family, high school, or city, to come "here." And so, when thinking about college, they took care to apply to a "safety school," or to a large number of schools, or to large popular universities like the Universities of Michigan or Pennsylvania.

Coming from such a background, girls find themselves already outfitted in the chocolate uniform. It may range in attractiveness, but it is always Conventional. Woolen scarves over the head, large plaids, sneakers, eyeglasses, and thick boots are common. When they are messy it is with dirty hair, bitten nails, and too-long skirts. And when they are well dressed, it is in a happily wholesome way, with pleated skirts, Loden coats, and the bulky cardigans that all of American teenagery is wearing. If they approach the tastefulness of the peach style at times (without ever really achieving it), it is perhaps because peachy dress serves as an epitome of fashion in many public high schools.

Chocolate friendships and romances are both casually groupy. One girl may have two or three close friends, who are not necessarily friends with each other. Cliques are not firm or obvious. Similarly, these girls often date many boys without being serious about any. Sometimes, however, a chocolate girl has few or no friendships, and she spends most of her waking life on schoolwork.

For achievement is very important to this style. They are active within the existing system. Recognized in high school by students or teachers, perhaps high scorers on national tests, they often major in functional subjects like Government, History, Economics, and above all, science. They chip away at PBH [Phillips Brooks House], at co-ed political clubs, at publications. Or else devote themselves intensely to getting high marks. They justify their behavior on pragmatic grounds, and worry most about careers and graduate school.

And they love to take Soc Sci 2, for it combines sociology and history into a rigorous but functional how-to manual. There the girls who address envelopes for the Young Democrats meet the boys who aspire to the Senate, and on rainy days the girls look more rained on than in other classes.

Whether the girl is noisily career minded or a silent academic recluse, she is likely to have a certain chocolate attitude toward college. To her, the experience of Harvard-Radcliffe is most important for "the infinite opportunities it offers." She sees college primarily as a set of doors to be utilized, rather than a self-sufficient milieu. And so she chooses to compliment another girl by giving her some utilitarian and unfeminine attribute: like "brilliant," "down to earth," "conscious," "alive," or "great" and the like.

If both of these flavors are unsuitable, a girl can still do Radcliffe in lime. For this it is most useful to have been brought up in a family which is professionally intellectual: usually college professors, artists, or writers. It helps to have gone to one of the progressive private schools, where standards are predominantly individualistic and intellectual, rather than social. (With girls' schools these are more easily distinguished than with boys'.) And it is useful to have lived in a college town, a foreign country, or a sophisticated urban community; to have applied to a very small number of progressive and stiff colleges, like Swarthmore, Sarah Lawrence, Oberlin, and so forth.

Once all this is done, limeness is just beginning. The distinctive feature of this style is Style. Girls who adopt it are sometimes thought of as the Radcliffe stereotype, and probably give wholesome Harvard freshmen from Iowa their first proof that the East is indeed strange looking. Greek shoulder bags are extremely popular, as are ski jackets, black tights, pierced ears, half high heels, long unpolished fingernails, rain ponchos, "Marimekko" dresses, primitive jewelry, and long hair. The most well-dressed of them imitate a European sort of gray-beige, expensive simplicity; the sloppy ones wear ski polo shirts and dungarees and can be called (to their probable disdain) "beat." They have generally been to Europe, or hitch-hiked across America.

Upper-level English courses contain many of these girls, as do courses in creative writing, foreign languages, and the other humanities. They rarely participate in extracurricular activities, with the exception of creative arts. When they do act, write, paint, or play instruments, it is usually extremely well. Probably they wrote poetry when they were young.

Limes very seldom have groups of close friends, and never cliques. Instead they travel mostly alone, or with a serious boy friend. And their traveling often takes the form of gliding. Perhaps a little too thin, some cultivate a mysterious, ethereal, or merely composed look. They are most conscious of their sex and often the most beautiful of the girls. They decorate their rooms with taste, and more concern for art and individuality than do their fellow students. And a search for self-expression, for eternal, almost mythic verities, is implied in the adjectives they use to compliment another girl: "beautiful," "good," "nice," "womanly," "sympatico," "free."

This self-consciousness is usually of an assured quiet sort. They define the Radcliffe years as an arrow pointing toward them, with everything else fading into a grayish blur. What do they like best here? The privacy, the independence, the challenge, or some particular experience of the past, they answer softly.

Like the chocolates, this flavor wanted to liberalize the sign-out rules, but while the chocolate reason was an indignant "we are responsible enough," the lime reason was "they have no business interfering with our lives."

If you want to get in touch with anyone of a particular flavor and can't judge adequately from the Freshman Register, you should go to certain addresses. Peaches center about dorm living rooms, the Spa, Widener reading room, and organized social functions. Chocolates are upstairs in their room, in Mallinckrodt, in "Rad Libe," in restaurants, at their organization's headquarters, or eating early dinner. Limes are also in Widener (although more likely in the stacks than the reading room), in cafeterias and coffee shops, in the Fogg, and in people's apartments.

They all meet, to be sure — at registration and graduation.

[Awarded Dana Reed Prize "Honorable Mention" in 1963]

The Weathermen're Shot, They're Bleeding, They're Running, They're Wiping Stuff Out

BY JOHN G. SHORT '70

November 12, 1969

Walking over to Lincoln Park Wednesday night, I stop at a liquor store, buy a bottle of beer, and ask for an opener. I know what the Weather Bureau has got planned for tonight. Earlier, at the briefing at the Michigan-Wisconsin-New-England-and-New-York-State movement headquarters, they told us that after the speeches we were going to march through the city. The police would try to stop us. Police make me very uneasy. The beer fails to make me the least bit high.

At Lincoln Park the turnout for this, the first demonstration, is very small. About 300 people are gathered around a bonfire fueled by park benches. Another 200 newspapermen and spectators stand around the edges. It is very sad. They had announced 1500 would show, and were really expecting 800. It is undeniably terrible when any left political movement turns out to have far less support than it needs, when the people you thought you had won don't care to show.

I sit down on the grass at the edge of the crowd not listening to the speakers, watching the fire glowing through the legs of the people around it looking through the trees across the park to the cars going by on the expressway. I count the cars, and my friend, Kunen, keeps time. In 150 seconds, two and a half minutes, as many people whiz by on the expressway as there are Weathermen in the world.

How sad that only this few people are crazy. Where are the massed armies of insanity? A hundred thousand people marched on the Pentagon. Maybe it's because that was on a weekend and this is the middle of the week.

Quite suddenly a speaker is announcing "We're going to be moving out now. Stay with your groups, and follow the leadership." The march wants to get as far south as the Drake Hotel, which is next door to where the judge of the Conspiracy 8 trial lives. There are no police in the park; they are all in the streets outside waiting to move in if the Weathermen stay past the eleven o'clock curfew.

The Weathermen break into a run across the park on signal. They are wearing white helmets, which are all you can see bobbing up and down in the night. They are screaming and chanting, and suddenly start the high-pitched shrill used by the people of Algiers during the revolution. Ill-leel-leel-lil-ill-il-eel-eeeeeeeeeeee.

They pass a big square park building. Stones and bricks are hurled up out of the running crowd and smash to pieces the building's 20-foot-tall plate-glass windows.

Now they are across the last bit of park and running into the street. There are no police around anywhere. The police have somehow been faked out. The crowd charges up Clark Street, one of the main streets of Chicago, wiping out store windows on both sides. And then a florist shop takes a stone right through its front window. Lots of flowers are knocked over.

This is when I decide to put a distinction between me and the Weathermen. Their action is really against the people. Kunen is running up the street alongside me. He says, "What are they doing hitting a florist shop?" I don't know, but I don't feel as bad about it as he does. We move out of the crowd and start running up the sidewalk.

A bottle thrown out of the crowd hits the side of a building just in front of me. A girl with long blonde hair is showered with glass but isn't cut. A boy from the crowd yells at us, "Get into the street." But it looks like everyone in the street is going to be shot and arrested pretty soon. The sirens are beginning to scream.

The crowd slows down to a fast walk every so often to allow itself to be amazed. They have taken control of the street. They have proceeded entirely unchecked by opposition. The police squad cars pull across each new intersection only to drive screeching away when the crowd gets near.

Their sound is echoing off the tall buildings around them. Their boots are thumping like a forced march. A new window goes shattering to the ground every two seconds. They begin wiping out cars.

The brighter lights of the Loop are far up Clark Street. But the crowd swings into a turn left onto Goethe Street. The kids are all staying very close together. When it turns, the crowd seems to act as one, its arms waving, its helmets bobbing, flowing into the smaller street like a river rushing through a canyon.

They hit State Street and head back down toward the Loop again. They have foxed the police. It is very hard to keep track of the crowd in the night.

Some of the girls don't have helmets on. Their hair is streaming back behind their heads as they run. They all pass some construction sites where people run over to pick new stones and bricks. No paving stones in Chicago. A guy is going past a Rolls Royce. Imagine a Rolls Royce. He plants one foot ahead of him. Stops, pivots like a shortstop bringing his arm

down in a big arch. His club takes out the windshield. Someone else opens the back door, rips out the phone or something,
and leaves. Middle-aged people looking out from the lobby of
the hotel and standing in furs on the street are visibly upset.

Now the police are zooming in to take a stand at Division
Street. The crowd charges forward to get there first before the
police can set up. But the police are ready, and they move in
on the running crowd as it enters the intersection. Tear gas is
fired.

The Weathermen have been divided. Some made it through
and they are now circling back north to join the rest of the
group.

I stand half a block from the intersection. People are running full speed past me the other way. A girl stops and lights
a phosphorous smoke bomb. The intersection is filled with gas
and smoke. Through it I can see the revolving blue and red
lights of police cars. Police are pushing their captives into the
wagons.

A squad car is coming up Clark Street against the flow of
the retreating Weathermen. It is blocked. Its windows are
smashed in seconds. The driver drops it into first and speeds
through the crowd.

The crowd, on the run, winds east on the first side street to
rejoin the smaller part of the group, which had been cut off.
After they pass an apartment building, one of the stragglers in
the group is grabbed by a bystander. They start fighting. Another Weatherman comes in to help the kid. They get the
man, who is in a gray suit and is about 30 years old, down on
the ground. One of the two starts kicking the man while he's
down. His fur-draped mother starts screaming to let him
alone. The kids back off and one is grabbed by some other
men and dragged into a building, where he is beaten. A policeman drives up on his motor scooter. Someone yells to him,
"A man in there has pulled a gun." A crowd is gathering.
There are no other police anywhere around. The cop splits.

I leave to find where the Weathermen have gone. It isn't
easy. Their line of march is only about half a block long, and
they move so fast that by the time you find them they're either on top of you or gone again.

I find them going north on Astor Street back up toward Lincoln Park. They seem to have been traveling in S-type patterns, constantly changing their direction to avoid the police.

Astor Street is a very quiet street; it has trees, sports cars, and ripple-front brick apartments; it is a lot like Georgetown. The Weathermen seem to have momentarily lost the police. They are wiping out cars and the windows of the more expensive-looking places. Doormen are surprised. A dusty Volkswagen bus is left alone.

A boy and his girl driving up the street in his car are engulfed by the crowd. They stop the car and sit there as the people in helmets pour by. The back windows of the car are broken, while the two sit looking straight ahead.

But the Weathermen are now going in the exact opposite direction from their objective, the judge's hotel. They hit North Avenue, which is the street immediately south of Lincoln Park. They are in a very bad position.

Once more they turn east, and one block later are at the corner of North and the Lakeshore Drive expressway. They have led themselves into a corner. They must get themselves back into the city to survive. They turn north parallel to the expressway, followed now by patrol cars. They take the first right back into the city and run into an ambush a block later.

Buckshot zings into the trees over the heads of the kids.

Two or three policemen step out front and level their pistols at the crowd. Blam, blam, blam, blam, blam. They empty their guns at the kids. Several people go down. But they are not hit; they're ducking. It takes about half a minute for the Weathermen to realize that those were blanks. But by then they are retreating. They have no guns.

A girl is lying in the intersection. She has been shot through the leg with a real pistol bullet. A boy has been shot in his shoulder and the side of his body. The police have a lot of people they grabbed pinned up against patrol cars.

Police come charging down their middle in a V. The group is split, running up two different streets. Several more shots are fired. I am toward the back of the group when two cars of plainclothes policemen come roaring up from behind. They leap out of their cars before they have even stopped and start grabbing people.

There is an alley to my right. It is the only way out. Half a dozen of us take off down the alley as fast as we can with the cops chasing us. Police come pouring into the area behind us. I am running.

I spin my head and my glasses go flying off. I think, "There go my glasses." I can't see, but I don't even slow down. The police are a few steps behind us. Some of the girls, who aren't as fast, are being caught.

The alley becomes dark, and all I see is the light at the end of it down on North Avenue. As I run, I am dreaming. There is something I can remember, somewhere where this whole piece of terror happened to me before. I remember, yes, it happened, running away from two boys who tried to hold me up with a razor blade one night in Harlem. I'm not aware of my legs lifting or my arms pumping or any part of running. I can't see. I am floating through a blur.

As I'm coming to the end of the alley all I can see is the flashing blue lights of police cars in front of me. All I can hear is the high tweet of police whistles being blown all around me. The police are coming at us from the other end of the alley, too.

Then, as we approach them, there comes an empty lot on our left. There is a wire fence as high as my chest. I, and one or two other kids, put our hands on it, and throw ourselves over.

Now I am running across the lot, stepping on things I can't see, surrounded again by police whistles and flashing blue lights moving parallel to us in the street.

I get to the other side and take a flying leap over the same fence. A police car turns down the street right in front of me. I put one hand on the trunk and twist around it, taking off down North Avenue, right next to the park, again.

The police are moving back in the other direction now to seal off the area I just got out of. They are all behind me. They can't leave their posts.

I stop running in a couple of blocks, and quickly take off my black leather jacket and wipe the sweat off my face and make like a pedestrian. I can't see anything and stop some people on the street to ask what street I'm on and which way to the nearest telephone. They point west.

I find a gas station, its phone, and a dime. It's an open phone, right out on the street. I dial the long-distance operator and call The Crimson to file my news. I get David Hollander in the newsroom. "David," I say, "everything's gone wild here . . ."

I stand on North Avenue for half an hour phoning in my stuff to Cambridge. Police cars are pouring by me into the area I just left. A detachment of helmeted tactical cops walk by in step with one another. They pass so close I could trip them . . .

I took a CTA (Chicago Transit Authority) train up to the movement center, where I'm staying. I am amazed to find that most people made it back OK. They say they only know of about six or eight who got captured and I'm the fifty-fourth to return . . .

The Weathermen leadership for this regional center is discussing how to organize things from now on while most people are crashing in the main room, which is a windowless volleyball court of the theological seminary where we're staying. To get in this room I pass a security check, which OK's my Weathermen ID card and frisks me for weapons I might be carrying. I go to sleep at 2 a.m.

At 4 a.m. one of the girls from the leadership comes in and throws on the lights all over the room, and yells, "Everybody up and do thirty jumping jacks. We're going to have a meeting."

I roll over in agony and drool into the wall, "I could just vomit." Most people get up and are ready to jump, when it is decided to put the whole thing off until the morning because it's important for us to rest.

Morning comes at 6:30 when the lights are turned on again, this time for good. People get up from where they've been sleeping, and collapse on the floor in a rough circle around the leadership. I pull on my pants and shiver, leaning against the wall with my blankets wrapped around my legs.

Girls make up much of the leadership in our center. And one of them is giving us an initial analysis of the last night's events. She wants to point out what went wrong, but tells us there were a lot of good things about it, too.

"There was a lot of smashing windows and hitting rich people's property and doing a lot of out-a-sight stuff. But," she says, "a lot of our people got ripped off, too. And that wasn't good."

People make the criticism that we should have fought the police more. They say that people would fight back when they were attacked, but that often groups would change their direction to avoid only four or five policemen when we could have overwhelmed them instead . . .

We talk about whether wiping out all the parked cars is an action against the people. It is generally understood that the area we attacked is where the oppressing class lives, and that people who associate with this existence are putting their cars on the line by their own act of will. It is, then, more or less these people's fault if their car is there. The Weathermen believe, after all, that there can be no spectators in the revolution — you're either part of it, or you are automatically acting against it. I am thinking that they are probably right, but, at the same time, they are demanding an awful lot, in fact too much, of people. Someone suggests that we spare Volkswagens and that sort of thing. The idea is passively accepted by the group spread around the floor . . .

. . . [The next night, after a few more demonstrations have taken place.] At midnight I go back to our movement center where they are holding a secret meeting of all the 250 or so Weathermen in Chicago to discuss what has already happened and to plan their strategy until Saturday. The entire Weather Bureau is there . . .

Mark Rudd talks, and then someone with red hair in a T-shirt begins a long rap about Weathermen political philosophy. I'm leaning against a post, summarizing, for my own use, Weathermen philosophy as follows:

1) Our economic structure in this country (capitalism, my father's corporations, your father's corporations) perpetuates a system. Our related social habits (thinking we are separate people, out on our own, not responsible to the poor around us), perpetuate the system. The system, whether or not it means to, keeps down the poor and the people in foreign countries where we have imperial interests.

2) Our jaillike schools make us unhappy, with the result

that we become oppressors defending the system to cover up our unhappiness. Family-inspired social conventions teach us subconsciously to do absurd things like giving an inferior role to women. And the values of our competitive capitalist economy teach us to squish anyone who's weaker than us.

3) Since the system makes us oppressors, no halfway effort to change the system, which cooperates with some of the values of that system, could ever win.

4) Only the kids and the blacks will join the struggle because they're the only ones whose lives aren't already tied up in the values of the system. The white workers won't join because they've got white-skin privilege.

5) There is a worldwide people's revolution going on right now. National boundaries don't cut us off from this because when the revolution is over, there will be only one people's government.

6) The first actions of this white revolutionary youth movement in the U.S. must be of a symbolic nature because its numbers are now small. They must show that the human spirit is capable of actual fighting even in spite of the peacefulness and obedience we were taught in school.

7) Finally, if people are shown that fighting can be, and is, done, then more kids will join in.

This is close to how the Weatherman in the street looks at things. I like it because it gets at the complexity of the world's guilt.

I could never act on it because I don't think any government will ever know how to run a country very well. Sartre said that revolution only changes the tyrants. "Revolution" means one 360-degree turn all the way round to the same place again.

I buy a sandwich, myself, and take the CTA back down to Chicago.

The next day it is raining [nothing happens] . . .

[On the day after, in Haymarket Square 200 Weathermen assemble.] John Jacobs, head theoretician of the Weathermen . . . stands up and shouts out a brilliant and passionate summary of the Weathermen philosophy before they go into their last battle in Chicago:

"There is a war in Vietnam and we are a Vietnam within

America. We are small but we have stepped in the way of history. We are going to change this country . . .

"The battle of Vietnam is one battle in the world revolution. It is the Stalingrad of American imperialism. We are part of that Stalingrad. We are the guerrillas fighting behind enemy lines . . .

"We will not commit suicide. We will not fight here. We will march to where we are within the symbol — the very pig fascist architecture . . . But we will make a political stand today . . ."

. . . The Weathermen start marching very quickly up Randolph Street toward the city, chanting, "Ho Ho Ho Chi Minh/NLF is going to win." The police lead the march, but hurry to stay in front of it.

When they are into the Loop area the march turns south on LaSalle Street, still moving very fast and still led by the police. But there are only about 12 policemen moving with the march. Others are standing 50 feet apart along the sidewalk on both sides for several miles through Chicago. But the Weathermen never have more than a couple of dozen police around them.

Two blocks later at Madison Street, they break. The leadership lets out battle cries, and 200 Weathermen go screaming through the police line out into the open street to the east.

The captain blows on his whistle and waves his arms. But they are already gone. The street around him is empty.

Rocks and pipes are thrown out of the running crowd into the windows of the stores all along Madison Street. Glass comes showering down right next to me. All the way up the street it goes crack, crack, crack, crack, crack, like a spreading earthquake . . .

. . . The Weathermen are on the loose again. There were only 200 of them and a couple thousand of the cops, but they still busted out. I'm racing down the street glowing in the wonder of people's eyes.

The Weathermen are going to get it. This area is being flooded by even more sirens. They won't be able to get out. It is daylight . . .

. . . I sneak up to the *Tribune* building at night with my

duffel bag. It is very dangerous to be a long-haired kid from out of state on the streets. They are still arresting people. I meet Parker [Donham '67('69) of *The Boston Globe*] and James Glassman ['69 of the *Herald Traveler*] in the *Times* office. Glassman gives me his suit coat so we won't get stopped. Parker drives us to the airport. And we take off out of there.

We are flying over lit Chicago, and I can see all the streets at once.

I am ambivalent. What the Weathermen were doing is suicide. My existence can still live with itself, it isn't screaming for a finish. And it doesn't want to color itself an unchanging gray by landing in jail for two years. The first thing the Weathermen have going against them, the main thing, the only thing that can seem really important, is the way their actions wipe out the self. It brings them down on you. Even if they are now slowly eating you away by the way they make you live, that seems better than being destroyed suddenly and totally.

Maybe to be a Weatherman you have to feel like nothing, to feel so crushed and fitted into the system that the only thing you want to do is break off and go smashing through the machinery with the hope that the other gears will come smashing with you. We are all guilty of racism and genocide. Just by living in the U.S., we are helping to maintain the status quo that burns the villages in Vietnam. All my happinesses are probably at the expense of others' sufferings. The world is like that. And it doesn't have to be, I don't think.

Everyone dislikes the Weathermen. Their fellow New Left political groups, the professors, the average student in the street, the general public of mothers and fathers, the policemen, and even the editorial page of this newspaper, of which I am an executive. They dislike the Weathermen because they can explain why the Weathermen are wrong and they think the Weathermen are stupid for not knowing it themselves.

I like the Weathermen because I hate everyone else. Everyone thinks they know. I don't know. I can't say the Weathermen are wrong. I can act; I can make decisions, and try to keep doing only those things that seem to make sense. But I don't know. I don't think I'll ever know.

It seems that the only *people* who get hurt by the Weathermen actions are the Weathermen themselves. Some people's property is smashed and a few people who are policemen are hurt. But the Weathermen say that those people are the big gears in the machine that's wiping people out all over the world. Just how true it is and how much "moral responsibility" people "owe" other people for the way they both live I don't know. I'm not even sure the "moral responsibility" exists. All feelings of morality that I have are not real things; they are just the values that my growing-up existence has worked into me.

One first feels his morality and then adopts a rationale for it later. My morality can have a great deal of sympathy with the Weathermen slogan "Bring the War Home." In other words, if they are going to perpetrate the war, let them experience their own work. Of course, morality is much more intricate than that. But that is just the point. The morality is infinitely complex: Nixon is not responsible for the war in Vietnam. No one in particular is. So the Weathermen are attacking that no one.

I have a great natural sympathy for crazy, anarchistic action. Preferably action that offers no further risk of guilt. I would like to blow up big stone banks, tip over the Washington Monument.

I also like disorder, chaos, riot, and entropy. The people who say they know don't know. I love to see them at a loss for words while I hug the unknown.

[Awarded the Dana Reed Prize in 1970]

PARANOIA

Walking the Streets

September 1, 1971

Any woman who has grown up in New York City is supposed to be accustomed to handling street hassles. If she hasn't been kidnapped at infancy from a baby carriage parked in front of the A&P, she will still have a good chance of being accosted by a drunken sailor (probably a fag, besides), robbed, heckled,

smoked out of a Madison Avenue bus by a pyromaniac lighting matches on the back seat, and altogether pinched so often
and in so many strange places that if the IRT subway line
could be held responsible and sued it would go bankrupt
faster than the Pennsylvania Central. And finally, if she gets
really lucky, like the five-year-old daughter of a minister I
once knew, she may get dragged up to the rooftop of some
apartment building and raped.

But of course, no one really expects anything better from
New York City. Hostility, violence, and histrionic acts of aggression are part of its mystique. The Kitty Genoveses and the
Galahads of this world and the next are essential for the en-
hancement of its reputation. For New York, as Mayor Lindsay
once so epigrammatically pointed out, is Fun City. Fun for
whom, he neglected to mention. Certainly, sexists and maso-
chists should be deliciously happy there.

I used to think I'd be a little safer around Harvard Square.
Not because its mystique was any less dramatic than New
York's, but simply because bicyclists and strolling lovers were
reputed to pre-empt the mad sailors and pyromaniacs.

The first week of my freshman year at Radcliffe, our dorm
resident held an introductory meeting to announce that five
girls had been raped on Garden Street and we should please
never walk through the Common at night without an escort.
This warning was met with nervous laughter and pseudo-
sophisticated scorn. Everyone continued to walk defiantly
through the Common, whether attended or not, no one got
raped without at least first giving her consent, and when, that
spring, a man wandered off the street into Jordan J and
stabbed a girl with an ice pick, only a few of the more misan-
thropic girls I knew began locking their doors before they
went to sleep at night.

The summer after that ominous beginning, I worked with a
bunch of pretty healthy young Canadian kids, went to California, and returned, my feelings about mankind altogether revived. Within one week of my arrival back in Cambridge, I
went innocently to take a midnight bath in the third-floor
bathroom of Barnard Hall. There before me I found an absolutely unknown naked man masturbating in the tub. Go

ahead and laugh, if you like. Of course there's something a bit comical about the scenario, shades of Portnoy or of Bruce Jay Friedman. Even more comical to remember that some girl in the dorm, a transfer student with more than the ordinary romantic-absurdist delusions about Harvard men, had seen the naked stranger wandering around the dorm all evening, but figured that he was only someone's boy friend having himself a good time.

Perhaps the encounter with the naked masturbator reveals more than the obvious elements of black humor. Certainly, it was a little frightening; officially so frightening, in fact, that the cops had to be called in, a fire drill held, and all of Barnard Hall evacuated at 2 a.m. so that every last room could be checked to make sure the poor naked dude wasn't lurking behind some bookcase. It was, also, unquestionably, a bit pathetic. Any man who has to get his kicks by displaying himself in front of a bunch of weary, bleary-eyed Radcliffe girls must first find himself in pretty desperate straits. But ideologically, the issue is even more alarming. For the moment, consider it an act of sexist chutzpah and listen to the remaining evidence.

The summer between last year and this cleared a few heads, blew a few minds, and raised a lot of consciousnesses. Kids who went to Europe returned appalled and nauseated by the generally carnivorous attitudes of the continental man on the street. Some who went to California said it was better than Cambridge, except for Telegraph Avenue, which was worse, and the ones who stayed in New York had no fixed opinions on street life whatsoever, having been forced to stay indoors all summer to avoid death by smog poisoning. There were also, of course, hundreds of kids dispersed across the country, picking watermelons in Georgia or salmon fishing in Alaska who were much too busy, too happy, or too far from the streets to worry about sexism or incidental acts of perversion. They are the lucky ones, but for the present purposes of consciousness raising will be bypassed.

I will admit that I did not come back to Cambridge this year expecting too much in the way of street liberation. Sure enough, the Harvard Trust had bricked up its front windows, the Bick was gone forever, and the male chauvinists were out in droves. I'd been back no less than three days when a kid walked up to me in the street and said, "Hey, are you married?" "No," I said, icily. "Well then," he demanded, giving me the old Don Ameche wink, and smirk, "howdja like to take me home with you?!"

What I answered was undistinguished, but the truth: "I'm awfully sorry. I have to go to tutorial now." Later I wished I'd just said "Fuck you" and left it at that. Though, of course, it's never tactically advisable to say "Fuck you" during a street confrontation. Someday someone might take you at your word.

Sybil is a typical Radcliffe street walker. She has typically long dark hair and lugs her books in a typically purple canvas satchel. She looks a lot like your roommate, or maybe more like your girl friend. Sometimes she rides a bicycle to class, but the morning under surveillance she has decided to walk.

She leaves Currier House at 11:45 a.m., just lucky enough to pass by a row of workmen who have quit work for lunch. All six of them immediately stop eating to stare at her, whistle, and make obscene remarks under their breaths. Since she is a brunette, they have no way of greeting her. If her hair were blond or red, they could have screamed, "Hey, blondie" or "Hey, red," and razzed her just that much more.

Safely out of the quad, she stops at a street corner to wait for the light. A car pulls up to the curb and a guy leans out and sneers, "Howdja like to do some modeling?" His face has the horribly lascivious look of Loerke, the demonic artist in *Women in Love*. Sybil ignores him. "It pays fifteen or twenty dollars an hour." She continues to ignore him. He drives away, on the prowl for a better broad.

She has walked about ten feet into the Common when two guys in tie-dyed shirts and bell-bottoms approach her, ogling and giggling. "Hey, classy Radcliffe girl," they taunt. "Got any spare change?" As she mutters she doesn't, she is immediately greeted by a guy strumming a guitar on a bench and whispering, "LSD for the Lady. LSD for the Lady."

By noon, she is safely out of the Common and standing on the traffic island waiting to cross into the Yard. She sees a bunch of little kids pedaling by on their bikes. She musters a weary smile. Children, she thinks, innocents, our only hope. And just then, one of the brats leans off his bicycle and pokes her in the boob.

Few Radcliffe girls may be privileged enough to experience all Sybil's electrifying confrontations in one fun-filled morning. All Radcliffe girls can check off at least a few and elaborate on them. But what is absolutely vital to every legitimately sexist street confrontation is that the woman must never feel as though she is being singled out for her individuality, her good spirits, or her charm. A street confrontation is never personal; it is always, in Buber's terms, an I-It relationship, never I-Thou. The woman must always be made to feel like an object under appraisal. Slim and rich, like a good cigarette. Soft, like a pair of slippers. Sleek as a Jag.

Street confrontations like Sybil's can drive the most mild-mannered, apolitical young Radcliffe thing to Bread and Roses. They can (and did) mobilize a group of New York City liberationists to stand on street corners and whistle at construction workers, complimenting them on their biceps and hard hats. And street confrontations can anger women like NOW's Ti-Grace Atkinson to remark that the only honest woman is a whore: at least she gets paid for walking the streets.

One fleeting, final confrontation. It is the end of a heavy autumn day, probably a Thursday. Sybil is walking back from the Coop, carrying all the books for two new courses, a lamp shade and a box of gingersnaps. Coming toward her, she recognizes Stanley, an old boy friend whom she has not seen since the summer. She looks up at him, and he stares at her, stares right through her as if they have never met. They have known each other for years, have exchanged birthday presents, have probably slept together. He looks right through her and doesn't speak. It is worse than all the "Hey, blondies" in the world.

— Elizabeth R. Fishel '72
[Awarded Dana Reed Prize "Honorable Mention" in 1972]

Tell Me, How Can I Get Tenure at Harvard?*
BY ARTHUR H. LUBOW '73

June 15, 1972

Dear Miss Getachair,

I am Lecturer in East Asian–American Relations at Harvard. Let me make clear right from the start that I don't need the job. Before I came here I was an important man on the National Security Council and in the United States government. I turned down the job of editor-in-chief of *Harper's* hoping I would get tenure at Harvard. Now it seems I won't be able to stay. Is there anything I can do?

CHARISMATIC

Dear Charismatic,

It's probably too late. "East Asian–American Relations" is much too fuzzy. Make up your mind: Do you want American, or do you want East Asian? If you want to stay at Harvard — and neither government nor *Harper's* (why not *The Atlantic*, for heaven's sake?) is the place for a young gentleman — you should look for another job. Have you ever thought of being a House master? Or, better — I'm told all these newspapermen came to Harvard each year as Nieman Fellows. Surely they need someone to take care of them.

Dear Miss Getachair,

I am an instructor at a state university in the Midwest. I want to be a Harvard professor. What do you think I should do?

YOUNG AND DETERMINED

Dear Y & D,

Join a women's auxiliary of a minority group.

Dear Miss Getachair,

I am rich, successful, and surrounded by important friends. All Harvard offers is crummy pay, a heavy teaching load, and a community infested with underfed hippies and overdressed tourists. So why am I beating my brains out to stay here?

BAFFLED

*Certain corrections have been made in this article. See David Landes's letter to The Crimson, December 19, 1972.

Dear Baffled,
  Good question. I'm baffled, too.

Good question, indeed. Why do so many scholars enter the Harvard rat race and compete for that elusive bit of cheese, a tenured appointment? Some cite their eminent colleagues, others the excellent library, the fine students, or the Boston location.

All stress the importance of the Harvard name. The prestige of Harvard does more than boost a man's ego; it usually boosts his career. Researchers in the natural sciences find that federal grants have a tendency to gravitate toward Cambridge. And for social scientists, the ivied paths of Harvard often lead directly to Washington.

But as the many state universities improve in quality, competitors to Harvard appear on the horizon. Although their libraries and faculties do not equal Harvard's, the salary and fringe benefit offers of these universities may lure individual members of the Harvard Faculty. This still does not happen very often. The Dunlop Report on the Recruitment and Retention of Faculty noted that in the decade from 1957-58 to 1966-67, only 24 tenured Faculty members left Harvard to accept academic positions elsewhere.

Harvard Faculty members are not being drawn away. But the Harvard magnetism has lost its attractive force for many academics at other universities. Fifty years ago, perhaps, middle-aged professors sat around and waited for the call to Harvard. These days, the call often goes unheard. The 1968 Dunlop Report noted that in the previous decade, about half of Harvard's offers to professors at other universities were refused. The report concluded that "once a man is settled and reasonably successful, it is hard to move him either to or away from Harvard."

If that is true, Harvard should be grooming its junior Faculty members for tenured positions. Instead, Harvard is an export factory which supplies the nation's universities with many of their brightest young professors. As its budding scholars fall off the vine, Harvard goes looking for "the best man available anywhere in the world" to fill each opening.

That is why this year, for instance, the History Department failed to renew the contracts of three junior Faculty members and extended futile offers to distinguished European historians who replied that they like it where they are.

Dear Miss Getachair,
   Why be modest? I am a bright young historian of modern Europe. For several years I have been working on a brilliant book which, alas, is still in manuscript. Now my contract is up for renewal and my department informs me that it wants a book, not a manuscript. The chairman keeps adumbrating something called the Graustein formula, which, coupled with the implications of the Dunlop Report, means (or so he says) that there is no longer a place for me at Harvard. Is he telling the truth? What is this Graustein formula, and what does it want from me?

                                                        UNAPPRECIATED

Dear Unappreciated,
   The Graustein formula is a rule. Harvard has many rules. When they don't want to give you something, they cite a rule. When they want to give you something, they find a way to bypass the rule. You wanted something that they didn't want to give you.

Named after the Harvard mathematician who did the statistical work, the Graustein formula was given to Harvard by the influential Committee of Eight in 1938. Professor Graustein estimated that the average tenured Faculty member stays at Harvard for 34 years. He then computed the number of annual appointments each department must make to remain at its current size. That figure — "the Graustein number" — more or less determines the frequency of appointments in each department. For example, if a department had 17 tenured members in 1938, it would be entitled to appoint a new member every other year.

   Because new departments and new fields within departments have developed since 1938, and because life in general does not always conform to written rules, the dean of the Faculty must, in his words, apply the Graustein formula "flex- ibly." If a department has a chance to pick up a hotshot pro- fessor, it can borrow ahead on its Graustein number and get him while he's available, even if the next scheduled appoint- ment in the department is several months or years hence. If a patron donates endowed chairs to a specific department, or if a particular field grows rapidly, the dean has two options. He can bring in new professors "above the line," and change the department's Graustein number. Or he can make "below the line" appointments, hiring a few extra people and postponing the decision to replace them until the time of their retire- ment.

"It's a useful managerial tool," Dean Dunlop commented last week. He said that the formula has three major advan- tages: it works to prevent retiring professors from hand-pick- ing their successors; it enables departments to adjust to changing fields of study; and, if handled properly, it creates an even age distribution in the Faculty.

The Graustein number is also a good figure for a depart- ment chairman to have ready when a disappointed assistant professor asks why he was not rehired. But this institu- tionalized mystification fools no one. "The Graustein is sim- ply a clothesline to hang appointments on," quipped one as- sistant professor.

One assistant professor of History whose appointment was hanged this year is Charles S. Maier '60. Maier was appointed an instructor in spring 1967. In fall 1969, after the enactment of the Dunlop Report's recommendation to phase out the po- sition of instructor, Maier became an assistant professor. Under the provisions of the changeover period, he opted for a four-year term. His contract came up for renewal this year, one year before its fourth and final year, 1972–73.

Maier hoped to be promoted to the tenured rank of profes- sor. Because he had already taught for more than five years, he was not eligible for a three-year term appointment. Before the Dunlop Report, the scholar shinnying up the Harvard Great Chain of Being served five years as an instructor and then, if his contract was renewed, another three years as an assistant professor. A regulation of the American Association of University Professors requires universities to grant tenure to academics who have taught at the school for eight years. So after serving his initial eight years, the assistant professor in the pre-Dunlop era would, if promoted, receive tenure and the title of associate professor.

Under the new, post-Dunlop system, a person begins as an assistant professor with a five-year contract. After those five years are up, he is promoted (if he is lucky) to associate professor, which is now a nontenured position. When that three-year contract expires, he is ready to become a tenured full professor.

When should an assistant professor be made an associate professor? The Dunlop Report is deliberately vague on that point. "Appointments to this rank should be limited to those who merit serious consideration for promotion to tenure," the Dunlop Report recommended. Elaborating on this point, Dunlop said last week, "There are two requirements. First, a person must be of a quality, given a further period of development, likely to show the kind of quality we are looking for in tenure appointments. Second, there must be reasonable prospects of a permanency."

Just what constitutes "reasonable prospects of a permanency"? Dunlop would rather not say. He maintains that a general definition cannot be codified. "I don't mind two or three people competing for a vacancy," he commented. "But I will not see the debasement of the associate professorship by having ten guys competing for one spot."

As dean of the Faculty, Dunlop must approve the promotions that each department recommends. This year, he cracked down on promotions and required department reasons for this policy: "We are interested in getting the best possible people, in looking outside as well as inside; and we want the record clear with regard to equal employment opportunities." He does not mention a third reason — the financial difficulties which demand stringency.

Whatever his reasons, Dunlop last fall vetoed the Government Department's recommendation to promote two assistant professors, Robert L. Jervis and James R. Kurth, to the rank of associate professor. You can only promote one, Dunlop told department chairman James Q. Wilson. When Wilson then presented a department recommendation to promote Jervis and let Kurth go, supporters of the more radical Kurth protested vehemently. After a couple of months of bickering, Dunlop finally agreed to let the two promotions go through.

Both Jervis and Kurth specialize in international relations. Dunlop's original reluctance to promote two men and let them compete for one vacancy may stem from his recognition that in the field of international relations, only half a vacancy exists. Presumably, both Kurth and Jervis are now vying for the spot that Henry A. Kissinger '50 once occupied. But Kissinger is only half gone. Although Dunlop says, "As far as I'm concerned he has resigned," the chairman of the Government Department says that Kissinger can return to his place if, sometime in November, he communicates his intention to leave the Nixon administration by the end of the year. The place that Kurth and Jervis are competing for may soon be no place at all.

No matter what happens, Kurth and Jervis are relatively fortunate. If they were in the History Department, they would probably be out looking for jobs. The History Department has never appointed a nontenured associate professor. By interpreting the Dunlop Report's guidelines so strictly, the department in effect has cut a man's trial period down to four years. Under the old system, an instructor who showed promise in his first couple of years would be rehired and would have five additional years to prove himself before his contract came up for review. Today a man with a Ph.D. starts as an assistant professor. He has four years before his appointment is reviewed. If his department interprets the term "promise" broadly, he will have another three years to produce written work. But if his department, like the History Department, thinks that to promote a man to associate professor is to promise him a tenured position, the assistant professor will have only four years to write a distinguished book.

Most people can't do it. When Charles Maier's contract came up for review last winter, his book was still in manuscript. While that may have been a factor in his case, the tenure bid of his colleague, Samuel R. Williamson, was also shot down. And Williamson had already written one prize-winning book and had another book in the works.

The regulation that a man must have published a book of proven value is one of those rules that can be cited or waived, depending on the sentiments of the department. For example, Edward L. Keenan '57 received tenure in spring 1970, almost two years before his book on Ivan the Terrible was published. Patrice L. R. Higonnet, who, like Keenan, became a professor in spring 1970, had completed his manuscript, but the book had not appeared at the time of his appointment. So even in the History Department, a man can get tenure without having published a book. And while scholars in some other fields produce primarily articles, historians are normally judged by the merits of their books.

Dear Miss Getachair,

I am an assistant professor. I have been offered the job of senior tutor. Should I accept?

HESITANT

Dear Hesitant,

As senior tutor, you will receive a secretary, a telephone, a free house, a private office, and a sure shot at a tenured position . . . at any university but Harvard.

After all the administrative drudgery that senior tutors perform, they must find it disheartening to learn that the position hurts, rather than helps, their chances for promotion in the Faculty. Since the post was created in 1952, there have been 63 nontenured senior tutors. Six of them have become professors at Harvard. "Most senior tutors do not make it at Harvard unless they're given tenure at the time of their appointment," observed Charles P. Whitlock, who as dean of the College acts as chairman of the Administrative Board of Senior Tutors. "But most senior tutors go on to be full professors at other colleges," he added.

When asked if he thought the job of senior tutor of Kirkland House hurt his prospects for tenure, Sam Williamson said only, "It didn't help." Williamson served as senior tutor during the hectic days of radical political activity. The chores of the position eat away research time. They also prevent a man from building his departmental reputation and keep him from doing the requisite number of favors for his senior colleagues.

Even if a man stretches his days to the bursting point, he will find his record as senior tutor a hindrance. Departments do more than ignore a man's contribution as senior tutor: they often count it against him. Academics apparently prefer scholars who are strictly scholars and not administrators, too. The senior tutors who make good usually have House masters slugging for them in their own department: consider Mason Hammond and Ernest May in Kirkland House; John Bullitt and Joel Porte in Quincy House; and Eliot Perkins and Franklin Ford in Lowell House.

Many conservative Faculty members felt especially hostile toward senior tutors during the late sixties, when they thought the Administrative Board should have been punishing student radicals more severely. These political considerations probably damaged the Harvard career of Cornelis Klein, associate professor of Mineralogy and former senior tutor of Leverett House.

Klein had advanced higher on the ladder than Maier and Williamson. In July 1969, the Geology Department raised him to the nontenured rank of associate professor. In spring 1971, the department recommended that he be promoted to full professor and be granted tenure.

When a department wants to hire an assistant or associate professor, the dean of the Faculty must approve the choice. When a department wants to give a man tenure, more elaborate approval is required. An appointment without limit of time, which lasts an average of 34 years, is a more serious matter than a term appointment of three or five years. The president of the University must approve each tenure appointment. Ever since the Committee of Eight Report revised the system in 1938, the president has convened an ad hoc committee to advise him in his decision.

After a department meets and recommends a candidate for tenure, the department chairman must submit to the dean a list of scholars, outside as well as inside the University. From that list, the dean and president select an ad hoc committee to judge the proposed appointment. This ad hoc committee then considers a pile of written material prepared and collected by the department chairman. Such material includes letters from the chairman and other members of the department, opinions of scholars inside and outside the University, a biography and bibliography of the nominee, a description of the search procedure, and a discussion of why this candidate is the person best qualified for the job. Meeting with the president, the ad hoc committee then interviews the department chairman and other experts. Finally, the committee reports to the president, and the president decides.

The ad hoc committee procedure is designed to help the president judge a candidate's qualifications and ensure that the department has checked outside the University in searching for the most eminent scholar available. The system also helps watchdog the distribution of tenure appointments among the fields within a department. Sometimes a department selects more than one name and asks the president and the ad hoc committee to choose the best person. More often, it proposes one candidate and requests his confirmation.

On May 25, 1971, one month before leaving office, President Pusey vetoed Klein's appointment. Such a decision is always unusual. In Klein's case, it was especially surprising, since his department unanimously had recommended his promotion. Characteristically, Pusey's motives were a subtly blended mixture of academics and politics.

The academic question went beyond Klein's personal qualifications. In fall 1970, Dean Dunlop had created a committee to investigate the status of Geophysics in the Geology Department. Francis Birch '24, the department's only tenured geophysicist, by then had already passed the retirement age. The small committee of scientists from outside and inside the University reported that Geophysics, the fastest growing and most glamorous area of Geology, was grossly understaffed at Harvard. It noted the abundance of Harvard mineralogists and suggested boosting Geophysics at the expense of Mineralogy. So, one year after Klein became an associate professor of Mineralogy, [which led him to believe his] work met the University's standards and that "reasonable prospects of permanency" existed, a special and prestigious committee was reporting to the president and dean that Harvard needed more geophysicists and fewer mineralogists.

The special committee's recommendations were no doubt important. But senior members of the department who testified before the ad hoc committee say that President Pusey himself played an extraordinarily energetic role. "He was clearly in command," one Geology professor recalled. Pusey easily dominated the men he had asked to serve on the ad hoc committee. One of these men had also sat on the special review committee.

One geologist speculated that his fellow department members described Klein's virtues less emphatically when questioned by a president who obviously opposed the appointment. After one of Klein's backers reminded Pusey that Klein had conducted a good deal of research despite the time-consuming duties of the senior tutorship, the president reportedly snapped back, "Franklin Ford was a senior tutor, and he did all right."

Klein's performance as senior tutor hardly endeared him to Pusey. No one objected more than the president to the Ad Board's lenient treatment of disruptive student radicals. Pusey's distaste for Klein's politics probably provided the passion behind his academic objections to the appointment.

"The only thing that I find an unresolved problem is the nonreaction of the department," Klein says in retrospect. "They had made two decisions: a promotion to associate professor, which was a unanimous decision, and then a unanimous decision to recommend me to the ad hoc committee. I find it odd that the department in no way reacted." Klein thinks that the chairman could have appealed the verdict to a new judge, President Bok, who took office a month later.

If the department had in fact not wanted to appoint Klein, it might very well have spared itself the unpleasantness of arguing his merits and simply sent his name to an ad hoc committee sure to shoot him down. Neither Klein nor his senior colleagues contend that is what happened. Such things have happened, however, in the History Department, which is notorious for its acrimonious debates and factional splits.

The History Department had its full share of unpleasant-
ness in the mid-sixties, when it debated the appointment of
Fritz Stern, a German history professor at Columbia. David S.
Landes, professor of History and Stern's good friend, sup-
ported the appointment enthusiastically. Oscar Handlin,
Warren Professor of American History, joined the opposition.
As usual, the sides split roughly along the American and
European divisional lines of the department.

The department recommended by a split vote that Stern be
hired. The ad hoc committee was unimpressed, however, and
President Pusey rejected the appointment.

Stern's supporters were bitter. They knew that Handlin had
gone to the top to voice his objections. They also suspected
that Franklin L. Ford, McLean Professor of Ancient and Modern History and former dean of the Faculty, was less than enthusiastic about the prospect of a new man encroaching on
his territory of German history. They realized that if Ford had
wanted the appointment, he was close enough to Pusey to
guarantee its approval.

Why was Stern blackballed? In such cases the academic
and political reasons tend to blur together. On the one hand,
Stern writes slowly and reputedly mistreats graduate students. On the other hand, his political reputation was mushy
left, which was anathema to conservatives like Handlin.

The wounds were still red when Patrice Higonnet's bid for
tenure came up in the spring of 1970. Higonnet was a continental historian who specialized in modern France and could
also cover Austria-Hungary. The department was looking for
someone to replace Crane Brinton, who had taught French
history. It also needed someone to do Austria. Higonnet
seemed to be the man.

Higonnet had even more going for him. His conservative
politics pleased Handlin and the other Americanists. His lack
of expertise in German history satisfied Ford. The departmental chores he had performed softened up everybody. And he
was well-liked by Stern's old supporter and Harvard's leading
Modern European historian, David Landes. Higonnet was in
the right place at the right time. The department united behind him, and the President confirmed the appointment.

Higonnet may have outclassed his competitor, Robert

Darnton of Princeton, on purely academic considerations, although in fact Darnton had published more written work. Whatever the case, the important point is that Higonnet did not have to battle with academic weapons alone. Politics, both personal and partisan, enter into decisions to hire as well as decisions not to hire.

Dear Miss Getachair,

I am a great teacher, and my students love me. Unfortunately I haven't published very much at all. You see, I've been too busy drawing up new courses and meeting with students. Do you think my department will understand? What are my chances for tenure?

ANXIOUS

Dear Anxious,

No. And nil.

Just as we, like Dostoyevsky, can imagine the modern Church crucifying Christ, so we can envision Harvard University terminating the contract of Socrates because he had produced no written work. Although all the written rules stipulate that "creative work," and not printed pages, determine a candidate's eligibility for tenure, in practice the dictum of "publish or perish" retains its force.

Scholarly work, and not teaching ability, decides the fate of the academic at Harvard. Defending the system, Dean Dunlop argues that the University must be able to predict a man's future. A professor's teaching ability can fluctuate sharply over the next 30 years, Dunlop maintains, but his capacity to produce creative written work will remain relatively constant. Ignoring the truth value of this dubious statement, we can still safely conclude that at Harvard, teaching comes second to research.

James C. Thomson Jr., lecturer in History and one of the three young historians who did not receive tenure this year, expressed the view of most junior faculty when he said, "The system is so constructed in theory and practice as to provide good teaching only by accident. On the one hand, those hired for permanency are not hired with an eye to their teaching ability. On the other hand, those who are junior faculty teach under conditions of such stress, overwork, and career anxiety, knowing the odds are 99 to 1 that they won't be kept here, that they put their energy into getting their theses and other publications into print to get themselves jobs elsewhere."

Although the charismatic Thomson did not receive tenure, he will stay at Harvard as curator of the Nieman Fellows program. Like most administrative posts, the appointment of curator is "without limit of time." The appointment extends indefinitely but can be terminated any time at the pleasure of the president. Such an appointment lacks the security of a tenured position. As one Faculty member observed wryly, "To get thrown out, a tenured professor really has to rape little girls. Lots of them. One wouldn't be enough." Presumably, for an administrator, one would be enough.

Thomson will continue to teach courses as a lecturer in History. His tenure appointment, like many others in the History Department, collapsed because it was spread too thin over different areas. Thomson specializes in East Asian–American relations. This field is just gaining scholarly recognition, but to the academically conservative Harvard History Department, it is still unestablished. The East Asian wing of the department supported Thomson's candidacy, but the Americanists opposed it. The Americanists won, and Thomson lost. In a similar episode, Ernest R. May, an American historian, backed the bid of Sam Williamson, a specialist in European diplomatic history. Caught between the two opposing camps of Americanists and Europeanists, Williamson was neither fish nor fowl. The department would not recommend his promotion.

One way to open a new field in a stuffy department is to raise money for an endowed chair. John K. Fairbank '29, Higginson Professor of History, is directing a fund drive for a chair in Vietnamese Studies, which will presumably be occupied by his protégé, Alexander B. Woodside, assistant professor of History. The going price for an endowed chair is $1 million. The income on that sum is primarily used for salaries, which average $24,000 and do not exceed $33,000.

Because Fairbank began the drive in 1967, when the cost of a chair was only $600,000, the University has set that amount as the target. The Ford Foundation donated half, and Fairbank has already raised another $150,000.

"It's rather difficult to drop a field," Fairbank said. "You come along with a new field and you have to raise money for it. A field once established usually doesn't disappear." A field did disappear when Fairbank was promoted to a place in Chinese history over 25 years ago. The history of the Spanish Empire has not been taught at Harvard since.

But Fairbank is the exception to the rule. If Woodside receives tenure at Harvard, he will have Fairbank to thank for it. In 1960, Fairbank came to Woodside with an idea.

"I suddenly realized in 1960 that Vietnam is a subject that isn't studied," Fairbank recalled. "That was a real giveaway. What was I doing around here? We were so occupied with China that we never thought about Vietnam. It was French, and no one ever went there."

"Luckily, an able man came along," he continued. "Woodside was at Harvard as a graduate student in Chinese history. I asked him if he was interested, and he said he was." Last year, Woodside published a book on the Chinese influence in Vietnam.

Some men do very well when they switch fields. John Womack Jr. '59, professor of History, moved from American to Latin American history when he was a junior faculty member. Now he has a brilliant reputation and a tenured position at Harvard that the History Department had wanted to fill for 14 years. But not everyone is so successful. Thomas E. Skidmore made a giant leap from medieval European history to Brazilian and South American history. He is now at the University of Wisconsin.

Dear Miss Getachair;
Could I be dreaming? Just yesterday my department voted against giving me tenure. Today I talked to ten senior faculty members and not one brought it up. Am I hallucinating? Did it all really happen?

SCHIZO

Dear Schizo,

You sound quite sane, but forgetful. Remember: you're no longer living in the real world. Now you are at Harvard.

If she came to Harvard, Lewis Carroll's Alice would feel right at home. The world of University manners becomes most surreal after a junior faculty member is not rehired. None of his colleagues mention it. "It's perfectly absurd," Klein laughed. "You've taught joint courses with these people, you've known them outside. Nothing is said, not even, 'Gosh, that's too bad.' It's very strange." Thomson also marveled at "the degree to which these things aren't spoken about," adding, "No one says, 'I'm sorry things didn't work out.' "

No one says a thing. The system keeps on plugging along: the frills change, but the premises remain the same. Occasionally, the bulky machinery causes hilarious blunders. Consider the episode of the secretary in the Department of Romance Languages, who accidentally mailed a letter inviting the wrong professor to come with tenure to Harvard. He accepted and he came. There was nothing the department could do.

But such gross mistakes are the exception. The system normally runs quite smoothly. It doesn't encourage good teaching, but it does let some good teachers through. It loses many bright young scholars, but it manages to hang on to a few. Lately, under pressure from the Department of Health, Education and Welfare, Harvard has increased its hiring of blacks and women. These days, if a clever department chairman wants to hire additional nontenured faculty he just looks around for an eligible woman or black. The president and dean also ask department chairmen to submit a list of blacks and women who were considered for each tenure appointment. Dean Dunlop may be cutting financial corners, but not at the expense of the University's affirmative-action plan.

It would be naive to expect promotions to proceed on purely objective, academic criteria. What is alarming about the present system is not the latitude it permits for personal considerations. Rather, it is the system's premises. The University should be a place for teaching as well as for research.

When a department or ad hoc committee is considering a man's record, his teaching ability is not the primary concern. Because departments at Harvard initiate appointments, the criteria for selection tend to be especially technical and book-oriented. At smaller colleges, the president usually directs the entire procedure and pays more attention to a candidate's teaching ability.

Harvard must find ways to develop and keep bright young scholars, or else it will lose the best men to the universities catching up from behind. While it is all well and good to disdain the superstar salaries and featherweight teaching loads that some universities give to distinguished professors, it would be unrealistic to think that Harvard can trade on its name alone for much longer. Once eminent men have settled down somewhere, it is very difficult to lure them away. Either you develop your own young scholars or you dangle out tempting bribes to attract big names from outside. Harvard must choose its course, unless it wishes to languish like an ancient battleship, a glorious but nonfunctional reminder of another era.

[Awarded the Dana Reed Prize in 1973]

Members of the Harvard Crimson

Selective Index

Members of The Harvard Crimson

INCLUDED BELOW are editors of The Harvard Crimson's News, Editorial, Photographic, and Business Boards; employees, designated by a dagger (†); and honorary editors, denoted by an asterisk (*). Deceased members have been noted with the symbol (d.) after the name and class year.

ABBOTT, John M. K. '22 (d.)
ABBOTT, Lawrence J. '24
ABRAMS, George S. '54
ACKERMAN, Marshall W. '49
ADAMS, Edward B. 1892 (d.)
ADAMS, Faneuil '19
ADAMS [WEISBROD], Jo R. '69
ADAMSON, William R. '38
ADDIS, Stephen L. '57
ADELMAN [WALTCH], Lilla M. '53
ADLER, James B. '53
ADLER, Jonathan R. '61
AFFELDER, Lewis J. '36
AGASSIZ, George R. 1884 (d.)
AGEE, Christopher R. '79
AGOOS, Julian E. '40
AGUIRRE, John B. Jr. '49
AIKEN, John G. 3RD '40 (d.)
AISENBERG, Jamie O. '81
ALBERS, William E. '42 (d.)
ALBRIGHT [ARLEN], Alice P. '62
ALBRIGHT, Nile L. '61
ALCOTT, Mark H. '61
ALEXANDER [NOVAK], Carol J. '55
ALEXANDER, Jeffrey C. '69
ALEXANDER, Jonathan '68
ALGEO, Warren H. '45
ALLAN, Charles F. '72
ALLEN, Carl F. Jr. '65
ALLEN, Charles C. 1884 (d.)
ALLEN, Ferry B. '23 (d.)
ALLEN, Frederick H. 1880 (d.)
ALLEN, Herbert Jr. '18

ALLEN, John L. '39
ALLEN, Joseph '37
ALLON, Eric R. '73
ALPER, Chester A. '52
ALSCHULER, Richard H. '37
ALTER, Jonathan H. '79
AMAN, Carol Greenhouse '71
AMATNIEK, Kathie '64
AMAZEEN, Edward S. '31 (d.)
AMES, James B. '32
AMESBURY, Walter R. Jr. '36
AMFITHEATROF, Erik '54
AMORY, Cleveland '39
AMORY, Harcourt 1876 (d.)
AMSTERDAMSKA, Joanne A. '82
ANDELMAN, Robert J. '66
ANDERSON, John F. W. '37
ANDERSON, Nancy C. '71
ANDERSON, Robert E. Jr. '23
ANDERTON, Walter P. '08 (d.)
ANDRADE, Eduardo '28 (d.)
ANDREW, Sumner B. '23
ANDREWS, James M. 4TH '28
ANGIER, Albert E. '20 (d.)
ANNIS, Kenneth J. '65
ANSLOW, Carolyn Simpkinson '55
ANSPACH, Mark R. '81
ANTELL [COLMAN], Maxine J. '63
APGAR, David P. '78
APPLETON, Francis R. 1875 (d.)
ARDERY, Philip P. Jr. '66
ARLEN, Alice Albright '62
ARLEN, Ann Warner '55

ARLEN, Jennifer A. '81
ARMSTRONG, James S. '38
ARMSTRONG [BANCROFT], Margaret A. '60
ARNOLD, Fred E. '60
ARONSON, Thomas L. '77
ARTHURS, Lee M. '82
ASHCRAFT, Richard E. '60
ASTON, Eugene N. 1874 (d.)
ASWELL, Edward C. '26 (d.)
ATHERTON, Alfred L. Jr. '44
ATKINS, David '80
ATTANASIO, Paul A. '81
AUCHINCLOSS, Kenneth '59
AUSPITZ, Josiah L. '63
AUSTEN, Ralph A. '58
AUSTIN, Alan K. '70
AYER, Frederick '11 (d.)

BACHRACH [SCOLNICK], Barbara '62
BACKUS, Hiram H. '27 (d.)
BACON, Francis M. Jr. 1884 (d.)
BACON, Robert 1880 (d.)
BAER, Theodore S. '44
BAGGOTT, Robert C. '78
BAILEY, Charles W. II '50
BAILEY, David W. '21
BAIRD, Jane B. '74
BAKER, Charles B. '54
BAKER, James S. '19 (d.)
BAKER, Jeffrey L. '71
BAKER, John H. '15 (d.)
BAKER, Louis W. '46
BAKER, Melville P. '22 (d.)
BAKER, Myles P. '22
BAKER, Richard S. '51
BALCH, Thomas W. 1890 (d.)
BALDWIN, Bertram C. 3RD '58
BALDWIN, Charles E. Jr. '26
BALDWIN, Stephen P. '43
BALDWIN, Thomas T. 1886 (d.)
BALDWIN, William H. 1885 (d.)
BALKIND, Benjamin H. '52
BALL, K. Joel '80
BALLANTINE Arthur A. '04 (d.)
BALLANTINE, Arthur A. Jr. '36 (d.)
BALLANTINE, John W. '42
BALLARD, Frederic L. Jr. '63
BALLMER, Steven A. '77
BALSAM, Aldo R. '23 (d.)
BANCROFT, Margaret Armstrong '60
BANCROFT, THAYER L. '21 (d.)

BANCROFT, Wilder D. 1888 (d.)
BANK, Theodore P. 2ND '45
BARACH, Jeffrey A. '56
BARBASH, Shephard R. '82
BARCLAY, George C. '19
BARDEL, Penelope Kline '62
BAREIKIS, Robert P. '59
BARGE, Kelly S. '70
BARISH, Jonas A. '42
BARKER, George G. '32 (d.)
BARKER, George S. Jr. '46
BARKER, LeBaron R. Jr. '26 (d.)
BARNES, Bernard '30
BARNES, Henry B. Jr. '33
BARNES, Joseph F. '27 (d.)
BARNES, William 1888 (d.)
BARNES, William S. 1886 (d.)
BARNET, Robert '42
BARNETT, Stephen R. '57
BARNETT, Theodore R. '41
BARNEY, Daniel R. '72
BAROL, William F. '79
BARONE, Michael D. '66
BARRETT, Anne E. '79
BARRETT, Donald V. '72
BARRETT, Frederick P. '37
BARRETT, Michael J. '70
BARRETT, Paul M. '83
BARRETT, Robert E. Jr. '30
BARTELS, Kenneth G. '73
BARTLETT, Anne E. '79
BARTLETT, Henry C. '28
BARTLEY, William W. III '56
BARTON, Frederick O. 1881 (d.)
BARTON, Rexford W. '21 (d.)
BARTON, Walter K. 1886 (d.)
BASKIN, Marc N. '73
BASS, Michael J. '83
BATCHELDER, Charles C. 1889 (d.)
BATCHELDER, Edward T. '30 (d.)
BATCHELDER, Roland B. '13 (d.)
BATES, Charles T. '29
BATES, Walter A. '46
BAUER, Nancy F. '82
BAUM, Marc L. '80
BAUR, Edward '27
BEACH, Bennett H. '71
BEACH, David E. '79
BEACH, John W. '33
BEACH, Reuel W. '06 (d.)
BEATON, Neal N. '75
BEAUMONT, John E. Jr. '33

BECK, Gordon M. '73
BECKER, Sidney K. '06 (d.)
BECKETT, William S. '73
BECKHART, Leslie K. '82
BECKSON, Mace '82
BEDARD, Deborah K. '82
BEDNARK, James D. '72
BEECHER, Jonathan F. '58
BEECHER, William M. '55
BEEKMAN, Jerome F. '64
BEER, Walter E. 1890 (d.)
BEERE, Sue Joel '54
BELGROVE, Angela M. '80
BELISLE, Eugene L. '31
BELKNAP, Michael H. P. '63
BELL, Ernest L. III '49
BELLER, Daniel J. '69
BELLI, Thomas A. '69
BELLO, Stephen F. '66
BEMIS, Harry H. 1887 (d.)
BENIGER, James R. '69
BENJAMIN, Laura R. '70
BENJAMIN, Robert M. '17 (d.)
BENKARD, James W. B. '59
BENKIN, Isaac D. '56
BENNETT, Amanda P. '75
BENNETT, Edmund N. '10 (d.)
BENNETT, Edwin K. '38
BENNETT, Mark R. '82
BENNETT, Ralph B. Jr. '42
BENNETT, Roger W. '13 (d.)
BENSON, Reuel A. Jr. '35
BENYAS, Eugene C. '43
BERGEN, Charles S. '77
BERGREEN, Laurence R. '72
BERING, Harriet A. '73
BERK, Donald J. '79
BERKELEY, Linda E. ' 73
BERNSTEIN [HUYSSEN], Nina '70
BERTOLINO, Raymond C. '80
BERZIN, Steven M. '72
BESSIE, Simon Michael '36
BEST, Marshall A. '23
BETSKY, Celia '73
BEVARD, Charles W. Jr. '64
BEYER, R. Andrew '65
BIDDLE, Geoffrey R. '72
BIDDLE, George '08 (d.)
BIDDLE, Sydney G. '13 (d.)
BIGELOW, Charles L. '39 (d.)
BIGELOW John M. '33
BILLER [COHEN], Audrey J. '68

BILLINGS, Franklin S. 1885 (d.)
BINGER, Eugene T. '46
BINGER, Wilson V. '38
BINGHAM, Andrew W. '57
BINGHAM, Norman W. Jr. 1895 (d.)
BIRCH, A. Francis '24
BIRDSALL, Stephen T. '31
BISHOP, James R. T. '18 (d.)
BISHOP, Michael J. '70
BISHOP, Robert L. '37
BISHOP, Shirley Wolman '71
BISSELL, Frederick E. '00 (d.)
BIXBY, Paul L. '77
BLACK, Robert B. '42
BLACKALL, Robert M. '12 (d.)
BLAINE, Graham B. '19 (d.)
BLANCHARD, Edward V. Jr. '74
BLANTON, Thomas S. '77
BLASS [SHAFFER], Ingeborg E. '54
BLATCHFORD, Walter L. '31
BLATT, Richard S. '78
BLATTEL, Marilyn Brown '68
BLECHMAN, Michael D. '62
BLINKEN, Donald M. '47
BLITMAN, Judith H. '61
BLONDEL, John D. '78
BLOSSOM, Carl W. '04 (d.)
BLOWERS, George A. '28 (d.)
BLUE, Rae '53
BLUHM, Jeremy S. '73
BLUHM, Robert G. '72
BLUM [YOAKUM], Alice E. P. '52
BLUM, James D. '74
BLUM, Jeffrey D. '70
BLUMENTHAL, David '70
BLUMENTHAL, Richard '67
BOAL, Stewart '29
BOAS, Gilbert H. '49
BOAS, Jean P. '55
BODIAN, Marion E. '69
BODMAN, Edward D. '45
BOECKELER, Benjamin C. '27
BOEDEKER, Edgar C. '64
BOFFEY, Philip M. '58
BOGART, Herman L. '35
BOGUMIL [SLONAKER], Helen L. '66
BOIT, Charles S. '53
BOLDING, Grady M. '73
BOLLARD, Ralph H. '05 (d.)
BOLTON, Mary P. '71
BOND, Nicholas P. 1878 (d.)
BONDER, Daniel B. '72

BOORSTIN, Daniel J. '34
BOORSTIN, David W. '71
BOORSTIN, Jonathan '67
BOORSTIN, Robert O. '81
BOOTH, Marilyn S. '77
BORDEN, Charles, S. '43 (d.)
BORGES, Edward M. '54
BOTT, Charles W. A. '82
BOVARNICK, Murray E. '44
BOWDEN, Priscilla '61
BOWDITCH, Edward '03 (d.)
BOWDITCH, John B. '37 (d.)
BOWEN, James W. 1882 (d.)
BOWERS, Peter A. '55
BOWERS, Paul S. '37 (d.)
BOWERSOCK, Justin D. III '29
BOWIE, Beverley M. '35 (d.)
BOWIE, Walter R. '04 (d.)
BOWKER, Richard J. '72
BOWLES, Sherman H. '12 (d.)
BOWMAN, Francis E. '24
BOWSER, Hallowell '44
BOXER, Sarah G. '80
BOYCE, Burke '22 (d.)
BOYD, Frederick V. '73
BOYD, Joseph M. '35
BOYD, Peter A. '72
BRAATEN, David G. '46
BRACKETT, John G. Jr. '39 (d.)
BRACKMAN, Jacob R. '65
BRADFORD, Robert F. '23
BRADLEE, Henry G. Jr. '26
BRADLEY, Charles W. 1880 (d.)
BRADLEY, John D. 1886 (d.)
BRAGDON, Henry W. '28
BRAND, Robert N. '58
BRAND, Steven M. '81
BRANDT, Conrad '41
BRANIGAR, Richard W. '31
BREAKSTONE, Jeanne Katz '63
BRECKENRIDGE [PIERREHUMBERT],
  Janet M. '75
BREGGIN, Peter R. '58
BREGMAN, Walter W. '55
BREINDEL, Eric M. '77
BRENHOLTS, Alfred R. Jr. '69
BREWSTER, Theodore O. '29 (d.)
BREWSTER, William R. '22 (d.)
BRICE, Stewart M. 1893 (d.)
BRICKEN, Jules '35
BRIDGES, Samuel W. '26
BRIDGMAN, Hugh '19 (d.)

BRIGGS, John D. Jr. '32
BRIGGS, Robert A. '34 (d.)
BRIGGS, Peter M. '74
BRIGHAM, Dwight S. '08 (d.)
BRIGHT, Jackson V. R. '22
BRINSER, Ayers '31 (d.)
BRITELL, Peter S. '63
BRODY, Daniel S. '71
BRODY, Julia Green '71
BROEKHUYSEN, Martin J. '63
BROH-KAHN, Jere '54
BROMBERG, Karen M. '77
† BROOKS, Lewis M. Jr. (Pressman)
BROOKS, Stephen H. '70
BROUGHTON, Arthur N. 1893 (d.)
BROWN, Alison G. '81
BROWN, Archibald M. '03 (d.)
BROWN, Cabot '21 (d.)
BROWN, Charles S. '08 (d.)
BROWN, Dennis E. '55
BROWN, Douglas A. '44
BROWN, Elisabeth E. '77
BROWN, Franklin Q. Jr. '27
BROWN, John P. '14 (d.)
BROWN [BLATTEL], Marilyn A. '68
BROWN, Reay H. '72
BROWN [ERHARD], Sallie Hope '50
BROWN, Susan K. '81
BROWN, Willa H. '81
BROWN, William C. Jr. '14 (d.)
BROWNE, Kingsbury Jr. '44
BROWNELL, George A. '19
BRUCE, John S. '80
BRUCE, Robert R. Jr. '66
BRUCK, David I. '70
BRYSON, William C. '67
BUCH, Richard P. '34
BUCHSBAUM, Andrew P. '79
BUDER, Eugene H. '38
BUELL, George C. 1882 (d.)
BUFFINGTON, Merrill '21 (d.)
BULKLEY, Robert J. '02 (d.)
BULL, Bartle '60
BULLARD, John C. '43
BULLARD, Stephen 1878 (d.)
BUNKER, Gerald E. '59
BURCH, James M. 1883 (d.)
BURDEN, William A. M. '53 (d.)
BURDETT, George A. 1881 (d.)
BURGHEIM, Richard A. '55
BURKE, Jack D. Jr. '70
BURKE, Roger M. Jr. '52

BURLINGAME, Frederic A. 1897 (d.)
BURLINGHAM, Charles '05
BURNHAM, David B. '55
BURNIM, Ira A. '73
BURNS, Monique L. '77
BURNSTINE [STRAUSS], Joanna '61
BUSSARD, Ellen '71
BUSSARD, Steven W. '70
BUTLER, Allan M. 1884 (d.)
BUTLER, Henry S. 1877 (d.)
BUTLER, Keith E. '75
BUTLER, Richard H. '60
BUTLER-THWING, Francis '13 (d.)
BUTTERFIELD, Alfred C. '37 (d.)
BUTTENWEISER, Paul A. '60
BUXTON [SOBOL], Anne P. '66
BYER [ITTELSON], Margaret A. '67
BYRD, Thomas H. '30
BYRD, William 1897 (d.)
BYRD, William M. '64
BYRON, Frederick W. Jr. '59

CABLE, Arthur G. '09 (d.)
CABOT, Christopher '71
CABOT, Harold '22
CADY, Stephen N. '48
CAHOUET, Francis M. V. '54
CAL, Raymond I. '78
CALABRESE, Michael A. '79
CALDWELL, Arthur L. '20
CALHOUN, Thomas H. Jr. '39
CALKINS, Benjamin '78
CALKINS, Evan '43
CALKINS, Hugh '45
CALKINS, Wendell N. '39
CALL, David H. '60
CAMERON, Donald F. '22 (d.)
CAMERON, Duncan H. '56
CAMERON, Kenneth D. '34
CAMPBELL, Robert M. '34
CAMPBELL, Robert P. '83
CANADAY, Frank H. '14 (d.)
CANADAY, Wilbur D. '17
CANEDY, Brenda Haram '54
CANTOR, A. Jay '70
CAPLAN, Lincoln W. 2ND '72
CAPLOE, David R.'73
CARDIN, Sanford R. '78
CARLEBACH, William D. '41
CARLESON, Jonathan P. '72
CARLETON, Philip G. 1899 (d.)
CARLETON, Richard H. 1898 (d.)

CARLSON, Justina K. '81
CARLSON, Timothy G. '71
CARMICHAEL, Donald S. '35
CARP, Paul I. '42 (d.)
CARPENTER, Benjamin 1888 (d.)
CARPENTER, Frederic I. 1885 (d.)
CARPENTER, Frederic I. '24 (d.)
CARPENTER, John A. 1897 (d.)
CARPENTER, Kenneth G. '08 (d.)
CARR, Ashton L. 1898 (d.)
CARRET, Donald '50
CARROLL, Rosamond '70
CARSWELL, Donald '50
CARSWELL, Robert '49
CARTER, Carol Fredlund '66
CARVALHO, David N. '76
CASEY, Edward M. '44 (d.)
CASEY, John F. '38 (d.)
CASEY, Thomas W. '40
CASEY, William F. '48 (d.)
CASLER Lawrence R. '53
CATE, Carl S. '09 (d.)
CATER, Douglass Jr. '46
CATURANI, George W. '34 (d.)
CAUGHEY, John L. Jr. '25
CAVELL, Cathleen Cohen '66
CEDARBAUM, Jonathan G. '83
CESTURI, Matthew M. '79
CHADWICK, Jerome A. '58
CHAMBERLIN, Dean '29 (d.)
CHAMP, Frederick P. '19 (d.)
CHANDLER, Porter R. '21
CHANLER, Winthrop 1885 (d.)
CHAPMAN, Stephen J. '76
CHAPPELOW, Kent '38
CHASAN, Daniel J. '65
CHASE, Harold T. 1886 (d.)
CHASE, Walter G. 1882 (d.)
CHASE, William L. 1876 (d.)
CHASNOW, Jeffrey B. '83
CHASTENEY, Robert W. Jr. '31
CHAZIN, Robert L. '58
CHENEY, George L. 1878 (d.)
CHESEBROUGH, Stephen W. '62
CHI, Emile C. '57
CHILDS, Henry D. '58
CHIRA, Susan D. '80
CHIU, Wei I. '68
CHRISTOPHER, Theodore A. '77
CHU, Franklin D. '70
CHUBB, Robert W. '15
CHURCHILL, Albert G. '29

CHURCHILL, Asaph 1888 (d.)
CHURCHILL, Asaph Jr. '28
CHURCHILL, Michael '61
CLAPP, Philip E. 3RD '75
CLAPP, Stephen C. '60
CLARK, Allen W. '18
CLARK, Anna K. '79
CLARK, Blair '40
CLARK, Charles M. '43
CLARK, Charles M. Jr. '28
CLARK, Frederic W. '61
CLARK, Henry A. 1874 (d.)
CLARK, Lincoln Jr. '41
CLARK, Richard C. '36 (d.)
CLARK, Richard N. '32
CLARK, Samuel B. 1874 (d.)
CLARK, Sidney E. '63
CLARK, Steve M. '81
CLARK, Walter D. 1889 (d.)
CLARK, William C. '03 (d.)
CLARKE David Jr. '78
CLAY, George R. '43
CLAYTON, Lewis R. '75
CLAYTON, William B. '66
CLIFTON, Gregg E. '82
CLYMER, Adam '58
COBB, Farrar 1890 (d.)
COBB, Jeffrey B. '66
COBB, John C. '41
COCHCRANE, John M. '43
COFFIN, Benjamin H. 4th '61
COGSWELL, William F. '13 (d.)
COHEN, Audrey Biller '68
COHEN [CAVELL], Cathleen J. '66
COHEN, Daniel E. '60
COHEN, Douglas M. '67
COHEN, Ethan R. '83
COHEN, Steven J. '57
COHEN, Joel E. '65
COHEN, Ronald I. '64
COHN, Alan D. '51
COLE, Bruce K. '76
COLE, Frederick L. '15 (d.)
COLE, Henry L. '24
COLEMAN, Deborah A. '73
COLLINS, Jerome A. '57
COLLINS, Randall A. '63
COLMAN, Maxine Antell '63
COMSTOCK, Craig '61
COMSTOCK, Margaret Von Szeliski '64
CONANT, Ernest L. 1884 (d.)
CONANT, James Bryant '14 (d.)
CONKLIN, Charles R. '48

CONNELL, Richard '15 (d.)
CONNOLLY, Francis J. '79
CONNORS, Laurence J. '68
CONRAD, Rona Harris '54
CONROY, William H. 1899 (d.)
CONSOLINI, Robert L. '53
CONSTANTINE, Eleni M. '77
CONSTANTINIDIS, Panos P. '80
CONTRERAS, Joseph L. '79
CONWAY, Richard F. '76
COOK, Chester W. '19
COOK, Edward H. '43
COOK, Robert S. '17
COOLIDGE, Louis A. 1883 (d.)
COOMBS, David I. '50 (d.)
†COOPER, Betsy R. (Typist)
COOPER, Ellen A. '75
COOPER, Oscar F. '02 (d.)
COOPER, Richard T. '58
COOPERMAN, Alan '81
COPAKEN, Richard D. '63
COPITHORNE, David A. '75
CORBETT, Dennis P. '75
CORDINGLEY, William A. Jr. '71
CORKERY, Paul J. '68
CORLIES, Thomas 1874 (d.)
CORNFELD, Leslie A. '81
CORSIGLIA, J. Patrick '81
CORTESI, Deborah Shapley '67
CORTY, Andrew P. '74
CORWIN, Howard A. '54
COSTIGAN, Henry D. '20 (d.)
COTLER, Stephen L. '65
COTT, James L. '81
COTTON, Richard '65
COTTON, Stephen E. '67
COUGHLIN, Edward J. Jr. '52
COULSON, John '13 (d.)
COVER, John F. '17 (d.)
COVILLE, Gilbert G. '50
COWAN, L. Geoffrey '64
COWAN, Paul S. '62
COWETT, Edward M. '52
COWETT, Wilbur A. '45
COWLES, Gardner Jr. '25
COWLES, John '21
Cox, Wilmot T. 1879 (d.)
COXE, Weld '51
CRAM, Robert J. '02 (d.)
CRAMER, Dwight L. '74
CRAMER, James '77
CRANE, Thomas S. '72
CRAWFORD, James W. '71

CREAMER, Winifred M. '73
CREELMAN, Brenton W. '35 (d.)
CRENSHAW, Albert B. '64
CRICHTON, John M. '64
CRICHTON [MARTIN], Sarah K. '75
CRIMMINS, Francis T. Jr. '77
CRITCHLOW, Douglas E. '76
CRIVELLO, Madeline S. '73
CRONIN, Philip M. '53
CROSBY, Robert A. '71
CROUSE, Timothy '68
CUDDIHY, Thomas M. '49
CUDHEA, David W. '53
CULBERT, Kenneth P. '17 (d.)
CUMMIN, Robert I. '35
CUMMING, George M. 1876 (d.)
CUMMINGS, Ellen Lake '66
CUMMINGS, Peter '66
CUMNOCK, Arthur J. 1891 (d.)
†CUMPSTON, Copenhaver '72 (typist)
CUNNINGHAM, Caroline C. '81
CUNNINGHAM, Robert A. '19
CUNNINGHAM, William P. '44 (d.)
CURTIS, Allen 1884 (d.)
CURTIS, Frazier 1898 (d.)
CURTIS [LENTZ], Jill '71
CURTIS, John A. Jr. '34 (d.)
CURTISS, Harold M. Jr. '39
CUSHMAN, John G. '25
CUSHMAN, Robert A. '23
CUTLER, Howard A. 1894 (d.)
CUTLER, Marshall 1877 (d.)
CUTLER, Ralph H. Jr. '40
CUTTER, Richard A. '22

DAHL, Erik J. '79
DAHLEN, Richard L. '65
DAKE, Michael D. '73
DALE, Paul W. '45
DALTON, Joseph W. '79
†DALY, Alan J. (Makeup Man)
DALY, Charles D. '01 (d.)
DALY, Christopher B. '76
DAMM, Christopher J. '80
DAMMANN, John F. Jr. '39
DAMMANN, Peter A. '42
DAMMANN, Thomas L. '35
DAMON, Theron J. '05 (d.)
DANA, Payson '04 (d.)
DANE, Ernest B. Jr. '27
DANIELS, George G. '49
DANIELS, Lee A. '71
DANSER, Harold W. Jr. '37

DARLING, Eugene A. 1890 (d.)
DARLING, Herbert H. 1889 (d.)
DARLING [PEALE], Jean J. '59
DARLING, Lynn M. '72
DARRAH, Dorothy A. '71
DAUKSEWICZ, William J. '76
DAVENPORT, James F. '25
DAVIDGE, Walter D. 1888 (d.)
DAVIDSON, Gerald R. '62
DAVIS, George H. 1879 (d.)
DAVIS [NEAL], Georgianne A. '51
DAVIS, Horace A. 1891 (d.)
DAVIS, Jack W. Jr. '69
DAVIS, Jonathan T. '75
DAVIS, Joseph A. '68
DAVIS, Kim G. '76
DAVIS, Lisa E. '81
DAVIS [GRIFFETH], Nancy H. '67
DAVIS, Paul D. '40
DAVIS, Robert G. '29
DAVIS, Ron L. '77
DAVIS [GEER], Sarah W. '71
DAVIS, Stuart A. '67
DAVISON, Paul E. '80
DAWSON, Harvey M. '37
DAY, John A. Jr. '72
DAY, Katherine L. '71
DAY, Stanton 1883 (d.)
DE GANAHL, Joe '25 (d.)
DE MILO, David A. '80
DE ROO, Deborah Labenow '51
DE ROODE, Albert '04 (d.)
DE SAINT PHALLE, Anne '70
DE WINDT, Heyliger '12 (d.)
DE WINDT, Heyliger A. 1881 (d.)
DE WITT, Addison '76
DEAN, James 1897 (d.)
DECHERD, Robert W. '73
DECKER, David J. '70
DEFRIEZ, Thaddeus C. 2ND '09 (d.)
DEGIVE, Josephine Fisher '65
DEMOS, John P. '59
DEMOTT, Joel H. '67
DENISON, David '46
DENISON, John A. 1898 (d.)
DENNIS, Melvin H. '23 (d.)
DENNISTON, Arthur C. 1883 (d.)
DENNY, Arthur B. 1877 (d.)
DENORMANDIE, Ernestine Rathborne '72
DENTON, Herbert H. Jr. '65
DERBY, Charles H. '03 (d.)
DERRICKSON, Ann L. '72

DEROW, Peter A. '62
DEVALL, Cheryl R. '80
DEVEREUX, Leslie W. '16
DIAMANTE, John C. '66
DIAMOND, David A. '59
DICKASON, James F. Jr. '44
DICKINSON, Francis R. '03 (d.)
DIECKERHOFF, Edward C. '31
DIEHL, Stephen K. '79
DIKER, Charles M. '56
DILL, Malcolm H. '20
DINERSTEIN, James C. '69
DINERSTEIN, Robert C. '63
DIONNE, E. J. '73
DIRECTOR, Mark D. '80
DIXON, Arthur '16
DOCTOROFF, Mark H. '82
DOERMANN, Humphrey '52
DOERR, Henry 3RD '41
DOHERTY, Richard J. '76
DOMRESE, Robert J. '66
DONAHUE, Deirdre M. '80
DONAHUE, Paul E. '75
DONHAM W. Parker '67
DONLEY, John W. '79
DORAN, Norbert A. '66
†DOWNES, Joseph A. (Janitor)
DOWNES, Thomas '34
DOWDELL, Donald A. '68
DOYLE, Conal C. '66
DOYLE, Richard N. '77
DOYLE, Robert C. '42
DOZIER, Rush W. Jr. '72
DRAY-NOVEY, Alison J. '65
DRINKWATER, William '04 (d.)
DRUCKER, Linda S. '82
DUBE, Elizabeth Healy '74
DUBOIS, Floyd R. '01 (d.)
DUBOIS, Cornelius '26
DUBOIS, John D. '24
DUBOSE, William C. W. '71
DUBROW [OUSBY], Heather J. '66
DUGGAN, Stephen P. '31
DUGGER, Celia W. '80
DUNBAR, Donald E. '13 (d.)
DUNCAN, Robert F. '12 (d.)
DUNGAN, Travis P. '74
DUNN, Jeffrey D. '77
DUNNE, Richard E. '72
DURFEE, Randall N. Jr. '19 (d.)
DURGIN, James H. '26
DURHAM, Robert G. '35

DURKIN, Edward C. '29
†DURSTON, Diana D. (Typist)
DUUS, Peter '55
DYER, H. Chouteau '57 (d.)
DYLEWSKY, William '82
DYSON, Esther '71

EAGLE, Joanna Shaw '56
EARLE, Morris '38
EATON, John M. Jr. '40
EATON, Richard '20
ECCLES, Mary Eisner '71
ECKER, Allan B. '41
EDDISON, William B. '46
EDELMAN, Richard M. '52
EDELMAN, Richard W. '76
EDELMANN [LUEY], Beth '67
EDELSTEIN, David B. '81
EDGERLY, Leonard S. '72
EDGERTON, Herbert H. '15 (d.)
EDGERTON, Seymour P. '24
EDISON, Julian I. '51
EDMONDS, Richard R. '69
EDMONSON, Amy C. '81
EDWARDS, Richard D. '41
EFSTATHIOU, S. Andrew '79
EGGERT, Elizabeth P. '75
EGGERT, Robert '73
EHLERMANN, Carl '05 (d.)
EHRLICH, William '25
EILBERG, James S. '57
EISNER, Mark J. '60
EISNER [ECCLES], Mary W. '71
ELIOT, John D. '06 (d.)
ELIOT, Thomas H. '28
ELKINS, Lorren R. '81
ELLIOTT, Frank W. '46 (d.)
ELLIOTT, Theodore H. Jr. '57
ELLIS, Laurence B. '22
ELLISON, Julie K. '73
ELLS, Stephen F. '56
ELLSBERG, Daniel '52
ELSER, William J. '44
ELY, Robert E. L. '76
EMERSON, Eugene '38
EMERSON Rupert '21 (d.)
EMERSON, William 1895 (d.)
EMERSON, William K. B. Jr. '16 (d.)
EMMERICH, J. Wyatt '80
EMMONS, Alfred P. 1890 (d.)
ENDICOTT, Henry 1897 (d.)
ENDICOTT, Thorndike H. 1899 (d.)

ENGEL, Monroe '42
ENGEL, Peter M. '81
ENGELKE [SHEPARD], Susan '65
ENGELMAYER, Paul A. '83
ENGLAND, Richard '42
ENGLISH, Maurice F. '33
ENGLUND, William A. '75
ENOS, George E. '37 (d.)
ENSIGN, Frank B. Jr. '52
EPPS, G. Garrett '72
EPSTEIN, Mark D. '75
ERHARD, Sallie Brown '50
ERICKSON, S. Osborn '71
ERON, George '62 (d.)
ERVIN, Spencer '08 (d.)
ESIELONIS, Karen L. '80
ESTRIDGE, Larry A. '70
EVARTS, Prescott 1881 (d.)
EVARTS, William M. '09 (d.)
EVERETT, Otis 1891 (d.)
EYRE, Lincoln L. 1878 (d.)

FAIER, Melinda B. '79
FAIR, Ellen B. '75
FAIRBANK, Nathaniel K. '24
FAIRFIELD, William S. '49
FALKENBERG, Giselle '80
FALL, Fabian '10 (d.)
FALLOWS, James M. '70
FALUDI, Susan C. '81
FARLEY, John W. 1899 (d.)
FARMER, Thomas L. '44
FARNSWORTH, Andrew C. '81
FARQUHAR, David M. '59
FARQUHAR, Francis P. '09 (d.)
FARQUHAR, Samuel T. '12 (d.)
FARQUHAR, William J. 1891 (d.)
FAULKNER, Arthur 1886 (d.)
FAULKNER, Francis C. 1874 (d.)
FAULKNER, Robert E. 1890 (d.)
FAULKNER, William E. 1887 (d.)
FEATHERSTONE, Helen Jencks '66
FEATHERSTONE, Joseph L. '62
FECHHEIMER [HEIMANN], Margaret E. '52
FEIGENBAUM, Joan '81
FEINBERG, David H. '81
FEINBERG, Lawrence W. '64
FELDBERG, Michael S. '73
FELDMAN, Albert J. '50
FELLOWS, Richard B. '41
FELS, Nicholas W. '64

FENN, Dan H. Jr. '44
FENN, Roger C. '15
FENTON, David W. 1895 (d.)
FERGUSON, Robert A. '64
FERNALD, Dana '46
FERNALD, Robert W. '07 (d.)
FERRARA, Peter J. '77
† FERRIERO, Seraphino (Linotypist)
FERRUCCI, Joseph T. '59
† FERULLO, Donna (Secretary)
FESSENDEN, Edward F. 1887 (d.)
FEUERSTEIN [HEYMAN], Ronnie E. '69
† FICKETT, Eunice V. (Bookkeeper)
FIELD, Daniel '59
FIELD, Donald T. '31 (d.)
FIELD [PIERCE], Ellen M. '53
FIELD, Frederick V. '27
FIELD, James A. '03 (d.)
FIELD, James A. Jr. '37
FIELD, Richard H. '26 (d.)
FIELD, Robert I. '74
FIELD, Whitcomb '05 (d.)
FIELDS, Arthur C. '46
FIELDS, Barbara J. '68
FIERO, Raymond R. '24
FINCHER, John H. '58
FINEBERG, Jonathan D. '67
FINEGOLD, Jonathan E. '77
FINK, Ira J. '75
FINKELSTEIN, Michael O. '55
FINLAY, James R. 1891 (d.)
FINLEY, Alexander '61
FINLEY, Robert L. '21
FINN, Vaughan '73
FIRST, Lewis R. '76
FISCHEL, Walter '02 (d.)
FISH, Robert A. '56
FISH, Sidney S. '43
FISHBACK, George W. 1884 (d.)
FISHEL [HOUGHTELING], Elizabeth R. '72
FISHER, Arthur '15 (d.)
FISHER, Emily A. '74 (d.)
FISHER, Floyd H. '19 (d.)
FISHER [DEGIVE], Josephine C. '65
FISHER, Richard T. Jr. '69
FISHER, Thomas H. '18 (d.)
FISHMAN, Mitchell S. '69
FISKE, Redington Jr. '20 (d.)
FITZGIBBONS, Dennis B. '78
FITZHUGH, Charles H. '77
FLAHERTY, Paul A. '72

FLANDERS, Jefferson M. '77
FLATHER, John R. '23
FLEMING, Carl J. '33
FLEMING, Donald B. '25
FLESH, George M. '68
FLICKINGER, Daniel N. '62
FLINT, Robert W. '43
FOLSE, Parker C. '77
FOOTE, Caleb '39
FOOTE, Wilder '27
FORBATH, William E. '74
FORCHHEIMER, Walter 1887 (d.)
FORD, Rebecca L. '80
FORDYCE, Clifton P. '23
FORDYCE, Samuel W. 3RD '21
FOREMAN, Christopher H. Jr. '74
FOREMAN, Evan H. '16 (d.)
FORMAN, Edward A. '75
FORST, Edward C. '82
FORSTER, William D. '67
FORSTER, William H. '44
FOSTER, Joseph '02 (d.)
FOSTER, Maxwell E. Jr. '51
FOSTER, Ronald M. Jr. '47
FOTI, Cathy M. '82
FOUQUET, Douglas M. '51
FOWLER, Charles Jr. '33
Fox, Edwin H. '44
Fox, Hugh C. 1894 (d.)
Fox, Jonathan M. '65
Fox, Rector K. 1896 (d.)
FRACKMAN, Jeffrey '65
FRANCHOT, Stanislas P. '32 (d.)
FRANK, Alan I. W. '54
FRANK, John V. '41
FRANKEL, David '81
FRANKLIN, Ruth Korzenick '56
FRANT, Howard L. '77
FRANTZ, Stephen W. '66
FRASER-CAMPBELL, Evan '06 (d.)
FRAZIER, Benjamin W. '31
FRAZIER, Mark C. '74
FREDLAND, J. Eric '64
FREDLUND [CARTER], Carol E. '66
FREEDBERG, Robin S. '75
FREEDBERG, Sidney P. '76
FREEDLEY, Vinton '40
FREEDMAN, Grace H. '83
FREEDMAN, Judith '71
FREEMAN, Jonathan '61
FREIBERG, Joseph A. '20 (d.)
FRENCH, Amos T. 1885 (d.)

FRENCH, Charles S. '30
FREUND, John G. '75
FRIED, Eric B. '80
FRIEDKIN, Don S. '42
FRIEDMAN, Bennett B. '45
FRIEDMAN, David L. '69
FRIEDMAN, Michael H. '76
FRIEDMAN, Raymond '43 (d.)
FRIEDMAN, Stanley J. '48
FRIEDMANN, John C. '44
FRIEDRICH, Otto A. '48
FRIEL, Michael K. '66
FRIENDLY, Alfred Jr. '59
FROSCH, James P. '71
FROTHINGHAM, Edgar V. 1896 (d.)
FROTHINGHAM, Francis E. 1894 (d.)
FRUMENTO, Aegis J. P. '76
FRY, Russell T. '17 (d.)
FRYE, James A. 1886 (d.)
FRYE, William R. '40
FUERBRINGER, Jonathan '67
FUERBRINGER, Otto E. '32
FULD, Alice Kinzler '61
FULLER, Edward 1882 (d.)
FULLER, R. Westwood '76
FULLER, Samuel L. 1898 (d.)
FULLERTON, Robert M. 1890 (d.)
FULTON, Robert E. Jr. '31
FULTON, Robert E. III '61
FURMAN, Dale B. '60
FURNAS, Joseph C. '27
FURNESS, Horace H. Jr. 1888 (d.)

GABEL, Matthew A. '75
GABLE, Carl I. Jr. '61
GADECKI, Patricia C. '81
GAFF, Thomas T. 1876 (d.)
GAGARIN, Nicholas '70 (d.)
GAGLIARDI, Peter A. '68
GALE, Mary E. '62
GALEOTA, William R. Jr. '70
GALLAGHER, Debra I. '82
GALLIE, Thomas M. '15 (d.)
GALLIE, Thomas M. Jr. '49
GAMBLE, Robert D. '60
GAMES, Edmund B. Jr. '59
GAMMACK, Thomas H. '20 (d.)
GANSON, John P. '62
GANZ, Robert N. Jr. '47
GANZ, Rudolf V. Jr. '63
GARAY, Martin R. '71
GARDINER, Doane '07 (d.)

GORDON, Watson M. Jr. '40 (d.)
GORE, George '34
GORMAN, Hollis E. '78
GORMLEY, Robert C. '78
GOTSCHALL, Mary G. '79
GOTTFRIED, Lili A. '70
GOULD, Maxwell '81
GOULDER, George V. '36
GOUVENEUR, Sallie T. '73
GOWING, Robert B. '29 (d.)
GRACE, Michael P. '40
GRADY, John E. Jr. '56
GRADY, Robert E. '79
GRAFF, Robert D. '41
GRAFSTEIN, Laurence S. '82
GRAHAM, Donald E. '66
GRAHAM, John M. '38 (d.)
GRAHAM, Mary Wissler '66
GRAHAM, Stephen S. '60
GRANT, Ellsworth S. '39
GRATWICK, William H. '25
GRAVES, Fletcher '15 (d.)
GRAVES, William G. '06 (d.)
GRAY, C. Boyden '64
GRAY, David 1892 (d.)
GRAY, Henry G. 1897 (d.)
GRAY, Horace '09 (d.)
GRAYSON, Bruns H. '74
GREELEY, Sidney F. '15
GREEN [BRODY], Julia E. '71
GREEN, Horace '08 (d.)
GREEN, Richard A. '47
GREEN, Sedgwick W. '50
GREEN, Thomas S. '09
GREEN, Wallace I. '46
GREENBERG, A. Frederick '60
GREENBERG [LEVINE], Jan '72
GREENE, Edmund '35
GREENE, Jerome D. 1896 (d.)
GREENE, Jerome D. 2ND '45
GREENE, Roger S. '01 (d.)
GREENE, Ronald J. '64
GREENHOUSE [AMAN], Carol J. '71
GREENHOUSE, Charles R. '45
GREENHOUSE, Linda J. '68
GREENMAN [MANOS], Katherine '53
GREER, Louis M. 1891 (d.)
GREVE, Charles T. 1884 (d.)
* † GREVILLE, William L. Jr. (Typist)
GREW, Joseph C. '02 (d.)
GRIFFETH, Nancy Davis '67
GRIFFIN, Thomas S. P. '13 (d.)

GRIGGS, Henry L. '76
GRILK, Charles 1898 (d.)
GRIMES, John S. '26
GRINNELL, Robert S. '14 (d.)
GRISWOLD, Herbert B. '38
GROSS, Patricia Hollander '63
GROSSMAN, Alan H. '60
GROSZ, John C. '61
GROTON, John M. '09 (d.)
GROVES, Herbert L. '12 (d.)
GROVES, James M. '05 (d.)
GROVES, Robert L. '10 (d.)
GROVES, Robert L. '40
GRUEN, Michael S. '63
GRUSON [VERNER], Kerry L. '69
GRUSS, Brenda '76
GUILD, Curtis Jr. 1881 (d.)
GUILD, Henry R. '17
GUINZBURG, Harold K. '21 (d.)
GUND, George '09 (d.)
GUND, Geoffrey De-C. '64
GUNN, Edwin P. '30
GUNN, Townsend M. '31
GUNZBERG, Guy W. '62
GUTHART, Leo A. '58
GUTMAN, Amy R. '82
GUTTENTAG, Michael D. '82
GWERTZMAN, Bernard M. '57
GWIRTZMAN, Milton S. '54

HACKER, Harvey J. '63
HAFF, Hopewell Rogers '60
HAGEN, Charles M. '70
HAGENBUCKLE, John D. '65
HAGLER, Elmer E. '16 (d.)
HAHN, Herbert R. '45
HAHN, Roger '53
HALBERSTAM, David L. '55
HALBERSTAM, Michael J. '53
HALBREICH, Jeremy L. '74
HALE, Edward E. 1883 (d.)
HALE, Herbert D. 1888 (d.)
HALEY, Edward '49
HALL, Robert C. '36
HALL, Samuel S. Jr. '15
* HALL, Tyrone J.
HALLETT, James B. '37
HALLOWELL, Gerald W. '10 (d.)
HALLOWELL, John H. '35
HALVORSRUDE, Elizabeth Millard '71
HAMBLETT, Robert B. '21 (d.)
HAMBURG, Margaret A. '77

HAMILTON, Allen B. '22 (d.)
HAMILTON, Charles J. Jr. '69
HAMILTON, Franklin E. E. 1887 (d.)
HAMILTON, Wallace '41
HAMILTON, William B. '72
HAMMOND, Harry S. Jr. '41
HAMMOND, John C. '19 (d.)
HAMMOND, Paula Trygstad '53
HAN, Margaret Y. '79
HANOWER, L. David '81
HANSCOM, Arthur L. 1880 (d.)
HANSEN, Otto R. 1885 (d.)
HANSON, Joseph O. Jr. '39
HAPGOOD, Powers '21 (d.)
HARAM [CANEDY], Brenda K. '54
HARDING, Victor M. 1889 (d.)
HARDY, Rodney C. '20
HARF, David G. '75
HARMON, David P. '30 (d.)
HARMON, David P. Jr. '59
HARMON, Howard L. '28 (d.)
HARPE, Michael G. '82
HARPEL, Elizabeth L. '83
HARRINGTON [MCDEVITT],
    Judith E. '61
HARRIS, Nathaniel L. '19
HARRIS [CONRAD], Rona C. '54
HARRISON, Selig S. '48
HART, Henry M. Jr. '26 (d.)
HART, Stephen A. '66
HARTMANN, Lawrence M. '58
HARTOCOLLIS, Anemona M. '77
HARTRIDGE, Alfred L. '31
HARTRIDGE, George G. '32
HARTSHORNE, Robert C. '58
HARTWELL, John M. Jr. '36
HARTWELL, John S. '32
HARVEY, Edmund H. Jr. '56
HARWOOD, Herbert E. '10 (d.)
HARWOOD, Robert W. '20 (d.)
HASKELL, William E. 1884 (d.)
HASKELL, William P. '36
HATCH, George K. '58
HATTON, Julian B '78
HAUGHTON, Richard '00 (d.)
HAVEMANN, Joel '65
HAVEN, George I. 1874 (d.)
HAVILAND, Henry F. '41
HAYCOCK, David W. '35
HAYCOCK, Joel W. '71
HAYDEN, Charles L. 1896 (d.)
HAYDEN, Edwin P. Jr. '50

HAYES, Bartlett H. 1898 (d.)
HAYES, Nicholas L. '63
HAYES, Thomas C. '65
HAYS, Alan S. '24
HAYS, Laurie '79
HAYWARD, Henry S. Jr. '39
HAZARD, Willis G. '29
HEADLEY, Russell K. '46
HEALEY, L. Christine '78
HEALY [DUBE], Elizabeth S. '74
HEALY, Michelle D. '81
HEARD, Joyce '73
HECKSCHER, Juretta J. '79
HEFLING, Stephen E. '73
HEILBRON, George H. 1883 (d.)
HEILBRONER, Peter L. '76
HEIMANN, Margaret Fechheimer '52
HEINEMAN, Benjamin W. Jr. '65
HEIST, Jeremy W. '67
HELLER, Steven M. '76
HELLMAN, Arthur D. '63
HELM, Mark B. '78
HEMINWAY, Truman 1877 (d.)
HENDERSON, C. Nellie '80
HENDERSON, James A. '14 (d.)
HENNEMAN, Suzanne Snell '66
HENRY, Bertram C. 1886 (d.)
HENRY, Diana M. '69
HENRY, Phineas M. '09 (d.)
HENSELMAN, Roger C. '42
HEPPEL, Alan B. '73
HERBST, Arthur L. '53
HERFORT, John A. '68
HERMAN, Jay B. '75
HERMANN, Andrew B. '82
HERMANN, George A. '54
HEROLD, Frederick G. '78
HERSEY, Richard M. '15 (d.)
HERSHBERG, James G. '82
HERSHKOFF, Helen M. '73
HERTZBERG, Hendrik '65
HERVEY, Charles S. 1888 (d.)
HERVEY, William A. 1887 (d.)
HERZENBERG, Stephen A. '80
HERZFELD, Stanley W. '39
HERZSTERN, Robert E. '52
HESSE, Nelson S. '27 (d.)
HESSEL, Arthur R. '64
HESSLER, Curtis A. '66
HEWITT, William J. '61
HEWSON, Martha S. '77
HEYMAN, Ronnie Feurstein '69

HIATT, Frederick S. '76
HICKOK, Robert D. '33
HICKOX, Paul M. '38
HIGGINSON, Edward 1874 (d.)
HILBOLDT, James S. '52
HILDER, David B. '78
HILDRETH, Robert J. '72
HILL, Anthony C. '73
HILL, Edward A. '19
HILL, Georgia A. '81
HILL, William B. 1879 (d.)
HILLARD, Charles W. '26 (d.)
HINCKLEY, Samuel N. '05 (d.)
HINDERT, Patrick J. '70
HINERFELD, Norman M. '51
HINERFELD, Robert E. '56
HINES, James J. Jr. '73
HINES, Thomas M. '81
HINKEL, Allen W. '08 (d.)
HIRSCH, David L. '57
HISS, Anthony '63
HOAGLAND, Alexander C. Jr. '50
HOBBS, Conrad '00 (d.)
HOBBS, Marland C. 1885 (d.)
HOCHBERG, Audrey Golden '55
HODDER, Gordon H. '52
HODES, Nancy J. '68
HOFFMAN, David G. '76
HOFFMAN, Elliot L. '51
HOFFMAN, Kenneth '74
† HOKE, Anna S. (Bookkeeper)
HOLBROOK, William S. '52
HOLDEN, Albert F. 1888 (d.)
HOLLADAY, Collis H. '20 (d.)
HOLLAND, Kurt I. '77
HOLLAND, Louisa M. '80
HOLLAND, Rupert S. '00 (d.)
HOLLANDER, David N. '71
HOLLANDER [GROSS], Patricia L. '63
HOLLANDS, F. Rockwell '40
HOLLISTER, George M. '18 (d.)
HOLLISTER, John J. Jr. '25 (d.)
HOLLISTER, Paul M. '13 (d.)
HOLT, Roscoe T. '04 (d.)
HOLWAY, Donal F. '65
HOOK, Walter E. '30
HOOPER, Bayard '50
HOOPER, Robert C. '31
† HOPKINS, Arthur H.
    (Chief Linotypist)
HOPSON, Howell H. III '46
HORN, Garfield H. '40
HORNADAY, John A. '31 (d.)

HORNBLOWER, Margot Roosevelt '71
HORNE, Thomas C. '67
HORNIG, Gregory W. '72
HOROWITZ, Irvin M. '45
HORVITZ, David '60 (d.)
HORWITZ, William H. '34
HOUGHTELING, Elizabeth Fishel '72
HOUGHTON, Alanson B. 1886 (d.)
HOUGHTON, Silas A. 1887 (d.)
HOUGHTON, William M. 1922
HOUSTON, Tom R. Jr. '64
HOWARD [PIRIE], Deirdre E. '59
HOWARD, Mary F. '82
HOWE, Albert S. Jr. '27
HOWE, George L. '18 (d.)
HOWE, George W. '21 (d.)
HSIA, Lisa C. '80
HSIAO, Karen K. '75
HUBBARD, Charles J. 1883 (d.)
HUGHES, Howard D. '04 (d.)
HULL, George H. '02 (d.)
HULL, Stockton L. '52
HUMPHREVILLE, John E. '69
HUNNEMAN, Carleton 1889 (d.)
HUNT, Edward L. 1893 (d.)
HUNTER, Timothy M. '68
HUNTINGTON, Frederic D. '12 (d.)
HUNTINGTON, James O. S. 1875 (d.)
HUNTOON, Robert H. '50
HURST, Carl B. 1891 (d.)
HURT, Harry III '73
HURTADO, Patricia M. '82
HUSBAND, Joseph '08 (d.)
HUTTER, James L. Jr. '33 (d.)
HUYSSEN, Nina Bernstein '70
HYLAND, Richard E. '69

IGNATIUS, David R., '72
IJAMS, John H. '07 (d.)
IMAM, Salahuddin I. '70
INGRAM, Dwight H. '16 (d.)
INGRAM, Osborne F. '35
IRVING, Colin F. N. '45
IRWIN, Herbert M. Jr. '37 (d.)
IRWIN, Steven D. '81
ISELIN, John J. '56
ISEMAN, Joseph S. '37
ITTELSON, Margaret Byer '67
ITTELSON, Thomas R. '68
IVY, Thomas P. 1881 (d.)

JABLIN, Burton F. '82
JACKSON, Isaiah A. '66

JACKSON, Rodney H. '26
JACKSON, Wendy B. '75
JACOB, Lawrence 1878 (d.)
JACOBS, Daniel B. '49
JACOBS, Herbert A. '26
JACOBS, Mary M. '79
JACOBS, Nehama '73
JACOBS, Scott W. '71
JACOBSON, Aileen E. '69
JAHN, Harold E. '36
JAKAITIS, Gary J. '76
JAMES, David L. '55
JAMES, Henry 1899 (d.)
JAMES, Robert Bronson Jr. '78
JAMES, Stephanie D. '82
JAMIESON, Ronald B. '35
JAMISON, Andrew '70
JANES, Thomas W. '77
JANIS, Ronald H. '70
JANTZEN, George H. Jr. '45
JANUS, Christopher G. '36
JASZI, Peter A. '68
JEAN, Alfred E. '80
JEN, Lillian C. '77
JENCKS, Christopher S. '58
JENCKS [FEATHERSTONE], Helen W. '66
JENCKS, Stephen F. '62
JENKINS, Marc J. '83
JENKINS, Walter E. Jr. '40
JOEL [BEERE], Sue B. '54
JOHNSON, Bruce E. H. '72
JOHNSON, Deborah B. '71
JOHNSON, Harold P. '05 (d.)
JOHNSON, Harold T. '60
JOHNSTON, Sim '73
JONES, Alfred W. '23
JONES, Boisfeuillet Jr. '68
JONES, John C. III '39 (d.)
JONES, Patricia C. '64
JONES, Rosalyn E. '83
JONES, Sharon E. '77
JONES, Victor O. '28 (d.)
JUNGE, Alexander L. '36 (d.)
JUERGENS, Ann E. '73

KAFKA, Ernest '54
KAHN, Charles M. '74
KAHN, Terri A. '76
KALATA, Marilyn F. '69
KALES, Albert M. 1896 (d.)
KALISH, Martin S. '75
KALLER, Candace J. '79

KANE, Edward R. M. '51
KANE, Joel M. '43
KANE, Oliver T. '72
KANE, Woodbury 1882 (d.)
KANG, Kaffee '75
KANN, Peter R. '64
KANON, Joseph A. '68
KAPLAN, Gilbert B. '73
KAPLAN, James I. '76
KAPLAN, John '51
KAPLAN, Martin H. '71
KAPLAN, Peter W. '76
KAPLAN, Richard D. '55
KAPLAN, Seth A. '77
KAPLAN, Stephen H. '68
KAPLAN, Warren '56
KARIKAS, Angela '74
KARNOW, Stanley A. '45
KARRON, Andrew T. '78
KARSON, Stanley G. '48
KASS, Rudolph '52
KASSMAN, Herbert S. '45
KASTEL, Howard L. '54
KATZ, Allan M. '62
KATZ [BREAKSTONE], Jeanne '63
KAUFER, Scott A. '75
KAUFMAN, Donald B. '62
KAUFFMANN, John A. '52
KAUFMANN, Myron S. '43
KAUS, Robert M. '73
KEARNEY, Gene R. '51
KEELER, Lawrence M. '36
KEFFER, Thomas W. '77
KEIDAN, David B. '66
KEITH, Eugene D. '42 (d.)
KELLEY, Augustus M. '35
KELLEY, Bartram '32
KELLEY, Nicholas '06 (d.)
KELLEY, Stephen F. '71
KELLEY, William D. '17
KELLOGG, Warren F. 1883 (d.)
KELTON, George H. 1893 (d.)
KENDALL, Isaac W. '01 (d.)
KENDALL, Michael D. '79
KENEN, Joanne L. '79
KENNARD, Delano M. '30 (d.)
KENNEDY, Caroline B. '80
KENNEDY, Clement E. '16 (d.)
KENNEDY, Harris 1894 (d.)
KENNEDY, John Fitzgerald '40 (d.)
KENNEY, William O. '10 (d.)
KENT, Samuel L. III '43
KERR, Gilbert A. '75

KERRIGAN, Gerald A. '44
KESSEL, Melvin J. '45
KIAM, Victor K. '82
KIEVE, Robert S. '43
KILDAY, Gregory J. '71
KILHAM, Lawrence '32
KIMBALL, Hannibal I. 1894 (d.)
KIMMEL, Richard N. '66
KING, James G. 1889 (d.)
KING, James G. Jr. '20 (d.)
KINGSON, Charles I. '59
KINGSTON, John C. '35
KINKEAD, Gwen E. '73
KINSLEY, Michael E. '72
KINSLEY, Susan F. '74
KINZLER [FULD], Alice E. '61
KIRK, Alexander E. '20
KITCH, James C. '69
KLAW, Spencer A. '41
KLEIMANIS, Karen Sobol '70
KLEIN, Andrew G. '70
KLEIN, Julia M. '77
KLEIN, Roger M. '79
KLEINMAN, Paul G. '73
KLEPPER, Lawrence R. '49
KLINE [SHARP], Marcia B. '68
KLINE [BARDEL], Penelope C. '62
KLINE, Richard B. '53
KNAFEL, Sidney R. '52
KNOWLTON, Winthrop '53
KOCH, Albert C. '34
KOCH, Robert A. '44
KOCUR, Mary A. Z. '81
KOENIG, Robert P. '24
KOFFSKY, Paul S. '73
KOGAN, Judith '78
KOO, Freeman F. '42
KOPELSON, Robert G. '68
KOPLOW, David A. '73
KOPP, Bradford B. '73
KORNS, Alexander '62
KORRY, Alexandra D. '80
KORZENICK [FRANKLIN], Ruth E. '56
KOVACS, Joseph A. '75
KOVASZNAY, Beatrice M. '72
KRAMER, George P. '50
KRAMER, Joel R. '69
KRAMER, Peter D. '70
KRASIK, Sophie A. '70
KREINDLER, Richard '80
KRAUSS, James L. '73
KRIM, Robert M. '70

KRIPKE, Scott A. '80
KRISS, Ronald P. '54
KRISTOF, Nicholas D. '81
KRITZLER [POTTER], Zoe Ann '68
KROHN, Lewis M. '44
KRONFELD, Edwin J. '52
KRUMBHAAR, Edward B. '04 (d.)
KRUPNICK, Mark L. '60
KRUSKALL, Stephen I. '67
KUCHARSKI, Anastasia '68
KUHN, Thomas S. '44
KUNEN, Mark C. '66
KUPFERBERG, Seth M. '75
KUTIK, William M. '70

LABENOW [DE ROO], Rita D. '51
LACHER, Irene M. '76
LACKNER, Francis A. Jr. '32
LADD, Maynard 1894 (d.)
LADER, Lawrence '41
LAIBE, Constance M. '83
LAING, Charles C. '53
LAING, Diana R. '79
LAING, Mercedes A. '77
LAKE, David A. '70
LAKE [CUMMINGS], Ellen '66
LAKIN, Herbert C. 1894 (d.)
LAM, Fung H. '76
LAMAR, Jacob V. '83
LAMB, Robert K. '28 (d.)
LAMONT, Corliss '24
LAMONT, Hammond 1886 (d.)
LAMONT, Thomas S. '21 (d.)
LAMONT, Thomas W. 1892 (d.)
LANDAU, M. David '72
LANDAU, Robert S. '45 (d.)
LANDON, Hugh M. 1892 (d.)
LANDRY, Peter A. '74
LANE, John P. '07 (d.)
LANG, Frances A. '69
LANG, Lisa L. '82
LANGGUTH, Arthur J. '55
LANSING, Livingston '36
LAPORTE, Cloyd, '16 (d.)
LARDNER, James M. '69
LARNER, Henry C. '37 (d.)
LASCHEVER, Jack A. '81
LASSER, Elliot C. '44
LATHAM, Stephen R. '82
LAUTERHAHN, Cecil M. '30
LAWLESS, Gregory F. '75
LAWRENCE, David S. '81

LAWRENCE, Edward P. '63
LAWRENCE, James III '58
LAWRENCE, William R. '01 (d.)
LAWTON, Frederick C. '36 (d.)
LAZRUS, Jay K. '44
LEACH, Eugene E. '66
LEAR, John '81
LEARNER, Leonard G. '76
LEAVITT, Russell S. '46
LEDECKY, Jonathan J. '79
LEE, Benjamin B. '01 (d.)
* LEE, Bill (Red Sox pitcher)
LEE, Chong H. '83
LEE, Richard T. '79
LEE, Thomas H. Jr. '75
LEHR, Richard D. '76
LEIDER, William B. '57
LEIGHTON, George B. 1888 (d.)
LEIGHTON, James H. '14 (d.)
LEIMAN, Elizabeth A. '81
LEIPER, George A. '50
LELAND, Oliver S. '22
LEMANN, Nicholas B. '76
LEMOYNE, Emily Wheeler '75
LEMOYNE, James G. '75
LENNIHAN, Marion Burke '73
LENNIHAN, Mark H. '78
LENNON, Peter D. '70
LENTZ, Jill Curtis '71
LENZNER, Robert L. '57
† LEONARD, Carolyn Pisano (Secretary/Typist)
LEONARD, Christiana M. '59
LEONARD, Elissa A. '79
LEONARD, H. Jeffrey '76
LEONARD, John D. '60
LEONE, John J. '70
LERNER, Michael A. '65
LERNER, Stephen D. '68
LEROY, Herman S. 1879 (d.)
LESSER, John A. '66 (d.)
LESSER, Wendy C. '73
LETSOU, Anthea '81
LEVENSON, Michael H. '73
LEVENSON, Thomas M. '80
LEVENTHAL, Robert S. '48
LEVIN, Michael I. '42
LEVINE, Faye I. '65
LEVINE, Jan Greenberg '72
LEVINE, Laura J. '79
LEVINE, Martin S. '66
LEVINE, Richard L. '63

LEVINE, Robert W. '59
LEVINE, Steven B. '78
LEVY, Edmond A. '51
LEVY, Jacques E. '49
LEVY, Julian C. '69
LEVY, Richard N. '59
LEWIS, Anthony '48
†LEWIS, Dorothy M. (Ad Makeup)
LEWIS, Frederic B. '51
LEWIS, Gregory M. '79
LEWIS, James M. '71
LEWIS, Philip C. '17 (d.)
LEWIS, Richard E. '40
LEWIS, William F. '23 (d)
LEWIS, Samuel W. '00 (d.)
LEWIS, Sarah Wood '73
LIBBY, Charles T. 1886 (d.)
LIEBMANN, Ruth E. '77
LIGHTHILL, David P. '50
LILIENTHAL, David E. Jr. '49
LILLEY, Tom '34
LIMAN, Lewis J. '83
LINDEN, L. Thomas '56
LINDER, Robert B. '23 (d.)
LINDSAY, Clyde E. '69
LINDSAY, David R. '37
LINDSAY, Dorothy A. '74
LINSCOTT, Roger B. '41
LIPSKY, Seth A. '68
LITMAN, Harry P. '80
LITTLE, Bertram M. '23
LITTLE, David M. '18 (d.)
LITTLE, Thomas W. Jr. '43
LLOYD, Alfred H. 1886 (d.)
LLOYD, Herbert M. 1883 (d.)
LLOYD, Robert B. Jr. '47
LOCKE, John R. '01 (d.)
LOCKE, Joseph A. '09 (d.)
LOCKETT, Arthur H. 1892 (d.)
LOEB, James 1888 (d.)
LOENGARD, John B. '56
LOEWI, Roger W. '39
LOGAN, David C. '70
LOGAN, James N. '23
LOITMAN, Bernard S. '50
LOMAX, Mark W. '75 (d.)
LONDON, Stephanie J. '78
LOO, Dennis D. '73
LORD, Peter P. '52
LORENZ, Joseph P. '53
LOTTMAN, Michael S. '61
LOUD, Edward P. '01 (d.)

LOUDERBACK, William J. Jr. '20 (d.)
LOVE, James S. '17 (d.)
LOVE, Cornelia S. '71
LOWE, John G. Jr. '49
LOWENFELD, Andreas F. '51
LOWERY, Woodbury 1875 (d.)
LOWRY, Edward G. Jr. '25
LUBBERS, Sherry L. '81
LUBOW, Arthur H. '73
LUCAS, G. Robert 2ND '65
LUDLAM, George P. '25
LUDLOW, James B. 1881 (d.)
LUDWIG, Frank C. '42
LUEY, Beth Edelmann '67
LUKAS, J. Anthony '55
LUKAWSKY, Edward M. '71
LUKINS, Kyle B. '80
LUNBECK, Robert A. Jr. '77
LUND, Fred B. 1888 (d.)
LUND, Joseph W. 1890 (d.)
LURIE, Carol P. '75
LURIO, Cynthia Reich '55
LUXENBERG, Steven M. '74
LYFORD, Joseph P. '41
LYMAN, Harrison F. Jr. '42
LYNCH, John E. Jr. '46
LYNCH, Sarah K. '75
LYNN, Kenneth S. II '45
LYNTON Carol R. '83
LYONS, Clifton A. Jr. '78
LYONS, John P. 1882 (d.)

MA, Christopher Y. W. '72
MACARTHUR, Frank 1876 (d.)
MACCOBY, Daniel H. ' 75
MACCOBY, Michael '54
MACGREGOR, Robert M. '33 (d.)
MACKINTOSH, Charles A. 1874 (d.)
MACNIDER, Hanford '11 (d.)
MACVEAGH, Charlton '24 (d.)
MACY, William K. '12 (d.)
MAGALIF, Jeff D. '74
MAGBEE, Guy F. '35
MAGIE, Frank O. Jr. '18 (d.)
MAGOWAN, Robert A. '27
MAHONEY, Joan McPartlin '49
MAHONEY, Flourence J. 1897 (d.)
MAIER, Charles S. '60
MAIER, Pauline Rubbelke '60
† MAKGETLA, Neva Seidman '78
    (Typist)
MAKOV, Oren S. '82

MALAWISTA, Stephen E. '54
MANDEL, Paul W. '51 (d.)
MANDELL, George S. 1889 (d.)
MANN, Clarence C. 1899 (d.)
MANNING, Susan A. '78
MANNING, William H. 1882 (d.)
MANOPOLI, Jane E. '70
MANOS, Katherine Greenman '53
MANZ, Robert D. '70
MARANS, Eugene J. '62
MARCH, Charles D. 1880 (d.)
† MARCUS, Felicia A. '77 (Typist)
MARCUS, James S. '51
MARCUS, Lawrence E. '38
MARDEN, Charles F. 1899 (d.)
MAREK, Margot Ravage '55
MARIANI, Lorenzo E. '77
MARKARIAN, Warren H. '54
MARKHAM, Richard B. '69
MARKS, Jonathan B. '66
MARKS, Stanley A. '48
MARLAS, James C. '59
MARQUAND, Joseph 1885 (d.)
MARRS, Jennifer '81
MARSHALL, Douglas G. '55
MARSHALL, Robert P. Jr. '68
MARTIN, Alba B. '30
MARTIN, George K. '32
MARTIN, Leonard E. '39
MARTIN, Sarah Crichton '75
MARVIN, George 1899 (d.)
MARVIN, Wilbur '41
MASLON, Patricia J. '56
MASON, Curtis E. '62
MASON, Bayley F. '51
MASON, Frank A. 1884 (d.)
MASON, Hugh Clark IV '75
MASON [NIEMIEC], Melanie T. '71
MASSING, Michael A. '74
MATHEWS [WOOD], Alison A. '52
MATHEWS, Edward R. 1896 (d.)
MATHEWS, Linda McVeigh '67
MATHEWS, Thomas J. 2ND '67
MATLOFF, Judith E. '80
MATSCHULLAT, Kathryn J. '77
MATTHEWS, Andre D. '66
MAY, Arthur L. '28
MAYER, Martin P. '47
MAYER, Timothy S. '66
MAZUR, Peter '49
MCALLARD, David '69
MCALLISTER, Bruce R. '58

McCABE, Aloysius B. '49
McCAIG, Jeffrey J. '73
McCANDLESS, Sandra Ravich '70
McCARTHY, Michael B. '73
McCLELLAND, David C. K. '69 (d.)
McCLURE, Donald F. '20
McCOLLOM, Marion E. '72
McCORMICK, Michael H. '50
McCORMICK, Morrison R. '28
McCUE, John J. G. '36
McCULLOCH, Patricia W. '65
McCUTCHEON, John T. Jr. '39
McDEVITT, Judith Harrington '61
McDONALD, Boyd E. '49
McDONALD, Robert N. '74
McDOUGALL, Harold A. 3RD '67
McELHENY, Victor K. '57
McFARLAN, Franklin W. '59
McGEE, Henry W. III '74
McGILLIS, Sarah M. ' 80
McGINLEY, John R. '31
McGINN, Thomas A. J. '78
McGINNIS, Brian T. '71
McINTIRE, H. Dickson '80
McINTOSH, Amy B. '80
McINTOSH, Rustin '14
McINTYRE, Henry P. '46
McKIBBEN, William E. '82
McKITTRICK, Thomas H. '11 (d.)
McLANE, Susan B. '71
McMAHON, Bernard J. Jr. '42
McMECHAN, Jervis B. '42
McMENNAMIN, George B. '45
McMURTRIE, David L. '50
McNEES, John E. '60
McNEILLY, Robert H. '45
McNULTY, John W. '48
McPARTLIN [MAHONEY], Joan '49
McPHERSON, John W. '29
McQUEEN, Michelle D. '80
McQUIRE, James S. '83
McVEIGH [MATHEWS], Linda G. '67
McVITY, Sarah L. '83
MEAD, V. Alexander Jr. '65
MECKLENBERGER, James A. '65
MEEKER, William H. '17 (d.)
MEHLMAN, Robert D. '52
MEIER, Clement R. D. '05 (d.)
MEISELS, Martha Miller '59
MEISENBACH, Richard '28
MEISLIN, Richard J. '75
MEISTER, Alton '42

MELAS-KYRIAZI, Theodose C. '81
MELNICK, Peter R. '80
MELODY, David H. '72
MELONE, Neil G. '37
† MELTZER, Mary A. (Typist)
MERNER, David R. '83
MERRIAM, George R. III '69
MERRIAM, John C. '71
MERRIAM, John M. 1886 (d.)
MERWIN, Davis U. '50
MERWIN, Henry C. 1874 (d).
MERWIN, Loring C. '28 (d.)
METCALF, Carleton R. '02 (d.)
METZ, Jeremy M. '79
MEYERS, Herbert S. '52
MEYER, Laurence P. '71
MEYER, Marc H. '78
MICHAELS, James W. '43
MICOU, Paul '81
MILBAUER, Marvin E. '67
MILDE, Walter J. '25 (d.)
MILLARD [HALVORSRUDE],
    Elizabeth V. '71
MILLER Charles P. '41
MILLER, Craig F. '79
MILLER, James N. '43
MILLER [MEISELS], Martha E. '59
MILLIKEN, Nancy '74
MILLS, Abbot L. 1881 (d.)
MILNE, George P. '01 (d.)
MINTURN, Robert S. 1884 (d.)
MITCHELL, James S. '64
MITCHELL, John K. 1881 (d.)
MITCHELL, Jonathan B. '41
MITCHELL, Marc D. '70
MITCHELL, Morton D. 1887 (d.)
MITCHELL, Roger S. '30
MITTER, Sara Sagoff '59
MOEN, Edward C. 1891 (d.)
MONRO, John U. '34
MONTANARI, Valerio R. '33
MOORE, Charles 1878 (d.)
MOORE, Charles P. '73
MOORE, Munro G. '52
MOORE, Philip W. Jr. '31 (d.)
MOORE, P. Wayne '79 .
MOORHEAD, James B. '76
MORAN [PETERSON], Nancy '66
MOREHOUSE, Clifford P. '25 (d.)
MORGAN, Charles D. '06 (d.)
MORGAN, Charles E. 1898 (d.)
MORGAN, Frank H. 1876 (d.)

MORGAN, Robert W. Jr. '46
MORISON [LEONARD], Christiana '59
MORISON, Elting E. '32
MORISON, John H. '35
MORISON, Robert S. '30
MORRILL, Culvin F. '34
MORRILL, Henry L. '32
MORRIS, Richardson '14 (d.)
MORRISON, George A. Jr. 1887 (d.)
MORSE, David H. '33 (d.)
MORSE, Edward L. C. 1877 (d.)
MORSE, John M. '07 (d.)
MOSELY, Philip E. '26 (d.)
MOSKIN, John R. '44
MOSKOW, Michael B. '55
MOSS, Alvin H. '71
MOSS, Gordon D. '74
MOTT, John C. '37
MOULTON, Franklin W. 1883 (d.)
MUCHA, Walter R. '65
MUESER, Peter R. '75
MULFORD, William '28
MULLAN, Fitzhugh S. M. '64
MULLEN, Thomas A. '78
MULLER, James W. '73
MULTER, Andrew J. '79
MUMFORD, James G. 1885 (d.)
MUMFORD, William W. 1884 (d.)
MUNROE, Henry W. '43
MUNROE, John '13 (d.)
MURAKISHI, Christine C. '73
MURDOCK, Harris H. '01 (d.)
MURO, F. Mark '81
MURPHY, Esme C. '81
MURPHY, John E. '41
MURPHY, John R. '55
MURPHY, Victoria Thompson '60

NADAS [SEAMANS], Elizabeth P. '69
NALLE, Horace D. Jr. '78
NASON, James R. P. '24
NAST, Charles C. '25
† NATHAN, Janet D. (Ad Makeup)
NAZRO, Arthur F. '03 (d.)
NEAL, Anne D. '77
NEAL, Georgianne Davis '51
NEALE, Laurance I. '06 (d.)
NEF, John U. '20
NEILSON, Alexander S. '58
NELSON, Bryce E. '59
NEMIROW, Martin S. '60
NEPOM, Gerald T. '72

NESBIT, Hugh M. '77
NESBIT, Thorpe '15 (d.)
NESBITT, Lois E. '81
NETZER, Jenny '76
NEUMAN, Robert H. '58
NICHOLL, Willard '43 (d.)
NICHOLS, Norman E. '51
NICHOLS, Walter C. 1893 (d.)
NICHOLS, William I. '26
NIEMIEC, David W. '72
NIEMIEC, Melanie Mason '71
NIGHTINGALE, Philip L. '37
NIRDLINGER, Charles F. 1883 (d.)
NITZE, Peter A. '80
NITZE, William A. 2ND '64
NOBLE, Gilbert W. '24
NOBLE, John H. 1885 (d.)
NOBLE, William B. 1885 (d.)
NOONAN, John T. '46
NORMAN, Andrew E. '51
NORQUIST, Grover G. '78
NORRIS, Thomas W. '24
NORTON, Eliot 1885 (d.)
NOVAK, Carol Alexander '55
NOVEMBER, Robert S. '58
NOVICK, Julius L. '60
NOYES, Eliot F. '32 (d.)
NOYES, George C. '20 (d.)
NOYES, Perley H. '06 (d.)
NUGENT, Daniel '11 (d.)
NULAND, James G. '45
NUTTER, Charles R. 1893 (d.)
NUZUM, Claude T. '59

OBERLE, Mark W. '70
O'BRIEN, Kevin J. '74
O'CONNELL, John R. '73
O'CONNOR, Blake '32 (d.)
O'CONNOR, Thomas B. '35 (d.)
ODOM, Karen A. '80
O'DONNELL, C. Patrick Jr. '67
O'DONNELL, Lawrence F. '49
O'DONNELL, Thomas F. Jr. '63
O'DONOGHUE, Mark H. '73
OEI, Kendall L. '74
OESTERREICHER, Arthur '52
OGILBY, Remsen B. '02 (d.)
OHLS, James C. '67
OLDENBURG, Richard E. '54
OLSEN, Russell G. '35 (d.)
O'NEIL, Robert Marchant '56
O'NEILL, Eugene '25 (d.)

O'NEILL, Grover '16 (d.)
O'NEILL, Katherine Garrett '76
ORDESKY Morrill S. '53
ORDIN, Diana L. '70
O'REILLY, Daniel E. '38
O'ROURKE, Michael J. '73
OSBORNE, Lithgow '15
OSBORNE, Richard '43
OSTRO, Ernest A. '54
OTIS, Edward V. '21
OTIS, Frank J. Jr. '27 (d.)
OTIS, Harold '04 (d.)
OTIS, James '25 (d.)
OTIS, William K. 1898 (d.)
OTTENHEIMER, Edward J. Jr. '52
OUSBY, Heather Dubrow '66
OYAMA, David I. '64

PADNICK, Glenn A. '68
PAGE, Edward F. '35
PAGE, Nancy R. '82
PAGE, Robert A. '30
PAHL, Henry D. Jr. '56
PAINE, George L. Jr. '22 (d.)
PAINE, John B. Jr. '23
PAINE, Robert T. 1888 (d.)
PAISNER, Bruce L. '64
PAISNER [WINIG], Maxine S. '66
PAISNER, Richard D. '70
PALCHES, Peter G. '55
PALERMO, Rose C. '80
PALFREY, John G. Jr. '40 (d.)
PALM, James W. '40
PALMER, Meredith A. '73
PALMER, Robert W. '73
PANIN, Ivan N. 1882 (d.)
PAPRIN, Judith E. '79
PARADISE, Richard R. '46
PARKER, Chauncey G. 1885 (d.)
PARKER, Franklin E. Jr. '18 (d.)
PARKER, Harry S. 3RD '61
PARKER, Newton B. '29
PARKER, Philip E. '34 (d.)
PARKER, Stephen W. '78
PARKER, Ross I. Jr. '42
PARRISH, James C. '07 (d.)
PARSONS, Geoffrey '30
PARSONS, W. Stuart '62
PASZTORY, Blaise G. A. '58
PATTERSON, John G. '35 (d.)
PATTON, Lewis F. '74
PAUL, Bruce B. '56

PAUL, Oglesby '38
PAUL, Rodman W. '36
PAULDING, James K. 1885 (d.)
PAULIN, Louis R. E. 1883 (d.)
PAVENSTEDT, Adolf F. '30 (d.)
PAYSON, Charles C. 1898 (d.)
PAYSON, Gilbert R. 1890 (d.)
PAYSON, Samuel R. '38
PEABODY, Charles N. 2ND '46
PEALE, Jean Darling '59
PEARCY, Glen J. '66
PEARSON, Henry G. '34
PEARSON, Robert W. '31
PEARSON, Theodore '25
PECK, Ann '66
PECK, Cornelius J. '45
PECKHAM, John J. '00 (d.)
PEDDIE, David D. '41
PEGE, Deborah A. '83
PEMBERTON, Frank A. Jr. '42
PENDLETON, Elliott H. 1882 (d.)
PENN, Mark J. '76
PENN, Rhesa L. III '76
PEPPER, Thomas M. '61
PERIN, Charles P. 1883 (d.)
PERIN, Edmund S. 1882 (d.)
PERKINS, Edward C. 1879 (d.)
PERKINS, Henry G. 1887 (d.)
PERRY, Carroll Jr. '31
PERRY, Francis U. '21 (d.)
PERRY, Lewis Jr. '36
PERRY, Rodney S. '77 (d.)
PETERSON, Nancy Moran '66
PETSCHEK, Paul M. '73
PFEFFER, Maxine S. '81
PHELAN, William D. Jr. '63
PHELPS, James C. '32
PHELPS, Reginald H. '30
PHILIPS, John N. '42
PHILLIPS, George N. '13 (d.)
PHILLIPS, James M. '43
PIERCE, Daniel '56
PIERCE, Ellen Field '53
PIERREHUMBERT, Janet
   BRECKENRIDGE '75
PINGREE, Frederick DeW. '24 (d.)
PIPER, Ralph C. '12 (d.)
PIRIE, Deirdre Howard '59
† PISANO [LEONARD], Carolyn C.
   (Secretary/Typist)
PITMAN, Harold M. Jr. '37
PLATT, Henry N. Jr. '44

PLIMPTON, George F. '14 (d.)
PLIMPTON, Kathleen Riley '76
PLOTZ, Paul H. '58
POLLACK, Daniel A. '60
POLLAK, Charles N. 2ND '40
POLLAK, Lee '56
POLLAK, William L. '78
POLLOCK [UNGAR], Beth L. '68
POOR, Harris O. 1890 (d.)
POOR, Henry V. '36 (d.)
POPE, Frederick III '72
POPE, John Jr. '56
PORTER, Daniel D. '72 (d.)
PORTER, John H. '75
PORTEUS, Richard R. '61
POSER, Norman S. '49
POST, James O. '30
POTTER, Huntington '72
POTTER, Pitman B. '14
POTTER, Samuel B. '53
POTTER, Stephen J. '70
POTTER, William H. Jr. '20 (d.)
POTTER, Zoe Kritzler '68
POTTINGER, J. Stanley '62
POWEL, Samuel '32 (d.)
POWELSON, Stephen V. N. '38
POWERS, John L. '70
POYER, Lisa M. '77
POZEN, Robert C. '68
PRATT, Frederick T. '22
PRATT, Henry N. '24
PRATT, John T. '55
PRATT, Laurence O. '26
PRESCOTT, Carl F. 1897 (d.)
PRESCOTT, John L. '27 (d.)
PRESSER, Stephen B. '68
PRESSMAN, Gregory P.'66
PRESTON, James F. Jr. '32
PRESTON, Morgan O. '39 (d.)
PRICE, Stephen C. '61
PRINCE, Judith A. '77
PRINGLE, Robert M. '58
PRINTZ, Harry W. '78
PROCTER, John R. 1898 (d.)
PROFFITT, Waldo Jr. '46
PROKOSCH, Michael '70
PROPP, Jonathan B. '81
PROPP, William H. '79
PROUTY, Lewis I. 1894 (d.)
PRYOR, Lawrence S. '82
PUGH, Andrew T. '81
PURCELL, John F. '38

PUTNAM, Charles S. '43
PUTNAM, George '10 (d.)
PUTNAM, Herbert 1883 (d.)
PUTNAM, William E. '32
PYLE, Roger N. '65
PYLES, Albert Z. '10 (d.)

QUELLMAN, Michael '79
QUIGLEY, Andrew P. Jr. '76
QUIMBY, Thomas H. E. '40
QUINCY, Josiah 1880 (d.)
QUINLAN, William H. 1891 (d.)
QUINN, Thomas H. '36
QUINT, Peter E. '61
QUIRIN, John H. '19 (d.)
† QUIRK, Jacqueline A. (Secretary)

RABB, Bruce R. '63
RABINOVITZ, Jonathan D. '82
RABINOWITZ, Daniel S. '77
RADNER, John B. '60
RAFSKY, Robert A. '68
RAGOZIN, Leonard '49
RAISZ, Lawrence G. '46
RAND, William 1888 (d.)
RANDALL, Robert I. '48
† RANDALL, Shannon (Typist)
RANDOL, William M. Jr. '30
RAPHAELSON, Joel '49
RASMUSON, Mark R. '70
RATHBORNE [DENORMANDIE],
    ERNESTINE N. '72
RATNER, David L. '52
RATNER, Jonathan D. '79
RATNOFF, William D. '74
RAUH, Joseph L. '51
RAVA, John A. '58
RAVAGE [MAREK], Margot L. '55
RAVEN, Marc E. '81
RAVICH [MCCANDLESS], Sandra E. '70
RAY, Joseph L. Jr. '46
REED, Dana '43 (d.)
REED, Henry H. '23 (d.)
REED, John D. Jr. '69
REED, Julia T. '71
† REED, Kenneth E. (Custodian)
REED, Steven G. T. '74
REED, Warren A. 1875 (d.)
REEVES, Bruce M. '57
REICH [LURIO], Cynthia M. '55
REICHLIN, Seth D. '73
REID, Louise A. '73

REIDY, John J. Jr. '38 (d.)
REINHARDT, Forest L. '79
REINHART, Robert '29
REINIG, James W. '76
REINKE, John R. '76
RELLIE, Alastair J. C. E. '58
REMICK, Frank E. '31
RENIERS, Perceval '16
RESTON, Thomas B. '68
REYNOLDS, Arthur W. '22
REYNOLDS, Edward '15
REYNOLDS, Peter R. '79
REYNOLDS, William H. '74
REZNECK, Daniel A. '56
RHINELANDER, David H. '58
RHINELANDER, Philip H. '29
RHINELANDER, Philip N. '18 (d.)
RICE, Henry N. 1891 (d.)
RICE, John A. '64
RICH, Dominic W. '18 (d.)
RICH, Edgar J. 1887 (d.)
RICH, Frank '71
RICHARDS, Robert L. '31
RICHARDSON, Weld '41
RICHARDSON, William K. 1880 (d.)
RICHMOND, Thomas J. '73
RICHMOND, William '18 (d.)
RIDGE, Mary B. '76
RIESELBACH, Allen N. '53
RIESMAN, David '31
RIESMAN, Jean A. '79
RIESMAN, John P. '34 (d.)
RILEY [PLIMPTON], Kathleen T. '76
RIORDEN, Shane E. '48
RIMSON, Ira J. '56
RINDERMAN, Richard L. '53
RIPMAN, Christopher H. '70
RITTER, Edward F. Jr. '31 (d.)
RIVKIN, Malcolm D. '53
RIVKIN, Steven R. '58
ROBBINS, Alissa R. '81
ROBBINS, Elliott W. '33 (d.)
ROBBINS, Herbert D. 1884 (d.)
ROBBINS, John C. Jr. '42
ROBERTS, Russell B. '64
ROBERTS, Steven V. '64
ROBERTSON, Archibald T. '28 (d.)
ROBINS, Cliff '80
ROBINSON, Judson B. '28 (d.)
ROBINSON, Lydia W. '73
ROBINSON, Marguerite Stern '56
ROCHESTER, Mark C. '70

ROCKEFELLER, David '36
ROCKWOOD, Albert M. '44
RODEHEFFER, Mary R. '75
RODELL, Suzanna '79
† ROGAN, Francis T. (Day Foreman)
ROGERS, David C. D. '54
ROGERS, Frederick V. D. '42
ROGERS [HAFF], Hopewell L. '60
ROGERS, Joel T. '18
ROGERS, Stephen C. '62
ROGERS, Theodore O. Jr. '76
ROGERS [GIDDINS], Susan M. '63
ROMERI, Michael N. '76
ROOSEVELT, Franklin Delano '04 (d.)
ROOSEVELT, Henry P. '38 (d.)
ROOSEVELT [HORNBLOWER],
    Margot '71
ROOSEVELT, Philip J. '13 (d.)
ROOT, Robert T. '54
ROOTS, John M. '25
RORER, James B. 1899 (d.)
ROSBERG, Gerald M. '68
ROSE, Lawrence '23
ROSEN [WAILAND], Adele '70
ROSEN, George H. '68
ROSENBERG, Erica S. '81
ROSENBERG, Manuel B. '51
ROSENBERG, Mark L. '67
ROSENBERG, Scott A. '81
ROSENBLATT, Rand E. '66
ROSENBLUM, David '08 (d.)
ROSENTHAL, Jacob '56
ROSS, Lisa A. '81
ROSSTON, Steven J. '81
ROTCH, William '51
ROTH, Linda C. '71
ROTHENBERG, Peter J. '61
ROTHSCHILD, Walter N. 3RD '76
ROWE, James H. R. Jr. '31
ROWE, John J. '07 (d.)
ROWE, Paul K. '76
ROWE, William W. '20 (d.)
ROWLAND, Walter S. '61
ROWSE, Arthur E. 3RD '43
ROYCE, David '53, '55½, '56
RUBBELKE [MAIER], Pauline A. '60
RUBIN, Lowell J. '57
RUDDOCK, Merritt K. '36
RUGE, Richard B. '63
RUHL, Robert W. '03 (d.)
RULAND, Irving 1889 (d.)
RUMSEY, John A. '39

RUPRECHT, Archibald L. '43
RUSSE, Frederick W. Jr. '32 (d.)
RUSSAKOFF, Dale S. '74
RUSSELL, Brenda A. '81
RUSSELL, Robert S. '35
RUSSIN, Joseph M. '64
RUST, David E. '51
RUTLEDGE, Gordon K. '75
RYAN, Elizabeth E. '81
RYAN, Michael Jr. '72
RYAN, Kenneth J. '81

SABEL, Charles F. '69
SACHS, Arthur G. '63
SACHS, Howard J. '11 (d.)
SACHS, James H. '29 (d.)
SACHS, Walter E. '04
SACK, Edward J. '51
SACK, John J. '51
SACK, Kirby '78
SACK, Paul '48
SACKS, Robert A. '79
SADOWSKY, Marc M. '78
SAFFORD, Franklin R. '57
SAFFORD, Ralph K. '31
SAGOFF [MITTER], Sara E. '59
SALMEN, Stanley, C. '36
SALTER, William T. '22 (d.)
SALTZMAN, Cynthia M. '71
SAMMONS, Wheeler '37
SAMP, Richard A. '74
SAMPSON, Calvin P. 1874 (d.)
SAMUELS, Elizabeth J. '74
SAMUELS, Emerson '35
SAMUELSON, Robert J. '67
SAND, Robert H. '58
SANDERS, Louis P. 1893 (d.)
SANDERS, Russell M. '20 (d.)
SANDFORD, Joseph W. Jr. '32
SANDS, Brian M. '83
SANDWEISS, Martha A. '75
SANFORD, Henry S. 1888 (d.)
SANGER, David E. '82
SAPPINGTON, Thomas S. '37
SARFATY, Mona '71
SARGENT, Daniel '13
SARIS, Patti B. '73
SARS, Edmund '59
SAUM, George N. '29
SAUNDERS, Pamela R. '81
SAVADORE, Laurence D. '53
SAVER, Jeffrey L. '81

SAVIT, Michael K. '78
SAWIN, Edward A. '25 (d.)
SAWYER, Richard M. '46
SAXE, Robert L. '56
SAXE, Stephen O. '51
SAXON, Olin G. Jr. '44
SAXTON, George A. Jr. '44
SCHAFER, Jack G. '55
SCHAFER, Roger S. '41
SCHANBERG, Laura E. '80
SCHEFFEL, John C. '80
SCHEFFER, David J. '75
SCHEFT, William Jr. '79
SCHELL, Jonathan E. '65
SCHEUERMANN, Robert A. '52
SCHLAMM, Haran T. '75
SCHOELLER, Arne L. '52
SCHOEN, Douglas E. '74
SCHOENBERG, Robert J. '55
SCHOENFELD, Bruce '82
SCHOLL, Anthony H. '66
SCHOOFS, Marlene T. '82
SCHORR, Steven '78
SCHRAGER, Victor A. '72
SCHULTE, Lucy '80
SCHULTE, Terry T. '72
SCHUMACHER, Mary Stokes '51
SCHUMER, Fran '74
SCHWAB, Armand Jr. '45
SCHWAB, Rowena Strauss '54
SCHWABACHER, Thomas K. '58
SCHWALB, Burton A. '57
SCHWARTZ, Harry K. '55
SCHWARTZ, Michael W. '63
SCHWARTZ, Paul W. '59
SCHWARTZ, Frederick A. O. '24 (d.)
SCHWARZ, Henry '64
SCHWARZ, Henry F. '29 (d.)
SCHWEPPE, John S. '39
SCOLNICK, Barbara Bachrach '62
SCOTT, Gavin R. W. '58
SCOTT, George C. Jr. '34
SCOTT, Hope T. '76
SCOTT, Mary E., '74
SCOTT, Janet P. '77
SCOTT, Richard C. '32
SCOVELL, Helen V. '82
SCUDDER, William M. 1899 (d.)
SEAMANS, Elizabeth Nadas '69
SEARS, Edmund H. 3RD '59
SEARS, Joseph H. 1889 (d.)
SEARS, Richard D. 1883 (d.)

SEDGWICK, Harold B. '30
SEDGWICK, Theodore '71
SEEGAL, John F. '68
SEFTENBERG, Stephen L. '56
SEGAL, A. Troy '80
SEIDMAN, Gay W. '78
† SEIDMAN [MAKGETLA], Neva '78
  (Typist)
SELIGMAN, Nicole K. '78
SELKOVITS, Lawrence D. '60
SELLINGER, David E. '71
SENDOR, Benjamin B. '73
† SENESE, Aglaia (Accountant)
SERBIN, Jon D. '83
SEYMOUR, Harold J. '16 (d.)
SHACKTER, Peter V. '57
SHAFFER, Ingeborg Blass '54
SHALIT, Nevin I. '83
SHANE, Peter M. '74
SHAPIRO, Lawrence '81
SHAPIRO, Margaret A. '77
SHAPIRO, Peter I. '74
SHAPLEY [CORTESI], Deborah '67
SHARAF, James A. '59
SHARLITT, Joseph H. '45
SHARP, Marcia Kline '68
SHARP, Rodman A. '51
SHARP, Roland H. '30
SHAW [EAGLE], Joanna M. '56
SHEAFE, William 1879 (d.)
SHEAR, Frederick M. '71
SHEELINE, Paul C. '43
SHEFFER, Jonathan B. '75
SHEN, Leonard H. '81
SHEPARD, Charles E. '76
SHEPARD, Joseph W. '58
SHEPARD, Susan Engelke '65
SHEPLEY, John '21
SHEPRO, Rick W. '75
SHERLOCK, Diane L. '78
SHERMAN, Morris M. '57
SHERMAN, Richard T. '28 (d.)
SHERRARD, Joseph A. Jr. '37
SHERRILL, Arthur M. '47
SHERRILL, Leicester H. '26
SHERWOOD, Arthur M. 1877 (d.)
SHIPMAN [SMITH], Carlota G. '55
SHOEMAKER, Paul T. '76
SHOHET, Stephen B. '56
SHOOK, Thomas L. '71
SHORT, John G. '70
SHORTER, Nicholas A. '75

SHORTLIDGE, Raphael J. Jr. '50
SHOTTER, Spencer O. '14 (d.)
SHUMAKER, M. James '65
SHURCLIFF, Charles H. '65
SHURTS [TISHER], Sharon L. '73
SIA, Richard H. P. '75
SIDORSKY, Robert I. W. '79
SIEBERT, Laurel L. '75
SIEGEL, Donald H. '69
SIEGLER, Ralph T. '43
SIGAL, Marlowe A. '52
SIGAL, William C. '57
SIGEL, Efrem J. '64
SILBERSTEIN, David A. '67
SILK, Michael L. '78
SILVER, Cathy Simon '53
SILVER, Charles W. '58 (d.)
SILVER, George A. R. '58
SILVER, Michael E. '80
SIMMONS, Gwendolyn D. '77
SIMMONS, William M. '52
SIMON, Barry S. '71
SIMON [SILVER], Cathy '53
SIMON, David L. '45
SIMON, Donald J. '75
SIMON, John A. '72
SIMON, John G. '50
SIMON, Robert M. '55
SIMONS, Anna '79
SIMONS, Joan Gardiner '51
SIMONS, Thomas C. '50
SIMOWITZ, Lee H. '68
SIMPKINSON [ANSLOW], Carolyn C. '55
SIMS, William S. '33
SINGAL, Daniel J. '66
SINGER, James W. 3RD '57
SINGER, Monroe S. '47
SINNOTT, Allen '39
SINNOTT, Roger W. '66
SINSABAUGH, Nancy J. '76
SISSON, John H. '40
SIVITZ, Tracy E. '82
SKINNER, George T. '36
SKOLNIK, Donald A. '65
SLACK, Charles W. '83
SLADE, Winthrop Jr. '21 (d.)
SLEATOR, William W. '67
SLEETH, Walter J. '65
SLINGERLAND, Harold B. '20
SLOAN, Clifford M. '79
SLOAN, David M. '71
SLOAN, Gerald M. '72

SLOANE, Barry R. '77
SLONAKER, Helen Bogumil '66
SMAIL, John '51
SMALL, Neal E. '45
SMITH, Arthur C. '14 (d.)
SMITH, Carlota Shipman '55
SMITH, Eileen M. '82
SMITH, Franklin E. '68
SMITH, Herman D. '21
SMITH, Joseph B. '44
SMITH, Joseph T. '80
SMITH, Louis G. '00 (d.)
SMITH, Mark D. '72
SMITH, Robert E. '62
SMITH, Robert T. '27 (d.)
SMITH, Roger L. '73
SMITH, Scott F. '76
SMITH, Winthrop P. '58
SMOCK, William H. '66
SMURRO, James P. '72
SMYTH, Henry L. 1883 (d.)
SMYTHE, Alexander C. '73
SNELL [HENNEMAN], Suzanne M. '66
SNYDER, Allen L. '40 (d.)
SNYDER, George W. K. Jr. '62
SOBEL, Robert '53
SOBIN, Harris J. '53
SOBIN, Jonathan '72
SOBIN, Julian M. '41
SOBOL, Anne Buxton '66
SOBOL [KLEIMANIS], Karen L. '70
SOHIER, K. Sage '75
SOKOLOV, Raymond A. '63
SOLMSSEN, Arthur R. G. '49
SOLMSSEN, Peter K. '52
SOLMSSEN, Peter Y. '76
SOLOMON, Stanley C. '74
SOMMER, Edwin J. Jr. '44
SONTGERATH, Richard '72
SORENSON, Richard P. '65
†SORRENTO, Patrick R. (Production Foreman/King)
SOSLAND, L. Joshua '82
SOSLAND, Morty D. '83
SOUTHWICK, Paul '43
SOUTHWICK, Peter A. '73
SOUTHWICK, Thomas P. '71
SPAETH, Edmund B. '42
SPALDING, Eliot '00 (d.)
SPALDING, Irwin E. '45
SPENCE, Donald P. '47
SPENCE, John F. Jr. '47

SPENCER, John F. '34
SPENCER, Robert C. '64
SPENCER, Thaxter P. '43
SPIELER, Emily A. '69
SPRAGUE, John C. '28 (d.)
SPRING, Suzanne R. '80
SPRINGER, W. Bruce '69
SRAGOW, Michael H. '73
ST. JOHN, George C. Jr. '33
STADLER, John A. '75
STAHL, Sarah A. '80
STALTER, Oliver R. B. '43
STAMAS, Stephen '53
STANTON, Stephen B. 1887 (d.)
STATES, David J. '75
STATES, Katherine P. '80
STEADMAN, H. Richard '70
STEARNS, David B. '42
STEARNS, Thomas H. '53
STEARNS, Wallace E. '23 (d.)
STEDMAN, William E. Jr. '76
STEEDMAN, Charles '57
STEEL, Lewis M '58
STEGALL, Mark D. '79
STEIN, Michael '46
STEIN, Michael D. '81
STEINBERG, Rafael M. '50
STEINGARD, Sandra '77
STEPHENS, Beth P. '76
STEPPACHER, John A. '45
STERN [ROBINSON], Marguerite L. '56
STERNHELL, Carol R. '71
STETON, Frederick W. Jr. '31
STETSON, Joshua 1877 (d.)
STEVENS, Abbot '11 (d.)
STEWART, Martha B. '75
STIFEL, Laurence D. '52
STILES, Robert H. '16 (d.)
STILES, William F. '62
STILLMAN, J. Whit '73
STILLMAN, Mark C. '76
STIMSON, Frederic J. 1876 (d.)
STOCKTON, Peter K. '34 (d.)
STODDARD, James L. '10 (d.)
STOKES [SCHUMACHER], Mary C. '51
STONE, Herbert S. 1894 (d.)
STONE, Jack A. '42
STONE, Melville E. Jr. 1897 (d.)
STONE, Warren R. '54
STONE, Wilfred S. '26
STONG, Elizabeth S. '78
STOREY, Charles M. '12

Storey, Charles M. Jr. '37
Storey, James M. '53
Stork, Carl '81
Storrow, Samuel 1887 (d.)
Storrs, Henry R. 1896 (d.)
Stout, Richard A. '29
Strackbein, Ronald G. '63
Stranahan, Michael '61
Strasfogel, Ian '61
Strasser, Richard F. '82
Strassner, Anne L. '77
Straus, C. B. Terry III '73
Straus, Donald B. '38
Straus, Francis H. III '81
Straus, Joseph N. '76
Straus, Robert K. '27
Strauss, Joanna Burnstine '61
Strauss [Schwab], Rowena V. '54
Streeter, Ruth C. '76
Strike, Anthony Y. '77
Strmecki, Marin J. '81
Strode, Elizabeth A. '78
Stromberg, G. Thomas Jr. '79
Strout, Henry F. 1890 (d.)
Strout, Richard L. '19
Sturges, Harry W. Jr. '30
Sturgis, Neville '46
Sturgis, Robert S. '47
Sullivan, Brian F. '83
Sullivan, Deirdre M. '79
Sundlun, Stuart A. '75
Sutton, Albert M. '54
Swan, Jonathan O. '53
Swanson, Daniel A. '74
Swart, William R. '19
Swartz, Marvin S. '72
Sweeney, Donald L. '26 (d.)
Sweetnam, George K. '79
Sweetser, Arthur '11 (d.)
Sweezy, Alan R. '29
Sweezy, Paul M. '31
Swett, Bradford N. '57
Swett, Steven C. '56
Swift [Glass], Eleanor B. '66
Swirles, Todd M. '76

Talbot, Winthrop T. 1887 (d.)
Tanzer, M. David '83
Tate, John T. Jr. '46
Taub, Peter B. '51
Taylor, Charles M. '59 (d.)
Taylor, Howard 1886 (d.)

Taylor, James S. '18 (d.)
Taylor, Martin A. 1889 (d.)
Taylor, Robert S. '72
Templeton, Payne L. '79
Tennant, William E. '67
Tentindo, Nancy A. '83
Tilles, Desmond L. '57
Thayer, Benjamin B. 1885 (d.)
Thayer, William H. 1889 (d.)
Thayer, William R. 1881 (d.)
Thayer, William S. 1885 (d.)
Thomas, Errold B. '16 (d.)
Thomas, Evan W. III '73
Thomas, Geoffrey L. '66
Thomas, George F. 2nd '44
Thomas, Patricia A. '79
Thompson, Clifford F. '56
Thompson, Howard H. '34
Thompson, Richard H. '30
Thompson [Murphy], Victoria '60
Thomson, Philip W. '02 (d.)
Thorndike, Joseph J. Jr. '34
Thorndike, Townsend W. Jr. '35
Thorp, Joseph G. 1879 (d.)
Thurston, William R. '42
Tiffany, Francis B. 1877 (d.)
Tifft, Steven J. '74
Tilles, Desmond L. '57
Tilles, Jeremiah G. '54
Tilton, Edwin O. '36
Tinkle, Marshall J. '79
Tisher, Sharon Shurts '73
Tisherman, William R. '82
* Titcomb, Caldwell '47
Tolman, Prescott A. '31
Tontodonato, Lino D. '80
Toobin, Jeffrey R. '82
Torres, Cynthia A. '80
Trafford, Perry D. 1889 (d.)
Trager, James G. Jr. '46
Trainer, John N. '00 (d.)
Tranchin, Robert W. '74
Trask, William R. 1885 (d.)
Traub, Margaret A. '80
Traub, Marvin S. '47
Travis, Albert C. '05 (d.)
Treichler, Rachel '73
Tripp, Gordon A. '57
Trobe, Jonathan D. '64
Trott, Stuart H. '53
Trygstad [Hammond], Paula A.
    '53 (d.)

TSIPOPOULAS, Dorothea M. '81
TUCK, Steven L. '71
TUCKERMAN, Bayard 1878 (d.)
TUFANO, Peter '79
TUGMAN, William M. '14 (d.)
TULLER, Martin A. '51
TURNER, Eric M. '78
TURNER, Mordaunt V. '17 (d.)
TURNER, Paul S. '75
TURNER, Richard R. '76
TWEEDALE, Douglas L. '80
TWILLEY, Joshua M. '50
TWOMBLEY, William G. 1879 (d.)
TYNG, William W. '41
TYSON, James L. '39
TYSON, James L. Jr. '81

UHLANER, Carole J. '71
UJIFUSA, Grant M. '64
ULE, Guy M. Jr. '61
ULLMAN, Richard H. '55
ULLMANN, Robert L. '77
ULLYOT, James R. '62
ULMER, James M. '77
UNDERHILL, Charles M. '30
UNDERHILL, David R. '63
UNDERWOOD, Edward S. '32 (d.)
UNDERWOOD, Sanford '12 (d.)
UNGAR, Beth Pollock '68
UNGAR, Sanford J. '66
UNGER, Roger C. '71
URBAN, Raymond A. '73
URBANY, Francis S. '55

VAN BUREN, Alice C. '73
VAN DUZER, Henry S. 1875 (d.)
VAN EVERA, William P. '37
VAN SANT, John D. '64
VAN VORT, Burton E. '44 (d.)
VAN VORT, Walter B. '69
VAUGH, Wilton J. A. '20 (d.)
VAUGHN, Peter G. '77
VENN, Tamsin H. '73
VERDIER, Lawrence J. '33
VERNER, Kerry Gruson '69
VIDALIS, Efthimios O. '76
VILLARD, Henry S. '21
VINCENT, Donald G. '51
VINCINANZO, David A. '81
VOGEL, Charles P. '18 (d.)
VOLK, Nicholas Jr. '53
VON MAYRHAUSER, Stanford '65

VON SZELISKI [COMSTOCK], Margaret R. '64
VOOSEN, John C. '64

WACHMAN, Alan M. '80
WACHTEL, Harvey J. '57
WADE, Ronald W. '76
WAGGONER, Robert C. '58
WAGNER, Robert F. Jr. '65
WAILAND, Adele Rosen '70
WALD, Stephen L. '57
WALKER, Charles C. 1892 (d.)
* WALKER, Johnny
WALKER, Lou Ann '75
WALKER, Richard D. '14 (d.)
WALKER, Richard D. Jr. '39
WALKER, Strother H. '34
WALL, Wendy L. '83
WALLACE, Michael B. '71
WALLACH, Richard W. '49
WALLER, John J. Jr. '46
WALTCH, Lilla Adelman '53
WALTON, Jonathan R. '63
WARBURG, Frederick M. '19 (d.)
WARBURG, James P. '17 (d.)
WARE, Francis M. 1879 (d.)
WARE, Henry 1893 (d.)
WARE, Thorton K. '10 (d.)
WARING, Guy 1882 (d.)
WARNER [ARLEN], Ann C. '55
WARNER, Lucien H. Jr. '45
WARNER, Milton B. Jr. '45
WAROFF, Deborah R. '70
WARREN, Edward H. 1895 (d.)
WARREN, Edward P. 1883 (d.)
WARREN, Samuel D. 1875 (d.)
WASHBURN, Harold C. '06 (d.)
WATERS, Edward A. 1898 (d.)
WATERS, George F. '43
WATERS, William W. '37 (d.)
WATSON, George H. Jr. '58
WATTLING, Richard L. '49
WEBER, William A. '62
WEHLE, Louis B. '02 (d.)
WEIL, Amanda E. '83
WEIL, Andrew T. '63
WEIL, Norman Jr. '54
WEINBERGER, Caspar W. '38
WEINHOLD, Timothy A. '74
WEINSTEIN, Robert H. '44 (d.)
WEISBROD, Jo Adams '69
WEISMAN, Richard S. '78

WOOD, Alison Mathews '52
WOOD, Cyrus '32 (d.)
WOOD, Howard 3RD '38
WOOD, Rawson L. '30
WOOD, Russell A. '03 (d.)
WOOD [LEWIS], Sarah M. '73
WOOD, Winthrop A. '19 (d.)
WOODMAN, Francis C. G. 1888 (d.)
WOODROE, Stephen C. '62
WOODRUFF, James N. '83
WOODRUFF, Robert L. Jr. '50
WOODS, James H. 1887 (d.)
WOODWARD, William 3RD '66
WOOTTEN, Rufus M. '27
WORCESTER, David '28 (d.)
WORCESTER, David L. '66
WORKUM, Fifield '20
WORTHINGTON, Robert '23
WRIGHT, Albert Jr. '22 (d.)
WRIGHT, Charles H. C. 1891 (d.)
WRIGHT, Christopher B. '78
WRIGHT, David H. '50
WRIGHT, Jared L. '64 (d.)
WRIGHT, Leonard M. Jr. '45
WRITINGTON, Dana C. '36 (d.)

WULSIN, Eugene '43
WYANT, William K. Jr. '35
WYMAN, George F. '27

YASUDA, Masako '82
YARMOLINSKY, Adam '43
YEAGER, Joseph H. '79
YOAKUM [BLUM], Alice E. P. '52
YOUNG, Charles W. '44
YOUNG, Harrison H. '66
YOUNG, John H. '65
YOUNG, Reginald 1877 (d.)
YOUNG, Robert P. Jr. '74
YUKINS, Richard E. '56

ZACKSON, Hannah J. '76
ZEITLIN, Charles E. '53
ZEITLIN, Jonathan H. '77
ZEITLIN, Lawrence R. '51
ZIMBLER, Brian L. '80
ZIMMERBERG, Betty '71
ZINSSER, Hans H. '38 (d.)
ZOBEL, Hiller B. '53
ZUKOSKI, Charles F. Jr. '19

Selective Index